The ROAD to
REBELLION

The ROAD to REBELLION

Class Formation and Kansas Populism, 1865–1900

Scott G. McNall

The University of Chicago Press
Chicago and London

SCOTT G. McNALL, professor of sociology at the University of Kansas, is the editor of *Current Perspectives in Social Theory,* vols. 1–7, *Theoretical Perspectives in Sociology,* and *Political Economy: A Critique of American Society.* He is the author of numerous works, including *The Greek Peasant* and, with Sally McNall, *Plains Families: Exploring Sociology through Social History.*

The University of Chicago Press, Chicago 60637
The University of Chicago Press, Ltd., London
© 1988 by The University of Chicago
All rights reserved. Published 1988
Printed in the United States of America

97 96 95 94 93 92 91 90 89 88   5 4 3 2 1

Library of Congress Cataloging-in-Publication Data

McNall, Scott G.
   The road to rebellion: class formation and Kansas populism, 1865–1900 / Scott G. McNall.
      p.   cm.
   Bibliography: p.
   Includes index.
   ISBN 0-226-56126-7   ISBN 0-226-56127-5 (pbk.)
   1. Populism—Kansas—History—19th century.   2. Farmers—Kansas—Political activity—History—19th century.   3. Social classes—Kansas—History—19th century.   4. Kansas—Politics and government—1865–1950.   I. Title.
F686.M4   1988
978.1′031—dc19   87-23736
                           CIP

To
Amy
and
Laura
and
Miles

Contents

Preface

It is more clear today than ever that democratic states and democratic institutions are the exception rather than the rule. Even in democratic societies, few seem to care about how democracy is created or maintained; liberties are taken for granted, even though they may be threatened; politics is seen as somebody else's business; and people happily retreat to what they perceive as the security of their private pursuits. The link between public and private worlds goes unrecognized, although the survival of democratic institutions depends upon our recognizing it and acting on it.

At the time of her founding, America's exceptional and fragile character was well understood. One of the first to comment on the problematic nature of the American experiment was the aristocratic French observer of American morals, Alexis de Tocqueville. Tocqueville was both fascinated and repelled by the American experiment. Would democracy survive, or would it devolve into a form of soft fascism, with people pursuing their private and individual interests under the watchful eye of a benevolent, authoritarian state? His greatest fear was that the individualism which built the country could also lead to its destruction. He was concerned that people would see themselves as solely responsible for their own destinies, that they would be cut off from the past and thus from a future. In his words, "Each man is forever thrown back on himself alone, and there is danger that he may be shut up in the solitude of his own heart."[1] A people shut up in their own hearts have no understanding of what they might do to protect the private realm and liberties they cherish.

Tocqueville's solution to the problem of the separation between the public and private spheres, as well as to rank individualism, was to link the individual to a larger moral community by way of family, friends, religious institutions, and local communities. To use today's terms, state and civil society had to be wedded. As Tocqueville said, "If men living in democratic countries had no right and no inclination to associate for political purposes, their independence would be in great jeopardy."[2]

The founding fathers, too, understood that there were tensions within the American system, but those fathers were divided along essentially two lines—Jeffersonian versus Madisonian or Hamiltonian—by their views of how to guarantee the survival of the republic. These divisions stemmed, in part, from different ideas about human nature.

Thomas Jefferson had no doubt that people were essentially cooperative and capable of self-government. He assumed that a full and rich life could not be a retreat to the private life. People needed to wed the public and the private. "The pursuit of happiness, in its dual interdependent facets, can provide a fully human life; but the pursuit of either at the neglect or expense of the other will lead to personal perversion in the individual and to social decay in the corporate world."[3] A society of small property-holders with the desire and obligation to participate in the public pursuit of happiness would assure individual freedom, limit the encroachment of the government into the private realm, and check arbitrary authority.

Jefferson's friend and constitutional antagonist, James Madison, looked out on the same political landscape and came to very different conclusions about what must be done to guarantee the survival of the body politic. Like Jefferson, Madison saw inequality developing, but he believed there was little to be done about it; according to his idea of human nature, a few would always profit at the expense of the many. He was even less sanguine when it came to the prospects of democratic rule, and once said, "Had every Athenian citizen been a Socrates, every Athenian assembly would still have been a mob."[4] A strong government was necessary, then, to protect individuals from one another; furthermore, the government should be so structured, mechanically, as to prevent any one group from achieving dominance. Multiple constituencies should be developed. Leviathan, controlled naturally by the best citizens, would guarantee freedom for all.

Alexander Hamilton's views closely paralleled those of Madison, particularly in terms of a people's ability to govern in its own or the country's best interests. Where Jefferson saw social beings, Hamilton saw market beings, rationally calculating their gains and losses. People would be happy, in Hamilton's view, when their interests could be maximized, but they could not do this by themselves. A strong pro-business government, providing progress and prosperity for all, was necessary. The implication, of course, was that prosperity would solve the problem of liberty. This is exactly what Tocqueville feared: that a strong government would act in the people's name to provide them with the material resources they desired. These resources would allow them to retreat to their private realms, shut up in their own hearts, while the government went on about its business. Theoretically, at least, the public and private spheres would be severed. As Matthews has argued,

> Hamiltonian economics, then, are the negation of Jeffersonian economics. Hamilton longs for empire, opulence, and glory for the nation whereas Jefferson seeks virtue, freedom, and happiness for the social individual. Jefferson believes that men are sociable, reasonable creatures, who, with the passage of time and the aid of science, can return to the garden. Hamilton, in contrast, views men as "ambitious, vindictive and rapacious," who, given the opportunity, will turn Jefferson's garden into a pigsty.[5]

One can debate when the fall from grace occurred, but there were many who argued, even before the country celebrated its first centennial, that the democratic experiment was a failure. Henry Adams, grandson and great-grandson of two presidents, son of our minister to England during the Civil War, had ample opportunity to observe the machinations of politicians and the development of our political system at close hand. In his autobiography, *The Education of Henry Adams*, he argued that the kind of political morality and democratic politics Jefferson had hoped would animate the American dream was dead even before the outbreak of the Civil War. In his view, political morality had given way to political expediency and many saw politics as simply another way of enriching themselves at the public's expense. Speaking of post–Civil War America, he noted that the political "vultures descended on . . . [Washington] in swarms that darkened the ground, and tore the carrion of political patronage into fragments and gobbets of fat and lean, on the very steps of the White House."[6]

Lawrence Goodwyn is more precise about when and why democracy died in America: it came to an end with the defeat of the nineteenth-century agrarian revolt. In his view "modern" politics dates from the time of the first battle between Bryan and McKinley for the presidency. "The economic, political, and moral authority that 'concentrated capital' was able to mobilize in 1896 generated a cultural momentum that gathered intensity until it created new political guidelines for the entire society in twentieth-century America."[7] When the light went out, what vanished was the promise of democracy itself: the willingness to consider alternative political and economic systems. Farmers and others who marched under the banner of the Farmers' Alliance and then the Populist party were struggling over the very *meaning* of America. Whether or not they lost the battle, and why, is one of major topics to be considered here, but the issue of democratic politics is deeply implicated.

In their recent work, *Democracy and Capitalism*, Samuel Bowles and Herbert Gintis argued that, in order to develop a "new" political philosophy and breathe life into the corpse of democratic politics, we must understand that the public and private are one, as are politics and economics. They are particularly concerned that people have lost sight of the fact that one cannot think of the polity as separate from the economy, or as a sphere separate from ideas or values. They recognize, just as the Populists and America's agrarian radicals did, that politics is "a contest over who we are to become, a contest in which identity, interests, and solidarity are as much the outcome as the starting point of political activity."[8] The inspiration for their vision comes in part from America's populists and the English Chartists of the 1830s and 1840s. The Chartist, Bronterre O'Brien, clearly understood and summarized the links between the political and the economic.

> Universal suffrage is . . . a grand test of Radicalism. . . . Knaves will tell you that it is because you have no property that you are unrepresented. I tell you, on the contrary, that it is because you are unrepresented that you have no property. . . . Thus your poverty is the result not the cause of your being unrepresented.[9]

As we will see, this idea—the recognition of the link between the political and the economic—was one of the animating visions of America's radicals.

A call to reestablish or reaffirm a democratic social order, a call appealing to our country's own history, makes it essential that we understand the conditions relating to the success and failure of America's greatest mass-democratic movement. The Farmers' Alliance, and the People's party to which it gave rise, mobilized hundreds of thousands of voters at the national level in 1892 and 1896, even more when one considers races for control of county governments or the governorship in individual states. Yet this movement which figured so prominently in the lives of Americans at the time and in our imagination today, which caused the two dominant political parties to reshape their agendas, was for all practical purposes moribund by the turn of the century. The question, of course, is why. A focus on one state, Kansas, seen by some as the center of the firestorm in the 1896 election between William Jennings Bryan and William McKinley, will clarify the reasons why people were drawn to these movements, as well as why they later abandoned them. Debates about how classes came into being, or how democracy is to be realized, cannot be settled in the abstract. Only by looking at the efforts of real people to control their own lives can we possibly begin to understand these processes.

It is also important to me to give meaning to the often quoted aphorism, "Men and women create history but not always in circumstances of their own choosing"; to show the orchestration of agency and structure, why each deserves its due in a disentangling of the development and ultimate decline of the Farmers' Alliance and the Populist movement. I will deal with farmers as rational, conscious actors, struggling against an entrenched class system, rigid and indifferent political parties, and an economic system and ideology that held little promise for them. I will examine the process by which a group of people tries actively to constitute itself as a class, though this story is of a class that fails to achieve dominance, fails to become a class for itself. I would have liked to show how a class can create itself as a radical class—one in opposition to the dominant political and economic system—and effect basic changes in the political and economic system. We need today, perhaps more than ever before, to understand not only how to structure alternative agendas but how to make those agendas a reality. Perhaps we can learn from past failures.

For American farmers to triumph, to alter the political and economic system, they had to create a distinct movement-culture, provide alternative explanations and solutions for the problems of nineteenth-century America that would win them allies among such groups as urban workers; above all, they had to improve, materially, the economic and political position of their class. Drawing on their own experiences, farmers created and offered an alternative, Jeffersonian vision of what life in America should be like. Farmers saw themselves as the source of the country's wealth and their labor as primary. They argued for justice and a fair rate of return for the efforts of their labor. But this message was not heard by workers, who did not identify with the farmers, while America's industrialists and capitalists heard the farmers' message as a threat to their Hamiltonian vision of how progress and prosperity were to be achieved.

One bitter irony, as we will see, was that farmers drew a political and economic vision from their own subjective experience, a vision which clearly radicalized them and caused them to offer essential challenges to the capitalist system, but this was not a vision that posed effective alternatives. In fact, it resulted in the mobilization of others against them. Objectively, farmers were petty capitalists or simple commodity producers, and saw themselves as such. Their slings were directed not against the dominant economic system, but against monopolists, middlemen, and parasites—people who would not play by the rules of the capitalist game. They wished to control or affect the political system in such a way that the rules of fair play would predominate. The republicanism of petty producers, then, combined what would prove to be incompatible visions.

The story of the Alliance and the People's party clearly reveals the dialectic between agency and structure. People posed alternatives, challenged the system, found some strategies wanting, and tried still others. The extent to which they could continue their struggle, offer new alternatives after defeat, and keep the movement together depended in large part on their ability to create a distinct class organization that would be effective in the context of American politics. They could not do this. The effort can be seen as a series of strategic moves between farmers, the movement they created, and the dominant political and economic system. It was a heroic struggle, one that holds lessons for the present and the future.

It requires an effort to penetrate barriers between the centuries, to understand what someone speaking a century ago meant. Throughout the text, I will let people speak for themselves whenever possible. I do not suppose that the voices which I have captured are representative of all farmers, workers, or merchants, though I am confident that they are sufficiently so to allow us to understand the struggles that were taking place and to see the different images of America that prompted the speakers. As with other historical studies, this one will disappoint those hoping for definitive answers to questions. The data, though extensive, are not comprehensive. I have made use of whatever fragments were available to make up a picture of this movement.

ACKNOWLEDGMENTS

I especially want to thank those who have read and commented on this manuscript or different versions of the chapters along the way. For their support and sometimes spirited disagreement I am indebted to: Dwight Billings, Michael Schwartz, Jill S. Quadagno, Donna Barnes, Ed Royce, James Divney, Craig Calhoun, Michael Kimmel, Bob Liebman, Gary McClelland, Craig Jenkins, John D. McCarthy, Larry Neuman, Richard Hogan, Robert L. Lineberry, Sally A. McNall, and my colleague Robert J. Antonio. I also want to acknowledge the fine help of the research assistants who saw me through the difficulties of gathering, assembling, and making sense of the archival data: Bridget Jones; Kathy Stanley; and Richard Hardin, perhaps the only mechanical engineer in the country who understands the complexities of the Alliance and the Populist movement. Those individuals who responded to my call for information on the Alliance in their counties deserve special thanks: S. M. Dell of McPherson County; Ruth A. Siegrist of Graham County; Evelyn Walden of Sheridan County; Marilyn Holzworth of Cheyenne County; E. Neil Carson of Clay County; Virginia Johnston of Lane County; Jackie Stephan of Woodson County; Alfred Ferguson of Greenwood County; Thelma Schroth of Cloud County; Carol J. Dage of Wynandotte County; Elsie E. Brown of Anderson County; Irene Blansit of Haskett County; Denise Morrison of Finney County; Ivan J. Newsam of the Albany Historical Society; Kathryn Littler of Chase County; D. Cheryl Collins and Jean C. Dallas of Riley County; Betty A. Strom of Morris County; Bonnie Forbes of Wilson County; Helen Henderson of Allen County; William Cuthbertson of Crawford County, and Mary Jo O'Brien of Johnson County. I wish to thank my typist, Pat Johnson, for her patience and good humor. Finally, Nicolette Bromberg of the Kansas Collection deserves special mention for helping me with the time-consuming task of locating and selecting the illustrations for this work.

Financial support for various portions of this study has been provided on three separate occasions by the Graduate Research Fund of the University of Kansas.

PART ONE
AGENCY AND STRUCTURE

1

The Farmers' Alliance and People's Party as a Class Movement

In the "Legislative War of 1893" Republicans and Populists squared off to do battle. Each side deputized officers who took up position in the Kansas House of Representatives. Courtesy Kansas State Historical Society.

Before the presidential election of 1892, America's farmers participated in a massive organizing effort. Meeting in small groups, men and women gathered in schoolhouses, churches, and family parlors to talk about falling farm prices, the railroad, beef, and cotton monopolies, and why their ceaseless toil seemed to get them nowhere. Their number grew with lightning speed in some states, and their determination increased.

Prices for agricultural products had fallen steadily since the close of the Civil War. To give some idea of the range, in 1866 a bushel of corn sold for sixty-six cents; it had dropped to thirty-one cents in 1878; when the large crop of 1889 came in, it sold locally in states such as Kansas for as little as ten cents a bushel, and was often burned in place of high-priced coal. The effect on the farmer can be imagined. One recalled:

> Many a time I warmed myself by the kitchen stove in which ears were burning briskly, popping and crackling in the jolliest fashion. And if, as we sat around such a fire watching the year's crop go up the chimney, the talk sometimes became bitter . . . who will wonder.[1]

Organized under the banner of the Farmers' Alliance, people turned to local politicians and state legislatures for help. They banded together, sometimes successfully, to elect people sympathetic to their cause. Yet even when legislation was introduced in their favor, it had far less effect than they had hoped, and farmers throughout the country began to see the dominant political parties as indifferent to their cause, if not at times outright hostile to it.

As the presidential election of 1892 drew near, many decided that they could help themselves only by forming another party. This they did in the name of the people by founding the People's party, commonly known as the Populist party. When the Populists met at their founding convention in Omaha on Independence Day, 1892, the delegates warmly applauded the words of Ignatius Donnelly:

> We meet in the midst of a nation brought to the verge of moral, political, and material ruin. Corruption dominates the ballot-box, the legislatures, and Congress, and touches even the ermine of the bench. The people are largely demoralized. . . . The newspapers are largely subsidized or muzzled; public opinion is silenced; business prostrated; our homes covered with mortgages; labor impoverished; and the land concentrating in the hands of the capitalists.[2]

Mary Elizabeth Lease, who supposedly told Kansas farmers that what they needed to do was raise less corn and more hell, left no doubts as to her feelings. She thundered, "Wall Street owns the country. It is no longer a government of the people, by the people and for the people, but a government of Wall Street, by Wall Street and for Wall Street."[3]

James B. Weaver was picked by the Populists as their national presidential candidate and captured 9 percent, or over 1 million, of the total votes cast in 1892. In states such as Kansas, the Populists swept to victory with control of the legislature and the governor-ship. The fortunes of America's farmers and the Populist party would vary considerably from state to state and from region to region in the following years. By the time the golden-tongued orator from Nebraska, William Jennings Bryan, challenged McKinley for the presidency, the Populists had fused with the Democrats and the campaign was dominated by the single issue of whether the federal government should engage in the free coinage of silver. Even though he was outmanuevered and outspent by the Republican political machine under the tight control of Mark Hanna, Bryan won over 46 percent (over 6 million) of the votes cast. After this, however, the fortunes of Populists and agrarian radicals fell rapidly, so that by 1900 their impact on the ballot box was scarcely felt. In the state of Kansas, the Alliance had claimed over 100,000 members in 1890, but by 1900 their number had declined to less than one-tenth that figure.[4] On their own—without support from the state's Democratic party—they had generated over 100,000 votes in the 1890 election for governor, 37 percent of the total. By 1902, they were but a memory.[5]

Why did the Farmers' Alliance and the People's party collapse in such a short period of time?[6] How could a movement that at one time captured the imagination, dedication, and commitment of so many people lose its base of support in such short order? One answer I will *not* give is that the collapse was inevitable, nor will I claim that people did not understand what they were doing. Outcomes are not predetermined but are the result of rational actors struggling to control their lives. The simple fact was that many nineteenth-century Americans did not accept as inevitable the domination of the country by financial and industrial elites, and they mobilized against it. They tried to create themselves as a class, one which would serve as a Jeffersonian counterweight to the power of entrepreneurs.

I have chosen to label these efforts as a class movement. A class movement is one in which the participants are involved in a struggle over the very definition of their political, economic, and ideological interests. All class movements have at their core an economic dimension and, like class relationships, are about relationships of power.[7] American farmers were aware that if they did not dominate in the political arena they had little hope of achieving economic justice or of maintaining a way of life that they held dear. Their struggle was, at its most fundamental level, about who would benefit from the results of their labor. The surplus that farmers produced was drained away by monopolists and by markets the farmers did not control, and by taxes whose burden fell on them rather than on investors and entrepreneurs. They saw corrupt politicians and an indifferent political system as responsible for this situation. Class movements, like class, have a processual or developmental character. This work, then, is about a group of men and women who began the long journey from being a class *in itself* to being a class *for itself*.

Defining Class

How does a class become a class for itself? In what is class consciousness rooted, and what role does it play in mobilizing people? We have come a long way since the days of the economic determinists, when class was seen as a simple reflection of one's economic position. E. P. Thompson in particular expanded our understanding of class formation. As he demonstrated in *The Making of the English Working Class*, classes are emergent.

> If we stop history at a given point, then there are not classes but simply a multitude of individuals with a multitude of experiences. But if we watch these men over an adequate period of social change, we observe patterns in their relationships, their ideas, and their institutions. Class is defined by men as they live their own history, and, in the end, this is its only definition.[8]

A class, in Thompson's view, is a "very loosely defined body of people who share the same categories of interests, social experiences, traditions and value-systems, who have a *disposition to behave* as a class, to define themselves in their consciousness in relation to other groups of people in class ways."[9] Class is defined in cultural terms, and in opposition to other social groups. People must see and describe themselves as distinct. As Thompson further argues, through people's lived experiences, confrontations with the world at large, and attempts to make sense out of those confrontations, classes emerge, and with them a willingness to act on the basis of class. "What we mean," he says, "is that changes take place within social beings, which give rise to changed *experience:* and this experience is determining, in the sense that it exerts pressures upon existent social consciousness, proposes new questions, and affords much of the material which the more elaborated intellectual exercises are about." [10] The oppositional element figures prominently in Thompson's theoretical framework.

> Class formations . . . arise at the intersection of determination and self-activity: the working class "made itself as much as it was made." We cannot put "class" here and "class consciousness" there, as two separate entities, the one sequential upon the other, since both must be taken together. Nor can we deduce class from a static "section" (since it is *becoming* over time), nor as a function of a mode of production, since class formations and class consciousness . . . eventuate in an open-ended process of *relationship*—of struggle with other classes—over time. [11]

In sum, Thompson's definition of class is probably the most useful one we have for understanding class as *process,* and for understanding the vital role of culture or ideology. Yet there is a flaw in Thompson's definition, for he assumes that if the conditions he outlines are met, a class will emerge, when in actuality history has seen the emergence of but a few autonomous classes. We need to understand why some groups cross the threshold and become a pure class while others do not.

Thompson has been criticized on both empirical and theoretical grounds for his view of the process of class formation and his ideas about when the British working class comes on the scene. [12] Two issues involved in this debate seem central for understanding class mobilization: the weight one gives to the rational class actor (agent) versus the social structure, and the extent to which one emphasizes cultural and ideological variables as opposed to "economic" ones.

The agency-structure debate has been pursued at length by Thompson in direct opposition to the ideas of Louis Althusser and Perry Anderson. [13] Briefly, Althusser, arguing from a structural position, rejected the notion of active human agents; people were simply the "bearers" of social structure. Anderson, in opposition to Thompson, said that modern history was best understood as the unfolding of the contradictions within society. If agents played a role, it was only with the rise of modern revolutionary movements. Thompson, in a pointed attack on the entire structuralist school, argued strongly for human agency: history *was* consciousness, *was* goal-directed actors pursuing their interests. Douglas Porpora, in an attempt to resolve the debate, suggested that crises may be brought about, as Anderson claims, by structural contradictions in society, and that human agents may react to these changes but in unpredictable ways.[14] Although Porpora is correct in giving structure its due, it is important to consider how class-conscious actors can generate within a system the very crises or contradictions that Anderson takes as given. This is one of the strengths of Thompson's position: he assumes that crises can be generated by active human agents. But, as noted above, a caveat is in order, for people's actions do not always produce the results they hoped for, and not all occupational groups become classes.

Craig Calhoun has also criticized Thompson for not being Marxist enough in his analysis of the formation of the British working class.[15] He says that Thompson failed to deal with people's *objective* relationship to the means of production. Calhoun argues that radicalism, which Thompson attributed to the working class, was actually rooted in artisanal communities. This is not to reduce class to simple economic relations, but to argue (as I do) for an understanding of class as culture, structure, and social relationships.[16] Calhoun's British artisans mobilized not only because they understood that they must do so to protest the loss of a way of life but because they belonged to true communities. To mobilize, "people must have strong emotional ties with each other, a faith in their strength, and an identification with the collectivity in which they are to act."[17] Calhoun also makes the point, which will be elaborated below, that traditional communities can in the long run inhibit the formation of the type of classes to which Thompson has reference. The point is not that we must ignore the economic position of human actors but that we must determine whether it is one which contributes to, or erodes, class formation.

William G. Roy, in his summary of recent work on class conflict, notes how, in the work of the neo-Marxists, the traditional Marxian perspective has been altered.

> Neo-Marxists disagree with advocates of economic determinist versions of Marxism who assert that collective action is motivated by class-based interests. The historical record is too full of examples of collective action propelled by religious, ethnic, regional, nationalistic, and other cross-class relationships to sustain such an assertion. They alternatively propose that collective action is historically decisive to the extent that it is rooted in class relationships, which analytically links the causes and consequences of class action.[18]

Classes, then, can even affect the mode of production. The social relations of production (a part of the mode of production), and sometimes even the social forces of production, are modified as a result of struggle. People may act to protect a way of life, a way of working and living. In organizing, in confronting the world in which they live, people develop class consciousness. Consciousness grows out of action and opposition. However, this consciousness is not created anew, but refined.

The importance of the lived experiences of people as the "material" out of which classes are constituted has been clearly demonstrated by, among others, Herbert Gutman.[19] Gutman points out that language, stories, and ideas of harmony and brotherhood make a people, and hence a class, unique. Ideology enters significantly into the formation of classes.[20] Ideologies are not more stagnant than any other part of social reality.[21] As Ron Aminzade has shown in his study of French artisans, they, like Calhoun's English artisans, were a consistently radical force in preindustrial France precisely because of their noneconomic interests. These interests were expressed, argued over, sharpened and defined, and grew out of informal gatherings and associations. In short, worker capacity for political and economic mobilization stemmed from a way of life, embracing both economic position and ideas about such things as the work process and the nature of the family.[22]

I am not arguing that ideology and class consciousness are equivalent, although the two terms are often treated as similar. The reason for drawing a distinction is that many groups of people possess ideologies, or to use Ira Katznelson's term, "dispositions,"[23] by which they make sense out of their everyday lives, and which structure their response to the world. However, class consciousness is more than this, though it certainly encompasses ideology, because it speaks not just to how one must make sense out of the world but also to the fact that a group acts in opposition to other classes, opposition born out of a struggle to control the economic and political environment. Class consciousness, then, contains both a cognitive and a material dimension. It involves ways of thinking about the world, as well as the concrete relations that give rise to it and the social bonds that sustain it. By distinguishing class consciousness from ideology, we avoid the trap of assuming that because a group possesses an ideology (which we can usually find if we hunt long enough) it is a class. This does not mean that we cast ideology aside as a crucial variable, only that we see it as part of the process of class formation and the development of class consciousness. We cannot, then, have a class without class consciousness (which is one of Thompson's central points), but we can have ideology without class.

Ideology remains as central an element as material force in shaping class action, and we need to give our attention to those mechanisms that allow for the expression and mobilization of ideology, as well as to those factors that inhibit it. Here I wish to emphasize the fact that, in American society, one of the ways people have learned about the nature of their oppression and about how to articulate the values they wish to protect, is through their participation in class organization. In mobilizing, in trying to actually change the economic and political system, people create themselves as a class. Politics, broadly defined, is not secondary but central to the process of class formation in American society. More specifically, political parties have often served as distinct class organizations.

Theda Skocpol has appropriately called our attention to American political parties as a means through which contesting groups both express and attempt to act on the basis of class interests.[24] She has been criticized, however, for ignoring social class and for failing to examine the means by which class contradictions become embedded in the modern state.[25] Skocpol tends to see party and state as independent systems, and to see neither party nor state policy as the result of class struggle. I would argue that it is often via the political party that class contradictions become imbedded within the state system. Class, party, and state are intimately linked. State structure and state policy are determined by the class contradictions imbedded within them.[26] Among the Western industrialized countries the political party has been, and can still be, a means for articulating and shaping class consciousness, which in turn forms the nature and structure of the modern state.

But it would be foolish to suggest the American political parties represent distinct social classes. Groups often compete for dominance within the party (within the Democratic party, for example, unions, industrialists, and ethnic groups compete, to name but a few), in order to shape national or state policy.[27] Much of the struggle between classes thus occurs as a result of their attempt to achieve hegemony within a party. The political process also masks class struggle. One could describe this process as a struggle over organizational capacities; in fact, as I will argue, the attempt of American farmers to create themselves as a class, and to develop class consciousness, was dependent in large part on organizational capacities.[28] This position is not unlike that which Marx articulated in *The Eighteenth Brumaire*.

> In so far as millions of families live under economic conditions of existence that separate their mode of life, their interests and their culture from other classes, and put them in hostile opposition to the latter, they form a class. In so far as there is merely a local inter-connection among these small-holding peasants, and the identity of their interests begets no community, no national bond, and no political organization among them, they do not form a class. They are consequently incapable of enforcing their class interest in their own name, whether through parliament or through a convention.[29]

A group's ability to become a class is affected by internal divisions, or structural capacities, and the overall nature of the class structure at any given historical moment. At any given time, the class structure of a society is made up of diverse economic locations or positions. Some people are white-collar workers, some blue-collar, others are managers and capitalists, or, in our case, they may be farmers or merchants. Each of these groups possesses different structural capacities for mobilizing as a class, and these are intimately related to their organizational capacities. For instance, miners have traditionally had a high degree of interaction, have seen themselves as occupying a distinct position in society, and as a result have acted in concert. Many service workers, on the other hand, are widely separated from one another, do not live and work in the same communities, and tend not to act in unison. A farmer's distance from his neighbors affected his ability to sustain a personalized political commitment. People's structural capacities also may be affected by the fact that they are divided from one another by religion or ethnicity. Class consciousness, in turn, is determined by people's organizational and structural capacities, and their attempt to *act* as a class *for* itself.

Class organizations loom large in our analysis as a factor not only in shaping class consciousness but in determining whether a class will be successful—whether it can become a class *in* and *for* itself. There is an inherent danger in even using the term "class consciousness," for it has been taken to assume an either/or condition. That is, a group possesses a class consciousness, assumed to be "correct," or it does not, and thereby is possessed of "false" consciousness.[30] In our model there is no such thing as false consciousness. Structural conditions and class capacities combine in such a way as to produce strategies which may or may not be successful in shaping state policy. People may choose strategies which isolate them from other classes, mobilize powerful elites against them, or allow their movement to be defused at the ballot box by the dominant parties endorsing elements of their platforms. In short, rational actors sometimes make strategic mistakes, and not because they were infected by "false" consciousness. (The conditions under which they might make fewer mistakes are treated below.)

Class theory can be an invaluable tool for understanding why class conflict exists, and for keeping our attention focused on the element of exploitation. However, traditional class theory has not helped us greatly to understand the processes by which people do or do not mobilize as classes, and why they succeed or fail in creating themselves as autonomous classes. I believe that our understanding of the dynamics of class formation can be enhanced by conceptualizing class formation as a social movement, keeping in mind that class movements involve a struggle over surplus value.

Class Movements as Social Movements

Sources of Solidarity and Bases of Mobilization

Something other than sheer economic distress must be invoked to account for the rise of a class movement. Usually, challenges to traditional values and a sense of community cause people to take up arms. Hundreds of thousands of farmers in the North and South joined the Farmers' Alliance in an attempt to halt the growing power of corporate America over their lives. Steven Hahn, in his study of those yeoman farmers from the Georgia Upcountry who joined the Alliance, said that it was because of changed social relations. Upcountry farmers were, in Hahn's view, reacting to a new law that would have required them, at considerable expense, to keep their livestock penned rather than roaming freely, as had been done for decades. This new law acted as a catalyst to "articulate and politicize the responses of petty producers to disruptive social change."[31] The proposed changes in grazing rights led to the farmers' fear that their whole lives were being subordinated to the capitalist market system. The Alliance, and then the Populist party which grew out of it, provided a means by which farmers could articulate threatened values and stand against challenges to their tra-

The Wichita National Guard unit was rushed to Topeka with their new Gatling guns to keep order during the Republican-Populist "War of 1893." Courtesy Kansas State Historical Society.

ditional way of life. As with early nineteenth-century artisans on the Continent, a threat to traditional value systems provided the impetus for mobilization. Yet, in the case of Kansas farmers, it was less that cherished values were threatened than that they felt capitalist America, of which they were a part, was treating them unfairly. They wanted to protect a way of life they cherished, but they wanted to do so by receiving a fair price for the goods they produced, by being successful capitalists.

The immediate social world of class actors plays a decisive role in determining whether they will become involved in a movement, ignore it, or abandon it at a later stage. As Mark Granovetter has said, "Actors do not behave or decide as atoms outside a social context, nor do they adhere slavishly to a script written for them by the particular intersection of social categories they happen to occupy. Their attempts at purposive action are instead embedded in concrete, ongoing systems of relations."[32] Hahn's Georgia yeomen abandoned the Alliance because ties of kith and kin reasserted themselves when the movement foundered. It is something of a paradox, then, that although people may mobilize on the basis of traditional values, and become radicalized as a result, often ties to local communities and age-old values can limit their possibilities. Sometimes people cannot transcend the localism that served to fire the original movement. In addition, as Mary Ann Clawson has so ably demonstrated in her study of fraternal organizations at the turn of the century, a substantial number of people were and are embedded in organizations that act to "deconstruct class as a basis for organization, mobilization, and solidarity."[33] (As we will see in chapter 4, Kansas farmers were embedded in organizations that cross-cut class.) To overcome such limiting contexts people must be educated, and must understand that they need to act as a *class*. How does this come about?

Strategy and Creative Escalation

One of the ways in which people learn to act in concert is through involvement in a social movement. The social, or class movement, serves several important functions. Movements help to translate grievances into a sense of injustice, a key element, as Barrington Moore noted, in sustaining mobilization.[34] People must come to feel that traditional social rules have been violated, that injustices have been created, and that they can do something about it. A class movement, then, must possess an effective protest ideology, one which can explain past failure, current defeats, and provide hope for the future.[35]

Though people come to a movement with definite expectations, they also develop new ones as a result of confronting the established political and economic order. Lawrence Goodwyn said that nineteenth-century American farmers developed a counterideology as a result of their involvement in the Farmers' Alliance.[36] That is, they met together, discussed their grievances, developed ideas about how to deal with their economic plight, and tried to put the ideas into operation by forming economic cooperatives. Having formed cooperatives, they found merchants and bankers allied against them, because their efforts threatened capital's control over labor power and over marketing and distribution systems. By trying to change the system, farmers learned who their enemies were and what they were up against. In this century, coal miners who mobilized against owners, and found themselves confronted with hired thugs protected by state and local governments, or even had public armies turned against them, learned that large capital and the state walked hand in hand. Kansas farmers, in their efforts to form a third party, found themselves locked in conflict with the dominant political machines, and were educated as a result. Kansas farmers were not, as Goodwyn suggests, educated in the alliances, but in the larger political world.

The strategies that a group of people use are seldom simple or limited to one technique, unless goals are very limited. A sit-down strike may be a way of achieving immediate wage concessions, but it will not be the way by which the working class comes to control the means of production. The history of groups moving toward dominance are replete with examples of the use of first one and then another strategy, as the group inches closer to its final purpose.

In the late nineteenth century, American cotton farmers found themselves facing ruin. The price of cotton had dropped to its lowest point since the Civil War, and many lived in conditions of debt peonage. Those farmers who composed the Texas Alliance first tried to work out simple trade agreements with local merchants; then, when the merchants would not cooperate, they tried to set up their own stores, mills, and cotton gins. Finding themselves again challenged, they tried to market their cotton by themselves; that effort was followed by a joint-note program designed to free them from the lien system. They staged a boycott against the jute trust (those who produced the jute used to bag the raw cotton); and finally, when that failed, they formed a political party.[37] The strategies that Kansas farmers adopted were, however, much more attenuated, for they were never really involved in cooperative economic endeavors. Their efforts were first and foremost political.

There is an important relationship between strategy, creative escalation, learning, and success.[38] Normally, it is the responsibility of the leadership of a social-movement organization to promulgate an ideology that will explain failure or externalize blame.[39] That is, if a group is blocked in its attempts to win concessions through a sit-down strike, or withholding rent payments, or rioting, blame must be laid at the door of those the group is opposing. For example, the opposition is said to have had the support of the local police, or it is said that the "management" was negotiating in bad faith, or that landlords do not care about people. If a strategy does not work, a group must move to another level, must creatively escalate the battle. Doug McAdam, in his analysis of the 1960s civil rights movement, described a process by which the leadership of civil rights groups *consciously* adopted new strategies when morale appeared to be waning.[40] There was a decision to stage protests in areas where the police were known for their violent behavior, so that civil rights protestors and groups would gain national support, and so that they could make the implicit and explicit point that this was a racist society. The success of new strategies is highly dependent on learning, however. Members of groups must know and understand why an old strategy has failed, and why new ones must be employed.

Creative escalation has its risks; it can create schisms within an organization. In class movements participants may not be willing to choose a revolutionary path, if the struggle appears long and difficult, and the results seem problematic. Without organized learning they may just as easily choose a reformist course. There is no magic formula, but one can say that strategies which are debated by the rank and file and are clearly understood by them are those likely to be supported. This is a major reason why "political" education has played such a prominent role among revolutionary cadres. The Vietcong, for instance, talked about the lessons to be learned from previous encounters, and these discussions served to cohere the group and boost morale.

Escalation poses yet another type of threat to the organization. Escalation can cause powerful outside elites to mobilize against the group in question, as Michael Schwartz has noted in the case of the Southern Alliance.[41] Elites, too, will learn during an extended struggle.[42] In the case of the civil rights movement, some southern law enforcement officials found that a strategy of violent response was counterproductive. Instead, they chose to adhere to the law and to enforce it in a nondiscriminatory pattern. In short, they put the civil rights leaders in positions where they either acted peacefully, and hence defused the movement, or acted violently themselves, and hence lost support they needed to gain concessions. The actions of Kansas farmers resulted in the mobilization of powerful probusiness groups against the farmers, groups whose image of what America should become was bolstered by a national ideology encouraging growth and development. A movement must be in a position to choose courses of action that avoid the extremes of mobilizing powerful opposition groups and exhausting its own momentum. The importance of *both* organization and learning looms even larger when we consider the issue of the rational actor.

The Rational Class-Actor
Selective Incentives and Moral Suasion

The extreme position in the rational-actor debate is taken by Mancur Olson, who argued that there is little reason to expect political organizations, unions, or social movements to act on the basis of the specific interests of the individuals who make up the movement, or to expect individuals to act on the basis of the collective. On the contrary, "unless the number of individuals in a group is quite small, or unless there is coercion or some other specific device to make individuals act in their common interest, *rational self-interested individuals* will not act to achieve their common or group interests."[43] Were this true, there would be little reason to believe that people could constitute themselves as a class and act as one. Yet the perspective deserves examination rather than simple rejection.

Much of the controversy surrounding Olson's theory revolves around the issue of solidarity versus selective incentives (see J. Craig Jenkins for a summary of the debates).[44] Anthony Oberschall, as well as John McCarthy and Mayer Zald, have argued that one of the primary reasons people mobilize is to secure benefits made available to them by movement entrepreneurs, or benefits generated by the movement through political action.[45] Bruce Fireman and William Gamson, in a spirited critique of this position, argued that although the "amount of resources at the discretion of potential constituents, the degree of previously existing organization among potential constituents . . . and—overall—the structure of the political economy constraining the mobilization and wielding of resources" are significant, the impact of these factors is often mitigated by the desire to achieve a collective good.[46] In short, solidarity and moral vision count. Social movements, and again by implication class movements, must

> offer the *collective incentives* of group solidarity and commitment to moral purpose. Group solidarity and purposive incentives are collective in that they entail the fusion of personal and collective interests. Movement supporters, like all socialized actors, act in terms of internalized values and sentiments as well as calculations of self-interest. The major task in mobilization, then, is to generate solidarity and moral commitment to the broad collectivities in whose name movements act.[47]

Bert Klandermans put the matter slightly differently. He, too, is uncomfortable with the strong version of Olson's argument. Klandermans found that people's willingness to participate in strikes depended, in large part, on their belief that other workers would participate and that there was a reasonable chance of success. "Ade-

quate diffusion of knowledge of the collective good is the corner-
stone," said Klandermans, "of every mobilization campaign."[48]

John A. Hannigan, in his review of the work of Alain Touraine
and Manuel Castells in social movement theory, also argued that
selective incentives must "be buttressed by the collective incentives
related to group solidarity and commitment to a moral purpose."[49]
More importantly, he noted that often these moral purposes, or
collective agreements about means, grow out of involvement in the
movement itself.

One must combine a rational-actor perspective with an understanding that people may join a movement for noninstrumental
reasons, and that an image of the collective good and solidarity can
grow out of action. Of course there will be those who join a cause
because they believe benefits will be forthcoming and who readily
exit when the benefits do not appear. The longer people are in an
organization and the tighter the networks are that brought them
together in the first place, the more probably they will come to
identify with the collective, and be willing to sacrifice short-term individual interests for the long-term gains of the group. People,
then, can make rational decisions to participate in collective actions
to produce collective goods from which they will benefit.

Yet another caveat concerning the rational-actor perspective
must be introduced. Rational actions sometimes have unintended
consequences, and what may be rational in the short term, whether
for the individual or the class, may not be rational in the long run.
Individual rational decisions may be a collective irrationality. Let us
clarify the point by an example. Calhoun, in his treatment of Marx's
designation of the working class as potentially revolutionary, noted
that Marx was correct to argue that only by behaving as a revolutionary class and acting in concert could working men and women
achieve their goals. But, he says, Marx was wrong to assume that
"class must supersede all other collectivities for the workers, and
that those interests which they had in common as members of the
working class must become their exclusive interests, and that, therefore, it was individually rational for each worker to participate
in the collectively rational overthrow of capitalist domination by
the working class."[50] Calhoun argued that it was rational for the
nineteenth-century British working class to choose options which
produced immediate benefits. To the extent that workers, or any
other group, had options other than engaging in pure class action—which could and did produce dire consequences—it was in-

dividually rational to pursue low-cost goals, even when the results did not advance the class as a whole (were collectively irrational). As we will see, it could be in an individual farmer's interest to vote with the Alliance or the Populist party for one election, and then be in his interest to vote with the Republican party in future elections, especially if that party could pass legislation which seemed to deal with the economic problems that confronted him.

Movement Formation, Size, and Power

If mobilization for action is rapid, the organizational structures necessary for learning to take place are weak or absent. If a movement is large in size (which a class movement must of necessity be), learning is inhibited. Claus Offe has provided a detailed statement of the relationship between individual interests and the propensity of a group of people to mobilize and engage in prolonged action, which I will modify for my purposes.[51] Offe developed his model on the basis of a discussion about unions and argued that there was a contradictory relationship between size of an organization and the power it has to affect the larger environment. That is, the greater the size of a group, the less the propensity for any individual to be sufficiently motivated to sacrifice him/herself for the group's goals. In the case of a large union, a member might not see why it was in his/her direct interests (either economic, political, or organizational, in the sense that support would strengthen the organization and lend credibility to its demands) to act at the union's behest. For a union or any other form of class organization to be successful, people must be educated by the organization in the movement culture, and/or ideology; otherwise, they are not likely to support its long-term goals and purposes. Likewise, if the time between recruitment and attempted mobilization is short, then the likelihood of a group's success is diminished, because its members will not have had time to develop a movement culture or will not understand the organizational policies or tactics that lead to discipline. (As will be seen below in my discussion of Piven and Cloward, this means that although system crises may produce short-term gains, this very fact may lead to demobilization.)

There would be a direct and positive relationship between size and power were it not for the fact that size leads, inevitably, to a diversity of interests, which reduces the ability to motivate people for collective goals. (This is also true of speed of mobilization.)

Here is where the boundary debates can assume importance: by isolating the common experiences of those who sell their labor power, and identifying them to potential movement recruits so as to produce greater solidarity. Schwartz has recognized the paradox of size and power. "The group needs a larger membership to succeed; and at the same time, it needs success to grow."[52] However, this process will unravel if the organization cannot solve people's grievances or if it cannot educate members. Many would see the tendency toward bureaucracy or oligarchy as extraordinary and unfortunate. I see it as quite normal and potentially useful. That is, given the diversity of membership within the Alliance, and then within the Populist party, a centralized or bureaucratic structure was essential for welding together disparate interests. However, as will be seen, for a class movement to maintain coherence and continuity, the leaders must represent the interests of their constituents.

The Process of Bureaucratization

There has been a long-standing debate within the social-movement literature between those who see bureaucratization as inevitable within a successful movement and those who do not. William Gamson, for example, has suggested that groups with a well-developed division of labor and organizational structure are most capable of mobilizing constituencies with widely diverse interests.[53] Charles Tilly and his associates have documented the shift from communally based organizations, which engage in small-scale localized action, to those characteristic of modern industrialized societies, in which centralized, formally organized movements dominate.[54] Summarizing the position, J. Craig Jenkins has noted:

> The growth of industrial capitalism and the building of modern states destroyed the autonomy of small solidary groups and forced claimants to compete in a larger national political arena in which large numbers and bureaucratic structures were keys to success. Furthermore, urbanization and the growth of the mass media reduced the costs of large-scale mobilization, making bureaucratized associations more feasible. Finally, the institutionalization of liberal democracy, especially mass electoral participation, furnished an environment well suited to movement organizations that could mobilize large numbers of supporters.[55]

Those who believe that bureaucratization is not inevitable usually point to small-scale personal-growth movements, or note that the civil rights or women's movements grew without a centralized bureaucracy, but they miss an important point: even though different civil rights or women's movements pursued somewhat different specific goals, and often represented different constituencies, they still shared a common set of assumptions.

As a group shifts from localized concerns—the very issues that may have drawn people into a movement—to national concerns, bureaucratization may be crucial to the group's success. If a group lacks a centralized hierarchy, or has few links among local leaders and organizations and the national unions or parties, the group's chances of success are lessened. Whether a group has a well-developed organizational structure from which to mount a prolonged assault strongly affects its chance of success and, consequently, the extent to which the group can count on the loyalties of its members.

I have outlined a process whereby size leads to diversity of interests, which leads to bureaucratization (or conversely, negates full democratic decision-making), which then enhances the ability of the leadership to mobilize members and gain power. In the case of a large union, this model suggests that, in order to exercise or gain power, a group must command some needed material resource. Unions can threaten work stoppages, strikes, and boycotts, and their threats may be taken seriously, depending on the size of the organization and the extent to which the leadership is able to call the members out, keep them out, or prevent them from walking off the job. Individualistic interests must be suppressed in favor of an overarching goal, and this is usually accomplished through a centralized or bureaucratic organization.

In the case of the Kansas Alliance of the Populist party, one of the only threats that farmers could wield over the system was their vote. In meeting after long meeting, farmers talked about reform of the system through the ballot box. Initially, they picked slates which they thought would favor their cause: then, with the formation of the People's party, they ran their own candidates. At all times, it was their votes which sent shock waves through the political system. Once the party was formed, the link between size and power caused the movement to unravel. Candidates were chosen who did not represent the interests of all of the farmers, and farmers lost the chance to play an active role in choosing who would and who would not run. With the sudden death of the local alliances, farmers lost their chance to play a directly active role in shaping the party's platform, which is one reason why the cause of silver came to dominate discussions in 1896. In short, the foundation that gave rise to the movement was quickly eroded, and a leadership structure emerged which was out of touch with the very base it claimed to represent.

Organization, Success, and System Crisis

Gamson's detailed study of groups that have challenged the dominant political-economic order isolated several variables that relate to success.[56] His dependent variable was defined as full acceptance, meaning that the social-movement organization was recognized as a central political actor (that is, it made a difference, and its concerns were taken into account as, say, were the concerns of Jesse Jackson's Rainbow Coalition during the 1984 presidential campaign) and that the movement had actually achieved its goals and objectives. First, he found that size was positively related to acceptance, though not necessarily to success. Therefore, dominant political parties will try to absorb renegade movements either by coopting the leadership or through the selective endorsement of the movement's less radical demands. Gamson argued that bureaucratization and centralization were central to success, because most attempts to challenge a given order demand long and sustained political conflict.

> Bureaucratic organization provides a solution to the problem of combat readiness—a cadre of reliable workers with coordinated tasks. Its contribution to the management of internal dissent is minimal; bureaucratic groups are at least as likely to experience factional splits as nonbureaucratic ones. But their ability to act quickly also depends on their having solved the problem of internal division. Centralization of power is an organizational device for handling the problem of internal division and providing unity.[57]

Gamson also found that bureaucratic organizations which narrowed their goals could offer members definite resources for participation, and those which were unruly during periods of political crisis were most likely to achieve success. Tilly and Skocpol have both demonstrated that a group's chances of success are substantially increased during periods of crisis, whether economic or political.[58]

Can a class movement succeed only if it has at its core a solid organization of dedicated members ready to seize upon weaknesses in the political-economic order? Frances Fox Piven and Richard A. Cloward argue powerfully to the contrary.[59] In their study *Poor People's Movements*, they claim that movement organizers who concentrate on building an organization risk the very goals they hope to realize.

> During those brief periods in which people are aroused to indignation, when they are prepared to defy the authorities to whom they ordinarily defer . . . those who call themselves leaders do not usually escalate the momentum of the people's protests. They do not because they are preoccupied with trying to build and sustain embryonic formal organizations in the sure conviction that these organizations will enlarge and become powerful.[60]

Piven and Cloward say, even more precisely, "The poor can create crises but cannot control the response to them."[61] According to them, poor people must seize whatever benefits the moment presents, not waste their precious time and resources building organizations which will, in the long run, be co-opted anyway. The American political system is supposed to be particularly vulnerable to mass protests and demonstrations, after which people settle for what they can get, rather than hold out for long-term "revolutionary" change. If there is a strategy for movements of the poor, it is to wait for and identify those situations in which the system is particularly vulnerable and in which politicians will make concessions. (This is not a bad strategy, especially if the concessions relate to an increased share of the surplus value, which is what class conflict ultimately comes down to. It is a weak strategy if people cannot sustain continued demands.)

One of Piven and Cloward's main contributions has concerned how protest is institutionally determined and shaped—what is, and is not, permitted—and why the protest of the poor is often aimed at very specific targets rather than at what one might think of as social structures. It is aimed at specific people or companies because working men and women "do not experience monopoly capitalism," they experience the factory, the assembly line, the foreman, the pay packet, and the employer; the people on relief "do not experience American welfare policy," they experience shabby waiting rooms, overseers, caseworkers, and the dole.[62] This is exactly why education through action, guided by an organization, is so important.

In his masterful summary and critique of Piven and Cloward,

Eric Hobsbawm has pointed out that what "the situation permits protestors to do depends on how the protesting groups have organized their everyday lives and labor."[63] The unorganized poor *can* withhold their support from the system, refuse collaboration, and rebel "against the rule and authorities associated with everyday activities."[64]

According to Piven and Cloward this localized protest is the most effective. But as Hobsbawm correctly emphasizes, mass protest cannot be an end in itself. Labor unionization or organization in the United States developed *out of* the mass protests and mobilizations of relatively unorganized workers. Piven and Cloward are right to criticize organizing efforts which get in the way of mobilization but mistaken in arguing that lasting gains can be achieved without organization. If unionization occurred because of mass protests, workers made gains in the years that followed not because they disbanded but because there were organizations that represented their interests. Organizations sustain people's efforts to change their lives.

I agree with Hobsbawm that the poor, "indeed, any subaltern group, become a subject rather than an object of history only through formalized collectivities."[65] Change does not occur through blind reaction—challenging the system to see how elites respond—but through organized efforts (see Mark Traugott for a discussion of the importance of organizations in crystallizing and mobilizing class sentiment).[66] Organizations grounded in people's own experiences, organizations that represent people's interests, have the greatest likelihood of wringing concessions from the state and winning control of the political and economic system. Organized groups, whether of the poor or the middle classes, have always posed the greatest threat to state power. It is organized protest, today as in the past, that authorities seek to prevent. That is why, in the late nineteenth century in America, the cry went up from bankers and merchants that farmers and workers were attempting to pass "class" legislation. Indeed they were.

Alternative Perspectives

One cannot, of course, consider populism without reference to John Hicks's classic, *The Populist Revolt.* In this sympathetic treatment of the farmers' plight, Hicks reduces the origins of the movement to economic grief and sees its failure as due, largely, to the farmers' inability to significantly change the political and economic course of the day. In his view, the Alliance and the People's party were "the inevitable attempts of a bewildered people to find relief from a state of economic distress."[67] Richard Hofstadter, in his direct counterattack on Hicks, *The Age of Reform*, argued that Populism arose primarily as a result of the status anxiety felt by farmers as the country became increasingly industrialized and the needs and concerns of the farming class were devalued. In his view, Populism failed as a movement because it was made up of reactionary misfits who did not want to join the parade of progress.[68] One of the most obvious problems with these two opposed views is that each author sees a direct link between economic problems and political behavior or ideology, whereas the process by which a social movement translates economic concerns into political action is anything but immediate or direct. Ideology and class consciousness were shaped within the movement, as economic concerns and inequalities were translated into a claim for justice. Second, to see this movement as springing from status anxiety is to degrade it, and to fail to understand that people were involved in a fight over the shape of America's political and economic institutions. Hofstadter was writing history backwards. Accepting the institutions of the 1950s (when his book was published) as inevitable, he looked back in history and saw challenges to these institutions as retrograde. This meant that he, and those who followed similar styles of analysis, could not see the fundamental class struggles which shaped the emergence of American institutions.

One of the works that has most profoundly influenced my effort is Goodwyn's monumental *Democratic Promise*.[69] Goodwyn had articulated a process by which he believed farmers developed a democratic political consciousness. He said that one could sum up the origins of Populism in one sentence: "The cooperative movement recruited American farmers, and their subsequent experience within the cooperatives radically altered their political consciousness."[70] He went on to elaborate a four-stage process of democratic movement building, which involved, first, the creation of an autonomous institution (in this case the Alliance) in which people could develop images and explanations of their plight that differed from those of the dominant classes. Second, there had to be a tactical means to recruit people to the movement; that is, economic cooperatives with distinct benefits encouraged people to enlist in the Alliance cause. Once in the movement, they could be educated— the third state—through the Alliance lecture system. And finally, in their assault on established institutions, people would form an autonomous political organization, which they did when the Populist party was created.[71] This is an imposing theory and has decided benefits. Chief among them is the fact that movement formation is seen as a sequential process, and success is seen as dependent on education and on the creation of an autonomous political organization. But as a description of what transpired in a state such as Kansas it is wrong.

The linchpin in Goodwyn's theory is an economic cooperative, or suballiance, in which people are educated through trial and error, in which they learn to practice democracy, in which they develop solidarity and achieve a sense of efficacy. However, as Stanley Parsons argued,[72] and as I demonstrate here, economic cooperatives, let alone those affiliated with the Alliance, were scarce on the Great Plains. Second, in the case of Kansas, there was not a slow progression from economic cooperation through the development of an Alliance infrastructure to a political movement. The Alliance exploded on the scene, its growth was extremely rapid, and it was involved from its very inception in politics. Thus, I also disagree with Goodwyn's primary understanding of what the Alliance was about, certainly what it was about in Kansas. Goodwyn sees the shift to politics as the final stage in movement evolution. I am arguing that the movement was always about politics—the desire to achieve power.

With that said, however, it is also possible to see much of what I have done as a confirmation of Goodwyn's ideas. How can that be? I believe that Goodwyn's model of what a *successful* democratic movement must do, and must be, is essentially correct. That is, there must be an organization in which people can practice democracy and develop counter-hegemonic ideas. They must be able to learn from past mistakes and, above all, they must possess an autonomous organization; in our society this implies a political party that will represent a distinct set of class interests. A key to the failure of the movement in Kansas was just this: the inability to sustain an autonomous political organization. Thus farmers could not pass legislation that would alter in any basic manner the dominant capitalist institutions.

Another scholar whose work shaped this project was Michael Schwartz, who developed an elaborate model for understanding the potential success and failure of protest movements through his examination of the Southern Farmers' Alliance in *Radical Protest and Social Structure*. Schwartz, like Goodwyn, located the rise of the movement in the economic conditions of southern farmers, though he clearly understands that people translated economic misery into action through the Alliance. He shows the economic degradation experienced by yeoman farmers, how they were at the mercy of town merchants, and how many of them were driven to the level of debt-peons beholden to store owners, or became sharecroppers for the larger plantation owners. He also argues that the slow evolution of the Southern Farmers' Alliance played a primary role in educating, politicizing, and mobilizing these same people. It was within the Alliance that people learned to articulate their grievances, formulate possible solutions such as the subtreasury scheme, and act. Schwartz also makes the significant point that people sometimes act "incorrectly," and thereby fail.

But if people failed to act correctly it was, according to Schwartz, because they were not allowed to learn from their mistakes—were, in fact, actively prevented from doing so. His chief explanation for this phenomenon was that the Alliance was dominated by an oligarchy—a planter class whose interests differed from those of the yeomen who made up the rank and file. (Dwight Billings found this same pattern in North Carolina.)[73] Because the planters' interests differed from those of ordinary farmers, members could not practice democracy and hence could not learn what would or would not make the movement successful. There were other factors which contributed to the demise of the Southern Alliance (racism, the counterattack by the Democratic party), yet Schwartz strongly implies that the Alliance would have succeeded if: (1) people had been in a position to learn; (2) people had learned what would and would not work in real political terms; (3) the movement had continued to grow and the Alliance had addressed farmers' concrete problems; (4) they had been able to maintain organizational discipline, which would have given them political and economic power; and finally, (5) oligarchy had not reigned, undermining the democratic structure and the learning process necessary for sustained action. In sum, Schwartz's explanation for the growth and decline of the movement is that farmers, because of economic problems, formed cooperatives and became politicized as a result of their involvement in them. Although farmers took economic and political action, they ultimately failed because the movement was undercut by the establishment or assertion of oligarchy. He also argues, while I find to the contrary, that speed of mobilization contributed to success. I believe that speed of mobilization contributed to the movement's failure.

Schwartz's position parallels that of Goodwyn in many ways. Be-

sides tracing the origins to economic problems, both writers tend to
see the degradation of the Alliance occurring with a shift to politics,
albeit for different reasons. Goodwyn argued that the shift to politics eroded the cultural claims that made the movement unique,
and that followers became demoralized in the face of defeat and
the dominance of an oligarchy. Schwartz suggested that the shift to
politics contributed to planter dominance. Schwartz saw oligarchy
as incipient in the movement, while Goodwyn implied that it occurred because politics necessarily led to compromise, deradicalization, and the dominance of the many by the few.

This theme has been echoed by Argersinger, who said, "Populism died because it failed to transcend the American political system. It was killed by those very factors of politics that its founders
had intended to kill: prejudice, elite manipulation, corruption."[74]
The language of democracy and cooperation, which had origi-
nated outside of the political system, could not, in Argersinger's
view, bridge the gap between a mass movement and the formation
of a political party. Once professional politicians came to dominate,
the "*party became increasingly oligarchic.*"[75]

My dispute does not have to do with whether the movement became oligarchic—for this certainly happened in Kansas—but with
why an oligarchy developed, and what the implications of this are
for democratic movements. It is worth remembering that neither
the Alliance nor the Populist party were of a piece. When Schwartz
writes about the Southern Alliance and Goodwyn describes the
Texas Alliance (which is where most of his data come from, though
he tries, inappropriately, to generalize to the movement as a whole),
they are describing very different organizational models. Oligarchy
occurred in Kansas, not because of class differences embedded within the organization, and not just because it turned to politics. It occurred because there was no organizational structure that allowed
people to learn from their mistakes or to debate new strategies, and
because many of the leaders had reform interests which differed
from those of farmers. I will eventually argue that oligarchy is the
rule rather than the exception, and that it need not necessarily lead
to the degradation of a movement. In fact, it is my position that a
strongly centralized, bureaucratic organization is essential for long-
term struggles.

This movement and its evolution must be understood within a
specific social context and the existing social formation, and at the
level of the national political economy as well as at the state and re-

gional levels. Hahn, in *The Roots of Southern Populism*, argued, as already noted, that kinship ties were more powerful than class ties, so that when results were not forthcoming, Upcountry farmers withdrew their support from the Alliance and the Populist party. He and I are describing different social movements. Ties of kin were weak in Kansas partly because it had been settled in a remarkably brief period of time. The kind of community which Hahn describes for Georgia simply did not exist in Kansas. Midwestern farmers were not protesting, as were their southern brothers, the shift from being subsistence yeomen to being capitalist farmers. Midwestern farmers came to the Great Plains to make money, and risked a great deal to do so. They did not oppose the capitalist system per se, but a system which treated them unfairly. The reasons they mobilized, the form the mobilization took, the language they used to describe their plight, and the reasons for their success and failure, differed considerably from the situation in the South. Different structural, material, and ideological circumstances produced different responses in different regions. By disentangling a portion of the movement, we can see more clearly some of the conditions that led to its success and failure.

The focus of the analysis will be the state of Kansas, which was the epicenter of the shock felt when Bryan ran against McKinley for president. It was a state with a long history of reform, the state to form the "first people's government on earth." It elected a Populist governor along with a Populist House and then Senate, and it sent Populist senators and congressmen to Washington. Kansas gave some of America's most powerful and popular orators a platform: Mary Elizabeth Lease, Annie Diggs, William Jennings Bryan, "Whiskers" Peffer, "Sockless" Jerry Simpson trooped to scores of small towns throughout the state and spoke before crowds of hundreds.

Kansas was, and was not, unique. It was unique in the speed with which the movement formed and in the initial electoral success of the Alliance. It was a state whose institutions and people came into being almost exclusively after the Civil War. But though Kansas was unique, it was not isolated from the effects of the national political economy, and debates that took place in urban America concerning the legitimacy of reform and reformers were heard on the prairie. In chapter 2, I examine the larger social formation and its impact on the state of Kansas. The class-structuring that occurred as a result of a war and the feelings that Americans had about this are

examined. Of particular concern was the fact that a sense of griev-
ance was slowly building among agrarians, and that neither of the
dominant parties seemed interested in doing anything other than
promoting business. A battle was in the making over the very definition of America, about how progress and prosperity were to be
achieved.

Chapter 3 details the unique history of Kansas, in particular the
fact that it was settled as a free state after a bloody conflict and the
Republican party's early rise to dominance. All political conflicts
within Kansas would be played out against the backdrop of the
Civil War. Chapter 4 examines the specific class structure of the
state and concentrates on two communities for greater specificity.
Class structure would be an inhibiting factor in the development of
a class movement, and it would make potential alliances between
workers and farmers difficult. How members of different classes,
e.g., farmers, merchants, and workers, talked about their society,
and what grieved them, is the subject of chapter 5. It is clear that
farmers and merchants came to hold almost diametrically opposed
views as to how progress was to be achieved in the state. Chapter 6
traces the rise of a movement culture, and considers the contradictory interests that were embedded in the movement from the outset. Who actually joined the movement, and why, is detailed in
chapter 7, and attention is given to the diversity (economic and
ideological) of recruits. The speed of movement formation is taken
as a primary reason for the failure of recruits to learn a movement
ideology and develop class consciousness. Finally, in chapter 8 I examine the impact of the Alliance and the Populist party upon
voting behavior, and I consider the consquences of a group of leaders whose interests differed from those of their constituents. The
epilogue asks the question, "Were there any circumstances under
which American farmers could have triumphed?"

PART TWO
THE STRUCTURED WHOLE

2

The National Political Economy

As agricultural prices soared, the Great Plains boomed. Here men have just gotten off a train in Horton, Kansas, to buy lots in a town that had just begun to build. Circa 1880s. Courtesy Kansas Collection of the University of Kansas Libraries.

No social movement or social class arrives suddenly on the stage of history. Each develops slowly and unevenly over time. The Farmers' Alliance and Populist movement, along with late nineteenth-century class and class consciousness, were decades in the making.

The decades which preceded the rebellion of the 1890s played a major role in shaping and determining future possibilities. Walt Whitman, celebrator of America and the opportunities the country offered the laboring man, had by 1871 come to the conclusion that democratic possibilities were fast disappearing from the land. In *Democratic Vistas*, Whitman saw signs of "exceptional wealth, splendor, countless manufacturers, excess of exports, immense capital and capitalists," all of which represented "a sort of anti-democratic disease and monstrosity."[1] Whitman was not alone in his view that something had gone desperately wrong with the Jeffersonian dream.

In the period immediately after the Civil War, American society changed dramatically, moving from a weak federal system to one in which the government played a major role in stimulating investment and acting on behalf of industry. Instead of a nation of yeomen, America became a nation of people who sold their labor power to the highest bidder, rarely in circumstances that favored the laborer. The post–Civil War period coincided with the first great waves of immigration. By 1870 immigrants made up over one-third of the industrial labor force. Polite society came to define laborers and immigrants as possible saboteurs of the great engine of progress.

Anthony Giddens[2] has called the structuring properties of a society the backdrop against which people make life-decisions. These properties do not predetermine people's fate; rather, they serve as the clay out of which history is formed. Structuring conditions may be labeled as ideological, political, and economic, but no magic inheres in this trinity. It only serves to remind us what complex of factors gave rise to the Alliance and the Populist movement. People's attempts to shape a new history were responses to a growing polarization of social classes, a degradation of labor, a delegitimation of economic reform, political parties that ignored laboring men and women, and a federal government that seemed to serve the interests of the rich. The issues that Kansas farmers would come to confront and the language they would use to express their discontent were part of a larger, national dialogue. How, then, was the order that farmers attempted to change in the 1890s structured in the post–Civil War period?

America as a Class-Dominated Society

The concentration of wealth in American society can be traced to colonial times.[3] However, between the period of the Revolutionary War and the outbreak of the Civil War, "the distribution of wealth appears to have undergone an episodic change."[4] Those in the top 10 percent of the population increased their share of the nation's wealth almost threefold. Even so, the line between what we think of as the working classes and the emergent industrial or mercantile elite was not finely drawn in either people's imagination or actions.

Though independent artisans in cities such as New York would struggle with attempts to curb their power over the flow of work, these artisans did not see their lot as similar to that of simple wage laborers, some of whom they employed as journeymen and apprentices. Even wage laborers seldom saw their lot in clearly defined terms. Many hoped to become masters of their own shops, and some, like Jefferson's imaginary yeomen, longed for land and a farm of their own. Nor were antebellum merchants and industrialists cast in a uniform mold, though there were marked similarities in their worldview.

Many of the new industrialists saw themselves as the creators of a new civilization. Men such as Caleb Woodhull of New York wanted to build parks, improve the living conditions of those in the slums, and in general provide for the general uplift of the working classes.[5] Woodhull was not alone in his view that because he was about God's work—the improvement of civilization—he had every right to call in hired thugs to suppress the demands of those who wanted to stop the parade of progress as he envisioned it.

Workers, as well as farmers, would eventually react to the paternalism of the "humanitarian" capitalists. The opposition, when it came, arose first among those in established trade unions or artisanal associations, for it was the artisan whose work was directly affected by mass production and the importation of products produced by foreign laborers, or in "colonies" such as the South. Neither of the dominant political parties was responsive to the demands of the urban laborer or the recent immigrant, so there was no sharp articulation of concerns, or development of alternative policies and strategies. When the dawn of class agitation broke in the United States, a variety of different groups, with substantially different goals and purposes, had rallied: trade unions, artisans, immigrant societies, socialists, and land reformers. Not unexpectedly, then, the "movement" that emerged in the post–Civil War period was a noisy assembly of divergent programs, theories, and ideas. Thus the radical or reform movement was divided from the outset, although it was uniform in the public consciousness. Reform and reformers, as we will see, fell on hard times in the years to follow, while the ideology of industrial America came to dominate by the beginning of the twentieth century.

The antilabor press, even before the Civil War, was quick to label the efforts of workers as socialistic and to raise the specter of the Paris communards. Workers' organizations often took great pains to point out that they were neither socialist nor communist, though a handful were. Most laboring men and women argued for simple justice and fair play. Through struggle, through refinement of ideas and strategy, a growing number of men and women came to see themselves as set apart and often allied against business *and* government—precisely because government was active in suppressing labor agitation. Both labor and capital had begun to define the proper role of the government in achieving national progress and prosperity. Many of those who came to states such as Kansas after the close of the Civil War were native-born Americans, who came out of the cities to farm; they were not people who had been isolated from the debates of the prewar years concerning the proper role of labor and capital. The Civil War did not heal the deepening chasm between classes or halt the formation of class consciousness; on the contrary, the struggle over the very meaning of America—over the power to define and control the country— had begun.[6]

In 1865, President Lincoln commented on the new specter that had arisen. In his words,

> We may all congratulate ourselves that this cruel war is nearing a close. It has cost a vast amount of blood and treasure. The best blood of the flower of American youth has been freely offered upon our country's altar that the nation might live. It has been indeed a trying hour for the Republic, but I see in the near future a crisis approaching that unnerves me and causes me to tremble for the safety of my country. As a result of the war, corruption in high places will follow. The money power of the country will endeavor to prolong its reign by working upon the prejudices of the people until all wealth is aggregated in a few hands and the Republic is destroyed. I feel at this moment more anxiety for my country than ever before, even in the midst of war. God grant that my suspicions may prove groundless.[7]

The concentration that Lincoln feared took place. According to one estimate, by the year 1890 there were four thousand millionaires and billionaires in the country, whose aggregrate property was worth about $12 billion.[8] The effect of this concentration was that the total income of the poorest 50 percent, the majority of the population, was less than a yearly poverty line of $500, and over half of all American families had no property whatsoever.[9]

America was also fast becoming a nation of wage laborers rather than independent yeomen. The Civil War brought about a substantial increase in the number of small entrepreneurs or manufacturers[10] and a decline in the number of those who were independent craftsmen. By 1870, close to half of the nation's work force was employed in nonagricultural pursuits, though a great deal of the manufacturing took place in rural areas. If one combines the figures for those employed in agriculture with those employed in nonagricultural pursuits by 1870, close to two-thirds of all laboring Americans were employees.[11] Moreover, most of these employees were native-born Americans. The ideological dilemma, therefore, was that a nation of free people, who had just fought a war for freedom from slavery, found themselves to be, in their own words, *wage slaves*. This changed class structure would prove to be an important element in thwarting farmers' attempts to forge alliances with working men and women.

At the close of the war, 1.5 million men were demobilized.[12] Some sought to find a place in the manufacturing industries of the North, others turned toward the Great Plains to take up the plow. Prosperity was hard won, and policies and issues surrounding the financing of the war would continue to dominate in the years following. Farmers and workers increasingly came to feel that they had not only picked up the bill for the war but that it was one which they were continuing to pay. It seemed to many that neither the Republicans nor Democrats spoke for the growing mass of the disenchanted. "Everywhere—North and South, among Republicans and Democrats—business and financial entrepreneurs had achieved effective control of a restructured American party system."[13] How this happened, and how political concerns were expressed and refined, is of importance for understanding the context within which the Populists would play out their struggle. Later, speakers in all parties (Democrat, Republican, Greenback, Union Labor, and Populist) would use the language developed in the pre- and postwar period to articulate their political concerns, to attract voters, to explain America.

The Dominant Political Parties

The war had brought about a basic realigment in both of the dominant parties. For the Democrats, there emerged a solid South, concerned primarily with Reconstruction, opposition to the Republicans, who were seen as the source of their miseries, and the re-

establishment of white hegemony. With the departure of the antislavery bloc of Democrats from the party in the North and the loss
of its rural base, "it became even more than before the party of immigrants and their descendants, and increasingly so as immigration
swelled; and a political line of cleavage on ethnic and religious lines
that had long existed—old-stock Protestants in one party and new-
stock Catholics in the other—was sharpened."[14] With the reform
element absent, the party became, and was seen as, the party of the
professional politician.

The Republicans dominated in the North and in the states making up the great heartland of the American continent. Divisions
within the Republican party in the prewar years were eroded, as
the war went its weary course. The Whig party moved almost intact
into the Republican ranks, bringing with it policies apparently
heightened and legitimated by the war effort: the beliefs that the
federal government should play an aggressive role in developing
manufacturing and commerce through restrictive, protective tariffs, that it should expand the banking industry, push forward
internal development by promoting a transcontinental railroad system, and encourage settlement of western lands through the Homestead Act.[15] There was also a reformist element within Republican
ranks, though for the time being the reform that would be preached
was one which encouraged men to improve by turning their backs
on the liquor bottle.

The Radicals, those who had stood for no compromise on the
issue of slavery within the Republican party, seem from today's perspective a curious lot, for their radicalism took the form of trying to
find a path that would secure peace through prosperity in the postwar years. Samuel Johnson, one of the most prominent of the reform leaders within the party, was particularly concerned about the
Knights of St. Crispin (an organization that represented shoemakers). In a series of articles Johnson acknowledged that although labor's protests against monopoly power and the railroad
were legitimate, organizing was not. From Olympian heights he
calmly reasoned that "The true industrial problem for our politics
is not, how shall majorities prove the extent of their power, but how
shall they learn to respect the principle that the rights of labor and
the rights of property are mutual guarantees."[16] The rights of capital and the rights of labor were, then, seen as equal. No longer was
labor the primary source of wealth. The capitalist, too, contributed
to the process of expansion. The laboring classes were supposed

to see themselves as *partners* in progress; they were not to make special demands based on their class position. The worst thing that laborers could do, according to men like Johnson, was to try and solve their problems through an *immoral* manipulation of the currency.

The Currency Debate

The currency debate was to become the whirlpool that drew everyone in. The war had been financed primarily by bonds sold through major banking houses, such as that of Jay Cooke. In order to make the bonds attractive, Congress passed an amendment providing for payment of the interest in gold coin. In order to raise the necessary monies to pay this interest, a tariff system was enacted, calling for payment in specie (gold). At the same time, greenbacks were put into circulation. A dual currency system quickly evolved, with gold for the bondholders and importers, and greenbacks for everybody else. The Populists, as we will see, were to refer time and again to the class dinstinctions represented by the currency system and supported by the U.S. Treasury. It was not an idle claim or a yearning for a pre-industrial past that led Alliance and Populist orators to claim that gold benefited rich monopolists.

At war's end, there was extremely high inflation, because the greenbacks had become a depreciated currency and because gold prices had been manipulated by bondholders. The secretary of the treasury, McCulloch, tried to bring order by slowly withdrawing greenbacks from circulation. The result was a contraction of the total currency. Manufacturers raised their voices and blamed the postwar economic decline on McCulloch's policies, which were then reversed. Manufacturers also successfully resisted attempts to end the tariffs that protected them. In 1867, they founded the American Industrial League, which set about educating the electorate in the evils of free trade, arguing that it was in the interests of all Americans—industrialists and working people alike—to promote America. Both political parties, in one fashion or another, were struggling with the issue of currency reform and the question of the tariff, but the struggle was resolved in favor of bondholders and the commercial classes. Not everyone accepted this outcome, and third parties were to make much of a government operating in the interests of the few. However, third parties had more to deal with than currency and class legislation; they had to deal with a particular moral climate, one extremely hostile to their attempts. Third parties stood outside of the accepted boundaries within which change was to take place.

The debates in the late 1860s assumed a moral character that was to persist until McKinley defeated Bryan in 1896, and the mentality of the salesman and entrepreneur triumphed. Those who advocated payment in specie—the hard-money advocates—did so on moral grounds, arguing that only a demagogue would propose that debts should be payed for with debased currency. On the other side, those stumping for greenbacks kept referring to them as the "people's money," and to the people as supreme. The advocates of the tariff saw it as the salvation of American business and claimed, also, that the tariff would protect the worker from cheap foreign imports. Those in the other camp argued that the tariff simply drove up the price of necessities for the common people. Initially, there were divisions within both parties as to how currency/tariff problems should be resolved.

A substantial portion of the nation's postwar debt was in the form of 5-20 bonds (payable in five years, redeemable in twenty), some of which were payable on April 30, 1867. Though it was clear that the interest was to be paid in gold, it was not at all clear how the principal was to be paid. Some argued it should be paid with a new national currency offered by the government (greenbacks), and others that it could be paid only in gold, for to do otherwise would be to "repudiate" the national debt. It would, in short, be immoral. The majority of the Republican party came to support the national bonds and their payment in gold. (Ultimately this was to mean the support of a gold standard and a shrinking of the money supply.) Jay Cooke, who had masterminded the sale of the bonds to other bankers during the war years, launched a massive campaign in their favor and, importantly, in the name of "the little people."[17] People saw the bonds as standing for the Union they had fought for, which helped to silence Democratic opposition. Although bankers and speculators held a sizeable portion of the bonds, hundreds of thousands of Americans—farmers, laborers, and small merchants—also held them, and believed that their prosperity depended on redemption in gold. The Republican party, rightly or wrongly, then, came to be identified in the minds of many American citizens as the "responsible" party, the one concerned with the progress and prosperity of the nation. Those who challenged the Republicans would also have ringing in their ears the charge that they were leading the country down the road to ruin. (Such was the case, as we will see, in Kansas.)

When Democratic politicians did enter the fray, they argued that there was nothing sacred about the government debt, that it should be paid in greenbacks controlled by the federal government, and that the bondholders represented the rich, who should be taxed. But the situation in the South was of more consuming interest to them. Frank P. Blair, Jr., in accepting the Democratic party's nomination for vice president in 1868, summed up the situation for the South. He said that it was "idle to talk of bonds, greenbacks, gold, the public faith, and the public credit" before the country dispersed "the carpet bag state government."[18]

The election of General Grant to the presidency marked an end to the "radicalism" which had flared briefly in both parties and had fared poorly. Grant's election victory was celebrated as a "victory for peace," for the equality of all (bondholders and debtors) before the law had been established, and the effort to establish a greenback currency had been effectively labeled as a crime against progress. Motley, writing about the election of 1868 and the triumph of the Republicans, argued that America was a nation of freemen, who had expressed the general will in refusing to reestablish something "much resembling slavery by means of vagrancy laws and the denial to freemen of civil rights, and the repudiation of the national debt by the assistance of those by whose rebellion it has been created." If people were honest or honorable, then, they would repudiate greenbacks, and "get rid of this irredeemable paper currency, which converts us all, whether we like it or not, into a nest of gamblers."[19] Even though it would be over two decades before the Populists figured as a political force in American life, the issues with which they would have to struggle and the language of the contest were being laid down. However, people did not wait until the late 1880s or early 1890s to begin to mobilize. They were doing so in the 1870s; future movements would build on this discontent.

Third-Party Movements

Though the Grant administration began with great expectations, it became synonymous with corruption. Politicians descended on Washington like great birds of prey, in the words of Henry Adams,[20] ready to tear the flesh from the body politic. Cause had been replaced by patronage and party discipline. "Businessmen saw to it that politicians shared in the opportunities for enrichment offered by the conquest of a continent. The politicians rode on free railroad passes, bought stock at preferential prices, and moved freely from the halls of Congress to corporation presidencies and back again. It was the period of the Crédit Mobilier and the Tweed Ring, of Jay Gould and Jim Fisk, and of corruption and spoilmanship that made up 'Grantism.'"[21]

The "liberals" who were left in both parties did not sit idly by, but their proposals for change took such forms as advocating the institution of a civil service system or voting out Grant and his cronies. They offered no response to the issues which were about to fire the agrarian revolt.

Precipitating Conditions: A Sense of Injustice Builds

The railroads.   The Homestead Act of 1862 threw open the doors to western development, but it was not until the war's end that America experienced the internal mass migration that was to be the greatest in her history. The federal government, in a desire to spur growth and development and increase the tax base, went to great lengths to encourage the railroads to build lines into areas that were sparsely populated or not populated at all. Congress awarded railroad companies vast tracts of public land. The usual procedure was to give a railroad alternating 640-acre sections of land in a checkerboard pattern along the entire length of a line. Sometimes, however, all of the property along a line was reserved for a railroad until a line was completed and the company could choose the sections it wanted.[22] Railroads became the farmers' bêtes noires and served as a symbol of corporate America.

Opportunities for abuse were considerable and were seldom passed up. One of the greatest scandals was that of the Crédit Mobilier; it became a rallying cry for farmers in the 1870s. Crédit Mobilier was organized as an agent to build the Union Pacific Railroad from Omaha, Nebraska, to the Pacific Coast. In the course of its development it corrupted a number of congressmen, robbed its stockholders, and made fortunes for the principals. First, Crédit Mobilier contracted with itself, through varying schemes, to build the road at exhorbitant prices. It then managed to get Congress to pass an act that gave it one-half of all of the land for twenty miles on each side of its right-of-way; the government also loaned the company close to $32,000 for each proposed mile of the line. Next, the company issued $10 million worth of stock. Having done that, Crédit Mobilier, as the agent or holding company for building the road, transferred all assets to itself, including the government loans. Thus, all of the liabilities were the responsibility of the shareholders and other investors, who had second liens on the assets of the corporation, while the directors had first liens and control. In "this position, the holding company, or financial agent, drained money as long as possible from the Union Pacific Company and the government and then allowed the road to be stripped of practically all of its earnings by diverting traffic to other competing roads, especially the Southern Pacific."[23] As one of those who told the story for farmers said, "Reduced to plain English, the story of Crédit Mobilier is simply this: The men entrusted with the management of the Pacific Road made a bargain with themselves to build the road for a sum equal to about twice its actual cost, and pocketed the profits . . . this immense sum coming out of the pockets of the tax payers of the United States."[24]

Debt. Farmers had good reasons other than Crédit Mobilier for being aggrieved. For them the railroads came to symbolize the difference between ruin and prosperity. Though the Homestead Act was supposed to provide free land, many ended up buying land from the railroad, because the railroad had already selected the choicest parcels, or because speculators had beaten them to the best land. This meant that the pioneer farmer was often faced with the choice of buying at the railroads' or speculators' inflated prices. It has been estimated that less than one acre in nine of government land went to homesteaders.[25] But even those who managed to claim their 160 acres still had substantial expenses, because farming on the Great Plains was a relatively capital-intensive business. Before a man and his family could hope to make a living, they needed a team of oxen and a plow to break the dense prairie sod, a wagon, hoes, shovels. Perhaps there would be expenses for digging a well and putting up a dwelling, even a sod house, cut down into the ground. One estimate indicated that the average northern farmer at the turn of the century had to invest about $785 in machinery alone, which was more than most farmers made in a year.[26] To buy machinery, to purchase seed, to get through the first years, farmers borrowed. Data were never kept systematically, but Fred Shannon determined that in 1880 the average farm mortgage was $1,224.[27]

In debt, then, many farmers depended on their ability to work long hours, on sufficient rainfall, and on an absence of natural disasters to be able to raise a substantial crop. But the farmers' markets were no longer local markets. Their wheat, corn, hogs, or cattle needed to be moved to markets in St. Louis, Chicago, New York, and even, in some cases, to markets on the Continent. Railroads and their agents lay between them and those markets. As Hallie Farmer said, the farmer "saw the cause of all his troubles in the capitalist; and chief among his capitalistic enemies he ranked the men who owned the western railroads."[28] The cost of moving grain and livestock to market was crucial to the farmers' welfare, and they believed they were being exploited. Some estimated that freight rates absorbed from one-third to one-half the price of their corn, oats, and wheat. Often farmers were left with no option but to sell their grain to an elevator owned by the railroad, or one favored by the railroad. The Populist orator "Sockless" Jerry Simpson was later to sum up the situation: "When the farmer sends his surplus to market, the railroads lie in wait for him. . . . All the benefits growing out of the great invention are given to the large corporations which are enabled to rob the people through special privileges granted by laws passed by a Congress whose election has been secured by the use of money wrung from the people by the charge upon watered stock."[29]

The situation for American farmers took a dramatic downward turn in 1873 and helped forge a link in their minds between their own fortunes, the railroads, and a Congress that acted at the behest of monopolists. Specifically, Jay Cooke, a prestigious banker, had spent a major portion of his bank's resources on the Northern Pacific Railroad, whose expansion had depended in large part on foreign capital, which disappeared with the Franco-Prussian War of 1870. In May 1873 there was a panic on the Vienna stock exchange; European investors sold most of their American holdings, chiefly railroad stocks. On the American side, there had been wild speculation in railroad securities, allowing the railroads, operating at a loss, to expand into the vast unpopulated regions of middle America. When the worth of their railroad securities were in doubt, Cooke's partners shocked the public by closing the doors of Jay Cooke and Co. on September 18, 1873. The resulting panic on the New York Exchange drove prices so low that the exchange had to close for two weeks. The result was a six-year depression affecting both the United States and Europe. Farm prices dropped and foreign markets shrank. Railroads, in an attempt to cover their losses, began to raise transportation rates. The federal government's response was particularly devastating, and would be referred to in the years that followed as the "Crime of 1873."

The Grant administration's response to a downward drift in the economy was to put the country firmly on the gold standard. In 1873, Congress demonetized silver, and in 1875 passed the Specie Resumption Act, which was to retire greenbacks slowly from circulation. The effect was a rapid contraction in the currency supply. For farmers, for debtors of any sort, money to pay debts became more dear each year, while what they had to sell brought less and less in the marketplace. The Bland-Allison Act of 1878 was something of a compromise. It required the United States Treasury to buy between $2 and $4 million worth of silver each year; however, it did not solve the problem of falling farm prices, relieve the burden on debt-ridden farm owners, or increase the prices of farm products. The silver issue would continue until the elections of 1896 and 1900.[30] Farmers seemed to have few friends. Their standards of justice, fair play, and the very meaning that work held for them were under assault. Both economic conditions and changed economic relations played a part in stimulating discontent.[31]

Though there was increasing income concentration, there was also a general improvement in the actual economic position of most Americans, including farmers, at the very time that the Populist movement took hold. Allan G. Bogue and Douglass North have argued separately that mortgage rates were not that high and that most farmers had experienced an actual improvement in their economic circumstances.[32] Why, then, were farmers angry? Was it because, as Hofstadter and others have argued, the farmer felt dispossessed, threatened by a loss of status?[33]

The farmer as businessman.   There is some truth in this argument, but it cannot be used as a way to dismiss the Populist movement as a retrograde yearning for the past. The fact was that farmers were quite clear about who it was they were angry with at the time. They did not experience monopoly capital in the abstract, they experienced it in the form of "railroad companies, banks, mortgage companies, and middlemen who were 'exploiting' . . . " them.[34] The farmer was reacting to a commodification of land, labor, and money, to the shift from a system in which he produced for local markets to one in which his welfare was dependent on his being a businessman.

Anne Mayhew argues that there is an important distinction between agriculture in the pre- and post-civil war periods. In the prewar period, many of the capital inputs in farms came in the form of simple labor. If a farmer wanted to speed the process of capital formation he *could* do so by working longer hours, finding new markets, and hauling his products greater distances, though he did not *have* to do so. There were, however, limited opportunities until the postwar period, when the introduction of railroads made it possible—indeed, necessary—to expand.

> It is not surprising that the farmer borrowed and that he shifted rapidly to production for the market. Had he not done so he would have been ignoring opportunities for which all writers on earlier periods in American history agree that farmers were eager. But even if he was not eager, he probably had very little choice. As the plains were settled, farmers found it increasingly difficult to be self-sufficient because of the limited range of crops which could grow, and increasingly difficult to get along without credit because of the need to purchase land to add to that which could be claimed under the Homestead Law.[35]

The farmer became a businessman, and found himself judged accordingly. But the cash nexus threatened many of the values that the farmer held dear, among them community and independence. It was not capitalism, per se, that infuriated the farmer, but monopoly relations. The twentieth-century reader will notice some of the contradictions in the farmers' position; it is difficult to have a system that combines a free marketplace with communalism. However, this is precisely what many farmers wanted. As we will see in an analysis of the ideology of Kansas farmers, the contradictions in their position made it difficult to formulate an alternative to industrial capitalism.

The attack on capitalism would take on a definite moral tone, and the proposals would be designed to soften the blow of industrialism, without entirely blocking it. Farmers wanted to alter the capitalist system "in order to make it more responsive to human needs, to reduce the suffering it had so far produced. They did not consider such reforms incompatible with the continued, even increased, tempo of industrial expansion as they variously understood it."[36] The farmers' class position, then, stood in the way of a full understanding of the "impersonality, inhumanity, and amorality of the industrial and financial capitalism at which they aimed their severest criticism."[37] In the South, Alliancemen wanted black support without giving up white dominance. Throughout the country, they wanted to prevent large-scale landholding while retaining their position as owners. They wanted a government that would control monopolies in their interest while remaining economical and small. They wanted an end to harmful competition while retaining a market system that would let them succeed as businessmen. They wanted a moral society when the rest of America was firmly committed to the goals of economic prosperity and progress, whatever the cost.[38]

The Farmers' Rebellion

As a result of worsening economic conditions, changed working conditions, monopolists who seemed determined to have their pound of flesh, and an indifferent Congress, discontent grew among the agrarian classes. The Granger movement, as it was called, had its roots in the immediate post–Civil War period. Under President Andrew Johnson's guidance, an organization was formed for the general purpose of educating and aiding farmers. Though it was concentrated in the South, it quickly spread throughout the country, so that by the time it held its 1874 convention in St. Louis, thirty-two state and territorial granges, representing over 500,000 members, were present.[39] The Grange, in 1873, made a direct attack on what its members saw as a source of their misery: the railroads.

In the state legislature in Illinois, farmers had attempted to pass laws affecting railroad rates. It must be emphasized that, during the initial period of agrarian mobilization, farmers directed their sights on the state capitols; they believed that if they could elect legislators sympathetic to their cause they could change their circumstances. Naturally, they focused on their immediate circumstances; they wanted state legislators to pass laws setting favorable railroad rates and rates of interest, and laws to protect the debtor. In any event, the Illinois Supreme Court struck down the laws that had been passed to control railroad rates, and the farmers reacted with anger. Meeting on the Fourth of July in 1873, they passed a Farmers' Declaration of Independence that served as a manifesto for groups throughout the country. It began with the sentence:

> When in the course of human events it becomes necessary for a
> class of the people, suffering from long-continued systems of op-

pression and abuse, to rouse themselves from an apathetic indifference to their own interests, which has become habitual . . . a decent respect for the opinions of mankind requires that they should declare the causes that impel them to a course so necessary to their own protection.

They went on to declare that:

we will use all lawful and peaceable means to free ourselves from the tyranny of monopoly, and that we will never cease our efforts for reform until every department of our government gives token that the reign of licentious extravagance is over, and something of the purity, honesty, and frugality with which our fathers inaugurated it, has taken its place.[40]

Declaring themselves free of all political parties and prejudices, they said that they would give their suffrage only to those politicians who would support their ends. The failure of the Illinois Supreme Court to uphold the railroad legislation only fueled the farmers' efforts in that state. The Grangers ran "antimonopoly" candidates in 66 of the state's 102 counties in the fall elections, won 53 of the races, and obtained 54 percent of the vote in the 66 counties. They had pushed the Republicans aside as the state's dominant party and passed even more restrictive railroad legislation.

This model was adopted throughout the old Northwest and Great Plains states. Farmers ran antimonopoly slates in local and state elections, usually in opposition to the Republican party. The Democrats in some cases gave way gracefully, or endorsed the farmers' candidates, as a way of attacking the Republican party. (This is one of the reasons why farmers' movements were greeted with disdain in such states as Kansas; the Republican faithful could argue that many of their supporters were simply Democrats in disguise.) And, for a time, farmers' political efforts were markedly successful. "The entire fusion slate was elected in Wisconsin. . . . Two state officers were elected in Minnesota. The new parties captured the lower house of the Kansas legislature, attained a tie in the Iowa house, and won a balance of power between Republicans and Democrats in California."[41] But it did not take the Republicans long to rebound in those states, and by 1876, only three years after it had begun, the Granger revolt burned itself out, though many of the issues would continue to haunt the dominant parties in the decades to follow.

There were several reasons for the "failure" of the Granger efforts. One was that railroad legislation was too narrow a base upon which to build a movement. That is, once the legislation was passed, interest rapidly waned. Furthermore, not all farmers supported an antirailroad party. Many of them lived in areas remote from rail transportation and were resorting to fairly elaborate schemes to coax railroads into building lines nearby. Finally the organizational structure of the antimonopoly parties was exceptionally weak at the state level, and nonexistent at the regional or national level.[42] The problem of organizational structure would prove insoluble for the Alliance and People's Party in Kansas.

The Grangers were not alone in their efforts to try to change the political system. In 1873–76, the country saw the emergence of the National Union party, the National Labor party, and the Greenback party. All of them were antimonopoly parties, standing for many of the same principles. It is important, however, to understand why efforts at reform took place *outside* of the dominant parties.

No matter how cynical one chooses to be about the origins of the Civil War, the fact remains that many Americans saw the war in clear moral terms. For them, slavery was an evil, and black men were to have the same rights in a reconstructed South as white men. On a more practical level, many Republican politicians were primarily concerned with establishing their party's rule in the South. They attempted to do so through the Reconstruction Acts of 1867. In the years that followed, real accomplishments were made by the "black and tan" governments (so-called by their opponents to give the impression that the Republican party in the South was made up of former slaves and mulattoes): the economic infrastructure was improved, and public schools and hospitals were built. All of this was achieved in the face of concerted opposition from white landowners and businessmen, who successfully reestablished their dominance through "radical violence, intimidation, and coercion."[43] This was the era of the Ku Klux Klan and other secret organizations whose aim was to drive blacks and Republicans from power.

There were strong differences of opinion within the Republican party, and among the northern Democrats, as to what should be done to bring the South to heel. A "liberal" wing within the Republican party, as well as a few northern Democrats, urged that the federal government show its mettle, a development that resulted, in part, in the Force Acts of 1870 and 1871. These acts gave President Grant broad powers in the use of federal troops to stop voter fraud and violence in the South. The Klan was declared illegal, and Congress conducted an investigation resulting in a thirteen-volume litany of horrors perpetrated by whites against blacks. Nevertheless, the fact is that not much was done by the Grant administration about the southern problem. Other issues loomed larger for many northerners.

> As Klansmen met in dark forests to plan their next raid in North Carolina in 1869, the Central Pacific and Union Pacific railroads met at Promontory Point, Utah, completing the transcontinental railroad. As black farmers were "haggling" over work contracts with white landowners in Georgia, the National Labor Union and Knights of Labor were being organized by white workers in Pennsylvania.[44]

Economic prosperity rapidly replaced moral reform as the chief concern of the Grant administration.[45] The "liberals" of both parties struggled for a brief time to shift the ground of the national debate back from economics to morality, particularly in the election of 1872, when, unable to prevent Grant's renomination (despite evidence of widespread corruption and graft) they nominated Horace Greeley to run independently for president. Greeley was soundly thrashed, so much so that he said, "I hardly knew whether I was running for the Presidency or the Penitentiary."[46] Both parties came to see the efforts of political reformers as detrimental to party control.

Those interested in independent political action had to find other routes to reform. As the depression of 1873 worsened, and the problems of both urban laborers and farmers remained unsolved, the initiative was taken in 1874 by a group of Indiana citizens to form the National Independent (or Greenback) party.[47] Like other parties, it declared itself in favor of the moral reform of the old parties, but it also singled out the money issue. The solution to America's problems, proclaimed the Honorable James Buchanan, "was to have the government issue greenbacks direct and to have sub-treasuries or depositories in all the large cities where bonds could be exchanged for currency and then reconverted at the pleasure of the holder."[48] In less than two years, the new party mounted a presidential campaign, but in only three states did it capture as much as 3 percent of the vote. After 1876, however, the party picked up support.

A deepening depression and falling wages gave rise to the most extensive and bloodiest strikes the country had yet experienced. As the powers of government at all levels were used against the strikers, workingmen's political organizations sprang into being, and the Greenback party seized the opportunity to embrace the workers' cause and call for joint action under the greenback banner. By this time, too, the currency issue itself had taken a new turn; a drop in the price of silver compared to gold had led to a proposal that the former metal . . . be restored to currency to permit payment of the public debt in cheaper dollars.[49]

Western agrarians and eastern laborers came together under the banner of the Greenback party in state and local elections in the period between 1876 and 1878. Here they had their greatest success, electing candidates who ran on a platform that was an amalgam of issues: free silver, reduction of working hours, railroad legislation, opposition to monopolies, and a demand that more land be made available to prospective homesteaders. The movement reached its peak in 1878, when over one million voters supported its candidates.[50] By the time that General James B. Weaver (who would later run as a Populist) staged his campaign in 1880 for the presidency, the movement had begun to unravel. Out of a total of almost nine million votes, Weaver captured a little over three hundred thousand, or 3 percent. The usual explanations for the failure of his candidacy are that the severe depression of the 1870s was nearing its end, which appeared to vindicate the hard-money advocates and hence to discredit the Greenback philosophy, and that many people moved back to their traditional parties for the national election, believing their votes would have more effect. Furthermore, the Greenback party suffered a problem faced by other parties: it was unable to successfully fuse the interests of western farmers and eastern laborers, either organizationally or programmatically.[51] But this did not mean the end of insurgency; the protest forces continued to build.

In the words of Henry Demarest Lloyd, a radical nineteenth-century social theorist, the years from 1880 to 1890 were crucial ones in the "history of the struggle for human rights" in the United States.[52] A generalized protest movement grew on two separate fronts, urban and rural, and then came together at the close of the decade when delegates from the Knights of Labor and the Farmers' Alliance met in St. Louis to draft a platform of general principles.

The membership of the Knights grew rapidly, mostly in response to wage reductions forced on workers in 1883. In a single year, 1885–86, 4,000 new assemblies and 600,000 members were added.[53] The leaders of the Knights tried to avoid the mistakes of the Greenbackers, who had come to grief on the shoals of partisan politics, and urged their members to throw their efforts into nominating pro-labor candidates in either party. The membership did not heed their advice. In fact, there was little evidence that the leadership had any control over the vast membership, which represented diverse class and craft interests. Local affiliates of the Knights ran separate tickets in the elections of 1886 with varying degrees of success. Time to mobilize at either the state or national level was not sufficient. But attempts were made to capitalize on this new insurgency.

Joseph R. Buchanan, in his *The Story of a Labor Organizer,* explained what he saw as necessary "to wipe the old parties off the face of the earth and secure the establishment of a people's government." Specifically, there would have to be a union of "The Union Labor Party, United Labor Party, American Reform Party, the Grange, the Tax Reformers, The Farmers' Alliance, Anti-Monopolists, Homesteaders, and all other political and politico-economic organizations of breadwinners."[54] The result was the Union Labor party, which unsuccessfully contested the national election of 1888. Its failure was not surprising, considering the wide range of interests represented in this strange alloy. The party received less than half of the votes (147,000) that the Greenback party had in 1880.[55]

Though much of the visible protest of the 1880s seemed to be urban in scope, a movement had continued to build in the farms and fields of America. The roots of the Farmers' Alliance could be traced to the late 1870s, when a group of poor Texas farmers banded together to form the Knights of Reliance. The group saw its purpose as organizing to "more speedily educate ourselves."[56] The organization decided against immediate political insurgency and began a long campaign of educating farmers. A traveling lecture system was set up with S. O. Daws, a dynamic lecturer, talking wherever a group of interested farmers could be assembled about the evils of the crop lien system, "denouncing credit merchants, railroads, trusts, the money power and capitalists."[57] Daws urged farmers to form trade stores, cooperatives, and their own sub-alliances to continue the work. The model proved so successful, and the conditions of farmers were such, that the organization eventually expanded into forty-three states and claimed 2 million members. Most of this original growth was in the South, which meant that when the organization eventually entered the political arena through the Populist party, it did so with an organizational base that was better developed in the South than in the old Northwest and Great Plains states, where the Alliance did not really begin to build until the late 1880s.

The opportunity to form a bond between all working men and women came, in the eyes of the southern Alliance leadership, with the "Great Southwest Strike" of 1886. The Knights of Labor felt they had won a battle against Jay Gould and the Missouri-Pacific railroad line in 1885, only to find Gould determined in his effort to crush their union in the following year. Union members were dismissed from their jobs and strikebreakers were brought in to keep the trains running. The Alliance leadership, chiefly William Lamb, recognized that the farmers' fate was linked to that of the workers: without changes in the political and economic system, farmers would be forever locked into a system of debt peonage. In support of the Knights, the Alliance called a boycott. Support for the workers grew among Alliance members and "went beyond boycotting to include joint political meetings with Knights of Labor assemblies and direct aid to strikers."[58] The stage was set for a formal agreement between Knights and Alliance forces, and for the Alliance to shift to partisan politics with the St. Louis platform of 1889. That platform showed the indebtedness of the Alliance to Greenback ideas concerning currency, for the first plank called for the federal government to issue fiat money. There was also a call for railroad regulation, the free coinage of silver, and a reclamation of excess lands held by the railroads.[59] Remarkably little in the platform addressed workers.

If there were divisions between wage laborers and farmers, there were also divisions within the Alliance itself. Originally the growth of the Alliance had been concentrated in the South, and it was the southern forces that led attempts to bring together the northern Alliance and the southern. That attempt was made at Ocala, Florida, in December of 1890. In many respects, the Ocala platform was similar to that of the St. Louis delegation. The Ocala convention, however, highlighted an important and radically new demand, not only that the government expand the money supply but that the government create a subtreasury scheme. The idea was that the government should set up warehouses to store farmers' crops until prices favored selling, and that the federal government should make available low-interest loans, to the value of 80 percent of the crop, until the time of sale. As it was clear to many that neither major party would support such legislation, the Alliance advocated the formation of a third party—a party that would soon come. The tension over whether to operate as a third party or to support profarmer candidates through the traditional parties was an important one in the organization. The northern and southern Alliances were further divided over which issues were most significant. For the southern farmer, trapped in a lien system which was impoverishing him, the subtreasury scheme was of considerable importance. Western farmers were more interested in railroad legislation, for they tended not to be indebted to local merchants.[60] Western farmers, unlike southern ones, wanted more land and low-interest loans to expand their operations. Southern and northern forces would also divide over the great "lard war."

An editorial entitled, "Hog Politics," in an 1890 edition of the Dallas *Morning News* said that, "It appears . . . that the farming interest of the North is making a grab at profit at the expense of the farming interest of the South."[61] At issue was the Conger lard bill, which would have had the effect of protecting the price of pure pork lard, an obvious benefit to hog-raising states and an indirect one to the farmers who grew the corn upon which the hogs were fattened. The bill was an attack, joined by midwestern diary farmers, on the interests of small southern cotton farmers and western ranchers. It would have placed severe restrictions on the production and sale of oleomargarine, which was made in large part from cottonseed oil, and/or beef lard. Some farmers, such as the dairy farmers of Wisconsin, the corn and hog producers of Iowa, or those with mixed farms in the northeast with ready urban markets, were doing far better, economically, than the cotton farmers of the South, or those who had risked all in the areas of sparse rainfall on the Great Plains. States such as Iowa and Wisconsin would later prove to be "immune" to the Populist movement. Several things, then, were happening simultaneously.

First, there was a movement building with a growing agenda at each stage. Monetary policy captured center stage, but, in an attempt to attract the votes of labor, farmer organizations would add to their agenda recommendations for the elimination of convict labor, and would have placed limits on child labor as well as on Chinese immigration. They also wanted an income tax, antimonopoly legislation, and more public land. Later, in the 1890s, new items would be added. Second, at the same time that a movement was growing, it was creating the conditions for later fractioning. In the absence of a strong centralized organization, there was no firm agreement on which issues were most important, or precisely how to deal with the needs of widely divergent actors. Third, farmer discontent continued to build, because economic problems had come to be seen as a major injustice, stemming from the nature of the political-economic system itself.

The major parties were slow to respond, and no party took an active role in courting the discontented until well into the 1890s. In the 1880 presidential election, neither party had anything to say about railroad legislation or control of monopolies, even though over a million voters had cast their lot with third parties.[62] However, as the contest between the dominant parties narrowed, each began to incorporate elements of the third parties into their platforms through the policy of selective endorsement. In 1876, the Republican Hayes captured the White House with only 49 percent of the popular vote—he had one electoral vote more than his opponent. The parties split the presidential vote—48 percent each—in 1880, but the Republicans were again triumphant. The Democrat Cleveland won in 1884 with only .3 percent more of the popular vote than Blaine. (Interestingly, it was a Kansan, John St. John, who, running on the Prohibition party ticket in New York, split the Republican vote in that state, giving New York's electoral votes and the election to Cleveland.) The election of 1888 saw the Republicans dominant, but only .7 percent separated the two major parties, with third parties capturing 3.5 percent of the vote. In 1892, Cleveland was reelected with 46 percent of the vote, while General Weaver secured 9 percent of the popular vote. This continuing situation made it easier for discontented voters to receive a hearing.

There was a growing tension within the Republican and Democratic parties. Though the national leadership might focus on "irrelevant" issues such as the tariff, there was a growing pressure, mostly from Democratic congressmen, to deal with railroad legislation and currency reform. Thus, even before 1890, western congressmen showed themselves to be flexible on the silver issue, and a strong silver-bloc was developing within the Democratic party.[63] Because local representatives were as responsive as they could be and remain members of the majority parties, efforts were focused on working within the party system. State legislatures served as a focal point for protest and mobilization; thus efforts to form an organizational structure that would confront issues on a national basis were undercut. Third parties and reformers confronted a system that was amenable to change because of the narrow differences between the two dominant parties, and because of the growing tensions within them. However, because they often focused on single issues they would be subject to undercutting by selective endorsement. A greater obstacle lying in the way of reform was ideology.

I have already suggested some of the reasons why the reform movement was ideologically vulnerable. First, the ideology was not consistent. Third-party platforms represented an amalgam of issues and interests. Second, and unlike Goodwyn, I do not believe that farmers were imbued with the spirit of Alliance ideology. Mobilization was rapid in many areas, diverse groups of farmers were drawn in, not all agreed on strategies, and many supported the cause only until they saw that it could not deliver the desired resources. But all reformers faced an exceptionally difficult task, because reform itself was held in disrepute.

Discrediting Reform

By the close of the century, Populist leaders would take pains to define their programs for change as "manly." They would also make an effort to argue that they were not anticapitalist and that nothing in their programs smacked of socialism. They would claim that their membership was made up of the best elements of society,[64] and they tried to disassociate themselves from the rabble. Yet, in the eyes of many, they were the rabble. The attempt to discredit reformers as communists and anarchists predated the Civil War, though it would take a more virulent form in the years following. Reformers would come to be blamed by the dominant classes for literally all of the unrest in the country, and those who attempted to aid Native Americans, workers, or blacks would be seen as "soft" and effeminate, as opposed to being hardheaded, businesslike, and practical. The only type of reform which was acceptable was reform that lead to the regulation of behavior.[65] Thus, reform which would create a docile, sober, and industrious working- or agrarian-class was acceptable, while reforms which would lead to a redistribution of wealth, or to the creation of alternative political and economic systems, was not.

After the assassination of President Garfield in 1881, an Iowa

Free land and the chance to grow rich drew hundreds of thousands to the Great Plains at the close of the century. Here Boomers are lined up in the streets of Wellington, Kansas, waiting for the gun to sound for the opening of the Oklahoma Territories. Those who jumped the gun came to be known as "Sooners." Courtesy Kansas State Historical Society.

Republican paper ran an editorial declaring that "for ten years the snake of the Commune has been trailing its insidious poison through the lower orders of society in this nation. . . . It grew up first in the dark and noisome places of New York City." The blame for Garfield's death was laid at the door of the Greenback party, "a fungus growth of that part of the public mind which grew morbid during the late hard times." [66] How was it that the visions of reformers called down such abuse? To understand, we must examine transformations in the postwar politico-economic structure.

The realization of a yeoman's paradise seemed within the grasp of some after the passage of the 1862 Homestead Act. The act was also seen by Free Soil Democrats and Liberal Republicans as a safety valve for urban workers and as a way to develop a large internal market for American products. The irony would be, to use Alan Trachtenberg's words, that "incorporation took swift possession of the garden, mocking those who lived by the hopes of cultural myth." [67] The reason was that access to the garden depended on iron rails, telegraph and telephone lines; in short, vast amounts of eastern capital. The West was penetrated with government encouragement of the entrepreneur, the railroad tycoon, and the monopolist. Agriculture, as we have already seen, was simply assimilated into this process. Eastern entrepreneurs, the business class in general, saw the western lands as theirs to exploit for the general benefit of the entire country. They would act on behalf of *all* classes. The West would require "civilizing," however; Native Americans were to be driven from their homelands to reservations. Civilizing the country began also to take on a larger meaning. Laborers, farmers, and other reformers would come to find themselves equated with the Indian.

As Richard Slotkin has suggested in his brilliant work *The Fatal Environment,* the end of Reconstruction in the South brought an end to democratic politics. It meant that both northern and southern elites were agreed on the need to control unruly classes, whether made up of blacks or urban immigrants. The war also had the indirect effect of legitimating the model of the soldier-manager. The war had been won through the organization of superior capital resources; federal troops had been used to put down draft riots and strikes in the interest of industrial and social harmony. The state, working in harmony with soldier-entrepreneurs, would rationalize the development of the country. If workers and farmers did not realize that America was "no longer a republic of Anglo-Saxon farmers, but a semiurbanized industrializing state"[68] with limited resources, businessmen did. Many were also coming to accept what Lincoln could only contemplate with horror: a permanent, landless proletariat. In postwar ideology the "condition of permanent proletariat was associated with the status of blacks, women, and chronic paupers," people whose "natural" endowments made them ready subjects for dominance and entrepreneurial paternalism.[69] American prosperity could not accept idle classes, which meant, essentially, anybody who would not hold a steady job in a factory, who struck for higher wages, or who demanded that the government control rapacious factory owners or railroad companies. Progress and industry required discipline and self-sacrifice.

The "evils" of reform came to a head with the Grant administration. In 1874, the yellow-haired Civil War hero, Custer, claimed to have found gold in the Black Hills of South Dakota. The reporters he took along to write of his triumphs quoted him as saying that it lay thick upon the ground. (Ground held sacred by Native Americans.) The rush was on, and the Indians were to be "pacified," for the country needed the gold. Custer's death at the battle of Little Big Horn in 1876, interestingly enough, was seen to be the fault of those who had been responsible for "coddling" the Indians, which meant basically supporting some of their rights. Reformers within and outside of the administration were also reminded of what their attempts at reform had supposedly wrought in the South: carpet-baggers and a black underclass unwilling to accept the yoke of wage labor. Native Americans were defined as the equivalent of blacks and wage workers; people who wanted something for nothing. Philanthropy could only lead down the road to economic decline.

One may gain some idea of the image that workers held in the popular mind of the middle classes by looking at the newspapers of the day. Philip Foner, in a sampling from a July 1877 edition of the *New York Times* which reported on the railroad strikes that had rocked the country, found the men characterized as:

> Disaffected elements, roughs, hoodlums, rioters, mob, suspicious-looking individuals, bad characters, thieves, blacklegs, looters, communists, rabble, labor-reform agitators, dangerous class of people, gangs, tramps, drunken section-men, law breakers, threatening crowd, bummers, . . . enemies of society, . . . robbers, . . . idiots.[70]

One newspaper made this equation: "The Indians can avoid extermination only by accepting civilization on the same terms offered to the urban working classes: obey the law or die, 'work or starve'."[71] The battle lines could not have been more clearly drawn. The agrarian reformers of the late nineteenth century, then, faced a combination of political, economic, and ideological barriers. As we will see, a great deal of attention would be given to trying to seize the ideological high ground; to define reform as legitimate.

Summary

The factors that set American farmers on the road to rebellion are to be found in the original debate over what America was, and what it should become. Many of the contradictions between the dream and the reality were revealed in the period surrounding the Civil War. Wage laborers saw a new, centralized government acting in the name of an emerging entrepreneurial class and wondered why they should not be helped. People given the opportunity to pioneer with the Homestead Act of 1862 found they needed money and credit to make it a possibility. Instead, they saw their government generous in its support of railroads and other monopolies, and saw the supply of credit dwindle so that bankers could grow rich. Though these, and other factors, were instrumental in mobilizing people, they did not predetermine their path. People would experiment with many alternatives before they chose to act in the name of the Alliance and the People's party in 1890.

At the level of the economy, it was changed market relationships, rather than simple economic problems, that caused people to seek new solutions. Though farmers would experience cycles of boom and bust, and would even see their conditions gradually improve during the very time they mobilized, they came to believe that they were being dealt with unfairly. The nascent movements of farmers and workers helped people translate immediate economic concerns into a feeling of generalized injustice, one that would ultimately have to be dealt with outside of the regular political party system. People lived lives in which they actively confronted not an abstract system of capitalism but one made material in the form of iron horses, steel rails, and buyers for monopolies who would not give them a fair price for the products that represented long and difficult hours of toil.

The Democratic and Republican political machines were slow to respond to growing unrest. At the end of the war, both parties were dominated by elites, whose main interest lay in spurring development or in reestablishing white dominance in the South. Both parties had abandoned moral reform in favor of economic reconstruction, and both were more concerned with how to maintain themselves in office than they were with developing agendas to address the needs of laboring Americans. In the late nineteenth century, politics tended to be localized, with people concentrating their efforts on electing state legislators who would pass laws favorable to their cause. Sometimes they were quite successful. However, as the margin of victory narrowed between the dominant parties, and state parties saw themselves swept from office by reformers, concessions began to be made. Within the two dominant parties, splits developed between hard- and soft-money advocates, between those who would make minimal concessions and those who would not. The opportunity for impact, though, still lay at the state and local levels, for it was not until the 1890s that either party adopted as part of its national program currency reform, or legislation designed to curb some of the major abuses of the railroads.

Many of the early reform movements and third parties were focused on a single issue. If the problem could be dealt with, rapid demobilization took place or the movement was undercut by selective endorsement on the part of a majority party. People turned to third parties when they found they could not move either Democrats or Republicans. These early movements captured an extremely diverse constituency. Their party platforms were an amalgam of issues designed to attract as many people as possible and mobilized powerful forces in opposition to them. But the protest movement, whether agrarian or urban, continued to build in the late nineteenth century. At each state there was an accretion of issues which were not dealt with within the context of either of the dominant parties.

Marching under the banner of the Greenbackers, the Knights of Labor, the Farmers' Alliance, and later the Populist party, a vast mix of different class groupings assembled. This diversity of class and interest would later prove to create problems in maintaining loyalty and cohesion. Reform and reformers were seen in the harshest light. Workers, agrarians, Native Americans, blacks, were all groups in need of being civilized by soldier-entrepreneurs who claimed all of America as their domain. The struggle over whose vision would dominate was as important as the struggle over the political and economic system, for all were mutually reinforcing.

The struggle of the Kansas farmer, to whom we will turn in the next chapter, was played out in the context of these national debates. The issues the Kansas farmers confronted and the language they used to express their discontent were part of a larger dialogue. How they translated this language, and what they chose to do was determined by conditions unique to the state.

3

Kansas: Ad astra per aspera

Kansas experienced a devastating drought in the 1860s. To reassure prospective settlers from the East, Henry Worrall drew this cartoon in 1869. Courtesy Kansas State Historical Society.

In the year 1541, Coronado, in search of the New Eldorado, entered what is now southwestern Kansas. It is reported that he strangled the guide who had led him there.[1] Over three centuries later, covered wagons would be seen moving slowly eastward, away from the drought-stricken plains of Kansas, with the words, "In God We Trusted, In Kansas We Busted," painted on the side. Yet many pioneers had come to the state full of hope, proclaiming it to be a prairie Zion. Kansas, whose state motto is *Ad astra per aspera* ("To the stars through difficulty"), was, and is, a land of contrasts. It was the home of John Brown, Carrie Nation, "Wild Bill" Hickok, Wyatt Earp, and "Bat" Masterson. Its Dodge City was to be fixed in the imaginations of millions of American viewers by the television program "Gunsmoke." Kansas was home, in the mid-nineteenth century, to a vegetarian immigrant colony, to a commune of Danish socialists who had read about the state in railroad brochures circulating in their country, and to a free-love movement. It was also a state that, long before others, passed legislation giving women the right to vote in municipal and then state elections. It passed a prohibition amendment in 1880, and stood at the forefront of political, social, and moral reform and rebellion. The *New York Times* would proclaim in 1887 that Kansas was "the great experimental ground of the nation."[2] It was not chance that pushed Kansas into the ranks of reform. It was the bloody controversy surrounding her admission into the Union, the people who chose to come to the state, her geography, economics, and politics that made the difference. But the national political economy described in the preceding chapter strongly affected possibilities in Kansas.

Early History

The settlement of the Great Plains was bound up with the issue of whether a state, on being admitted to the Union, would be free or slave. Congress had been involved in a heated debate about whether to finance a transcontinental railroad, and had settled on a southern route. However, Stephen Douglas, Illinois Senator and heavy speculator in western lands, wanted a northern route, which would run from Minneapolis-St. Paul through what is now North Dakota, and across the country to Portland, Oregon. In order to persuade his congressional colleagues to accept the northern route, Douglas had to show that it passed through an area of settlement. Hence, in January 1854, he introduced a bill to created the Nebraska Territory, which more or less encompassed the present states of North Dakota, South Dakota, Wyoming, Montana, and Nebraska.

To entice southern senators into voting for his bill, Douglas adopted the concept of "popular sovereignty." This bill flew in the face of the Missouri Compromise of 1820, which prohibited slavery north of the 36th parallel. Some of the southern senators wanted to repeal the Missouri Compromise so that any western state could choose slavery. The "solution," which was to prove disastrous for Kansas as well as the country, was the Kansas-Nebraska Act, which divided the area into the Kansas and Nebraska territories, with Nebraska free and the fate of Kansas left to popular sovereignty.[3]

"Bleeding Kansas," as it came to be called throughout the country, was up for grabs. In 1854, even before Native American claims had been settled, the federal government opened a land office. Both proslavery and antislavery forces rushed to settle the area, each side determined to prevail. Proslavery forces, whose sentiments were reflected by Senator David R. Atchinson, of Missouri, boasted: "We had at least 7000 men in the Territory on the day of the election, and one-third of them will remain there. . . . We are playing for a mighty stake; if we win, we carry slavery to the Pacific Ocean."[4] The New England Emigrant Aid Company and other societies financed the settling of entire antislavery towns. In July of 1854, twenty-nine men set off from Boston to establish the free-state settlement of Lawrence, Kansas, called "Yankee Town" by the southerners. It would figure prominently in the border skirmishes which characterized the pre–Civil War period.

Most of the proslavery forces flooded across the border from Missouri, though there were immigrants from the Deep South who helped establish such communities as Atchison, Lecompton, and Leavenworth. The free-staters countered with Wabaunsee, Osawatomie, and Oskaloosa. In less than a year, the two groups clashed, when in December 1855 over a thousand men surrounded Lawrence, Kansas. The "Wakarusa War" was in response to the efforts of the Free-State party to draft a state constitution outlawing slavery. The free-staters charged that the territorial elections had been rigged by proslavery forces when they encouraged hundreds of Missourians to cross the border and cast illegal ballots. The weeklong siege of Lawrence came to an end when the territorial governor negotiated a truce.

Proslavery forces held most of the elected positions in the territory, which effectively meant eastern Kansas. Much to the annoyance of the opposition, the Free-Soilers of Lawrence had continued to publish two inflammatory newspapers. They had also established a "Free-State Legislature" in Topeka. Not about to let this challenge go, a proslavery jury indicted a number of Lawrence men on charges of treason, and declared both the two free-state newspapers and the Free-State Hotel to be public nuisances. The grand jury also suggested, not too subtly, that such nuisances could be removed. Needing no further encouragement, the proslavery sheriff first arrested those named in the indictments and then rode into town with eight hundred men who burned the hotel and dumped the newspapers' type into the Kansas River. The home of the free-state "governor," Charles Robinson, also went up in flames.

Retaliation was swift and deadly. Three days after the sacking of Lawrence on May 24, 1856, five settlers living near Pottawatomie Creek, "were taken from their homes at midnight and hacked to pieces with broadswords, or heavy knives."[5] The blame was laid at the door of John Brown, fanatic abolitionist, and his sons. The result was a continued round of guerrilla warfare that lasted for almost a year. The nation focused its attention on Kansas, where many saw a drama being played out that affected everyone, a drama that involved the very meaning of the word "Union."

The poet and essayist Ralph Waldo Emerson spoke to the Kansas Relief Meeting in Cambridge, Massachusetts, on September 10, 1856. He began by noting that, "We hear the screams of hunted wives and children answered by the howl of the butchers." The abolition forces were suffering the most extreme cruelties, he noted, and yet asked only "for bread, clothes, arms and men, to save them alive, and enable them to stand against these enemies of the human race. They have a right to be helped, for they have helped themselves." He told his listeners that if the abomination known as slavery were to be ended, they must make sacrifices as great as those of their Kansas brothers and sisters. "We must learn to do with less, live in a smaller tenement, sell our apple-trees, our acres, our pleasant houses. I know people who are making haste to reduce their expenses and pay their debts, not with a view to new accumulations, but in preparation to save and earn for the benefit of the Kansas emigrants."[6] Help was forthcoming, but it would be several years before free-state forces established their dominance in the state.

The Democratic territorial governor, Geary, helped to establish a temporary and uneasy peace in the state, which may have helped the Democrats capture the 1856 national election in a campaign that revolved almost entirely about the "Kansas question." However, free-staters continued to arrive in Kansas and finally, on their fourth try, in July 1859, they drafted a constitution barring slavery from the boundaries of the state. The bill went to the U.S. House of Representatives, where it passed, in April 1860, but the southern-controlled Senate refused Kansas admission to the Union. Once again, Kansas was a national issue. The Republican platform included as one of its major planks the immediate admission of Kansas to the Union; not until the Republicans won the election and the South seceded was the Kansas Bill passed. In 1861, Kansas became the thirty-fourth state in a fractured union.

The impact of the Civil War on Kansas was indelible, and for many years people would heed the call to "vote as you shot." By its end, Kansas had contributed twenty-three regiments and four artillery batteries to the Union army—a substantial number of men, given the size of the state's population. Moreover, Kansas sustained the highest death rate in the Union, with over 8,500 casualties, and an untold number of injuries.[7] There were deaths in addition to those suffered on the battlefield, as communities along the Kansas-Missouri border suffered from a form of guerrilla warfare. On the dawn of August 21, 1863, William C. Quantrill almost succeeded in eliminating Lawrence, Kansas, from the face of the earth. Riding into town while most of the citizens slept, he and his men torched the town, shooting people as they fled or tried to stand and fight. Though over 150 died in the conflict, the town rapidly rebuilt. With the surrender of the South and demobilization, the growth of the state began in earnest, though the pattern of that growth was determined by the state's ecological diversity.

The Land

Kansas is at least three separate states, if one takes climate as a criterion. Would-be farmers who headed west in the 1860s would not have been struck by any remarkable changes as they crossed over the Missouri border into eastern Kansas, for it is similar in climate and geography to such states as Illinois or Indiana. They would have found hickory, walnut, and oak growing on the rolling hillsides. Here, the humid belt of the state receives between 37 and 42 inches of rainfall a year, and here most of the early settlers began to homestead, where timber needed to build a home, barn, or corral was immediately available.

As our prospective settler moved west, however, the geography and climate would begin to change. The state gradually slopes up from an elevation of 750 feet on the eastern border to 4,000 feet on the Colorado border. The trees begin to thin out, following the beds and tributaries of the two major rivers—the Kansas and the Arkansas—that drain the state. The railroads would follow the valley routes of these rivers on their western journey, and farmers, too, would first try to find a spot close to water and timber to build. Soon, the rolling hills would give way to open vistas, and the heavy grasses of the eastern and middle portions of the state would dwindle away to an ocean-like cover of buffalo or short grass.[8]

At the Colorado border the annual rainfall is about 15 inches a year. Those who chose to homestead in the middle and western portions of the state often had to build their homes out of the prairie sod itself, for little or no timber was available. Their farms would

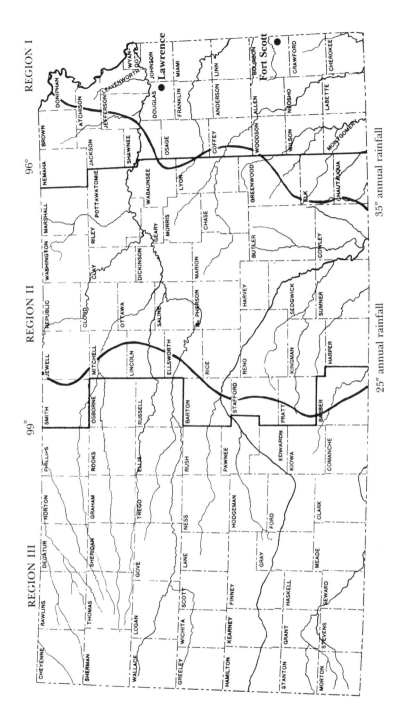

Fig. 3.1   Regions of Settlement and Average Rainfall Distribution for Kansas.
Rainfall data from Clark and Roberts, *People of Kansas*, p. 37. Map courtesy of the
Kansas Collection of the University of Kansas Libraries.

eventually be larger than those in the eastern portion of the state, because they would need to break more of the virgin sod, and put more acres under cultivation, in order to make a living.

The distinction between the eastern and western portions of the state was, and is, clear. The central portion is the most geographically diverse and has the most erratic weather. In this region, running from about the 96th to the 99th meridian, average annual rainfall varies from 35 to 25 inches (see fig. 3.1). This area itself can be broken up into five separate physiographic areas, of which the most distinctive is the Flint Hills, heavy with the blue-stem grass that supports cattle ranching. The rest of the region lent itself to farming, though success was dependent on rain. Rainfall figures, however, are averages, "whereas the climate of Kansas is notoriously given to extremes."[9] One year the rainfall may be 20 inches, another year 40. Even this wide variation does not tell the whole story, for in such areas as western Kansas the rain comes in great torrents in the spring and fall and runs rapidly off the ground, which is quickly dried by hot winds which can blow for days. The pioneer history of Kansas was marked by severe droughts in 1860, 1874, and one lasting from 1884 to 1887, just before the Populist upheaval in 1890. The son of a Kansas settler described the conditions of one drought and its effect.

> The summer that followed was the kind that turns men's hearts sad and sour. Dry weather early in June burned the oats yellow, and the wheat filled with shriveled kernels that were barely worth the cutting. Corn began to fire before Rosie and the children had finished hoeing, and did not even make fodder, except in the river field. The pasture dried up, and in the late summer and early fall the cows had to be herded along the road and along the railroad right-of-way. . . . Some of the mover wagons that jogged westward in April were on their way back in September. Times were so hard that, as the Downs *Times* said, "The Lord's Supper, with the original cast, would not draw a full house in any town in the West."[10]

Stephen Crane, writing about the afflictions that had befallen the people of Nebraska, cast a similar struggle in almost biblical terms.

> The farmers helpless, with no weapon against this terrible and inscrutable wrath of nature, were spectators at the strangling of their hopes, their ambitions, all that they could look to from their labor. It was as if upon the massive altar of the earth, their homes

and their families were being offered in sacrifice to the wrath of some blind and pitiless deity. The country died. In the rage of the wind, the trees struggled, gasped through each curled and scorched leaf, then, at last, ceased to exist, and there remained only the bowed and bare skeletons of the trees. . . . [11]

The weather would not be the only "natural" disaster visited upon Kansas's farmers. In 1874, a plague of grasshoppers caused some to believe that God had truly forsaken them. A pioneer in Jefferson county described his family's reaction. "They're here! The sky is full of 'em. The whole yard is crawling with the nasty things." [12] Funk, a Mennonite settler in Marion county, recalled the grasshopper invasion of 1874.

> Then with a whizzing, whirring sound the grasshoppers came from the northwest and in unbelievable numbers. They lit on everything. I was covered from head to foot. When they hit my face or hands the impact was like missiles and at once the insects began to eat. The ground was covered, in some spots to a depth of three or four inches, and trees along the creek were so loaded with grasshoppers that large limbs were broken off. The chickens came out of the hen house and gorged themselves on hoppers and then stood around sad eyed that they could not eat more. [13]

The grasshoppers ate the harness off his horses standing in the field, the clothes his wife had hung out to dry, and stripped his field of corn—cobs, stalks, and all.

People fought back as best they could, using grasshopper rakes to gather the insects before burning them. The situation was so serious that Governor Osborn, in 1874, issued his famous "Grasshopper Proclamation" and called the legislation into session. Other than the suggestion that grasshoppers should be outlawed, not much of consequence was accomplished. In fact, from the farmers' perspective, the response of the legislature and of townspeople was less than satisfactory. It set a pattern for what followed: the non-farmers' opinion that the farmers' problems were theirs alone. Some indication of the attitudes involved can be gleaned from a letter written by an angry farmer to the Wichita, Kansas, *Eagle* (July 17, 1874). The farmer was responding to previous comments by a "lady of the town," and said,

> What is to be done for the poor and destitute of this country? Let them . . . suck their thumbs as the generous lady said, or "let

them starve and be damned" as a high toned gentleman in Wichita said last week? . . . A majority of those needing help have families of small children to support. One lady in Wichita said last week that they had no business to have a lot of young-uns to support. . . . But it is a fact, and it can't be got over.[14]

Early farmers in Kansas did not anticipate the natural calamities that would befall them; they had little understanding of the diverse climatic conditions within given regions; they did not even have a good idea of what they ought to plant.

The Process of Settlement

Where people decided to settle and try their luck was dependent in large part on the railroads. The development of Kansas is unique in that the main railroad lines (the Union Pacific and the Atchison, Topeka, and the Santa Fe) were laid down first, towns followed, and *then* the farmer came. Settlement occurred in two primary waves: immediately following the Civil War and in the early 1880s. For many of those who came determined to farm, this was a highly experimental adventure.

There is evidence that many of those men and women who came to Kansas did so with no actual farming experience at all. In 1877, Howard Ruede came from Pennsylvania to Osborne, Kansas, to claim his 160 acres. From his letters home to his family, it is clear that he knew nothing about farming; he was, in fact, a printer. He had to learn from his neighbors how to plow, how to reap, and what to sow. From a neighbor, he learned how to dig a well and lay the well's interior stone walls. A farm wife taught him how to make his meals over the small fire in his "soddie," and he and his neighbors slowly learned what would and would not grow in a land of little, or erratic, rainfall.[15]

The first attempts at farming in Kansas followed an eastern model, partly because farming was concentrated in the subhumid region of eastern Kansas. It was also, before the Civil War, a self-sufficient type of agriculture, since roads were few and markets limited. The farmer planted corn and potatoes, some cereal crops and vegetables, and eventually fruit trees. As farmers moved on to the prairie, their techniques changed and new problems confronted them. No longer near water, they needed to dig wells; wood might have to be hauled a considerable distance; the prairie sod posed special problems. "The sod was so thick and tough that an ordinary

team of horses could not pull a plow through it." Instead, one
needed "the strength of at least a yoke of powerful oxen, or a team
of heavy draft horses, to pull the plow and break the sod."[16] The
old moldboard plow gave way to steel clad plows. As the sod was
turned over, the first crop of corn or potatoes would be "planted"
in holes chopped in the coarse soil with an axe. "Cultivation" would
be provided in the first year by rain, and by freezing and thawing.[17]
It normally took about two years to establish a farm, and most
farmers could bring only about ten acres under the plow. The
situation would change dramatically with the introduction of the
drill, the reaper, the mower, and the thresher. With their use, literally hundreds of acres could be farmed by a single family. But farm
machinery required greater and greater amounts of cash or of
credit.

Before long, Kansas farmers had the plains to themselves. The
railroads had pushed westward toward Denver by 1870, and the
great buffalo herds were exterminated. Buffalo hunters provided
meat for railroad workers, and shipped east, via the railroads, hundreds of thousands of pounds of meat, hides, and horn. Early
settlers would also pursue the buffalo, a sorely needed supplement
to their diet, and a source of cash; on the treeless plains, they benefited indirectly from the buffalo, since dried buffalo chips could be
burned to warm their small homes and cook their meals.

The days of the cattlemen were also numbered. Though cow-
towns such as Dodge City and Abilene still figure prominently in
peoples' imagination, their lifespan was remarkably short. In 1867,
Joseph McCoy, pondering the fate of over five million Texas long-
horn cattle foraging the Texas plains, hit upon the idea of driving
the cattle up the Chisholm Trail to Abilene, and shipping them
from there to points east. In three years, Abilene had become a
town of ten boarding houses and a dozen saloons. The growth of
Dodge City and Wichita was equally rapid. However, Joseph Glid-
den's invention, barbed wire, commercially available in the 1880s,
allowed farmers to fence their lands, and eventually eliminated the
great cattle drives. Cattlemen tried to fatten their herds on en-
closed ranges, but the great blizzards of the winter of 1885–86
killed millions of head of cattle throughout the Great Plains.

Indians, too, were gone from the scene. The last battle between
whites and Indians in Kansas occurred in 1878. The settler, eager
for land, was happy to see the Indians pushed onto reservations in
Kansas and Oklahoma. A settler in a small town in western Kansas

said in 1871, "One year ago the savages held sway here. Yesterday, the white man held possession." [18] Ironically, the farmer-settler, by legitimating the use of force to civilize the Indian, ultimately legitimated the use of force to put down his own revolt in the 1890s.

In their enthusiasm and ignorance, farmers tried farming almost everywhere and planting almost anything. In addition to corn, wheat, oats, barley, and sorghum, early Kansas farmers tried cotton, tobacco, and even planted vineyards, until prohibition in 1880 made that an uneconomical enterprise. They looked for riches in the silk industry, and planted thousands of mulberry trees to feed the silkworms. Their wives and daughters were to spin the silk. Here and there a woolen mill was part of the landscape, for Kansas had been touted as a fine place to raise sheep. In short, there was almost no agricultural endeavor that was not tried. They would learn, but it would take time, and some of their experiments would prove to be disasters.

> The wholesale invasion of a land so recently an untamed wilderness, and so different in climate and topography from the timber zone from which had been derived the previous agricultural experience of most settlers, was inevitably fraught with serious hazards. Merely to occupy the land, to erect rude shelters, and to begin cultivation was relatively easy. But to establish agriculture on a basis sufficiently secure to withstand drought, hail, insect pests, and market slumps required decades of dogged endeavor. [19]

The tide of immigrants would sometimes become an ebb tide of emigrants, washing out after drought or the fall in agricultural prices. The different waves of population growth and decline, where and when people settled, have implications for the rise and decline of the Alliance and Populist Party.

Though Kansas was a state of immigrants, those immigrants were almost exclusively native-born Americans. At no point did European immigrants ever constitute more than 13.3 percent of the total population, a figure that was reached in 1870. By 1900 only 8.6 percent of Kansas's population was made up of foreign-born whites. In 1890, this population of the foreign-born came primarily from—in descending order—Germany, England, Sweden, Ireland, Canada, Russia (the Mennonites), with lesser numbers from Scotland, Switzerland, Denmark, and Bohemia. The foreign-born would, however, constitute over 20 percent of the labor force on the railroads and in the mines. Most of those moving to the state in

Table 3.1   Population for Demographic Regions of Kansas, 1860–1900

Year	Region I	Region II	Region III
1860	91,967	15,239	—
1870	284,986	75,576	2,837
1880	447,692	451,111	96,963
1890	600,444	647,818	178,834
1900	673,143	637,410	159,942

Source: Adapted from Clark and Roberts, *People of Kansas*, p. 44.

the 1860–1900 period came from states loyal to the Union. By 1890, the states of Ohio, Indiana, Illinois, Pennsylvania, and New York had contributed a heavy share of the population.[20]

I will divide the state into three regions for purposes of analysis and discussion. These regions have been used by other researchers in discussing patterns of settlement and patterns of voting within the state. They correspond, roughly, to the areas of rainfall, with the 96th meridian serving as the cutoff point for the eastern third, Region I, and the 99th meridian serving as the western border of Region II. Region III lies, then, to the west of the 99th meridian. The regions have been further refined by taking into account population density. County density is highly correlated with geographic features, especially rainfall. Region I, then, consists of twenty-six counties lying within the humid belt, having a population density of 19.7 people in 1870; Region II, with thirty-seven counties, had a density of 2.5 people; while Region III, with forty-one counties, had but 0.1.[21] (I will refer to these as Regions I, II, and III, or, respectively, the eastern, central, and western regions.)

In 1860, the population of the entire state stood at about 107,000. In a decade, 1860–70, it would almost triple to 364,000 people. It would triple again, so that by 1880 there were 996,000 in the state, and by the time the Populist party was a reality, in 1890, there were 1.43 million inhabitants. The population growth was not even, as Table 3.1 shows.

The western third never attained the growth of the other two regions, but Regions I and II had almost the same number of inhabitants in 1880, even though Region I had a far greater number of people than did Region II in 1870—285,000 as opposed to 77,000. One can also see that Region II experienced a drop in population between 1890 and 1900, as did the far western region of the state. The reasons for the growth and decline must be considered in detail. Chief among the reasons for rapid growth were a boom mentality and high agricultural prices, as well as high prices for land. The primary reasons for the decline were a prolonged drought and falling prices, but all of these factors varied from region to region.

The Boom and Subsequent Collapse

The railroads had a complex effect on the boom and on people's response to it. Large bond issues were passed to entice railroads to lay tracks to a particular town or area, and small villages took on massive debts. The railroads were anxious to sell the lands they had acquired and needed to attract people to the state to do so; they sent agents throughout the world to attract prospective immigrants. They posted handbills, some of them quite misleading, everywhere. However, railroads were not the only agencies trying to entice settlers to the region. State agricultural agencies, for instance, told settlers that everything they hoped for could be found within the borders of Kansas. One "objective" report of Kansas told immigrants that "the sunlight falls upon its matchless landscapes as softly as upon the limpid waves of Naples Bay. It is something to live in a land where Apollo may tend flocks on the hills and Sappho turn dairymaid, singing her sweet songs in the shadows of the blue mounds."[22] If the settler was worried about the drought of 1860 or the grasshopper invasion of 1874, he was sent sketches showing men harvesting grapes as large as bushel baskets, and sheaves of wheat piled high to represent a yield of fifty bushels an acre. Thousands received brochures that said "The climate of Kansas is, without exception, the most desirable in the United States. . . . Since the year 1860, the State has been blessed with an abundance of rain. . . . The oldest inhabitants universally agree that the drought of 1860 was the only one of any consequence that ever visited Kansas."[23] No amount of intellectual ingenuity was spared in explaining why the settler need not worry about rain. One explanation was that the railroad lines would bring rain, because everyone knew that iron attracted lightning, which brought rain. If that was not convincing enough, people were told that rainfall occurred where there were sizeable numbers of people. Therefore, as the population of Kansas increased, so would the rain.

And, for a time, it did rain in Kansas. In the late 1870s and early 1880s the average rainfall actually increased, so that people thought the conditions they were witnessing were normal. The prairie bloomed. A Topeka doctor turned farmer wrote to his mother,

"Crops this year have been good. The soil is rich. . . . This country would beat Illinois in many farm products."[24] Another farmer said, "The harvest is great, and yield is bountiful. Prices are liberal, and every inhabitant . . . *ought* to be happy and contented."[25] Smalltown newspapers and hucksters of every description urged people to spend. The enthusiastic editor of the Kansas *Belle Plaine News* (February 27, 1886) urged his readers to ignore caution.

> Do not be afraid of going into debt. Spend money for the city's betterment as free as water. . . . Let the bugaboo of high taxes be nursed by old women. Do all you can for Belle Plaine regardless of money, and let the increase of population and wealth take care of the taxes. Double, treble, quadruple our expenditures . . . and Belle Plaine will boom.

And the towns did, indeed, tax themselves. Often it was for railroads. Convinced that their prosperity depended on a railroad line, towns would compete with one another over the size of the bond issue they were willing to underwrite. The citizens of Ladore, Kansas, for example, quarreled and failed to come to terms with the Missouri, Kansas, and Texas Railway. "As a result the railroad built through Parsons instead of Ladore. Not long afterward the people of the little town placed their houses on rollers and moved to Parsons, leaving the once promising town to die."[26] Very often the railroads built into remote areas, laying down thousand of miles of line in a short period of time, simply to secure the bond money.

Bonds were also voted by towns and counties for sewer lines, water lines, road improvement, wells, or sometimes for the direct

Table 3.2   Municipal Debt for Anthony, Kansas, 1885–1900

	Railroad Bonds	Refunding Bonds	Total Bonds	Total Outstanding Net Debt
1885–86	$ 961,000	$1,593,629	$ 3,172,390	$17,473,347
1887–88	8,544,551	2,378,750	13,388,062	30,733,935
1889–90	804,250	3,419,030	7,576,689	36,491,660
1891–92	315,000	1,154,240	3,271,831	37,075,740
1893–94	56,500	299,661	1,501,028	36,805,599
1895–96	—	712,900	1,719,677	34,604,246
1897–98	200,000	1,074,000	2,104,552	32,276,339
1899–1900	31,500	4,509,140	6,401,333	32,398,799

Source: Compiled from reports of state auditor and Board of R.R. Commissioners. Reported in Boyle, *Financial History of Kansas*, p. 95.

support of a company that promised to bring jobs and prosperity to its citizens. As a consequence, some towns had a staggering debt level that far exceeded the assessed valuation of the town and its ability to pay. For example, in 1889 the small town of Anthony, Kansas, had a total assessed valuation of $512,000. In the space of nine years, this value dropped to a low of $171,000, and the town's population fell from 2,252 to 1,074. While the town's assessed valuation was falling, its debt was skyrocketing (see table 3.2). By 1897, the year the town declared itself bankrupt and repudiated its debts, it had voted a total of $32.4 million worth of bonds for itself.

Farmers, too, were in debt; they needed money, and borrowing was made easy. As farm prices started up in the late 1870s, easterners were anxious to cash in on what they saw as a boom. Companies were formed for the sole purpose of channeling money to the West. So eager were people to lend money, in fact, that they urged farmers to borrow at the full value of the inflated land prices. Agents chased down prospective clients, urged on by easterners who said, "Get me a Kansas mortgage!" Some farms were mortgaged at the rate of 100 percent, and often even livestock and their prospective progeny had a mortgage hanging over them. Because many banks were prohibited by law from making loans on land, farmers were heavily in debt to private lenders and deeply involved in cash-cropping to pay the interest and principal on their loans.[27]

For a time, there seemed to be a good reason for optimism. Stories were told of fortunes made by trading on town lots. In Wichita a man boasted that he had made $100,000 in 100 days trading town lots, and then reinvested all of his profits in more real estate.[28] Though a farmer might have a $1,000 mortgage to pay off, there were examples of many who paid off their loans from the proceeds of their first year's crop.[29] Small wonder that the price of land increased. Farms which had been purchased for $3 an acre, or had been claimed as homesteads, sold at the height of the boom for as much as $250 an acre.

It is important to emphasize the fact that in the early 1880s mortgages were not something inflicted on farmers by the machinations of capitalists but were willingly incurred because the farmers, too, hoped to do well. Of course, other mortgages were written during hard times, but people were very reluctant to lend money to those who might not be able to repay in cash; they had little or no interest in reclaiming land or livestock. Compared to the United States as a whole, Kansas had more than its share of mortgages. In 1890, for example, 60.32 percent of all acres in Kansas were mortgaged,

Table 3.3   Farm Mortgages for Kansas and Other Selected States, 1890

State	No.	Amount	On Acres No.	On Acres Amount	On Lots No.	On Lots Amount
Kansas	298,884	$243,146,826	203,306	$174,720,071	95,578	$ 68,426,755
Nebraska	155,377	132,902,322	107,105	90,506,968	48,202	42,395,354
Missouri	192,028	214,609,772	103,161	107,718,625	88,867	112,891,147
Colorado	54,600	85,058,793	20,484	30,195,056	34,116	54,863,737

Source: U.S. Bureau of the Census, *Report on Real Estate Mortgages, Eleventh Census of the United States, 1890.*

whereas the figure for the United States as a whole was only 28.86 percent.[30] The amount of total indebtedness was also considerable, compared to that of other states.

Kansans had mortgaged 203,306 of their acres, compared to their neighbors in Nebraska, who, in a state of similar size, had mortgaged only 107,105 (see table 3.3.) A primary reason for the difference was that Kansas seemed a more likely place to succeed, so that speculation there was greater. The amount of the Kansas debt on farmland totaled about $175 million, compared to $90.5 million for Nebraska.

Townspeople, farmers, and eastern mortgage companies were all speculating on Kansas land, expecting the boom to continue forever. Though Kansas was an agrarian state, and farming was the principal concern of many of her citizens, there were still a substantial number who were there for one reason: speculation. A character in one of Willa Cather's short stories thought about what might happen when the bubble burst.

> Often as he sat watching those barren bluffs, he wondered whether some day the whole grand delusion would not pass away, and this great West, with its cities built on borrowed capital, its business done on credit, its temporary homes, its drifting, restless population, become panic-stricken and disappear, vanish utterly and completely, as a bubble that bursts, as a dream that is done. He hated Western Kansas; and yet in a way he pitied this poor brown country, which seemed as lonely as himself and as unhappy. No one cared for it, for its soil or its rivers. Every one wanted to speculate in it. . . .[31]

The boom did come to an end, but how this affected farmer or merchant depended partly on when they had come to the state, and the region in which they lived.

After the grasshopper plague of 1874, population growth had risen steadily. Agricultural prices, too, began a climb after the effects of the 1873 depression tapered off. In 1881 farmers received the highest prices for wheat and corn since the Civil War. Some believed a fortune was to be made in agriculture, and a human stampede was on. In 1880, the population of the central sector of Kansas stood at about 451,000, but it grew to 685,000 by 1887; the greatest surge occurred in a two-year period, 1885–87. The population of the far western sector jumped from 97,000 to 234,000 between 1881 and 1887, the greatest growth there, too, occurring between 1885 and 1887. Population growth, though upward, was far less dramatic in the eastern third of the state.[32]

The surge in agricultural prices, accompanied by the new wave of immigration, contributed to a rapid inflation of land values, whether in the towns or on the farms. If one were paying more than $100 an acre for farmland, one was likely to go into debt. Individual debt, for farms and equipment, as well as public indebtedness for railroad or municipal bonds, took a sharp upward turn. The new-mortgage debt per capita was, in 1885, twice what it had been in 1880, and in 1887 it was three times as large.[33] This debt was concentrated in the central and far western sectors of the state, for it was in them that the boom had had its greatest impact.

Before the boom began in 1881, eastern Kansas was relatively well settled; over half of its counties were established by the year 1856. Its population would increase by 6 percent in the 1885–87 period, while that of central Kansas increased 28 percent and that of western Kansas 160 percent. Yet during the boom, the value of eastern Kansas land went up, too, and some of the older, established residents took the opportunity to sell, usually to newcomers who could put down a substantial amount of cash for an improved farm. Though sizeable mortgages were incurred in this area, they were usually written in the period prior to increases in agricultural prices. Eastern Kansas might best be described as composed of settled and established farm families during this period, though they would not be insulated from the collapse that was coming.

In the middle region mortgages hung over the majority of the population. Between 60 to 75 percent of all farm owners in this area were in debt. "Tenantry was much less commonly practiced in this region than in the East, so each mortgage represented a family whose whole wealth was bound up in the endangered family home."[34] The men and women in this sector had undertaken their mortgages during a time of high prices and optimism. The situation in western Kansas was markedly different. Half the counties in this area were not incorporated until after 1885. Here growth occurred primarily in a one-year period, 1886–87, but at this time free land was still available, or one could purchase land from the railroad, or school lands, at relatively low prices, e.g., $3 an acre. There is some evidence that western Kansas was settled either by cattlemen, who had come earlier, or by speculators, who hoped to profit from the cheap land. For example, in 1890, most counties in western Kansas had no more than 10 percent of their land under cultivation, and the total value of all agricultural products for half of them was under $100.[35] Each county, then, seemed to contain in varying proportions people who were primarily speculators, or farmers, or townspeople, whether merchants or workers. Western Kansas contained the speculators, the middle sector had people who had recently arrived and who meant to farm, and eastern Kansas had the more stable population, of both farmers and merchants.

Prosperity in all sectors was tenuous, based as it was on inflated land prices, debt, and the expectation that agricultural prices would continue their upward spiral. The first blow for Kansas came in 1887 when a prolonged drought brought an end to speculative fever. The second came with the fall in farm prices. By 1889, corn was not worth shipping to market and the price on wheat was little better. John Ise, speaking for one of his neighbors, said,

> Of course everything was cheap. Henry kept his wheat, hoping for a better price later, but the next spring he had to fan it and sell it for less than he could have got at harvest. The local elevator was closed for a while, because neither corn or wheat was worth shipping. At twelve cents a bushel corn was a cheaper fuel than coal, and some of the neighbors burned it in their stoves.[36]

Response to the collapse varied. Almost half of the people in western Kansas simply left the region between 1887 and 1897. Many of these were speculators who had taken out mortgages with the sole intention of leaving with the money.[37] In a sense, it was easier for western Kansans to leave, because, as the figures given above indicate, they had less invested in the region. The western "farmer" came late and left early. The situation was different for those in the middle sector, though here, too, people left—the population dropped from a high in 1887 of 697,000 to a low of 575,000 in 1896. Eastern Kansas continued its steady upward growth.

The boom was not just in rural areas but in the small towns and cities of the middle sector. When the collapse came, financial ruin struck particularly hard at speculators in town lots, merchants, and others who had hitched their fortunes to the agricultural boom. Raymond C. Miller has calculated that the loss of population in cities—towns with over 4,000 people—was 36 percent in the period from 1887 to 1892. By his estimate, the rural loss—of people living on farms and in towns with under 4,000 people—was only 13 percent.[38] The calculations of James C. Malin, however, would indicate that the loss of farm population was higher than that. Considering only those who were farm proprietors, he found that 51.3 percent of those in the eastern sector persisted between the years 1885 and 1895. The number for the middle sector was 45.6 percent, and for the western about 35 percent.[39] Malin's figures exclude those living in rural areas—in cities of under 4,000 people—who were not farmers. Taken together, the two sets of data indicate that population loss was considerable in the cities, as well as on the farms, though not as high in the small villages. In either case, the loss of farm population meant that many potential recruits for the Alliance and the Populist movement left the region or state. The great losses within the cities not only drove speculators away, they also caused working men and women who could try their luck elsewhere to return to the East or continue on to the West. But it also meant that those who stayed had a stake in the political and economic struggles that were taking shape, and it meant that many of them were concentrated in the middle sector of the state. Here farmers lived close to the margin so that "any sudden emergency, a crop failure, any fall in prices, the loss of some stock, would mean disaster."[40] In the words of one farmer,

> It's always bad luck. Anyhow, that's what you have to figure on. If it isn't hot winds, it's chinch bugs, or grasshoppers, or black leg, or cholera, or distemper, or something you didn't expect. Interest is a terrible thing anyhow, a terrible thing, the way it eats and eats, due twice as often as it ought to be, and always at the hardest time. I never saw interest come due when it was easy to pay, never.[41]

It is true, as Bogue and Severson have argued,[42] that interest rates were not exceptionally high, certainly no more so than for other sectors of the economy. However, for farmers who had taken out a mortgage in 1885 or 1887, to find that by 1888 the value of their land had decreased by half or more (not to speak of what crops were worth), interest was high. To the midwestern farmer, growing wheat and corn as his principal cash crops, any program which contributed to monetary expansion, inflation, and a raising of the price of his crop looked good. This is one reason why silver would become a significant issue for western farmers as opposed to the subtreasury scheme that attracted southern ones. Midwestern farmers did not need to escape the grasp of the "man" who ran the general store, or the plantation owner who held the mortgage on their crops; they wanted more money and protection from the railroad monopoly.

Plains farmers belonged in a different sector of the national economy than southern cotton farmers. They had come on the scene later. Theirs was a capital-intensive business, and their debts were often to eastern mortgage companies. There were also, within the farming sector on the plains, people who had done quite well. Crops, at least until the late 1880s, brought high prices. Plains farmers saw themselves as independent entrepreneurs, simple commodity producers, responsible for their own destiny. If others made a profit from their efforts, it was not immediately obvious, for this took place through the medium of the market. The source of the southern farmers' grief was more apparent and more immediate. Thus, when farmers began to mobilize they did so around different issues. Southerners often tried to establish cooperatives that would allow them to operate independently of the system of debt peonage in which they were enmeshed, whereas western farmers wanted more money. It would, though, not take long before the Kansas farmers understood who was exploiting them and how this was taking place.

Resentment against the railroads had been long in building. To begin with, the railroads had been granted almost 10 million acres, or 20 percent of all of the land in the state. It was also some of the choicest land, since the railroads followed the major river valleys in their routes west. Though settlers anticipated the sale of railroad lands, the railroads were in no immediate hurry—either because they wanted to wait for the value of the land to rise or because they wished to keep the land off the tax rolls. A violent riot in 1871, in which settlers seized a railroad office and burned 26,000 railroad ties, caused the railroads to start selling the land. It was not until 1886 that the state was finally able to tax all railroad lands. The railroads were also seen as having too much political power and as responsible for the active corruption of state legislators.[43] As the crunch set in after 1887, people were not pleased that a substantial portion of their bonded indebtedness was in the form of railroad bonds. Railroads were of concern to both rural and city folk, one reason why the state Republican party could recommend legislation to control rates; the rates affected almost everyone.

The railroads were creative in setting rates, and seldom responsive to local concerns. Rates charged west of Kansas City to move grain or machinery were often double those charged in the East. Also, the rates to move grain from a point in western Kansas, say Hays or Garden City, were higher than those to move the grain from Atchison or Leavenworth to Chicago. The farmer living in the middle and western regions of Kansas, then, often faced exceptionally high freight charges, though there was a decline in rates to move grain from Atchison to Chicago between 1870 and 1900. (Corn, for example, cost 18 cents a bushel to ship in 1870, and about 10 cents in 1900). During the same period, the price of grain dropped. (Corn dropped from over 40 cents per bushel in 1872 to about 10 cents in 1898, which meant that a farmer's profits would disappear into the coffers of the railroad.) However, the drop in farm prices and the drop in rates was not simultaneous, and this could have been responsible for part of the farmers' anger. Between 1870 and 1900 there was a tendency for freight rates to drop during the time grain prices were high—but the rates remained stable when the price of grain declined.

> Such a relationship between one of the major costs of agriculture on the one hand and the prices of agriculture on the other would tend to increase optimism during the good years and pessimism during the bad. Hence as settlers saw falling costs and good prices making handsome returns in the late seventies and early eighties, they were willing to go into debt to reap what appeared to be . . . continuing benefits.[44]

I must not leave the impression that farmers were the only class with grievances. Workers in the city as well as merchants were concerned about the troubles that had been visited upon the state. However, merchants would come to see the farmers as the problem, either because they were guilty of overproducing or because they were frightening capital away from the state with their incessant agitation. Workers had taken action against their employers in the 1870s, and would do so again and again as the century came to a close. Workers, however, tended to focus on issues such as protection from "cheap foreign labor," and on legislation to protect their health and safety. But whatever the class, and whatever their concerns, there were limited opportunities for expressing dissatisfaction.

Kansas Politics

It would not be much of an exaggeration to say that the Republican party "owned" the state of Kansas. From the time of the first gubernatorial election in 1859 until a Populist governor was elected in 1892, the Democratic party won but one election. That was in 1882, when the previous Republican incumbent, John P. St. John, ran as a third-term candidate and was defeated by a Democrat. The reasons he lost are interesting and tell us something about politics in Kansas, but let us first examine the state's political climate in the context of that of the country as whole.

Kansas, as we have seen, was settled as a free state, and figured prominently in the border wars leading up to the Civil War. The early politics in the state revolved around the issue of abolition. In one northeastern Kansas county, Doniphan, a secret organization was formed to shoot any Democrats moving into the area, for the Democrats were firmly associated with slavery and its attendant evils. After hostilities ceased, many of the new settlers were from Union states or were Union soldiers. Those running as Democrats or those who made suggestions that the Democratic party might have something to offer were branded as "traitors," "turncoats," "rebels," and worse. The "bloody shirt," as it was called, was waved by the Republicans at literally every election, and the Kansas Populists would have to include planks in their platform showing that they were just as loyal and pro-Union as the Republicans. Attitudes would change, slowly, as more and more people came to the state, ready to put the memory of the war behind them. The masses who moved to Kansas in the period between 1881 and 1887 were probably not as strongly tied to the Republican party as the earlier immigrants.

In the period before the 1890s, politics in Kansas, as on the national level, was largely symbolic. That is, the issues that captured the attention of the major parties and the voters were not economic. Both parties posed as the champion of the progress, the friend of the businessman, workingman, and farmer. Within Kansas, the liberal or radical wing of the Republican party held greater sway than it did nationally. Kansas Republicans did not abandon the idea of Reconstruction, favored strong sanctions against the South, and supported Greeley's candidacy against Grant. They decried corruption in all its forms, whether of the body or body politic.

The liquor question figured prominently in early Kansas politics. "It was discussed at every constitutional convention, and as early as 1855 the legislature had taken steps to control liquor sales. Even in territorial days the ladies had engaged in 'spilling parties' and prayed over the habitués of the local grog-shops."[45] The Women's Christian Temperance Union was founded in Kansas in 1873, and in 1874 the state Republican party endorsed a prohibition amendment for Kansas and the nation. The national Prohibition party captured 100 votes in that year's election. In 1878, John P. St. John was elected governor on the Republican ticket. He had the strong endorsement of the Temperance party, which cross-cut Republican party membership. In 1879, St. John introduced legislation to control drink, but it was not until his second term as governor that he was able to pass the legislation necessary to ban the public sale of alcohol in Kansas. There were problems with the legislation from the start. Not only was it difficult to interpret the law, but many people were less than eager to enforce the legislation. But the Republicans had firmly committed themselves to prohibition.

In the election of 1882, St. John, much to the distress of the party leaders, decided to run for a third term.[46] The St. John men controlled the nominating convention, which selected him and endorsed a platform that called for vigorous enforcement of the prohibition amendment, control of the railroads, and women's suffrage. This would be the first election the Republicans would lose since 1859. It is not clear which issue—women's suffrage or liquor—spelled St. John's defeat, but the Democratic call for resubmission of the liquor issue to the people of Kansas drew a number of ethnic and working-class votes. It would continue to do so in the years that followed. This strong reform element within the party, and the party's willingness to deal with issues such as railroad legislation, were of particular concern to the farming class. Women's suffrage and prohibition were troublesome issues for both parties. Republican party regulars dropped women's suffrage in the 1884 election and portrayed a vote for the Democratic governor, Glick, as a vote for a "reign of rum." The Republicans won. Tensions within the Republican party, however, extended beyond these issues.

The Liberal Republicans, or Independent Republicans,[47] as they called themselves in some communities, lost firm control of the party in 1872, and shifted their allegiance elsewhere, e.g., to Union Labor or Greenback parties. Some of these men would surface in the Alliance and Populist crusade. Their ideas would linger as important issues for many voters. As a flyer for one of their tickets said, "Vote Against Corrupt Combinations." The corrupt combination might simply be the party in power, but it usually referred to real and sometimes imagined misdeeds on the part of elected officials. For example, many Republicans, not just farmers, felt that some of the legislators were no more than paid agents of the Santa Fe Railroad. Thus, when the Alliance erupted on the scene, as a reform movement challenging political corruption, it attracted a number of the Republican faithful. Later, when the movement was seen as pitted directly against the Republican party, and in league with the Democrats, many who initially had been involved withdrew their support.

At the local level, the notion of a county or courthouse "ring" took on real meaning. Especially in the rural areas, Kansas was a cash-poor state. In the first difficult years of farming, a man might walk ten miles every day to earn 50 cents so that he could buy the supplies he needed.[48] Cash was often concentrated in the county treasury, having been collected as tax monies from the citizens, or in some cases from the railroads. The money was spent for a variety of purposes: grading and improving roads, putting in a town's water supply, or building an impressive county courthouse. These jobs went to the party faithful, which meant that control of office brought real material rewards, and sometimes opportunity for abuse. But even without abuse the resources were concentrated.

In 1876, the Republican county commissioners of Osborne spent money on such diverse items as: the poor, printing legal announcements, rent for the building in which they met, and stationery. They also authorized payment of salaries to ten county assessors, the overseer of the poor, the doctor who cared for them, the courthouse janitor, a sheriff and his deputy, the probate judge, the county treasurer, jurors, witnesses, and attorneys who had appeared in a local case, and the person who drew the jurors' names out of a hat;

they made payment to local merchants for such things as "hauling," and "medicines." They did not neglect their own salaries.[49] Contests for office, then, involved bitter competition for resources.

The Republican faithful were also concerned about the possibility of corruption of their party at the national level, particularly with what had happened during Grant's administration. They believed that the body politic had to be redeemed. That is partly why parties such as Union Labor and the Greenbackers, which supported such things as civil service reform, were attractive to some Republicans. These parties, too, were also influenced by the Liberal Republicans who moved into their ranks.

The Republican party in the state of Kansas experienced considerable internal pressure from reformers. That meant that the party was "vulnerable" to appeals from farmers calling for railroad legislation to protect them from monopolists. It meant that a third party, with a strong reform orientation, would attract Republicans in the event that their own party failed to respond to the needs of citizens in the state. Unlike the national party, then, the party at the state level was permeable. In order to stay in power it had to give its attention to local needs. People understood this, so much early agitation took the form of trying to work within the party framework. The state party, however, operated within national constraints. It was not in its power, for instance, to pass legislation increasing the supply of currency, or to establish subtreasuries. Only certain strategies could work at the state level, which meant that pressures for national third-party movements that could address currency reform, or reform in general, continued to build. The Republican party experienced the greatest vote swings in the period from 1890 to 1900, partly for the reasons just identified: tensions within the membership and the speed and ability of the party to respond to different factions. Though the party would lose its temporary hegemony in the 1890s, it would firmly reestablish it by 1900.

Summary

Kansas was born in the strife surrounding the Civil War. The struggle to become a free state would significantly affect its politics. Kansas sent a greater percentage of its population and saw more of its men die in that war than any other state in the Union. It was, in the early years of settlement, a land of experiment, of hope, and of opportunity. Utopian and socialist colonies were established, together with farm communities and small towns.

Early settlers, however, were not prepared for what they found in the state. Drought and grasshoppers destroyed their crops; they had to learn how to manage the dense prairie sod and what would grow. Many of the early immigrants had to learn how to farm; some failed while others were richly rewarded.

Growth was constant after the Civil War, but it was the high prices for agriculture commodities in 1881 that spurred the sharpest increases. During the years 1885–87 a boom was on, and merchants, speculators, farmers, and others rushed to the state. In anticipation of continued agricultural prosperity, people mortgaged their farms, crops, and town lots. The boom came to an end with the prolonged drought that began in 1887 and the downward drift of agricultural prices that hit bottom in 1889.

The impact of the collapse was not evenly felt throughout the state, in large part because of the pattern of settlement. Eastern Kansas had been settled in the first wave of immigration before and after the Civil War, but the far western and central regions were not settled until the boom period of 1881–87. In central Kansas, where people had taken up residence late, borrowing to buy their land and make the necessary improvements, mortgage debt was high. This area would provide a disproportionate number of recruits for the Alliance and the Populist party. In the far western reaches of the state, over half of the population left the state in the period of the long drought, but many of these were speculators, or farmers who did not have as much invested in their land as did those in the middle sector. Fewer left central Kansas; more people abandoned the towns of the central sector than abandoned the farms. The outmigration eliminated, in both the towns and the rural areas, potential recruits for third-party movements. Those farmers who hung on through the years of desperation had made a significant commitment and would turn to parties that promised relief.

Much of the farmers' resentment was directed, not towards capitalism in general, but to specific targets such as the railroads and their agents. They saw their welfare as intimately bound up with the rates charged for moving their crops to market, and demanded that the state legislature "do" something. They were also in need of a program that would contribute to an expanded monetary supply and would make it easier for them to pay their debts. They were, in short, subscribers to a capitalist economic system, but one that was fair and just. Even before the Populist movement was officially launched, then, there existed the potential for later division, especially in terms of ideology. This would also affect the farmers' organizational capacities, because it meant that the group which formed to deal with their plight, drawing on an ideology that was not a coherent or consistent attack on capitalism per se, would attract people who had very different ideas about what could and should be done to right political and economic wrongs. There would be limits to the farmers' ability to create themselves as a class, because it would be difficult for them to develop a class consciousness that left them in stark opposition to the national political economy.

Farmers initially tried to work through the state's Republican party to effect change, but that party's immobility, as well as limits on what a state party could do, contributed to the attractiveness of a third party, at least in the short term. There was growing opposition within the state to the Republican political machine, and many of those who had bolted to reform parties early in the state's history were eager to find a means to deal with what they saw as a corrupt political system. Thus, when the Alliance rose on the political horizon, many were drawn to the organization who were not farmers, or who had an agenda that was largely irrelevant to the economic needs of the farming class. Furthermore, some of those skilled in reform politics and desirous of capturing office to pass their programs came to assume positions of leadership within the Alliance and then the Populist party.

The diverse constituency of the Alliance would serve as an inhibiting factor in the development of a distinctive ideology and an autonomous organization. At the inception of the Alliance, Republican and Democratic farmers voted for "farmer" tickets. But when the Alliance became the Populist party, and the Populists fused with the Democrats to capture office, many good Republicans abandoned their brothers in the Populist party because they saw it as a direct attack on a party to which they still had a commitment. Many Kansans had historical reasons not to abide the Democrats, and saw fusion as a corruption of the movement's main purpose and intent.

The Republican party was also a party which contained a strong reform element within it, as well as group of astute politicians. Many Republicans were eager to make some concessions to the farmers because they believed in their cause, and those more cynical understood that through a technique of selective endorsement they might be able to woo disaffected Republicans back to their ranks. In either case, it was again the unique history of the state that shaped both mobilization as well as its possible outcome. However, Kansas and its farmers were not isolated from the larger society. The Republican party, while making limited concessions, would come to tout the ideology of progressivism—the ideas of the merchant and the entrepreneur. Farmers would have to find their voice in third parties.

PART THREE

CREATING SOCIAL CLASS AND CLASS CONSCIOUSNESS

4

Class Structure and Society
Farmers, Workers, and Merchants
in Two Kansas Communities

A drawing made in 1859 of a worker cutting limestone blocks for the Presbyterian church in Lawrence, Kansas. In the distance a steamboat can be seen on the Kansas River. Courtesy Kansas Collection of the University of Kansas Libraries.

In the *Lawrence Daily Journal* of March 8, 1890, there appeared a notice under the heading of "City Gossip." Readers were informed that "Willie Dodd, a stunted bit of humanity, 49 years old, 3 feet 9½ inches tall, and weighing 60 pounds has taken up abode in the city making his living by singing songs at 5 cents apiece." Willie probably did not do well in this line of work, for future editions of the paper fail to refer to him, and his name does not appear in the census records. The same edition of the paper does, however, note that others were doing quite well. That week farmers were hauling corn, oats, and wheat to market, and benefiting from some of the highest prices for commodities since the close of the Civil War. Captain William Yates, the paper announced, had sold his farm and would retire to Lawrence on the proceeds. The paper carried advertisements for many of the local businesses, and the customers of Mrs. Eva Savage were informed that she was about to leave on her spring buying trip to the East; those desiring items "in the millinery line" were urged to place their orders ahead of time.

In Fort Scott, Kansas, 80 miles to the southeast of Lawrence, the local paper celebrated the increased prosperity of the town and told people how to line up for the Fourth of July parade. First would come the president of the parade committee, an old-time community member and local merchant. The town's brass band was to follow immediately behind him. They would in turn be followed by the local branch of the Grand Army of the Republic and all ex-soldiers. Behind the soldiers were to come the "Knights of Labor and any others who wish to march with them." Next in line were the cigar makers, to be followed by anybody else who wished to join the parade.[1]

Fort Scott was the home of Eugene Fitch Ware, a harness maker turned lawyer, and a poet who wrote under the name of "Ironquill." Ware would eventually turn his pen and jibes against the Alliance and the Populists, but when he began writing he was concerned chiefly with celebrating the wonders of business. In an 1876 piece, "A Corn Poem," he began by noting that history had paid far too much attention to the wonders of ancient civilizations, and had neglected to note "What built the cities, and what made them great." For Ironquill it was neither kings, monarchs, nor battles that made cities and states great, it was trade.

> Old Business is the monarch. He rules both
> The opulence of nations and their growth.
>
> He builds their cities and he paves their streets,
> He feeds their armies and equips their fleets.
> Kings are his puppets, and *his* arms alone
> Contains the muscle that can prop a throne.[2]

What does the plight of Willie Dodd, the order of the parade, and a poem championing trade have in common? They all represent the view that business and the entrepreneurial class are preeminent. Dodd is made the butt of the paper's joke, not just because he is short, but because he has to make his living singing songs. Casual laborers of any kind were a category of people to be ignored, ridiculed, or brought into line. Farmers on the other hand were fine, provided they brought their crops to town, spent their money, and acted like businessmen. The parade lineup, too, is suggestive of the way in which townspeople viewed different categories of people. As Robert Darnton has suggested in *The Great Cat Massacre*, community rituals often serve as a mirror of the larger social order. In the case of the parade, it is a merchant who rides at the head, followed by loyal Union troops. Laborers and cigar makers bring up the rear.

The explanations for the emergence and dominance of a national entrepreneurial class have already been traced in chapter 2. There we looked at the structuring conditions which caused businessmen to amass political power and which allowed them to begin the process of legitimating their ideology. Their dominance was established early, even where agricultural classes were at least numerically dominant. Rural America was tightly linked to the larger society—politically, economically, and ideologically. In a sense, states like Kansas were colonies or outposts of industrial society.[3] Capital flowed to these regions in order to establish the infrastructure for the transfer of scarce and desired commodities—in this case corn, wheat, and meat products to the urban centers. Many of those arriving in the region, then, came not to settle farms but to participate in trade and commerce, or simply to speculate in the boom. Towns sprang up overnight in regions where there were few, if any, settlers. The class structure of early Great Plains communities reflects the fact that they existed to serve the agricultural sector in a very specific sense: merchants and tradesmen would provide a link in the national chain between the farmer and the urban consumer. Goods and services would flow through the towns and villages; a class of merchants would control the welfare of farmers and laborers.

The pattern of growth and development in a state like Kansas was such that small towns and businesses were boomed ahead of the rural sector. A town's entrepreneurs not only saw a chance to do well but saw themselves as carving a new civilization out of the raw prairie. The fortunes of these early business pioneers varied greatly. Some became wealthy, while others failed, dropping back into the ranks of the skilled craftsmen out of which others rose. Those who stayed in their communities and prospered came to serve as the political elite of their counties and came to control the resources of the surrounding area for the purpose of pushing business forward. As businessmen had taken for themselves all credit for the creation of civilization, an attack on them was interpreted as an attack on the foundations of society. Merchants would try to turn back farmer protests by referring to the protestors as unenlightened, ignorant clodhoppers. The challenge of farmers was seen as a direct challenge to the economic and political power of the business class.

States such as Kansas had well-developed class systems. By this I do not mean that class boundaries were impermeable or unchanging from the time of settlement until the 1890s. However, there were distinct class groupings, whose members saw themselves as differing from those in the other classes. The two principal divisions would occur between farmers and town dwellers, and more particularly between farmers and merchants. In the next chapter I deal with the ideological differences between the classes. Here I am concerned with establishing what the class structure of the state actually was. I have argued that the ability of a class to create itself as a class—that is, one with distinct structure, organization, and consciousness—is determined in part by the class structure of the society as a whole. Though I have not argued for the primacy of economic position, I have said that how people earn their living—their relationship to the mode of production—determines in part how they experience and interpret their everyday economic experiences. Farmers responded in a particular way to the economic troubles of the 1890s, because they *were* farmers. As I have already argued, they would often express their discontent in terms shaped by national debates and by a national language. Also, because the objective economic position of workers and farmers was different, the potential for cooperation between them was limited. And, finally, even though the objective economic position of farmers and merchants was similar—one might define those in each group as members of the petite bourgeoisie—they found themselves on different sides of the political fence for a time because they played very different roles in the expansion of industrial America, and because each group, or class segment, had placed its hope in a different image of America.

But farmers, merchants, and laborers cannot, obviously, be treated as three uniform categories. There were well-to-do farmers, just as there were wealthy entrepreneurs. There were laborers who climbed into the ranks of businessmen, some who became farmers, and some who remained laborers for the whole of their lives, never realizing the dream of owning their own land, or being their own boss. However, many studies of social movements, including the Alliance and Populist party, have treated these groups as though they had fixed memberships. In fact, the actual fluidity among distinct class segments within the larger categories of farmer, worker, and merchant, goes far to explain why the Alliance and Populist revolt unraveled so quickly. The movement, at different stages, attracted people with diverse class interests. This made it more difficult for the movement to sustain itself during the long period of time necessary for an assault on the established political and economic order both within Kansas and nationally. Diversity occurred at three levels: within two communities, Fort Scott and Lawrence, Kansas; within the two counties, Bourbon and Douglas, in which these communities are located; and at the state level. Later in this work I will show how the class divisions within the community and county relate to voting patterns. Specifically, with whom did workers side in the political divisions of 1890? How did the farmers within a pro-Republican county vote, as opposed to those living in the towns? An examination of the actual process by which classes were structured shows how and why merchants came to dominate and over what issues people would divide.

The Growth and Development of Industry in Kansas

Early Kansas industry, in the period immediately preceding the Civil War, was concentrated in the eastern third of the state, and such manufacturing as is worth mentioning was restricted primarily to the timber "industry." Oak and walnut were cut for use primarily in the building of local homes, hotels, and livery stables, though there were a few furniture factories in eastern towns such as Leavenworth, Atchison, and Fort Scott. These industries were located close to the larger streams of eastern Kansas because they provided the source of power. Some enterprising soul or souls would build a dam to turn a large wheel. Attached to the wheel, in varying ways, were the belts that drove the saws, lathes, and millstones of the local businesses. A town's "industrial" district was often a maze of belts slinking down the block in brick-lined tunnels. Breakdowns were frequent, and injuries not uncommon.

Agriculture was preeminent in this period. The fertile valleys of eastern Kansas provided the bulk of the state's wealth in the form of corn, wheat, and oats. In 1860, for example, over 5.5 million bushels of corn were produced, 200 thousands bushels of wheat, and about 100 thousand of oats.[4] The corn and wheat were turned into meal and flour by the millstones of eastern Kansas and used almost exclusively for local consumption. Often the person who ran a lumber mill or furniture factory would mill grain on the side, sometimes even at a loss, in order to accommodate the local settlers. There appears to have been a great deal of mutual accommodation among the early settlers as they worked together to establish a new civilization on the frontier.

By the 1880s, use of water power for milling would give way to steam generators, powered by local coal. Kansas coal was concentrated in the southeastern counties of the state, principally in the region of Fort Scott and Pittsburg, and it provided a great boost to the economies of those regions. (Much of the coal would be used to fire the engines of the Santa Fe Railroad.) The Fort Scott area also had supplies of natural gas and natural cement, or limestone. Cheap fuel, coal, or gas, enabled the southeastern sector of the state to develop minor industries; much of the cement that went into building early railroad bridges, as well as bridges that carried pedestrians and the horse-drawn wagons of teamsters, came from Fort Scott.

Kansas had other natural resources, such as oil, but those fields were not discovered until later in the century and did not play a major role in the development of early industry. Isolated pockets of resources, e.g., salt wells and salt mines, had little or no effect on the development of the state as a whole. In short, the natural resources of Kansas, such as they were, were concentrated in the eastern sector of the state, and did not give rise to large industrial complexes. Rather, they generated a number of small businesses usually geared to a local market. In fact, it is localism that characterizes early manufacturing efforts. Brick kilns, lumber mills, blacksmithing establishments, quarries, and related activities were all geared to the post–Civil War period of growth.

Table 4.1   Kansas Labor Force, 1875 and 1885

	1875			1885
	Males	Females	Both	Both
Agriculture	71%	27%	68.6%	61%
Professional and personal service	10.4	57	12.8	15
Trade and transportation	7.3	0.7	7.1	10
Manufacturing, mining, mechanical	11.3	15.3	11.5	14
N	131,677	7,232	138,909	331,694

Sources: Kansas Board of Agriculture, *Fourth Annual Report*, pp. 524–25; *Fifth Biennial Report*, p. 56. Of those women listed as members of the agricultural labor force in 1875, over 95 percent are listed as farmers, rather than farm laborers. Women in the professional and personal service category are, first, domestic servants (50 percent) and, second, teachers (36 percent). The majority of women (62 percent) employed in manufacturing were milliners or dressmakers. These ratios are essentially the same for the 1885 data.

After the war, population began to grow in earnest, but the early growth reinforced the "industrial" structure, as well as the existing class structure and existing relationships of power. The farmer needed plows and other heavy equipment to begin farming and bought them from local blacksmiths. The merchant needed lumber to build a crude store from which to peddle groceries or drugs. The barber, newspaper editor, butcher, and lawyer also needed places to do business as well as homes or boarding houses in which to live. The craft industries, then, grew at a rapid pace and many of those employed in this period were either independent owners or skilled workers plying their trade in local towns and villages. Kansas was becoming a state of small businessmen.

Manufacturing spread slowly westward across the state and by 1870 forty-one counties claimed to have some sort of industry, compared to twenty-one in 1860. The number of manufacturers increased sevenfold in this decade, while the number of men employed increased ninefold. However, the actual value of the product only increased fivefold. This was the period of small businesses, and with the exception of the railroad—repair and manufacture of equipment—Kansas was a state of small entrepreneurs. A few people made fortunes in the coal fields of eastern Kansas, or got rich milling the flour of farmers, but most merchants did not. Though people hoped for something quite different, trade and manufacturing, as table 4.1 indicates, would continue to play a minor role in the state's overall economy. Lumbering continued to be the dominant industry until the 1880s, with flour-milling in second place in terms of value of the product. This shifted in the 1880s, because of the introduction of hard winter wheat (the turkey red brought by the Mennonites) into the state. At first flour mills were also widely distributed across the state and were small, the average capital being about $1,000 per mill.[5] Small, too, were the carriage, harness, and implement makers; however, they were located in eastern Kansas. In the early 1870s, then, only seven towns figured as manufacturing centers in Kansas and could be said to have a laboring class: Lawrence, Fort Scott, Emporia, Atchison, Topeka, Leavenworth, and Junction City. Kansas City, Kansas, was primarily a point for the transshipment of goods and would not figure as an industrial center until later in the century. These towns emerged as central in the early development of manufacturing because they were also railroad centers, where the farmer could ship his grain or the blacksmith receive his raw materials.

The competition for railroad lines was intense. Towns rightly saw railroads as directly linked to their welfare, and went to elaborate lengths to attract them, passing bond issues that mortgaged their future. By 1890, there were almost 15,000 miles of railroad lines in Kansas, moving coal, wheat, corn, and cattle to market. The welfare of both those in town and field was linked to the railroads. Ironically, it was railroad rates that provided for the early growth of many Kansas towns, and it would be railroad rates that proved their undoing.

The freight rates on finished goods, e.g., plows and agricultural implements, were extremely high, much higher than on raw materials. This encouraged the development of local industries that could turn the raw materials into furniture, agricultural implements, buggies, soap, beer, and clothing. Hand labor, then, received a boost, as did the small businessman who wanted to manufacture for the surrounding area, or even points west. For several decades, these nascent industries were protected from their eastern competitors. This protection would come to an end at the close of the century, and hundreds of the industries would be driven out of business.

A person writing about Leavenworth in 1910 noted,

it is an interesting fact that twenty years ago the town had more factories . . . and establishments used in the trades, such an carpentering and the like, than it has now. It had then the largest wagon factory in the state and four smaller, but active factories; its seven flour mills included the largest and best equipped mills in this section [of the state]. . . . Its iron foundries employed 500 men, and were growing rapidly; it had six furniture factories, including the pioneer and largest in the Middle West. Besides these industries the town had the only boot and shoe factory in the state, and one of the first packing houses west of the Missouri river.[6]

Collapse of industries in small towns occurred simultaneously with centralization. That is, with Kansas markets open to eastern manufacturers, many small-town "industrialists" were placed at a severe price disadvantage. The hand-made gave way to the mass-produced. The products of Kansas became even more exclusively agricultural, and even those products were in the hands of monopolists. The railroad served as buyer and shipper of grain, and the packing plants, representing eastern capital, were concentrated in Kansas City, Kansas, and Missouri.[7] How did the communities of Fort Scott and Lawrence, Kansas, fare during this process? How did the early history of these communities affect the development of the class structure, and how did merchants come to dominate the political system?

Class Structuring in Fort Scott and Lawrence

Fort Scott and Bourbon County

Early Settlement   Bourbon county took its name from a county in Kentucky, named in honor of the Bourbon monarchy for the aid it gave the struggling American republic in the War of Independence. It shares an eastern border with Missouri in the southern third of the state. The town of Fort Scott sits high on a bluff overlooking the Marmaton River, which winds through farm land about 200 feet below. Like the rest of eastern Kansas, the land rolls gently, and the tree-covered slopes are covered with a variety of eastern hardwoods.

In 1842, General Zachariah Taylor was responsible for protecting Missouri and the western frontier from the "depredations of the Indian." He sent Captain Benjamin Moore, of the First Dra-

The Fort Scott town square on a typical day, circa 1880. Courtesy Kansas Collection of the University of Kansas Libraries.

goons, along with an army doctor and a handful of soldiers, to select the site of a fort. Their first choice, fifty-five miles south of the present Fort Scott, proved to be too expensive. A Cherokee Indian by the name of John Rogers wanted the shocking sum of $4,000 for his land. As the party had been authorized to spend no more than $1,000, they set out to look for cheaper land. The present site of Fort Scott was decided on. It commanded an excellent view of the valley, provided water and timber, and—as the land belonged to the federal government—it was free. A simple one-story long building, without a floor, was thrown up, and the cracks between the logs filled with mud. The army was now ready to begin the process of civilizing the country.

In the years immediately following, the government built a mill on one of the small streams that fed into the Marmaton. It was used primarily to saw lumber for the fort, which grew rapidly in size. When finished, at a cost of $200,000, these quarters were said to be the finest on the frontier.[8] Such businesses as there were grew up to service the post. Some of the officers became directly involved in business activities themselves. One Colonel Wilson, for example, purchased an interest in the sutlership (the right to provide provisions for the men) from a Mr. John Bugg. Wilson also became the postmaster. The government decided to abandon the post in 1853, and the buildings were put up for sale in 1855. Wilson then purchased one of the larger ones for himself, and after the Civil War ended, enjoyed the growth of the town. This pattern of development for military forts was not unique. Many officers made money from provisioning their own troops and sponsored business activities in towns near their garrisons. Some helped to form town companies and tried to "boom" the property, often staking claims before homesteaders had a chance to claim anything.[9]

Not long after the government abandoned the fort, it had to be reestablished. In 1856, immigrants from South Carolina arrived in the town, sponsored by the Southern Emigrant Aid Society, intending to make Kansas a slave state. Skirmishes between free-state and proslavery forces broke out. Initially, the free-staters got the worst of it, but by 1857 had established rough parity with the proslavery forces. Though the town was occupied by two hostile and opposing forces, growth continued, much as it did in the rest of the state. Small blacksmithing shops opened, along with grocery stores and hotels. The men of Fort Scott could have a suit made by the local tailor, and the ladies had a choice of several millinery establishments. G. W. Goodlander, a local carpenter, who would become one of the town's leading citizens, sold walnut coffins lined with alpaca.[10] But growth in Fort Scott's business sector was relatively slow in the pre–War period.

In March of 1861, aware of the impending crisis, the citizens of Fort Scott met to decide what they should do. A significant portion of local Democrats declared themselves loyal to the Union, a fact that would figure in the later legitimation of the Democratic party in Fort Scott and Bourbon County. By April, over 100 men out of the town's 400 volunteered for service in the Union cause. The town was fearful of an invasion by General Rains's rebel troops from Arkansas and Missouri. *The Fort Scott Democrat* told its readers:

> There is no time for hesitation. The country is in imminent and immediate peril. General Rains says that Kansas must be wiped out. The torch of an invading army from Missouri will be one of blood, fire, and rapine. Let us have protection at once.[11]

Protection came; Fort Scott was to figure prominently in the defense of the western territories. By 1861, there were at last 3,000

Union troops stationed at Fort Scott, and more would come. Sometimes up to 10,000 troops were camped there temporarily.

> Long wagon trains of Government supplies,—hardtack, bacon,
> beans, rice, coffee and sugar, of the Commissary department, and
> blue uniforms, boots and shoes, blankets, etc., of the Quarter-
> master department were constantly coming and going, and the
> grand chorus of a thousand voices from the mule corral was the
> first thing heard in the morning and the last at night.[12]

As one writer said, "there was an excellent opportunity to make money from the war."[13] An army surgeon stationed at the fort wrote to his wife that practically everybody in the town was getting rich from the war. "The merchants of Fort Scott have the contracts to furnish the army with corn which they supply at $1.17 per bushel while the papers of Leavenworth for August 12, 1863, quote it as 34 cents per bushel." He also noted that when the corn ripened, local farmers would probably receive no more than 20 cents a bushel while the speculators would make $1.00.[14] A merchant class came into being during the Civil War period and dominated in the decades to follow. The exploitation of farmers by merchants, middlemen, and monopolists had a long history.

By 1865, the town's population stood at around 3,000. There was a woolen mill, which had prospered by making cloth for uniforms, as well as a telegraph line linking the town to the outside world. Fort Scott's coal was being shipped north as far as Leavenworth, and there were eleven dry-goods stores, seven groceries, three hardware dealers, a bank, a bookstore, several livery stables, shoemakers, harness makers, barbers, physicians, and, according to a historian of the time who provided this listing, "Lawyers—Too many, as usual. The rest of the fellows kept saloons."[15]

Town Growth and Development   The citizens of Fort Scott were determined to make their town *the* major industrial center of southeastern Kansas, if not the major center for the entire region of Missouri, Arkansas, the Indian Territory (Oklahoma), and points south. Like the residents of other small towns, they saw the railroad as the key to their success. As soon as the Kansas legislature authorized towns and counties to issue bonds in aid of railroad development, Bourbon County residents did so—several times. Though there would eventually be three separate lines serving this small community, the town's Board of Trade issued a pamphlet in 1884 showing no less than thirteen railroad lines entering and leaving the city. The map of railroad connections contained an explanatory note, "There are slight errors in this map, occurring through mistakes of the engraver. It fails to show some of the completed connections of Fort Scott, and also fails to have placed in *dotted* lines one or two merely projected roads, *but the report itself fully explains the facts*."[16] Without the cooperation of the railroad lines, the city would not prosper.

Railroad construction did not proceed smoothly. There were disputes over what a particular line would be called once the bonds were issued—citizens wanted it made clear that the line passed through Fort Scott. There were bonds issued for which no lines were laid; and the railroad companies reneged on promised connections with other cities. A special bond issue, which would have brought one railroad's main repair shops to Fort Scott, was later canceled because of the failure of the railroad to keep its promise. Legitimate resentment of the railroad came early to the people of Fort Scott, especially to the merchants who had been responsible for pushing passage of bonds. In a report on what Fort Scott needed to grow and prosper, the railroads were mentioned as having inhibited the town's development. The railroads and their owners were interested in moving people west to settle on "starvation railroad lands," rather than helping them settle on the "almost unrivalled and overlooked lands of Southeastern Kansas. . . . The prior claims and superior worth of Eastern Kansas . . . [have been] subordinated to the interests of her subsidized corporations."[17] When the farmers, and then the Populists, raised a cry for muzzling the corporations, there were sympathetic listeners among the businessmen of the town.

Nevertheless, lines were laid and through shipments from cities such as St. Louis and Chicago were possible. Cattle, coal, and cement traveled north and east on these lines. Grain was sent by rail south to Memphis, and from there by freighter to points as far distant as Liverpool. Lines to the west brought farmers' crops to market, and allowed the business classes of Fort Scott to send their wares into Texas, the Indian Territory, and deep into the Southwest.

The year 1873 was a disaster for Fort Scott. Both farmers and merchants were affected by the national depression. Farmers met that year in a state convention and declared themselves opposed to monopolists. They urged uniting for the purpose of getting supplies at cost and securing a reduction in freight rates. The local Republican paper praised their goals,[18] and printed a statement in a later edition communicating the farmers' needs and linking them to the problems of the merchants.

> Why is business dull in Fort Scott? Solely because the farmers of Bourbon county have not money to spend. I think no one will deny this. I do not suppose there is one farmer in fifty but would have spent double what he has spent the previous year for the necessities of life and the improvement of his stock and tools.
>
> The farmers' wives today, when they leave our city to return to their homes, feel sad that they cannot take the dress that the merchant feels sad not to sell.[19]

Business received a further blow when an April fire swept through the central business district destroying or damaging over twenty-seven local businesses. But because of available supplies of coal, natural gas, cement, farm products, and general enthusiasm, rebuilding of the town's economy was rapid. By 1880, the town's population stood at 5,372, and that of the entire county at close to 20,000.

The town's principal industries in the 1880s were two large nurseries which, according to local sources, had "a sweeping business from Nebraska to Georgia and Texas, amounting to $400,000 a year." The town was also known for its flour mills, especially that of Goodlander, with "its daily capacity . . . (of) 325 barrels of flour, and 150 barrels of meal." The Fort Scott Foundry and Machine Works manufactured steam engines, boilers, mining equipment, drilling machines, and provided the wrought iron for jails. It employed 125 men. The town also boasted of a cement plant, a planing mill, a carriage works, a woolen mill, a broom factory, and a plant that turned out 7,000 gallons of castor oil each year. The value of its agricultural products was placed at over $2 million, and that of all merchants and industrialists at $4.3 million.[20]

The Class Structure   The three primary classes of Fort Scott and Bourbon County prior to the turn of the century—workers, merchants and businessmen, and farmers—did not have firm boundaries. A number of those we would class as workers, e.g., carpenter, plasterer, carriage maker, were independent businessmen. Some moved from the category of skilled laborer to independent craftsman, and into the ranks of the town's business leaders. Farmers, too, might move from the category of yeoman to that of merchant. The merchants and businessmen of the town were also a diverse category, ranging from those with large capital investments to those

Table 4.2   Comparison of Bourbon and Douglas County Industries, 1888

	Bourbon (N=30)	Douglas (N=12)
Average capital	$33,630	$37,792
Average value of product	48,493	42,681
Average value of total wages	15,053	6,282
Average number employed		
Men	29.60	19.25
Women	.83	25.25
Youth	.53	11.08
Average daily wages, skilled		
Men	2.44	2.31
Women	1.00	1.02
Youth	—	—
Average daily wages, unskilled		
Men	1.45	1.29
Women	.80	.65
Youth	.64	.47

Source: Kansas Bureau of Labor, *Fourth Annual Report,* p. 98.

whose hold on prosperity was a tenuous one. For the most part, businesses were small.

In 1888, for all of Bourbon County, there were 30 industries, mostly concentrated in Fort Scott, that employed 888 men, 25 women, and 15 children. The average of 30 employees for each manufacturing establishment compares with that of the state as a whole. (For Douglas County, where Lawrence is located, there were only 12 industries, even though Lawrence had the larger population—11,000 compared to 9,000 for Fort Scott.) As table 4.2 also suggests, the rate of return on investment was high, during the period of time that industry was protected by differential freight rates. Business was, however, exceptionally risky, and there were a number of contributing factors.

First, the merchants' prosperity was linked to the farmers': when farm prices dropped, farmers stopped buying not only dresses for their wives but basic necessities. Merchants were as vulnerable as farmers to the economic downturns of 1873 or of the late 1880s. Second, their prosperity was false insofar as it was based on protection from national markets. This protection would end with mass production and lower railroad rates. (Lawrence industries were particularly vulnerable to these forces.) Third, competition among the merchants themselves was intense. In Fort Scott, for example, in 1890, when the total population stood at about 10,000, there were 45 grocery stores, 10 shoe stores, 15 lumber yards, 8 butcher stores, 11 drug stores, 9 dry-goods stores, 7 general stores, 13 hotels, and 28 restaurants. There were also milliners, sweet shops, and pool halls. Many of these businesses had entered in the boom period of 1885–87, and many exited in the collapse of 1889.

But even though business was risky, some did exceptionally well. The real possibility of prosperity drew many to the small towns of the Great Plains. It is not surprising that, when faced with actual or potential ruin, merchants reacted strongly. Their ire was, however, not directed toward the capitalist system of which they were an integral part but against "cheap foreign products," and farmers who "frightened" capital away from the state. The number of failed merchants was very high; in simple percentage terms the rate of failure may have been higher than that for farmers.

The Dun and Mercantile Company, later to become Dun and Bradstreet, began publishing information on the assets and credit ratings of Kansas businesses in the year 1865. I examined the available records for the years 1865–1900 to determine the range of enterprises that existed, the level at which they were capitalized, and their rate of failure. As table 4.3 makes clear, most of these businesses were extremely small, even by the standards of the day. The Dun and Mercantile Company Records give an average range of capital wealth from $250 to $1 million. To put this in perspective, there were a total of 904 establishments doing business in the city of Fort Scott between 1865 and 1900. One of these businesses had assets of a million dollars, but that business lasted only one year. Most of the highly capitalized businesses, e.g., those with more than $475,000, were banks and mortgage firms, which had a very poor record of success.[21] *Over half of all businesses were worth less than $1,500* (262 had an average value of $1,500, 132 of $750, and 78 had $250 or less).

The failure rate for the 904 businesses that existed in Fort Scott between 1865 and 1900 is extremely high. If we take the percentage of those in the category of $1,500 worth of assets, of which there were 262, only 42 of these businesses—16 percent—lasted more than five years. One hundred and fifty-six of the businesses failed in one or two years. In fact, out of 904 establishments, only 245 survived beyond five years, and by the time we reach 1881, just sixteen years later, only 61 of the original 904 are left. (Many of these failures were concentrated in 1873–74 and 1887–89.)

Table 4.3   Persistence of Businesses in Fort Scott, 1865–1900, by
Category of Wealth

Average Assets	Years in Business			
	1–5	6–10	11–16	16+
$1,000,000 +	1			
750,000	0			
625,000	0			
400,000	0			
250,000	2	2	—	—
162,500	2	—	—	—
100,000	5	1	1	—
62,500	3	3	3	2
42,500	13	4	2	1
27,500	28	13	8	4
15,000	73	34	22	13
7,500	115	50	26	15
4,000	141	37	23	8
2,500	49	20	8	3
1,500	262	42	21	8
750	132	25	13	4
250 –	78	14	8	3

Source: Dun and Mercantile Company Records for the state of Kansas, Douglas
and Bourbon Counties (Library of Congress).

Note: The table underestimates the failure rate. Because of gaps in the Mercantile
Company Records, I had to use five-year intervals for organizing the information.
The figures in column one (1–5 year rate of persistency) represent 100 percent
of the cases. For those businesses whose assets totaled $250 or less, then, only
18 percent persist beyond the five-year period. For those cases for which more
complete data are available it appears as though most businesses failed within one
or two years. There is an inverse relationship between level of assets and rate of
failure.

There is another figure which is equally revealing of the circumstances of town merchants, and provides support for the claim that
when the farmer hurt so did the merchant. If we compare the assets of businesses in 1890 with the assets of those left in 1900, we
find that the assets have shrunk considerably. The average assets of
the two mortgage agents that survived until 1900 went from a high
of $42,500 in 1890 to a low of $9,500 in 1900. Those who sold
building materials saw a decline in average assets from $24,000 to
$5,000 in the same time period, and the decline was equally pre-
cipitous in the building trades. The six remaining dry-goods stores
had average assets of $18,500 in 1900, whereas the nine that were

Table 4.4 Average Annual Earnings for Selected Occupations, 1897 and 1899 Compared

Occupation	Average Annual Earnings		Average Cost of Living		Average Annual Surplus/ Deficit	
	1897	1899	1897	1899	1897	1899
Agents and operators	$610.10	$656.68	$399.62	$640.04	+$210.48	+$ 16.64
Barbers	490.10	505.60	405.92	493.03	+ 84.18	+ 12.57
Butchers	492.66	407.80	343.37	461.38	+149.29	− 53.58
Brakemen	668.70	660.18	529.46	655.06	+139.24	+ 5.12
Railway blacksmiths	682.00	618.75	452.00	532.94	+230.00	+ 85.81
Carpenters	442.67	471.10	414.60	497.59	+ 28.07	− 26.49
Conductors	1,020.00	998.14	810.00	912.74	+210.00	+ 85.40
Clerks	531.00	460.39	438.08	428.19	+ 92.92	+ 32.20
Locomotive engineers	1,085.00	1,200.64	715.00	1,116.61	+370.00	+ 84.03
Locomotive firemen	728.78	674.57	503.00	648.36	+225.78	+ 26.21
Laborers	242.10	293.93	228.91	314.66	+ 13.19	− 20.73
Machinists	—	720.27	—	605.64	—	+114.63
Miners	332.94	344.06	401.88	370.19	− 78.94	− 26.13
Painters	—	409.40	—	449.56	—	− 40.16

Source: Kansas Bureau of Labor, *Sixteenth Annual Report*, pp. 128–54.

in business in 1890 had average assets of $62,857. This pattern was repeated over and over again in practically every business and trade in town, and throughout the state of Kansas. The fortunes of local merchants were linked to those of the farmers, but their desired solutions to those problems differed considerably.

If the economic circumstances of the merchant were precarious, what of the laborer's? We must first note that the category of worker is an amorphous one. There was movement between the ranks of artisans and merchants, which meant that some laborers cast their political lot and identity with that of the business classes. There were few concentrations of workers in the state and few opportunities to develop what we would think of as a working-class culture. Finally, and partly as a consequence of this, there were no organizational structures developed to deal with the interests of the working men and women of Kansas. In table 4.2 figures for Bourbon County show that skilled male laborers were paid an average of $2.44 a day, while the unskilled were paid $1.45. It is unlikely, though I have no hard data on this, that these men would have worked a full six-day week, or eight hours a day. Some early industries, canning for example, were seasonal, and breakdowns in machinery which could idle the labor force for several days were not uncommon. State-level data for this period, indicate, too, that few laborers worked full time during the year.[22] Table 4.4. presents average annual earnings for workers, most skilled, which will allow us to speculate about the conditions of workers in Fort Scott and, later, in Lawrence.

In the period 1890–1900 the poverty level stood at about $500 for a family of four.[23] Many skilled workers in Kansas reported an income above that, though they were concentrated in the railroad industry. Fort Scott, by virtue of the three main railroads that passed through it, numbered a significant portion of its population—10–15 percent by my calculations—as railroad employees. (Although many railroad workers wanted legislation promoting job safety, they differed from farmers on the regulation of rates, for they thought that might threaten their jobs.) Table 4.4 also reveals that a number of workers had more expenses than income in the year 1899. In particular, we find common laborers (who earned far less than a poverty-level income), miners, painters (who would have been affected by the economic downturn in the 1887–89 period), and butchers.

If we look at farm laborers as a separate category (table 4.5), we find that they cannot be said to have done well, especially in the

Table 4.5   Farm Labor Statistics for Bourbon and Douglas Counties, 1893

	Bourbon	Douglas	State Averages
% of farmers employing laborers by the month	75%	21%	27%
Av. no. of months laborers are employed	6	10	6.4
Av. daily wages, computing board, for laborers employed by the month*	$1.03	$1.11	$1.27
Av. daily wages, computing board, for laborers during harvesting and threshing season*	$1.40	$1.58	$1.81
Av. daily wages, computing board, for other farm work*	$1.15	$1.30	$1.48
Av. daily wages, computing board, for female help on farm*	$0.72	$0.86	$1.00
% of farm hands, employed by the month, who are married	10%	7%	14%
% of farm hands, employed by the month, who are over the age of 21	40%	47%	51%

Source: Kansas Bureau of Labor, *Ninth Annual Report,* pp. 62, 166.

*Note: "Board" includes food, lodging, washing, and mending. Average value of board in Bourbon County was $0.40 per day, in Douglas County $0.58 per day.

1890s. To take the state as whole, if the average daily wage was $1.27 (which would include board at about 50 cents a day), and the average number of months worked was 6.4, then the cash in hand for the year would be $195. This was hardly sufficient to live on, if we look at the annual cost of living as reported by workers in table 4.4. Often, a large part of the transient population within villages and towns was made up of the laborers who worked part time when seasonal work could be found. Alma, Kansas, for instance, with a total population of 957 people in 1890, had over 100 transient workers.[24] Part of the farm-labor category is made up of other farmers who were working for wages to supplement meager earnings from their crops.

By the 1890s, the reported unemployment rate for Bourbon and Douglas counties was high. In 1893 the state's Bureau of Labor Statistics sent out questionnaires to all county courthouses in the state. The townships (divisions within the counties) were asked to report on local conditions. Unfortunately not all bothered to respond, but those that did give a grim picture for both laborers and farmers. In Drywood Township of Bourbon County, for instance, 203 farm homes were listed. The officials of the township reported that 50 farmers, 51 farm hands, 50 day laborers, 35 mechanics, 30 women, and 49 other people were unemployed. The conditions in Marion Township were reported to be even worse. Here there were 450 farm households, and no farmers were listed as seeking work, but 500 farm hands were looking for work, as were 100 day laborers, 100 mechanics, and 250 women. Within the town of Fort Scott itself, there were 300 day laborers without work, as were 287 mechanics, 50 women, and 150 with unspecified occupations. In Lawrence, Kansas, things were not much better. Here, for the same time period, 225 laborers were unemployed, along with 150 mechanics, 75 women, and 300 other people.[25] The condition of the worker was as bad as, if not worse than, that of the farmer or the failed merchant.

Yet during the economic downturn, the local papers did not refer to the plight of workers. In some communities they remain almost invisible, as if people assumed that the category of laborer was a transitional one. Of course there were workers who planned on moving out of this status and did not define themselves as members of a working class. Certainly Kansas had no real factory towns, or experience with working-class communities. Richard L. Douglas, writing in 1910, commenting on Kansas City, Kansas, said, "it is rather a remarkable fact that there is not as yet a true factory class even in the oldest of industries." There had not developed a "class of labor trained from childhood in the trade." Douglas supposed that this might have to do with "the independence, or democracy, or freedom, or whatever it is that characterized the west."[26]

Labor unrest was restricted in terms of industry and locale. As I will treat the question of the ideological differences in the following chapter, let me simply note here that labor unrest began as early as the 1870s, and involved primarily the coal mining industry and the railroads. The first railroad strike broke out in Holton, Kansas, where 150 men, who had not been paid for two months because the line they were laying track for was in financial trouble, vowed "no pay, no track laying." The Kansas Central Railway Company brought in strikebreakers, who were presumably going to get paid. After one of the striking workers was killed, unrest spread to other railroad towns. In some cases, railroad workers vowed to pro-

Table 4.6 Labor Unrest in Kansas, 1883–1886

Industry Employees	Reason for Strike	Called by Labor Org.	No. of Firms Struck	Av. Length (Days)	Successful	% Gain/Loss in No. of Employees	% of Striking
Building trades	for wage increase	No	1	3	No	0	100%
Tailors	for adoption of fixed-price list	Yes	4	44	Yes	0	100%
Horsecollar makers	against wage cuts	No	1	3	No	−50%*	50%
Smelter workers	for wage increase and/or reduction in hours	No	4	5	No	−21%	100%
Coal miners	against wage cuts	No	15	76	66.6%**	0	100%
Compositors	for discharge of obnoxious foreman	Yes	1	2	No	−41%	41%
Cigar makers	for wage increase	Yes	4	22	No	−28%	100%

Source: Kansas Bureau of Labor, *Third Annual Report*, pp. 296–308.

*The loss in number of jobs reflects the fact that those employees who struck were fired and replaced with new workers.

**The strike was successful in ten firms but failed in five.

tect the company's property against lawless strikebreakers. The other major labor conflicts centered around the coal mines in Cherokee and Crawford counties in southeast Kansas.[27] (Coal miners, like railroad workers, were more likely to be foreign immigrants than those in other occupational categories in Kansas.) All in all, labor organizations were not strong throughout the state, and had limited success in achieving their ends.

There are some limited data on strikes in Kansas, although not for the two major periods of economic downturn. Table 4.6 shows that strikes were few in Kansas, were as likely to be called by a labor organization as not, and were not often successful. Those of longest duration and intensity were in the coal mines. Although the Alliance and the Populist party would call for a union of farmers and workers, these organizations were dominated by farmers, and the life experiences of those who might belong to a labor organization differed from those who were farmers. Actual contact, as well as organizational contact, was lacking. Laborers might well vote for the Populists as a means of protesting the policies of the state Republican party, or the control exercised by the local machine. But they would then abandon an Alliance/Populist ticket when they felt that their interests were to be served by voting for one of the dominant parties. (The voting patterns suggest that workers did, initially, vote for protest parties, and stuck with them in places such as Cherokee and Crawford counties, but then voted for the state Republican candidates, as well as the national Republican ticket, because they believed that a strong tariff would protect their jobs and bring prosperity.)

Though there were a substantial number of men and women working in the industries of Fort Scott, their voices were not heard in the rebellion of farmers in the state, although Fort Scott did have a chapter of the Knights of Labor and was the only city in Kansas, perhaps in the entire region, where a short-lived socialist college for the producing classes (workers and farmers) was organized, listing Eugene Debs as a member of its governing board.

If things were difficult for laborers, so were they for farmers. As table 4.7 shows, farmers within Douglas and Bourbon Counties had been steadily losing money. Both in relative and actual terms conditions had taken a turn for the worse, and no immediate upturn was foreseen. So, although North may be correct that nationally, and over the period between 1860 and 1900, the farmers' lot improved, circumstances differed for those in Kansas.[28] (Recall

Table 4.7   Farm Losses, 1883–1893, for Bourbon and Douglas Counties

	Bourbon	Douglas	County Averages
Bushels of wheat raised in 10-yr. period	648,053	3,783,280	2,902,876
Price received	$318,289	$2,135,912	$1,495,044
Value at av. price for preceding 5 yrs.	$536,200	$3,173,089	$2,324,008
Loss by decline in price	$217,911	$1,037,176	$828,964
Bushels of corn raised in 10-yr. period	19,832,873	18,955,606	13,905,286
Price received	$4,922,415	$5,425,986	$3,169,566
Value at average price for preceding 5 yrs.	$7,040,772	$6,996,533	$4,564,687
Loss by decline in price	$2,118,357	$1,570,551	$1,395,121
Total loss, wheat and corn	$2,336,767	$2,607,727	$2,224,085
Amount of farm mortgages in 1890	$1,602,984	$1,059,328	$1,576,840

Source: Kansas Board of Agriculture, *Ninth Annual Report,* pp. 60, 164.

Table 4.8   Cost of Producing 40 Acres of Corn, Bourbon and Douglas Counties

	Bourbon	Douglas	State Average
Av. cost except labor of man and team*	$ 98.00	$111.77	$ 88.15
Av. cost of man's labor	117.52	133.72	144.87
Av. cost of team	146.60	141.45	138.41
Total cost of 40 acres	362.12	392.94	371.43
Total cost per bushel	0.33.5	0.34.8	0.32.8
Freight per bushel to K.C.	0.04.48	0.03.36	—
Av. price per bushel paid to farmers	0.27.1	0.28.2	0.24.6
Av. loss per bushel	0.06.4	0.06.6	0.08.2
% of farmers obliged to sell on account of debt	80%	71%	77%

Source: Kansas Board of Agriculture, *Ninth Annual Report,* pp. 61, 165.

*Averages are for 5-year period, 1888–92.

that Bourbon and Douglas Counties were located in the eastern part of the state where economic circumstances were better than in the middle sector.) Farmers had lost money because prices were declining, and because the cost of growing their crops exceeded what they got for them in the marketplace. From table 4.8 it is clear that

Table 4.9   Cost of Producing 40 Acres of Wheat, Bourbon and Douglas Counties

	Bourbon	Douglas	State Average
Av. cost except labor of man and team*	$228.13	$202.31	$185.46
Av. cost of man's labor	62.92	79.92	89.01
Av. cost of team	80.25	63.95	73.14
Total cost of 40 acres	371.30	346.28	347.61
Total cost per bushel	0.66.7	0.70.1	0.65.3
Freight per bushel to K.C.	0.06.00	0.04.20	0.08.50
Av. price per bushel paid to farmers	0.61.2	0.63.0	0.58.6
Av. loss per bushel	0.05.5	0.07.1	0.06.7
% of farmers forced to sell because of debts	80%	71%	77%

Source: Kansas Board of Agriculture, *Ninth Annual Report*, pp. 61, 165.

*Averages are for 5-year period, 1888–92.

if it cost an average of 32.8 cents to raise a bushel of corn in the state, and the farmer only got 24.6 cents on the average, he was not going to stay in business long, and his level of debt would rise. The same was true of wheat (table 4.9), where the farmer lost 6.7 cents every time he sold a bushel of it. Especially intriguing, in view of the demands that farmers would make to control railroad rates, is a comparison of the farmers' losses with what it cost to ship grain to market. In the case of wheat it is exactly the same. That is, the farmer lost 6.7 cents on the transaction, and it cost, on the average, 6.7 cents to send the wheat to market via the railroad. For corn, the pattern is the same: 6.4 cents to send a bushel from Fort Scott and a loss of 6.4 cents. Of course there is something a little too neat about these figures. They may well have been prepared to show that railroads were the source of the farmers' problems, but they were issued by a Republican-controlled state government, not the Populists.

Residence and Socioeconomic Status   As Fort Scott developed, definite class patterns emerged in areas of residence, with workers occupying smaller homes in the industrial portions of town along the Marmaton, to the east, or clustered in some of the boardinghouses and hotels that lined the town's main street. Those who were more well-to-do lived in the large houses on the shaded red-brick-paved streets that extended back from the site of the old fort. The town also had a small black community, former slaves who had lived there before

Table 4.10   Socio-economic Characteristics of Ward and Township Residents in
Fort Scott and in Bourbon County, 1895

	Fort Scott			
	% White	% Foreign-born	% Professional	% Skilled and Unskilled
Wards				
I	95	13	1.6	74
II	83	14	7.0	52
III	80	14	15.0	58
IV	90	10	13.0	50
V	92	08	2.0	67

	Bourbon County		
	% Foreign-born	% Farmers	Average Land Value
Townships			
Drywood	11	92	$2,706
Franklin	3	90	2,748
Freedom	22	94	2,587
Marion	9	100	3,134
Marmaton	3	73	3,028
Mill Creek	13	82	1,872
Osage	13	82	3,140
Pawnee	4	72	1,800
Scott Township	12	68	3,472
Timberhill	0	100	2,738
Walnut	18	100	2,905

Source: Based on a 10% sample of the 1895 Kansas agricultural census. The category of skilled and unskilled makes no distinction, because one cannot be made
based on the census data, between those who were employed and self-employed. It
includes carpenters, ordinary laborers, railroad workers, domestics, and similar occupations. The category of professional refers to doctors, lawyers, teachers, and
ministers. The foreign-born are those native whites not born in the United States.
The value of the land refers to the average assessed value of an individual farmer's
homestead.

Kansas became a free state, or who had fled to the city during the
war. Table 4.10 gives us a rough estimation of the general socioeconomic characteristics of the different wards, or voting districts,
within the town, as well as that of the townships that make up the
county. Wards II and IV tended to represent the "better" sections
of town, while the other wards, particularly I and V, were where
workers made their homes. Those townships close to Fort Scott,

naturally, have fewer farmers in them than do those lying at a greater distance, e.g., Timberhill. We will return to these wards and townships when I discuss voting behavior in chapter 8, and we will see that distance from a town such as Fort Scott or Lawrence correlates with whether people voted for the Alliance/Populist tickets. I do not intend to suggest, however, that there was a clear relationship between job, or socioeconomic position, and voting behavior, for there were many factors that inhibited the formation of a strong class consciousness.

Social Organizations and Cross-Class Membership   Consider first that between 1859 and 1888 seven churches were formed in the town of Fort Scott, and thirteen in the immediate area. Some churches, such as the Presbyterian, counted among their members many of the abolitionist town settlers and some of the successful merchants, while other churches had strong working-class congregations. Nevertheless, people of different class groupings mingled together for prayer and Sunday worship. The town also had a substantial number of the secret societies formed prior to the close of the nineteenth century—such as the Masons, the Independent Order of Odd Fellows, and the Ancient Order of the United Workmen. As Clawson showed in her work on nineteenth-century fraternal orders, such organizations had a diverse class base; laborers, merchants, traveling salesmen, and doctors met together.[29] There were also numerous study and civic groups in Fort Scott, bringing a wide variety of people together, e.g., the Current Literature Club, the Magazine Club, the Pierian Club, the Women's Christian Temperance Union, and, especially, the Grand Army of the Republic.[30] These organizations cut across class ties, though they were primarily middle-class in their ideology. The effect was to inhibit the development of an alternative class-consciousness, and to inhibit the development of autonomous working-class or farmers' organizations.

The Dominance of the Merchant Class   The merchants, however, emerged as the politically dominant class; the politics of the community revolved almost exclusively around the issue of how to boost business. The means by which people rose to positions of power and dominance were remarkably ordinary. That is, they arrived in town with capital, or a skill, or sometimes just an idea for making money, and stayed to do so, and to serve their community.

(As will be demonstrated for Lawrence, the community's leaders were long-time residents.) Some made money because the initial competitive advantage that railroad rates provided allowed them to offer local citizens something they needed to begin farming, or to establish themselves in business. Many independent craftsmen who arrived in town in the 1860s became businessmen. Let us briefly consider the lives of some of Fort Scott's community leaders.[31]

Charles W. Goodlander, who served as mayor of Fort Scott in 1893, arrived in town in April 1857, apparently the very first passenger to come by stage from Kansas City. A young man of twenty-three at the time, he had received some high school education in Pennsylvania, and had followed the trade of carpentry. He had little difficulty finding work as an independent craftsman, for the town had begun its growth. Soon he opened a mill and lumberyard, and later purchased a brick kiln. According to one source, he, like other merchants, lost much of what he had in the panic of 1873. A boiler explosion of 1876 destroyed part of his mill and his grain elevator. He "retrieved his fortune by returning to his old business of building and contracting, bought back his mill property and suffered a heavy loss by fire in 1887. The mill was rebuilt." He later became president of a local bank, and bought and operated the Goodlander Hotel. He eventually purchased the old home of his father-in-law, the former commander and post-sutler, John Wilson, and converted it into the Goodlander Home for Children.[32]

Benjamin F. Hepler, M.D., was another Pennsylvanian. He came to Fort Scott during the Civil War, served as the physician for the local state militia, and opened a drugstore. Shortly thereafter he helped to see that free public schools were opened. Forsaking his medical business, he worked hard to help develop the town, and secured the charter for the first railroad that came to the area. He served on the board of directors of two railroads, was one of the principal proprietors of the Fort Scott Paint and Cement Works, and served as president of a town company formed to boost a community that existed in Cherokee County only in the minds of the proprietors. Eventually, he returned to his medical practice.

H. M. Mayberry was born in Illinois in 1830 and was raised on a farm. When he was twenty he went to work in the coal mines of Illinois, and in 1851 drove cattle in California, passing through Kansas on the way. In 1859, he moved to Fort Scott and claimed a homestead outside of town. Instead of farming, however, he began to dig for coal, and became the proprietor of the Mayberry Coal Mines, employing at times up to seventy-five men.[33]

Such stories were repeated scores of times. Farmers became the owners of butcher shops or hardware stores. Small businessmen became bank presidents, while some craftsmen became leading industrialists. There was a great deal of mobility and most people took their business to be business: they wanted to participate in the growth and expansion of the town. A wide spectrum of citizens, then, wanted railroad bonds passed, water lines laid, a sewer system installed, and roads improved. Merchants predominated in this category, because their interests were clearly linked to an improvement of the town's infrastructure, and it was merchants who were able to translate their growing economic power into political power. As in other towns, merchants dominate throughout the history of Fort Scott, in all of the important elected positions: they were the mayors, the city councilmen, the county commissioners. These positions were of more than symbolic significance. The councils and commissions controlled the tax monies which could be spent for improvement of the town, which translated into jobs, and they controlled the hiring of all the appointed officials in town.

In 1891, the mayor of Fort Scott owned a saddle and leather shop on Main Street. The council was composed of one man who owned the local pottery plant, another who ran an express company, and three others who were lawyers. Another member of the same council owned a shoestore, another a butcher shop, and the remaining two were combination salesmen and brokers. As was typical, the Republicans dominated the local political scene. (The Democrats, however, put up spirited fights in many elections, particularly in the 1890s, and fared better in Fort Scott than elsewhere because of allegiances to the Union Democrats, and because, when the Democrats fused with the Populists and the Alliance, the combined ticket attracted a number of votes from laborers within the town.)

The councilmen spent the city's money on three city engineers, two city clerks, a treasurer, a marshall and his assistant, two night policemen, and a policeman who worked in the day. They paid their own salaries as well as that of the mayor. Money went to several people who did various jobs for the city, such as repairing the hook and ladder wagon, and repairing the gaslights and poles. The newspaper was paid for running public notices, and a local businessman received rent for the building in which they held their meetings. Even if they spent the money wisely, and there is no evidence they did not, considerable patronage was involved. Their most important activity, whether directly or indirectly, involved organizing and using the town's resources, and sometimes even their own and those of other businessmen, to encourage the flow of capital to the town. Thus, when the farmer movement posed a threat to the flow, merchants saw their best efforts being undermined. The growth and prosperity of their towns was not linked in their minds with the agricultural sector. In fact, the "booming" of the towns was, in part, an artificial phenomenon which fed on itself. The businessmen of Fort Scott had formed a Board of Trade. In 1884, they published a statement explaining why people should come to their town. In addition to the natural beauty of the area, they assured readers that "cheap living" and "cheap homes" were to be found, along with cheap fuel and plenty of water. They pointed out that there was an abundance of opportunities for education and worship.

> Among these may be noted her cathedral and many churches; her Normal College, high schools and common schools; her fine Opera House and other halls of fraternity and amusement; her first-class hotel and numerous good ones; her efficient fire brigade and fire apparatus; her superior water and gas works; her fine pavements and miles of Macadamized streets; her new horse railroad and her convenient public fountains and hydrants, and all the usual conveniences and comforts of an advanced civilization common to the most advanced cities of her class.[34]

The growth of Fort Scott would not be matched by the enthusiasm of her founders. Industry would move out of the area and she would eventually become an agricultural service center. The fate of her sister to the north, Lawrence, was not appreciably different. In examining the growth of class structuring in Lawrence and Douglas counties, I will offer some examples and data that are not precisely parallel to those for Fort Scott; comparable data is seldom available.

Lawrence and Douglas County

Early Settlement   Douglas County and the city of Lawrence lie approximately forty miles west of the present towns of Kansas City, Kansas, and Kansas City, Missouri. The fertile bottomlands along the Kansas and Wakarusa Rivers, which run from west to east through the county, make up about 20 percent of the land. Along the shores grow native cottonwoods, and further back along the rolling hillsides are elm, hackberry, oak, ash, and walnut, which the early pioneers were able to use for building their homes. The remainder of the county was part of the tall-grass region of eastern Kansas.

It was not until May of 1854 that the land was opened for settlement by whites. Prior to that time, the county was part of the reservation of the Shawnee Indians, but the Shawnee ceded most of it in a treaty settlement, reserving lands to the east in what is now Johnson County and the site of one of the wealthiest suburbs in the United States. (Needless to say, the Shawnee have moved elsewhere.) Travelers crossed Kansas many times before 1854; one of the great routes to the west, the Santa Fe Trail, passed directly through it and Douglas County. Along this California road, as it was called by some, the first settlers or squatters located.

Lawrence figured prominently in the struggle between those who wished to see the state settled either by abilitionist or proslavery forces. In July 1854 the New England Emigrant Aid Society sent out two explorers, Charles H. Branscomb of Holyoke, Massachusetts, and Charles Robinson, who would become governor of Kansas, to secure a promising place for a town site. The Lawrence site was selected, and on July 17, 1854, a party of twenty-nine men left Massachusetts by train for St. Louis. There they boarded the steamer *Polar Star* for passage to Kansas City. In order to get all of their supplies and equipment to Lawrence, they decided to buy a team of oxen and a wagon. Traveling on foot and at night because of the hot summer sun, they reached Lawrence four days later. The men hurried to claim homesteads, and some returned immediately to St. Louis or to New England with the intention of coming back the following spring. Those who stayed went about the business of building log homes. B. R. Knapp, a member of the party, said:

> It costs some $50 to build a log cabin, and there is a good demand for carpenters and laboring men. I shall build a cabin for myself forthwith, and have already commenced log-cutting for my cabin. It is rather hard work for a green hand. . . . Our company is all broke up, and every man now works on his own hook. I am sorry to say that we have some trouble about the establishment of our land claims—one of our party had his camp utensils, tent, and all his fixings removed into the California road a day or two since, because he had squatted on the claim of Nancy Miller.[35]

The composition of the early party tells something about the different motives of the people who came to Lawrence and to Kansas itself. The merchants arrived first, took control of the towns, both literally and figuratively, and the farmers followed behind. The Emigrant Aid Society contributed to the formation of the town, but it was fully expected that the town would become self-supporting and that it would prove profitable to the original backers.[36] In the party were one attorney, two people who listed their occupation as "speculator," as well as a banker. Two physicians came along to claim land and minister to the sick. Slightly over a third of those who pitched their tents in Lawrence that July were skilled laborers—mechanics and craftsmen. Two men intended to open stores to serve those expected to pour into the area, and one reporter hoped to find work. It is not clear what George Thatcher, who listed himself as a "sportsman," intended to do. Only five men, however, or about one out of every six members of the party, intended to till the soil.[37]

Just one month later, a second party of sixty-seven, including some women and children, set out from the railway station in Boston. Before departing, the group sang a hymn written especially for the occasion:

> We'll seek the rolling prairies,
>   In regions yet unseen,
> Or stay our feet unweary
>   By Kansas flowing stream;
> And there with hands unfettered
>   Our altars we will raise,
> With voices high uplifted
>   We'll sing our Maker's praise.[38]

For the first year Lawrence was a city of tents, although the saw mill, built with funds from the Emigrant Aid Society, would make it possible for many to have wooden homes by the next year.

One of the first large buildings constructed was the Free State Hotel, another Emigrant Aid Society project, designed to house those flowing into the region. Also built in short order were a number of business establishments to serve this pioneer population, principally dry-goods and general-merchandise stores. Almost all was lost on May 21, 1856, when proslavery forces pillaged and sacked the town. Rebuilding, however, was rapid. In 1859, there were several churches, and under the auspices of the Presbyterian church, $2,000 had been contributed toward the erection of a single college building, which would become, in 1861, the Lawrence University of Kansas, and eventually the state's university. Once more, the town's fortunes took a turn for the worse when, in the dark of August 21, 1863, the Confederate raider, Quantrill, rode into town with his men and torched the central business district, burning people's homes and shooting those who ran out into the night. A witness, writing about the devastation, claimed that at least seventy-five buildings on the town's main business street were destroyed. It rose again immediately from the ashes. "Before the fire was out," according to this eyewitness, "rebuilding commenced. Five large brick stores, commenced before the raid, were pushed at once to completion. Every burnt store, whose walls were left standing, was at once repaired. A large number of new stores were commenced. Some one hundred and fifty buildings have been built, rebuilt, or moved in since the raid. . . . Churches and schools have been kept up without interruption. One year will almost obliterate the real marks of Quantrill's steps."[39] And, indeed, by 1865, the town's fortunes were on the rise. It was easy to see why people saw civilization itself residing in the towns, with their rich mix of social institutions and opportunities for advancement and improvement.

Town Growth and Development   By 1870, Lawrence's population had grown to 8,320, while that of the county as a whole stood at over 20,000. The period between 1860 and 1870, in fact, witnessed the most rapid period of growth, though by 1898 the town had 11,391 souls and the county 24,251. Those who settled Lawrence expected it to be the dominant industrial, business, and educational center of the state. It was, in fact, second only to Leavenworth as a commercial center at the close of the war. By 1900, however, it had lost its preeminence as a business center and would remain for many years an agricultural center, as well as a center of education. Let us briefly examine this process.

The enthusiasm of the business classes was unbounded. As early as 1855, the local *Herald of Freedom,* editorialized under the heading of "Capitalists":

> We are acquainted with no place which holds out advantages for the investment of capital equal to those in this city. There is a certainty of Lawrence becoming a great point. . . . Half a dozen steam saw mills could be set to work immediately to advantage, and kept constantly supplied with timber. An iron foundry and

the finishing shop would monopolize for years the business of the Territory. There is none, in fact, of importance between this and St. Louis.[40]

The paper was quite right to emphasize the fact that opportunities existed simply because there were no other great manufacturing cities in the region. It meant that the community could temporarily support a variety of activities such as the manufacture of farm implements, soap-making, iron casting, furniture- and pottery-making.

The Kimball Foundry, established in 1858, was typical. The Kimballs had experience working in a foundry in Massachusetts. They purchased an iron lathe and planing machine, to take advantage of the fact that Lawrence was three hundred miles from a railroad and base of supplies. "If a carpenter needed irons for his building, no matter how odd in form, the Kimballs could furnish them. If a farmer broke a plow or a machine, the Kimballs could replace the broken part. They had to make their own patterns, often to manufacture their own tools, and sometimes to secure their own material by gathering old iron about town."[41] Lawrence was similar to Fort Scott in that a large number of business enterprises flourished in this early period specifically because they had a competitive advantage.

The building trades also prospered in the early history of the town, and small saw mills were set up along the banks of the Wakarusa and the Kansas rivers. Even in 1860, commerce dominated. The 1860 federal manuscript census for Lawrence, Kansas, listed 603 people as being employed. A number of "workers" (15 percent) were concentrated in the building trades as independent carpenters, bricklayers, and cabinetmakers. Only 7.5 percent of the population listed themselves as farmers, and 11 percent gave their occupation as simple laborer. The vast majority of those people listing an occupation claimed they were small businessmen—a barber, an architect, butcher, engineer, dentist, hotel keeper, grocer, or jeweler. Even when everyone who might possibly have been employed by somebody else is counted, this does not yield a particularly high figure, perhaps 20 percent of the total population.

In the period preceding Quantrill's raid the principal industries in town were a plow factory; a factory making bookcases, desks, and other bits of furniture; a tannery; a tallow works; several grist mills, often run in conjunction with the saw mills; a pottery; and many smaller firms making harnesses, barrels, uniforms, and shoes.

The fortunes of the town improved in the postwar period due to two factors: the building of a private bridge and the coming of the railroad. The bridge linked the area north of the Kansas River to the town and provided easier access to Leavenworth and Atchison, to the northeast. (However, when the river was frozen, people would walk across the ice rather than pay the tolls. The issue of tolls would provide some political controversy in Lawrence, and there would even be a ticket of Liberal Republicans who ran on the platform of "no tolls." When the bridge washed out in 1879, and had to be rebuilt, it became public property. The business community had argued strongly for a public bridge.)

The city's bridge was only eleven months old when many of the town's citizens crossed over in a day of celebration to welcome the arrival of the Union Pacific from Kansas City. At the urging of the business community, the county voted upon itself an enormous burden of debt, which had to be scaled down in the collapse of the 1870s.[42] A plan was hatched to build a line to the Gulf, in order to make cotton, sugar, molasses, and pine lumber available to Kansans at low cost. Nothing came of this project, but the Union Pacific did run a line from Lawrence to Leavenworth and one south, about twenty miles, to the town of Ottawa. The citizens of Lawrence issued $200,000 worth of bonds for the Lawrence and Southwestern Railroad Company to bring coal north from Carbondale, which lay thirty miles to the south. With coal, it was said, Lawrence could become a major manufacturing center. In a few years, as the coal fields of Carbondale proved inadequate, only the rusty rails linking the two towns remained. The most significant scheme was that of the Pleasant Hill Railroad, for which another substantial bond issue ($125,000) was passed. The line would be constructed to run from Pleasant Hill, Missouri, forty miles south of Kansas City, to Lawrence, by way of De Soto, to Lawrence's east. The point was to bypass Kansas City and directly tap the St. Louis trade. The idea that Lawrence, rather than Kansas City, should serve as the commercial metropolis of the region was not an unreasonable one at the time; in terms of population and resources the communities were then nearly equal.

The history of the business enterprises of Lawrence reveals a number of failures. Some were linked to the economic misfortunes of the farmers in the 1870s and the late 1880s; others were due to changed technologies, to the fact that businesses left for more convenient locations, where improved water and rail transportation was available, and to the competitive power of eastern enterprises or disadvantageous railroad rates.

Let us take, as one example, the windmill plow works of Wilder and Palm. In order to harness the Kansas winds for their power, a massive stone and timber windmill fifty-five feet tall was erected. At first Wilder and Palm simply ground the wheat and corn of the local farmers. Then the business began making carriages and plows, and continued to expand into a major manufacturing establishment for plows, wagons to carry grain to market, and hay rakes and cultivators to harvest the crops. The scrapers they made for road building were distributed throughout eastern Kansas. The firm weathered the economic downturn which commenced in 1876, but by 1885 it was in receivership. The early eighties were ones of prolonged drought in Kansas, and farmers had been visited by another plague of grasshoppers. Because of credit problems some farmers could not pay for the tools and plows they had and could purchase no new ones. At the same time, the railroads had changed rates on finished products, which meant that plows from eastern firms, manufactured more cheaply, were brought into the local market. The windmill plow works simply could not compete with those that were closer to sources of raw materials and had a better source of power than wind.

Small businesses such as carriage works or furniture manufacturers, gave way to the larger industrial enterprises of towns such as Kansas City that concentrated both capital and large numbers of people. They were able to achieve efficiencies of scale that local businessmen could not. Kansas City began to make an active and concerted effort to attract the businesses of Lawrence. A flourishing chemical plant left for Kansas City, lured there by a promise of better facilities. Lawrence also had a viable meat-packing business, until the town of Atchison built a five-acre packing facility, using Atchison city bond money, for the Lawrence firm. The Lawrence woolen mill went out of business because it could not get wool, and the plant that made dandelion hair-tonic went out of business because men's tastes changed. The brewer went under with the passage of the prohibition law in 1880 and the determination of the local sheriff to prevent him from selling "medicine."

Lawrence businessmen did not sit idly by watching their town disintegrate during periods of depression, or when other towns came courting local industries. One of Lawrence's main problems was a lack of power. Coal from Carbondale had proved inadequate, and natural gas was not available. The solution was a 600-foot dam spanning the Kansas River, paid for by public script. Great things were expected from the dam, and contracts to share in its 2,500 horsepower were made with the city waterworks, the Kimball foundry, and flour mills. The great wheel concentrated business along the river. "Before long, cables strung from the water wheels over pulleys began to turn the machinery for the various enterprises taking power from the dam. Cables ran nearly 1,200 feet from the 56-inch water wheel to reach the Delaware Mills on the north side of the river."[43] The dam had problems: high water that broke its barriers, drought that slowed the river and stilled the wheel. A local man writing to the *Lawrence Daily Journal* in 1880 reflected the disillusionment of many:

> I recollect when we had no railroads. We all thought at that time, if we could only get the Kansas Pacific to come to Lawrence, that our fortune would be made. It came. Then we concluded we lacked a railroad to southern Kansas—that would make that rich portion of the State tributary to us. So we voted $300,000 in bonds. . . . That did not help us out. But we then decided it was a competing eastern outlet that we needed, so we proceeded to give about $450,000 to the Pleasant Hill railroad which was to have killed Kansas City and make Lawrence the commercial centre of the Kansas valley. Unfortunately for our hopes the grass grew soon over the track of that road. Again we were all wrong, it was said it was a coal fields [sic] connection with Osage County that was required to bring us cheap coal and make us a great manufacturing place. . . . After this . . . it was discovered that it was not railroads that we wanted, but a dam across the Kansas river.[44]

The early history of the town's growth and development, in which everything possible was tried to boost business, saw many businesses fail. Some failures were insignificant in terms of the numbers involved; one man and his family might move on to seek their fortunes elsewhere. In other cases, the failures were more dramatic. The local barbed-wire factory, for instance, employed almost two hundred men, who lost their jobs when the plant was bought out by an eastern concern which could supply the Kansas trade with cheaper products from Joliet, Illinois. Manufacturers in Lawrence, like those in Fort Scott, would also have reason for directing their anger against the railroads, because a local manufacturer who wanted to ship through Kansas City literally had to pay for transportation twice. Under the railroads' basing-point system, freight was first paid on the raw material from the eastern source to Kansas City, and then a high local rate was charged to move it to Lawrence. When it came time to ship the product, usually west in the case of Lawrence's industries, the freight rates were figured from Kansas City. This system inevitably made Kansas City a much more attractive place for business to locate.[45] Strong opposition to the railroads, among both farmers and merchants, was undoubtedly one reason the state's Republican party felt it could call for railroad legislation. Some businessmen and manufacturers, of course, did survive and prosper, and would come to dominate politically, economically, and ideologically the local scene.

The Class Structure Lawrence had fewer workers (see table 4.2) than Fort Scott, and evidently no active workers' organizations. If those who held the structural position of workers did speak of themselves as members of a unique group, it was usually as members of the "producing classes," the same term Alliance farmers and Populists used to refer to their position. There were some labor disputes in Lawrence, but they were more reflective of the power of the entrepreneurial classes and of the dominance of a pro-business ideology. Labor was scorned in Kansas as it was in the East.

Hauber Brothers of Lawrence were one of two large barrel-making concerns in town, and in 1895 they paid their coopers slightly less than the other firm. The men struck, and the *Lawrence Daily Journal* reported that

> The coopers working for Hauber Bros. in the east part of the city last night notified their employers that they would no longer work for the same money as they had been getting. This was repeated this morning, and Hauber Bros. at once paid all the men off and discharged them, and will not allow them to work longer under any circumstance.

The paper's reporter indicated that he had spoken to one of the Hauber brothers, and had been assured that the Haubers paid as much as anybody for such work. The paper went on to note that the sixteen discharged coopers were "loafing on the streets."[46]

About one week later the paper reported on the results of the strike:

The lock-out at Hauber Bros.' cooper factory is all over. Yesterday the firm put at work six new men and this morning three more were given jobs, and the full force will be on again in a very short time. The effort of the men to force their demands with the company has cost them all good jobs, and the cooper factory is again in shape to run its full capacity.

Mr. Hauber said this morning that he had anticipated no trouble in getting men and there were daily applications for places, making it a much easier matter than the dissatisfied men thought for, to fill their jobs with competent workmen.[47]

The message was clearly that anybody who struck was placing his job and livelihood in jeopardy. Jobs were hard to come by for working men, but they tended to place the blame for their economic problems on foreign immigrants and the lack of a strong apprenticeship program, rather than on the people for whom they were working.

We have already seen (tables 4.7, 4.8, and 4.9) that the farmers of Douglas County were caught in the economic downturn after 1887. They had been enthusiastic in their support of bonds to bring railroads to the area, for they saw their prosperity as linked to the railroads. Yet, like the merchants, they would come to see them as one of their major problems. The farmers of Douglas and Bourbon counties were, however, in a different economic position than those in the middle or western sectors of the state. First, they were closer to markets; they could sell fruits, vegetables, eggs, poultry, and milk locally. Second, having settled the state earlier, they had profited from the boom in agricultural land prices. Some sold out, some rented their property. That is why, for example, we find that 1893 only 60 percent of Bourbon County farms, and 71 percent of those in Douglas, were cultivated by owners.[48] (The averages for the different sectors of the state were: 71 percent owner-cultivated in the western sector; 58 in the central, and 59 in the east.) This is important because it means that one cannot argue, as Farmer did for instance,[49] that farmers became politicized solely because their status changed from that of owner to tenant. A close examination of the data reveals some important qualifiers. Those listed as tenants are very often relatives of farmers—a son or cousin getting started by renting a portion of family land.[50] A person classified as a tenant in 1890 may also have been an independent farmer who rented unused land from his neighbor to expand his own operation. The question arises, therefore, as to whether "tenants" were ideologically, socially, or economically different from those we think of as "independent" farmers. Tenant in Kansas meant something quite different than tenant in the South. It has also been demonstrated that in the case of Kansas the position of tenant was often a transitional one.[51] Farm laborers and tenants were usually young men on their way to becoming independent. Tenants were considerably younger than those classed as farm owners. The data also show an increase between the 1860s and the 1890s in the number of tenants, but that does not necessarily mean that farmers were being driven from their homes or were working for mortgage companies. It could just as easily mean that the value of land had increased. We will not, then, find any strong relationship between the rate of tenancy in a county or township and votes for the Populists. What relates to that vote is basically whether one was or was not a farmer.

The division between farmer and merchant was not so much one of economics as of ideology. Lawrence leaders did everything possible to attract business, and judged things and people in business terms. Farmers in distress were looked down upon as being bad managers, those who would frighten away necessary capital by their incessant complaining. Though farmers and merchants, then, began by together boosting growth and development, they rapidly divided over the meaning of growth, how it was to be achieved, and the standards by which people were to be judged. This parallels in some ways Stanley Parsons' image of the split which developed between the rural and village sectors in the state of Nebraska. Parsons attributes the rise of the Alliance and the Populist party in part to the contempt with which village leaders treated farmers. The merchants of the town accrued political, economic, and ideological power. Parsons cites a village editor in the 1890s, who expressed the feeling townspeople had for the farmer:

> What has happened to the old fashioned farmer who used to salt down his meat, raise all his own vegetables and take corn to town? The other day a farmer came into town with corn which he had sold for 15 cents a bushel and took home with him a bushel of apples at $1.50 and a bushel of potatoes at 25 cents. . . . All of these could be produced on the farm for 75 percent less money.[52]

Parsons' explanation, however, is primarily cultural. I am arguing that the ideas of farmers and merchants were shaped by their location within the economic system. Farmers and merchants were

Table 4.11   Occupations of the Citizens of Lawrence, Kansas, and
Their Wealth, 1860

Occupation	Average by Number of Responses		Average by Number in Category	
	Real Estate	Personal Property	Real Estate	Personal Property
Professionals (N=56) physician, dentist, teacher, lawyer, etc.	$4,870	$1,408	$4,272	$1,182
Merchants (N=104) factory and store owner, hotel owner, etc.	$3,567	$3,381	$2,618	$ 786
Public officials (N=8) Sheriff, registrar, treasurer, etc.	$2,893	$ 786	$2,893	$ 786
Farmers (N=45)	$ 933	$1,041	$ 998	$ 33
Skilled laborers (N=183) carpenter, bricklayer, blacksmith, etc.	$ 912	$ 321	$ 459	$ 172
Service and sales (N=44) clerk, agents, etc.	$ 613	$ 535	$ 396	$ 366
Unskilled laborers (N=15) hired hand, servant, general labor, etc.	$ 230	$ 203	$ 12	$ 86

Source: Federal manuscript census of 1860.

Note: In many cases no information on wealth was recorded for a respondent.
This might mean that the respondent had no wealth, or that the information was
not recorded by the census taker. I have, then, provided two sets of figures. The
first two columns represent the total wealth for an occupational category divided
by the number of responses, or bits of information about wealth. The second two
represent the total wealth for a given occupational category divided by the number
of persons in that category. Whichever figure is used, it is clear that professional
and independent proprietors have more wealth and personal property than laborers of all classes, e.g., skilled and unskilled.

divided, and wealth and resources were concentrated in the town.
Even in 1860, as table 4.11 indicates, professionals and merchants
had a far greater portion of the total reported wealth for the town
than laborers. These people also lived in different regions of the
town and county.

Residence and Socioeconomic Status   When building began in earnest
in Lawrence, those who had the greatest resources erected fine
homes at the foot of and on the slopes of Mount Oread, which had

Table 4.12   Socio-economic Characteristics of Ward and Township Residents in Lawrence and in Douglas County, 1895

	% White	% Foreign-born	Lawrence % Profes-sional	% Skilled and Unskilled	No Response
Wards					
I	80	18	11	56	0
II	92	10	10	26	33
III	80	23	3	45	28
IV	77	23	0	46	20
V	82	7	0	41	40
VI	68	0	0	59	18

	% Foreign-Born	Douglas County % Farmers	% Tenants	Average Land Value
Townships				
Clinton	11	82	7.7	$3,884
Eudora	43	90	14.8	4,344
Grant	21	99	40.0	2,520
Kanawak	17	100	5.6	4,458
Lecompton	12	94	12.5	3,400
Marion	21	82	6.9	3,392
Palmyra	16	89	2.7	3,445
Wakarusa	14	65	19.6	4,433
Willow Spring	22	100	13.0	3,404

Source: see table 4.10. The census enumerators for Lawrence and for Douglas county apparently followed somewhat different procedures than did those for Fort Scott and Bourbon County. For instance, in the case of Lawrence there are a number of men and women for whom no occupation was recorded. This could mean they were out of work, or, more likely, that they were in an occupational category—unskilled laborer, transient—that the enumerators did not bother with. It appears to be the case that those taking the census provided some information, e.g., occupation, on the basis of whether or not they knew a person. Thus, merchants and professionals are sometimes overrepresented, while workers are under-represented. There were no data on tenancy for Bourbon County, but the pattern was probably the same in both Douglas and Bourbon, i.e., it represents people getting started in farming and is a transitional category.

been named after a similar hill in Massachusetts and lay to the southwest of the river (Ward I). Some also built closer to the river, though to the east of the town's business district (Ward II). Foreign immigrants and workers made their homes to the east of the town, and in the business district which had a stockyard on its border along the river. These two districts (Wards III and IV) were characterized by substandard housing, and higher crime rates.[53] They also had a substantial (13–20 percent) black population in 1895. Most of Lawrence's black community was, however, concentrated across the river in the sixth ward, which was one-third black. Many of these men and women earned money as truck gardeners. The men were also blacksmiths or barbers, while the women were domestics or hairdressers. A substantial number of workers also lived across the river, in Ward V. The general characteristics of Lawrence's wards and of Douglas County's townships are given in table 4.12. Lawrence's professionals were concentrated in Wards I and II. The variations within the townships relate primarily to whether they have a small town embedded within them, e.g., Eudora, or whether they are contiguous to Lawrence, e.g., Wakarusa. To the extent that we can label a ward "black" or "privileged," there will be a predominate vote for the Republican party. Workers, too, tended to vote for the Republicans. It was the farmers in the outlying areas who voted as Populists. Lawrence, then, had a mix of class positions, and though there was some residential segregation there was also considerable overlap. This was, after all, a small town. People of different class positions also came together in the many social organizations within the community.

Social Organizations and Cross-Class Membership   Prior to 1900, Lawrence had sixteen established churches, with practically every major denomination represented. The Congregationalists were apparently first on the scene, having been intimately involved in establishing the founding party. "The organization was named the 'Plymouth Church' from the fact that the circumstances and aims of its founders, who were principally from New England, so nearly resembled those of the Plymouth Pilgrims."[54] They were followed by Unitarians, Baptists, Methodists, Episcopalians, Friends, and Catholics. There were also six "colored" churches, e.g., the Second Colored Baptist Church, the Colored Congregational Church, and the African Methodist Episcopal Church.[55] The churches, except for the black ones, drew from across the class spectrum.

The town also had its share of secret societies, literary, and self-help organizations. The Masons and Odd Fellows were well represented, and there was a Young Men's Christian Association. The Germans, who were concentrated in east Lawrence, Ward III, had two social organizations. People met in the evenings to discuss

Table 4.13   Occupations of Masons (Acacia Lodge No. 9, Lawrence, Kansas), 1869–1900

Occupation	N	%
Service and Sales	56	20.3
clerk, traveling man, agent, sales (real estate, insurance, agricultural implements, etc.)		
Merchants	45	16.2
factory and store owners, hotel and saloon keepers		
Skilled laborers	43	15.5
carpenters, bricklayers, blacksmiths		
Professionals	42	15.2
physicians, dentists, teachers, accountants, lawyers, editors, clergymen		
Unskilled laborers	12	4.3
hired hand, delivery man		
Public officials	10	3.6
judge, sheriff, land officer		
Farmers	8	2.9
Unclassified*	61	22.0
	(N=277)	(100%)

Sources:

Masons: *Anniversary History and Roster Celebrating the 100th Anniversary of Acacia Lodge #9, A.F. & A.M., Lawrence, Kansas.* (Lawrence, Kansas: The World Company, 1967).

Occupational Data: *Corbett Hoye and Co.'s Annual City Directory of the City of Lawrence for 1872* (Lawrence, Kansas: Kansas Tribune Steam Book and Job Printing House, 1872); *Green & Foley's Lawrence City Directory, City of Lawrence, Kansas, 1888* (Lawrence, Kansas: P.T. Foley, Printer, 1887); *A Directory for the City of Lawrence and Douglas County for 1893–1894* (Wichita, Kansas: The Leader Directory Company, 1894).

*No information could be found on the occupations of 22% of the sample. It is probable, then, that both skilled and unskilled laborers are underrepresented in this table, as they are the groups for whom information is often lacking in census records and city directories.

books and read plays together, in groups such as the Old and New Club (gentlemen only, to discuss the social sciences); the Ladies' Liberal Club, and the Friends Council No. 2, both literary groups.

There were many organizations, then, that cross-cut class ties and would have served to inhibit the development of a strong class consciousness, particularly one that posed an alternative to capitalism. Fraternal organizations drew together common laborers, those who were skilled, and merchants and salesmen. Clearly this was the case with the Masons in Lawrence (see table 4.13). I was able to secure a complete listing of all of those who joined the Masons between the years 1869 and 1900. Laborers make up at least 19 percent of the membership. Those in sales predominate, with 20 percent of the members, and there is an approximately equal number of merchants and professionals, e.g., 16.2 and 15.5 percent respectively. Farmers (2.9 percent) make up the smallest category of members. But even though social organizations drew from across the community, the merchants in Lawrence dominated politically, just as they did in Fort Scott.

The Dominance of the Merchant Class   Those who assumed positions of leadership in Lawrence were men who had made their money in trade. Justin D. Bowersock, who served twice as mayor and as a congressman from 1898 to 1906, is typical. Bowersock came to Lawrence from Iowa City, where "he set up for himself as a merchant and grain dealer and accumulated a tidy fortune."[56] He came to Lawrence to become a partner in his father-in-law's milling business. When his father-in-law died, he became heir to the dam which crossed the Kansas River, as well as to the Douglas County Mills. Bowersock played an important role in the town's development, putting his own money into a wide variety of enterprises, not all of which proved successful. He founded and served as the president of the Douglas County Bank, was director and vice president of the barbed-wire factory, and director of a flourishing chemical business as well as a patent-medicine business. He was involved in the search for gas and coal in Lawrence, and established a paper factory. He built the town's opera house, which stands today, showing foreign and classic films. He owned, or was involved in, at least five other businesses. Men who came with capital and were, like Bowersock, willing to invest it in the community were important to the town's prosperity. Not everyone came with Bowersock's resources, and not everyone had such an impact. Most came with a skill and hope, just as they did in Fort Scott.

Andrew Palm, president of the Lawrence Plow Company, came to the United States from Sweden in 1855. There he had been trained and apprenticed as a blacksmith. When he arrived in Kansas in 1858, he began making and repairing tools and equipment for locals. He accumulated a small amount of capital and bought a part interest in a saw and grist mill. Eventually, with his knowledge and more money, he was able to found the Lawrence Plow Company, which prospered for a time because he was protected from eastern competitors by high freight rates.

The Bowersocks, Palms, and others like them, made politics their business because it was necessary to pass bonds to get a railroad, to build a dam or a bridge. They set the tempo for the community. I examined the composition of the Lawrence city government (mayor and council) for the years 1868, 1875, 1887, and 1897. During these four administrations there were a total of forty-six positions. Out of all of these positions, only three were ever held by farmers. The rest were held by attorneys, grocery store and hardware store owners, lumber and implement dealers, as well as freight clerks for the railroads whose tracks passed through the town. Only one worker, a mason (who may well have been an independent contractor), held a position on the council. In short, there was a gradual concentration of wealth and power among the businessmen of the community. What did people make of this concentration? As we will see in the next chapter, it was the farmer who asked questions about the power of business.

Summary

The early economic history of the state of Kansas was like that of any colony. Traders, buffalo hunters, and squatters penetrated the wilderness, decimated the native population, and began to send the region's wealth to an industrial core. With the passage of the Homestead Act in 1862, Kansas's role as an internal colony solidified. Whatever people's motives for settling, the fact remained that Kansas's products—agricultural surpluses—were shipped east to feed a growing industrial class, or abroad to feed the hungry workers of England, France, and Germany. Though the agricultural classes acted within the state as independent businessmen, or simple commodity producers, they did not control the fruits of their toil. As the century progressed, they saw their labor power being appropriated through market mechanisms in the form of high railroad rates or monopolies that controlled the purchase of cattle, hogs, corn, oats, and wheat.

Entering the state in the same wagon trains as the farmers, and sometimes ahead of them, were the merchants and proto-industrialists. They came to make their money by trading agricultural products, selling the farmer the shovel he needed to dig his well, or manufacturing the plow he needed to break open the virgin sod. Some of these same men were also speculators; they came with the hope of making a profit from the sale of land. Town companies were formed and houses, churches, schools, roads, and canals were traced out on elaborate maps for the prospective buyer to see. These imaginary structures and improvements often remained just pipe dreams. However, towns did grow, some springing to life like mushrooms, and merchants prospered.

Workers, too, following the stream of westward migrants, flowed into the state. As villages and towns rose from the rolling prairie, there were jobs for skilled craftsmen, and carpenters, painters, blacksmiths, masons, coopers, and carriage makers found work. Many of these men opened shops of their own and carried their own tools to jobs for which they had contracted. Their economic welfare was not substantially different from that of the local merchant selling calico, flour, and tobacco. In the early stages of development, some accumulated small amounts of capital, or even came with resources which they were able to invest in small industries. Using their knowledge of blacksmithing, or their training as millers, they might dam a small stream, build a water wheel, and go into business as the town miller grinding grain and sawing timber. The carpenter might become a builder hiring other men, and might own his own lumberyard. Not infrequently some craftsman, whether self-employed or working for others, would decide to become a farmer and purchase land or claim his 160 acres. Farmers, too, might cross over and become carpenters in town, or merchants, or local industrialists.

Those businesses and industries which did exist in the state were small, seldom employing more than a handful of workers, though occasionally one or two in a community would employ upwards of a hundred people. Industry was also concentrated in eastern Kansas, where the population was concentrated, and where, initially, there were no railroad connections to the west. The prosperity of many of these early enterprises was of short duration. They produced almost exclusively for local markets and were protected from eastern competitors by high rates on finished products or, again, because the lines had not spread their web across the state. Later, when the railroads changed the rates, and these enterprises were no longer economically competitive, they collapsed or moved to Kansas City, where shipping charges on their finished products were less expensive.

The small size of local industries and the fact that the line between independent craftsman and local businessman was easily crossed meant that there was not a working class in most Kansas communities. No group of people defined themselves as workers, were members of working-class organizations, or possessed an ideology which clearly distinguished them from farmers or merchants. Working-class communities were separated by industry, region, and to some extent by ethnicity: railroad workers constituted a distinct segment of the class structure, but were isolated in three or four towns. The same was the case with Kansas coal miners, who were located in two southern counties, Cherokee and Crawford. While the population of the state as a whole was over 90 percent native-born whites, coal mining and railroading had a non-native white work force of more than 20 percent.

Class structure was fluid on the frontier not just because of opportunity but because of economic decline. When the effects of the national economic crisis of 1873 hit Kansas, and when the economic downturn began in 1887, many merchants shuttered their shops and moved on. Farmers, too, gave up after the long drought of 1887–88 and the collapse of farm prices in 1891, sometimes heading back to their relatives' homes in the East. Common laborers, as well as skilled, found jobs hard to come by during this time, and there were small communities whose populations swung between plus and minus 30 percent as transient workers moved in with the good times and out with the bad.

Nevertheless, there were three distinct class positions in frontier communities: workers, farmers, and entrepreneurs (merchants or industrialists). (There were also distinct class segments within these major groupings.) Members of these different class positions often came together to worship or belonged to fraternal organizations which cross-cut class ties. Organizations such as the Masons counted among their members not only shopkeepers but doctors, carpenters, clerks, salesmen, and common laborers; farmers were found infrequently in these secret societies. The business classes established their dominance and translated their growing economic power into political power.

This was possible because not only the merchant saw the town's reason for existence as business; so did the worker who hoped to become a craftsman, the craftsman who hoped to become a businessman. Farmers in the surrounding countryside were also eager to participate in the booming of the town, so land values would increase, they would have a place to sell their products, and when the railroads came, they could benefit from high prices in the East or on the Continent. Bonds were floated for a wide variety of enterprises from which an entire county hoped to benefit, and businessmen pushed for their passage. The farmers would withdraw their support for the business activities of the merchants after the collapse of the boom in the late 1880s.

Businessmen became the community leaders, serving as the mayors and councilmen for their towns. Village politics, such as they were, involved competition for patronage and did not involve party splits over whether everyone's efforts should be geared to booming the town. Both Democratic and Republican pioneer town fathers had the same goals.[57] Farmers seldom, if ever, served in positions of political leadership. As the century progressed, a political split widened between farmers, who had a different set of political, economic, and social goals, and the businessmen of the town. Each group would be vehement in its view as to what must be done to spur prosperity. The next chapter examines the form and nature of the ideological differences between these groups.

5
Languages of Class

James B. Weaver ran for president on the Populist ticket in 1892, capturing more than 8 percent of the total vote and 22 electoral votes. Cartoons such as this one figured prominently in the reform press.

"We are tired of class legislation, and want legislation for the people," said a Kansas miner in 1885.[1] A farmer said, "we are all, capitalists and farmers, threatened by monopolies."[2] The great leader of the Southern Alliance, Tom Watson, emphasized the fact that the Alliance was a middle-class movement; all farmers wanted was to participate in American prosperity.

> The great Middle Class is the mainstay of life. It is the judicious mixture of work and leisure which makes the complete man; the useful man; the happy man; the God-fearing man, law-abiding man. . . . Any system which will add to the great Middle Class,

where there is reasonable work and fair reward, secures to Society the best results of which humanity is capable.[3]

Kansas farmers and workers believed, simply, that legislation which benefited the few at the expense of the many was wrong. But other than arguing against class legislation, and for a just return for their efforts, in what language did the producing classes of Kansas couch their concerns? And, how did this language affect their chances for political success?

The Language of Politics

I have argued that there is a strong relationship between economic position and ideology, in the sense that both are equally important for an understanding of how a social class is actively created. I have also said that for a class to realize itself as a class it must have a unifying vision, for economic grievances are not in themselves sufficient to bring people to the barricades. If a group is to be dominant, a class language must provide for an understanding of political and economic realities, and it must allow people to explain and understand their defeats as well as their triumphs. People's languages are crafted from their actual experiences with work, family, political, and religious organizations. However, many people's lives are crosscut by social class; that is, they are embedded in churches, ethnic groups, fraternal and self-help groups that draw together members of many social positions, with different political and economic vocabularies. The result is sometimes a muting of a clear class language.

There are, nevertheless, conditions under which people are likely to sharpen their arguments, and to mobilize. When, for example, their basic sense of justice, of what is right and wrong, is violated, they stand as ready candidates for movements that promise to chasten the wicked. Kansas farmers were reacting not just to changed economic conditions but to changed relationships of work, to a political and economic environment that marginalized them socially and politically. No longer God's chosen people—the yeomen who supposedly formed the backbone of the country—they found themselves referred to by the larger society as unsuccessful businessmen. Language can translate a specific set of economic and social circumstances into an expression of felt injustice. A sense of injustice, which implies a vision of how people want the world to operate, and what their place in that world should be, grows out of and is shaped by confrontations with the dominant political and economic system.

When farmers came together to discuss their problems, they first tried to elect legislators sympathetic to their cause. At each stage in the evolution of the movement and movement strategy, they were blocked from realizing their interests. Unable to penetrate the class-dominated political parties of the day, or to get those parties to act on their behalf, they mobilized and formed people's parties. Class consciousness, therefore, grew out of attempts to change American society—specifically, out of attempts to participate in politics. Yet, when the battle ended, American farmers found themselves on the losing side; they had failed to keep America from choosing a future in which land, labor, and people would become commodities. The farmer would be judged by the standards of industrial society and the entrepreneur.

If farmers developed a language of politics and dominated the political scene for a brief period of time in many states, why were they unable to create themselves as a dominant or even autonomous class? Did they actually succeed in creating themselves as a class, which then failed? I believe that farmers developed a world view distinct from that of the merchant and worker. Though the class position of the farmer was fragmented by degree of economic success, this alone could not prevent the formation of a distinct class. However, farmers were also members of unique cultural groupings, whose loyalties pulled them away from class interest. As Paul Kleppner, in *The Cross of Culture,* has argued, in nineteenth-century America religious values were more important than economic values in determining how people voted.[4] In states such as Kansas, where the Republicans had shaped their agenda on the basis of pietistic religious values and came out strongly for prohibition, some farmers were going to be attracted to a Republican agenda, even when their long-term class interests might be better served by voting for the Populists. Because farmers were not a distinct homogeneous grouping, their structural capacities and their abilities to organize as a distinct class, were eroded.

From the inception of the Alliance and the formation of the People's party, tension was felt between those who did and did not want to work within the dominant parties, between those who wanted the movement to support women's suffrage and temperance and those who did not, between those who wanted to focus on issues of concern to all laboring classes and those who were concerned primarily with the needs of the farmer. These strains at the seams of the movement would prevent the translation of farmers' concerns into votes. A gap opened between the Alliance members and those men and women who spoke for the movement. These factors alone do not make the Alliance unique, for many other movements have overcome divisions within the ranks, and other class groupings have managed to weld together a committed band to work together on behalf of a class. The problem lies elsewhere, and brings us back to the question of language.

Farmers were possessed of a distinctive interpretation of American society but one that would fail as a unique class analysis. The Alliance and the People's party were founded on the belief that ultimately the people would be triumphant in their struggles against monopolists, capitalists, or the money powers. They argued for the equality of all people, and against those men and institutions that called into question agrarian values. The men and women of the Alliance were not socialists; they were simple Jeffersonian democrats. And therein lay one of their problems. If they argued that corrupt politicians were at fault, rather than the system itself, then a change in political leadership might be sufficient to still the incipient radicalism of the movement. If they demanded railroad legislation and it was forthcoming, the movement was again undercut. The very experience and traditions of those in the Alliance provided a political vocabulary which argued that America, as a capitalist society, could yet provide for the equality of laborers and farmers. *If* her institutions could be purified, *then* there would be justice for all. The Populist vision was of a pre-industrial America, but this vision was blurred by the supposedly egalitarian promise of capitalism. Farmers could not continue the struggle against capitalist America, because the language of Populism did not talk about modifying capitalist *institutions* or overthrowing them. Given the anti-agrarian and anti-reformist sentiment of the country as a whole, farmers often went out of their way to explain that they meant no harm to capitalism.

The Populists believed that their economic problems had a political cause. That is precisely why they mounted an assault on the political system; they understood that private and public spheres were not separate or autonomous, that their way of life was threatened if they did not achieve political representation. But in order to realize their dreams and emerge as a dominant political force, they had to attract other classes to their cause; they needed the support of workers. However, many workers saw in the Republican party's argument for high tariffs the protection of their jobs, while the farmer saw the high tariffs as depressing prices for farm products and inflating the costs of the necessities he had to buy. The worker was more concerned with excluding foreign immigrants, who competed with him in the job market, than he was with railroad legislation. The merchant felt that the farmers' demand for monetary expansion, or their threats to repudiate their debts, would undermine the basis of an industrial and entrepreneurial society. The Populists were constantly on the ideological defensive. Moreover, although Alliance and Populist leaders were united on general questions concerning equality and social welfare, they were divided among themselves, and hence from some of their supporters, on how changes were to be brought about in the political order. Some leaders supported fusion with the Democrats, others did not. Some spoke out strongly in favor of the subtreasury scheme as the only solution to the problem of credit for the farmer, while others saw the free coinage of silver as the answer to limited credit.

I must reaffirm the fact that language, or ideology, and class consciousness are not equivalents. An ideology involves an interpretive framework, a cognitive set, and a disposition to act. Class consciousness, on the other hand, as Thompson implied, occurs when a class is fully formed; that is, when structure, organization, ideology, and action become one. Class consciousness involves the disposition to act, and also the social and organizational bonds that sustain it.

Let us now look at the ideologies of the three major class positions in Kansas, and how, in the case of farmers and townspeople, these ideologies were developed in opposition to one another. We will also consider the general response of the dominant classes in Kansas to the question of reform and rebellion, which mirrored national responses. The village/rural split heightens in the debates between farmers and merchants over the future of Kansas.

The Voice of Labor

The litany of woes of Kansas laborers included some of the same concerns voiced by those in the large industrial metropolises of the country—that America was a class-dominated society, that monopolies ruled the lives of ordinary citizens, and that the government served the interests of the few rather than the many. In Kansas, some of the clearest statements about what was wrong with the conditions of working men and women came from those who were working for mine or railroad owners. But the expression of their discontent would also reveal the extent to which people still placed their faith in the dominant political and economic systems to make things right.

Mining was concentrated in Cherokee and Crawford counties. Those who dug the coal there felt that they were being cheated by the mine owners. Though the coal lay close to the surface, a miner or his team would have to spend time stripping off the top layer of rock and dirt. For this they were paid nothing. When they had to tunnel into the coal, and shore up the shafts with heavy oak timbers to prevent cave-ins, they were not paid. The companies weighed the ore after it had been screened, not before. When the companies did pay them, on a monthly, or at most biweekly, basis, it was in script which could only be redeemed for the overpriced merchandise in the company store. If miners spoke of unions and binding arbitration, they were usually dismissed.

A miner from Crawford county believed the owners showed little concern for their workers.

> Miners living in the company houses pay from three to six dollars a month rent for houses—or rather shanties—that never cost over $100 to build, and that would not rent for two dollars a month in any decent town. It is "skin" the miner with these companies, from the word "go."

Another miner from the region spoke of the unfair labor practices of weighing coal.

> I hope you [the commissioner of labor] will be able to do something for us Kansas miners about this five pounds per bushel that the company robs us of; it is the worst kind of stealing. The operators claim it is dirt, and yet they dock us from 100 to 200 pounds a box of coal if we send any dirt up in it. They take from us in this way 22 bushels of coal on every flat that we fill.

One miner said that the company, by giving him script to spend at the company store, prevented him from "expending the proceeds of his labor." Others said, "The Mexican peon never was more a slave than will be the married miners of this place, if times do not get better," and "My [yearly] expenses exceed my earnings by far—$26.70. I have had a great deal of sickness in my family this month, and have buried a three-year-old boy, and my sixteen-year-old daughter is just on the turn for the better; so you can see I am in distress just now. A poor man should have no sickness." "I am opposed to the railroads being permitted to run coal mines," complained one who was worried about the dominance of monopolies.

The miners called for government regulation to end the abuse, as would farmers and other laborers. "Don't forget to make and enforce laws against those who take from labor without return," said one. A man who worked in a Kansas City packing house told the commissioner of labor, "I think the working-people should unite and elect legislators who will grant us the same legislation that the business class obtains. Especially give us an arbitrating board like the Railroad Commission." A bricklayer echoed the need for an arbitration board in place of strikes. "I think strikes are detrimental to labor as well as capital, and believe a State board of arbitration, clothed with proper powers, could regulate the difference between employer and employee, and prevent them."[5]

Workers differed on the question of how government should be made to heed the interests of labor. Some felt that "What we want is honest legislators, who will try and make the wants of the working-people of America a study, and enact such laws as will compel employer and employee to settle all disputes by arbitration, so as to prevent any more strikes or lock-outs in this glorious country of ours." What would these laws be? A common laborer was quite specific:

> I think all wage-workers should join labor unions and become thoroughly organized. Then agitate vigorously for the repeal of the national bank act, and insist on the Government issuing . . . greenbacks to replace the notes of the banks . . . a careful revision of the tariff, by which the operatives would be protected from the greed and avarice of the capitalists, and they [the capitalists] in turn protected from the pauper labor of Europe. . . . Encourage our manufacturing industries so that our people may be all employed, and create a domestic market for our agricultural surplus, and avoid the necessity and expense of seeking a foreign market.

The need to organize for mutual benefit was widely accepted among laborers, but the form of organization and what it was supposed to accomplish were circumscribed. An old Union pensioner said, "I am getting to believe in labor organizations, although I be-

long to none. I believe the better organized labor becomes, the
more conservative it is." He thought both laborers and their organizations would become more conservative, because the organizations would "create a better understanding between capital and labor." The statements of working men and women often repeat the
assumption that labor and capital could and should work together
in harmony.

In a few occupations where labor organizations had grown, workers were more specific about what needed to be done to solve their
problems. A railroad worker on the Missouri-Pacific said, "pay us
once a week, in cash." Another, "I have to work 11 hours a day,
which. . . is too long." Thomas Sherman, a statistician for the Knights
of Labor, which represented many railroad workers, summed up the
demands of many:

> If the following laws were enacted they would be a benefit to labor
> and to the public generally:
> 1. Making Labor Day a legal holiday.
> 2. Compelling railroad companies to place guardrails on top of
> freight cars, for the security of brakemen.
> 3. Compelling trains to be run not less than fifteen minutes
> apart, for the security of the public.
> 4. Providing for the election of the Railroad Commissioners by
> the people.
> 5. For the encouragement of organization among working-
> people, that they may become educated and enlightened regard-
> ing the problems of the day.
> 6. To prohibit over-working of railroad trainmen, as many dis-
> asters are caused by this practice.

In short, Sherman wanted government protection and education.
Middle-class reform groups and working groups throughout the
country stressed the notion that an educated and enlightened working class would soon be middle class. The idea of escape from the
working class figures heavily in workers' proposed solutions to their
problems. If, for example, they could have land, they could live a
life of dignity. A railroad worker said,

> I believe the sale of land to private individuals was the greatest
> mistake the fathers of this Republic made. Land was not created
> to be sold, but for each person to occupy and cultivate, and sell his
> improvements that is his labor. This would prevent speculation,

and the poor could get possession of some, and that would be better than working for Jay Gould.

Both farmers and laborers were concerned with the issue of land, but this quotation also expresses another important idea of Alliance and Populist rhetoric: the land is sacred, something to be cherished and cared for, not subjected to the depredations of monopolists and speculators. It shows that laborers did not agree about which issues were most important to them—reform of the conditions of work and changes in the rates of pay, or how to escape altogether from the class of labor. A stonemason from Kansas City said, "If I had ten acres of good land I would let the rest of the masons do mason work. There are not enough tilling the soil, and too many in the towns." Another wanted the government to prevent people from acquiring large tracts of land. "The land should be equally distributed, also the wealth; and to do that, limitation of ownership should not extend beyond the capacity of the individual to occupy the land." Foreign speculators were a special source of concern to one bricklayer, "A man [should] be a resident of the United States before he can own more than $100 worth of real estate." A laborer from a western county echoed a common refrain of the Populists. "We, as wage-workers, must have the public domain opened to us for settlement so that we can get cheap lands for homes." There was at the time a great deal of public support for the idea of opening the Indian lands in Oklahoma—the Cherokee Strip—to settlement, and that support was common among both farmers and laborers.

A railroad section-hand in Atchison reasoned, "If I had a chance to get onto the land, and the State or National Government would organize a loan department by which greenbacks or national currency could be loaned to deserving poor men, at low rates as banks pay, to run 15 years, it would go far to settle the labor problem." In Kansas the Greenback party, and then other organizations which supported expansionary monetary policy, would have the ear of laborers who wished to till the soil, as well as those who had already done so. A worker in a village saw no reason why the federal government couldn't respond to individuals as they had to the banks. "We, as wage workers, demand that the Federal Government loan money directly to the people as cheap as to the national banks." A failed businessman from Emporia, who had fallen into the ranks of labor during the economic crisis of 1873, commented,

From 1865 to 1870 I was in business. I made money and paid good wages. But when the money was contracted I could not compete unless I cut my men down to starvation wages. I would not do this, and as a result lost all that I had made, and along with many others "went up" in the flames that consumed our money. I believe that the Government should issue money to the amount of $50 per capita, and keep it at that ratio. This, counting our population at 60,000,000 would amount to 3,000,000,000, or about the original amount of our war debt; then the money sharks who suck the life-blood of our industries could not corral it, and the workingmen and farmers would not be at their mercy.

Few successful merchants felt this way. This failed businessman's rhetoric directly parallels that of the Populists, and the figures he offers were frequently cited by Alliance and Populist speakers. Clearly, he was taken by their rhetoric as well as their ideas. He also went on to say that his ideas were not utopian or radical; they were the only practical solution to the problem.

Look at every new town in Kansas. Among the first comers is the infernal loan agent; he fastens his claws into every settler's land that he can, and the poor devil, after he had converted his raw prairie claim into a comfortable home, after he has gone through all the hardships and possibly worked himself and his family nearly to death, finds that he has expended his health and life for the benefit of some land-shark who never did an honest day's work in his life. If you want to stop strikes, if you want to do away with tramps, if you want to make our people happy and contented, the State will have to assume ownership of her highways, whether they be dirt roads or railroads; will have to control all avenues of communication, whether post offices, telegraph or telephone; will have to see that all able-bodied citizens find regular employment—not idle part of the time and working sixteen hours a day the balance in order to catch up. The hard-handed toiler should have as many leisure hours as the soft-handed clerk—work eight hours, education eight hours, and sleep eight hours.

Both laborers and farmers, then, would argue for state intervention, because they believed the state would protect their class interests. They saw nothing contradictory in arguing for a growth in the scope and size of the state's regulatory powers and also arguing for a government that would remain small, simple, and above corruption. They believed that the principles for which they stood *were* the principles of democracy. A government acting in their interests would be purified, above politics. They knew that the state had been acting at the behest of corporate power. As a tailor said, "the Civil War . . . brought class legislation, that concentrated money protection, [and] induced manufacturers to overstock the country with pauper labor." Now, they would ask the government to act for democracy. However, the road to this goal lay through the political marketplace, with all of its vanities. When farmers first mobilized, they did so with an appeal to principle, asking people to lay aside their party prejudices. For some, the party represented principle, which meant that to shift political loyalties, even when it was in their economic interests to do so, was not easy; for some, it was impossible. Because there was a great deal of "noise" in the political arena, the messages of the Alliance did not come through all that clearly. Both Republicans and Democrats, at the national and state levels, would apportion to themselves parts of the Alliance and Populist programs, and redefine other programs and ideas as dangerously radical and utopian. Such an atmosphere did not make one's individual or collective choices all that simple.

Though farmers and laborers agreed on a number of issues, there were concerns specific to the working man. He wanted an eight-hour day, protection from injury on the job, and laws that would restrict immigration, prevent the use of convict labor, establish an apprenticeship system to protect skilled labor, and restrict the hiring of women and children. As one printer said, "the most vital problem that labor has to contend with [is] . . . the usurpation of places held by men by women at lower price for the same work." If women were allowed to work, he reasoned, this "will make tramps and vagabonds of three-fourths of the working men." Others proposed slight variations on the problem of females in the work force. "Give women the same pay that men get" for the same jobs, said a meat packer. But the two most burning issues for the working men of Kansas were convict labor and immigration.

It was not an unusual practice in the late nineteenth century to employ convicts in prison shops, or shops controlled by private capitalists, to make barrels, wagons, or to dig coal. Though this practice was restricted in Kansas to the digging of coal for the state prison, it was more common in the surrounding states, and it antagonized the skilled workers of Kansas. A cooper in Lawrence noted that, "Prison convict labor [in other states] has about ruined my trade." A teamster in the same community said, "I want our Legislature to

pass a law prohibiting the introduction of convict-labor made goods
from other states, and to prohibit the hiring out of our own convicts." A laborer from the railroad center, Atchison, spoke, "I am
opposed to contract prison labor, but if prison goods must be made,
they should be branded so that purchasers may know what they are
buying." The use of convict labor was seen by a cigar maker to be
the doing of the large capitalists. "The State is flooded with cheap
cigars furnished by larger capitalists who work with . . . [convict]
labor, and who furnish the article so cheaply that our manufacturers cannot compete with them, causing the money to go out of
the State in payment for goods that should be manufactured here."
One worker's solution to the problem posed by convict labor was
simple: "Shoot all convicts."

Violent solutions were not limited to this suggestion. A mule
skinner said, "I am in favor of stopping all immigration of foreign
labor, and killing all Chinamen and Negroes." From the tone of the
Kansas workers' responses, one would have thought that they saw
in foreign immigration the root of all of their problems. A carpenter from Kansas City said, "If the blessed Swedes could be kept
out of here it would be a good thing. They are a little better than
the Chinese, but not much." Another carpenter in the same town
admitted, "I am a foreign-born citizen, but do not believe in pro-
miscuous immigration. . . . We can't afford . . . the ignorant hordes
of Italians and Hungarians who come here to earn a few dollars
and then return home." A tinner in Topeka lamented, "the immigration of foreign tinners is hurting my trade a great deal." A blacksmith's helper from the sparsely settled region of Lyons County demanded, "Stop heathen immigration, such as Italians and Chinese;
bring only civilized people or none—those who will build up labor,
not those who destroy it."

The Chinese were seen as a source of workingmen's problems,
not because there were any concentrations of Chinese workers in
the state, but because they stood as a symbol for the cheap "labor of
the tenement houses," as it was called, and because cheap Chinese
cigars were shipped into the state, undercutting local workers.
Many Kansas workers believed that the "unwashed hordes" in the
great industrial cities of America had been encouraged to come to
the United States by manufacturers who had no concern for "American" workers, and were only concerned with turning a profit. Kansas workers were aided and abetted in their anti-immigrant sentiments by local newspapers that carried reports on the tide of

immigrants washing up on both coasts and editorials which tried to make explicit the link between America's economic problems and this influx. Organized labor eventually took an anti-immigrant stance.

Much has been made of the irrational fear and general xenophobia of those who made up the Populist movement. They have been accused, by Hofstadter for one, of being racist, antiprogressive, and of believing in conspiracy theories.[6] However, they did understand that industrial America was moving forward on the backs of immigrant workers, and that the life of the small artisan would be crushed out as a result. Many Kansas laborers were independent "businessmen," or worked in very small enterprises where they had control over the flow of their work. They were not merely protesting against the use of immigrant labor but against the changed definition of work that occurred when cheap foreign labor was employed. About conspiracy, they were more than half right. Though there was not an active, or conscious, decision made to work in concert to do so, capitalists did consistently favor foreign immigration as a way of driving down wage rates. They had been aided since the Civil War by a state that first helped them bring in new laborers, and then gave them protective tariffs. The problem with a conspiracy theory, however, is that it restricts the field of vision. For workers, it meant that change in leadership, in individuals, rather than an alteration in the system of capitalism itself, was seen as a "solution." Like farmers, workers in Kansas fell into a pattern of supporting a system and asking that the government make modifications to control the rapacity of individual capitalists.

Farmers and laborers had similar concerns about an alteration in the nature of work, but proposed different solutions to their dilemmas. For the most part, Kansas workers used the language of the larger society—a self-help, social-gospel rhetoric—to analyze their condition. Cultural factors, rather than economic or political concerns, would divide workers from farmers, and also create divisions among themselves. Workers would disagree among themselves over questions such as the tariff, liquor, and precisely how one should control monopolies. The liquor issue was debated in Kansas even before the territory became a state. But as soon as a prohibition amendment passed in 1880, there were many who wanted it abolished. One reason offered by a number of workers was that it eliminated jobs. Noting the men were being put out of work, one worker said, "labor must be put to work on more luxuries. If such is the fact, I would suggest the repeal of the prohibitory amendment." A cigar maker lamented the decline in his trade, as cigars were often sold in saloons as an accompaniment to a cold glass of beer. "Our trade was very bad throughout the year, mainly caused by the attempts at enforcing the prohibitory law." Other workers, however, saw liquor as "the scourge of the working man." "Labor will never amount to anything, until workers stop drinking." "If labor expects to prosper, it has got to throw the saloons overboard," said a blacksmith.

The issue of temperance was both economic and cultural. Workers, farmers, and businessmen would all be divided over it; it would prove as vexing to the Populists as to Republicans and Democrats. Businessmen, whether Democrats or Republicans, saw liquor as a source of revenue. This was not an insignificant consideration in a period of economic downturn, which might explain why between about 1887 and 1894 the question of resubmission of the prohibition amendment was attractive in Kansas. The Democratic party sponsored resubmission to capture business and labor votes on this issue, and their initial success led many Republican party men to suggest that voters be given a chance to vote on the issue of whether they wanted the state to remain dry.

As a cultural issue, temperance pitted villages against the rural sector, exacerbated anti-immigrant sentiment, and was linked to the question of women's suffrage. Even in a state that did not have a concentration of immigrant voters, people talked about control of liquor as an answer to the labor question. Immigrants, labor, and liquor abuse could all be seen as part of the general problem of corruption. This was especially true if the Democrats were in power, for the Democrats were increasingly identified in people's minds with Tammany Hall and urban, ethnic, machine politics. As Parsons has shown in the case of Nebraska,[7] nativism was especially rife in the 1890s. In Omaha, where ethnic populations were concentrated, and the Democrats dominated for a time, the Republicans identified a vote for the Democrats as a vote for drink, Romanism, and corruption. Throughout the century, antiliquor campaigns aimed at the urban ethnic groups, blaming them for labor strikes, and also at agrarian radicals, for undermining the reform efforts of middle-class Americans. Labor, government, and human beings were to be regulated in the interests of progress.

A somewhat different tie existed between prohibition and suffrage. "In addition to teaching . . . foreigners respect for American law, the prohibitionists saw another solution to the temperance problem: give women the vote."[8] Temperance would follow from suffrage. As Mrs. Gougar, a Nebraska reform leader said, "If you give women the vote, you will have prohibition."[9] Progressive Republicans throughout the Midwest supported prohibition. Others saw that the question of women's suffrage was symbolic: a vote for suffrage was a vote against immigrants. Considering the dangerous complexities surrounding the issues, it is not surprising that Populist leaders in Kansas said, "We will not be sidetracked on the liquor question!" However, their failure to take a firm position at their first convention won them the immediate label, awarded by the state's Republican party, of "another liquor party."[10] To the extent that there were antinativist sentiments among Kansas's voters, the Republicans were the likely beneficiaries, and the Populists would be the losers, particularly when they fused with the Democrats. The Populists would also lose significant working-class support when, in 1894, at the urging of suffragists who held positions of leadership in the organization, they adopted a suffrage plank. It would be the last time they did so.

The tariff issue was also divisive. Perhaps no more eloquent statement of the problem of the tariff for the working man can be found than that of a mechanic from Atchison:

> Our tariff laws are claimed as a protection to home industries, but this is only the specious plea of the capitalist, who is never actuated by the principle of the greatest good to the greatest number. He well knows that if protected from foreign competition, how easy it is for capital to combine to keep prices up, while the lack of employment in other countries will force their wage-workers to seek our shores, and thus come in competition with wage-workers here, thereby reducing wages and the cost of production, and increasing profits of capital; while by combination, the prices to the consumer are kept up, and the wages of the *real* producer are forced down by foreign competition. Nor is this the limit of the evil. The large profits that return to capital stimulate over-production, and the unnecessary high prices paid by the consumer (the larger class always) have so impoverished him that he cannot be a liberal purchaser. Then . . . we hear the cry of "overproduction," and see the mills close and the wage-workers idle, while the capitalist looks idly on, indifferent, while his ill-gotten gains last. Now are we not children of one common father, and alike interested in the welfare of *all*, of every clime and nation? If

so why in the name of justice do we make laws to tax the many and enrich the few?[11]

For the most part, however, the issue of the tariff did not focus the interest of the working-class. It was primarily farmers who stood in opposition to the tariff, while Republican businessmen and industrialists supported it. Most workers, like the mechanic just cited, were agreed that equality was an important goal. This message of a need for fair play and equality echoed that of the social-gospel movement which was prominent at the time. Workers, farmers, and businessmen *all* made use of a rhetoric grounded in that of the American experiment. This commonality of language dulled the sharp edge of a distinctive class analysis.

Workers, like farmers, were of one mind on the need to control monopolies. They would be controlled by the government. The one real anomaly in Kansas occurred among railroad workers, some of whom feared that legislation could cost them their jobs. If there was a specific demand by railroad workers, it was usually that the railroads should shorten working hours and increase safety standards.

In the many comments received by the commissioner of labor in response to his questions about what should be done to effect changes, there were a few workers who called for radical changes. In 1885 a carpenter said, "A general reorganization of the Government, and the establishment of a socialistic form . . . is the only scientific and just method," for solving the problems of the working man. "Now in order to bring this about in a peaceable manner, which I hope will be done, it is necessary to have all working classes, and as many of the other classes as wish, to assist us in this matter, unite us with other organizations, and become educated in this movement." Generally, though, the position of workers was that, while monopolies were a problem, it was not the owner per se who was to blame. Owners defined themselves, and were seen by many Kansas workers, as members of the *producing class,* as opposed to the nonproductive class made up of monopolists and finance capitalists, or bankers.

A coal miner from Crawford county said,

> I think the laboring classes of our country are oppressed, more or less, in all callings. We cannot blame our capitalists, for they, too, are oppressed to an extent; but I think it is our rotten system of

government that permits laws to be enacted to protect monopolies and give them the power to rob us of our earnings by charging from 36 to 50 percent per annum for short loans, and also by giving away our lands to poor railroad corporations, and then bonding the people to build the roads.

A printer from Topeka echoed the same sentiment: "While I think that employees have rights which employers should respect, I also think that the employers have equal rights in the premises. The interests of both are mutual, and should work in harmony."

Kansas workers, then, often expressed the middle-class idea that labor and capital had equal rights and could work in harmony. It must be remembered that their experience with capital was of a limited nature. If they worked for others, it was in small enterprises where they knew their employers. Some had seen a town's businessmen and "industrialists" go under during the depression of 1873, and many were now witnessing similar problems in the collapse of the late 1800s. Their fears were far removed: immigrants, urban slums and workhouses, big capital. There was little that could be done at the state level, and unless a state-level movement pressed for changes in the daily lives of the workers, there was little reason for them to ally themselves with the cause. From a rational-actor perspective, unless workers really believed that monetary expansion would solve their problems, they were better off voting for a majority party that might pass legislation restricting immigration or tariff laws that would protect their jobs. Workers, then, did not develop a radical class language that farmers could appropriate. So conservative in fact was the language of workers that it inhibited the development of a common organizational structure for farmers and workers.

This, then, was the position of Kansas laborers. Labor was a diverse group, cross-cut by religious and ethnic divisions, as well as by type of work. Some groups, such as miners, did have well-articulated concerns and tried to act on them, but most occupational groups echoed the dominant progressive, social-gospel ideology of the day. Laborers as a whole were concerned about financial issues, or the need for credit, land, and control of monopolies, but there is little evidence that these concerns were as important for them as the questions of foreign immigration, the use of convict labor, or the liquor issue. Workers often used the same language to describe reality as did those who vilified reformers, minorities, immigrants, dangerous agrarian radicals, and even labor itself. Any ensemble of workers and farmers would be a delicate one, subject to fracture. Ironically, however, workers, radicals, and farmers were treated as one by America, even though they may not have acted as a coherent group.

"Solutions" to the Labor Problem

It is worth considering, if only briefly, how middle-class Americans felt the labor problem should be solved, for their views reflect both national and regional feelings about how unrest in general should be treated. It also reveals why middle-class Americans felt that the farmers were responsible for their own plight, and why farmers should not expect "relief." In 1896, the Kansas commissioner of labor opined that the labor problem was one of the gravest facing the country, though he noted that trying to get the "lower strata of the commonwealth" to bend their backs to improve a society, was an old effort. He offered a unique, if somewhat bizarre, insight into how one ancient civilization had dealt with the question of unemployment. "Egypt solved the problem by the magnificent undertaking of the erection of those vast piles, the age-old pyramids." [12]

Recognizing that "political economists, students of our social system and men prominent in the circles of organized labor" had labored hard to develop schemes to aleviate labor problems, he decided to solicit their opinions, and sent letters to university presidents, members of economics departments, and labor leaders throughout the United States. These men were simply asked, "How should the labor problem be solved?" The responses were published in the Kansas Bureau of Labor's *Eleventh Annual Report* under the heading "Sociology."

Professor T. N. Carver of the Oberlin College Department of Economics wanted it made clear that he did "not regard any measure of public relief, either in the form of goods or of employment, as a means of permanent improvement." His point was that, if you supplied the working poor with bread and milk, there would just be more working poor, and you would be right back where you started. His solution to the problem was to "increase the productiveness of labor." Wages must improve, but this could not be accomplished through organization, for that would not change the law of supply and demand as it related to labor. Rather, one must encourage "the accumulation of capital. This will reduce the rate of interest and encourage the extension of industry." At the same time, the supply of labor was to be reduced "by excluding foreign immigrants." Thus, both labor and capital would benefit. E. A. Ross, sometimes referred to as one of the founding fathers of American sociology, also thought that "A restriction of immigrating labor" was a good idea.

The social-gospel tradition is revealed in the assumption that everyone in society should strive for moral and spiritual improvement, in order to achieve a society free from acrimony, strikes, and protesting farmers. Willard Fisher, professor of economics and social sciences at Wesleyan University, argued for "Moral elevation: Cessation from intemperance and other forms of vice; cultivation of industry, frugality, and providence." The president of what is now Case Western Reserve, the Reverend Charles F. Thwing, said that the condition of workers would change once homes were improved. "If the home of the workingman were made thoroughly pleasant, I am sure that the saloon, the most destructive agency of the best interests of the common people, would lose much of its power." The acting president of DePauw University, H. A. Gobin, also focused on the home. "By means of lectures, tracts, and newspaper articles, give the laboring people some information respecting the sanitary conditions of their homes and the best conditions of thrift and prosperity. Urge upon them the idea that there is as much art in the proper spending of money as there is in its acquisition." Should they prove to be obdurate pupils, he also suggested that it be made "a penal offense for any one to be found begging from house to house."

The laboring classes were viewed as poor children, who needed to be educated to live in civilized society, who needed to be taught that capital had its rights, too. (Granted, there were some who felt that capitalists should be more considerate of the poor, but it was assumed they would when business got better.) This paternalism was well expressed by Professor Frederick C. Clark of Ohio State University. Laborers, he said, "must be taught the science and the art of work; taught through the medium of the night schools; taught by their superior fellows; even compelled, in some cases, to study during periods of rest the mechanisms entrusted to them; taught to save labor, material, etc.; . . . taught, most of all, to earn their savings and to save their earnings; finally, taught the science and art of living."

One might think that organized labor and its representatives would protest the paternalistic and pro-capitalist nature of these remarks, but in fact that happened infrequently. The general tone of labor's response can be gathered from E. E. Clark, the grand chief conductor of the Order of Railway Conductors of America. Writing from Cedar Rapids, Iowa, he said, "The socialistic or co-operative commonwealth idea, is, to my mind, impracticable until the whole nature of humanity has been changed." A cooperative commonwealth could be realized, however, only if "selfishness could be eliminated from the make-up of the people," and he was not very optimistic about this possibility. Therefore, the solutions to the laborer's problems lay in the passage of laws prohibiting convict labor, and a limitation of the labor supply. "I believe that, so long as we have a surplus of laborers seeking employment in our country, closely restricted immigration laws should be provided and en-forced." As for large capital, he believed that "Combinations of capital are essentially necessary to the successful carrying out of plans and improvements characteristic of the progressive age in which we live." His opposition to the employment of women and children was also couched in the ideology of America's progres-sives. "The man is the natural provider," and women should stay home. "Women accepting positions theretofore filled by men can have no time for the home, and the home must suffer. When the working man's home is no longer his lode star, the principal pillar will have been torn from under the structure of our republic." As for children, they "should be in school and should spend their time enjoying childhood, and fitting themselves to take their station in the world of work and responsibility."

Lee Johnson, grand president of the Brotherhood of Boiler-makers and Iron Ship-Builders of America, said that Americans need not worry about labor organizations, for "The true principles of organization are opposed to strikes, and favor the settlement of all grievances by arbitration, using all efforts to create and main-tain harmonious relations between labor and legitimate capital." James O'Donnell, speaking for the International Association of Machinists, did talk about real changes that trade unions would try to accomplish, though he also emphasized that their goal was so-cietal harmony, improvement of the general social welfare, and a strengthening of the family.

The grand secretary of the Order of Railroad Telegraphers, J. R. T. Auston, appealed to a sense of decency and justice to solve labor's problems. He believed that all citizens needed to work together to achieve a better society. "The curse of our time is human selfishness and greed, combined with an overpowering desire to accumulate wealth regardless of morality, justice, and equality. If it were possible to instill into capital these three elements, labor would receive its just reward." Capitalists needed to treat laboring people better "than brutes or machinery." "The doctrine of 'the survival of the fittest' should be superseded by 'Love thy neighbor as thyself,' and [capitalists should] assist him to rise superior to environments and influences which tend to dwarf the better part of his nature."

The social-gospel ideology of the day combined a fear of foreign immigration and the desire to control it, either by limiting it or by educating immigrants to good work habits; education as the means of overcoming one's class background or ethnicity was strongly supported. Workers, immigrants, and—by extension—farmers were people who needed to be educated and disciplined to the rigors of industrial society. This worldview, born of Enlightenment faith in the plasticity of human nature and wedded to Social Darwinism, placed strong responsibility for the condition of an individual, or of a social class on that person or that class. If farmers were suffering, they must have caused their problems by producing too much, or borrowing too heavily. If laborers lived poorly, they needed to learn thrift, good work habits, methods of sanitation, and scientific cooking. The progressives would provide society's malcontents with a chance to improve. They could stop drinking, they could use their leisure time to improve their minds, so that they could better appreciate the property of those for whom they worked. Many workers in nineteenth-century America bought into this ideology, which inhibited the development of a working class, and limited the potential of workers for allying with groups that challenged the probusiness ideology of capitalism. Where did farmers fit into this portrait of American society, and how did their ideology compare with that of workers?

Merchants and Farmers: Competing Ideologies

I will deal with farmers and merchants together because, in many ways, these groups defined themselves in opposition to one another in Kansas. Though the farmers might make an appeal to the urban worker, and the manufacturer might tell the laborer that his welfare lay with an expansion of industry, for the most part the programs and ideas of these two groups had little to do with the laborer.

David H. Ecroyd has said that,

> To the rural Populist, urban people fell into one of two classes, both of which were stereotypes: capitalists, or else laborers. . . . In reality, the Populist was pretty much opposed to all urbanism, because it symbolized the new marketing system which he didn't understand and which seemed to operate only to his disadvantage. He thought that his national and state governments were being perverted by money changers from the banking centers of the East and Europe. . . . The feeling of resentment was emotionalized in such a way that the Republicans came to represent Eastern capitalism to the Populists, and the Populists came to be seen as nothing more than hayseeds, worthy only of Republican contempt.[13]

If I have an objective to Ecroyd's characterization of the Populist, it is to his claim that the farmer did not understand the new system of marketing. He understood it all right; he objected to it, as well as to the control that urban centers, and village politicians, exercised over his life.

The rift between farmer and merchant did not first open in the year 1890, when the Populists came on the scene, but had been long developing. Wartime tariffs established to protect northern industries continued after the war, contributing both directly and indirectly to a rise in the prices the farmer and the laborer had to pay for their goods, as well as to a simultaneous shrinkage in the money supply. The farmer had seen the government boost the railroads, was aware of the Crédit Mobilier scandal, which enriched some politicians and beggared the people who held the watered stock of the corporation. They would soon become aware of the "Crime of 1873," when Congress passed legislation demonetizing silver and thereby contributing to a rapid contraction of the currency, in the same year that a nationwide depression, brought on by the closing of Jay Cooke's banking house, began. The farmer was in trouble as early as 1873, and the reaction of the eastern or urban press is instructive.

In an 1873 editorial in the *Nation*, an unidentified writer pointed out that the unrest among the debtor class was primarily the fault of farmers.[14] This was because they had moved into a barren land

and then voted on themselves a huge debt to entice the railroads to build in their direction. The farmers talked of repudiating their debts because, commented the writer sarcastically, they now found them "inconvenient." Lenders responded by either suing or threatening to sue Kansas municipalities. The writer noted that townspeople stood by their debts, partly, one assumes, because not to do so would mean that others would be afraid to lend them more money. He went on to note that "The people who defended the suits were the town officials; but the people who paid the taxes were . . . in a number of instances, and probably in most cases, farmers." Though he makes nothing of this, it is significant that it was townspeople, primarily merchants, who pushed the sale of bonds, whose benefits were most noted in the town. However, the property taxes to reduce the bonds were spread throughout the county, and hence paid by a large number of farmers. One of the concerns expressed by the farmers in the economic downturn was that property, such as bonds, was not taxed, yet land, whose value was falling, was. Farmers had objective, not imaginary, reasons for being displeased with the town politicians. Farmers' "surplus" was being appropriated both through the mechanism of the market and through a system of taxation. This was a true class struggle, a battle over surplus value.

In another *Nation* editorial of 1873, the writer blamed the farmers' problems solely on the farmers, and implied that they were simply poor businessmen, hardly the criterion by which farmers wished to be judged. As for railroad legislation, said the writer, "We believe . . . that if there is anything of which the country is thoroughly sick, it is of legislative or general governmental interference with the making and working of railroads."[15] The railroads, he went on to add, were under no obligation to send the farmers' goods to market without a profit for themselves. The farmer had moved too far, had produced too much, and any problems that resulted were his fault.

> If a man chooses to go out into the wilderness without roads, wagons, or any other means of reaching a market, and plant ten times as much corn as he and his family can consume, and then, in the fall, begins to wail and lament because he cannot find a purchaser for it, nobody pays any attention to him, or people content themselves with telling him that he ought to have thought himself of the market before he built his house or put in his crop. If he

begins to weep and ask whether he must use it for fuel, they tell him unhesitatingly that it is his duty and privilege to do so, if he cannot turn it to any better account. . . . If he were still to refuse to be comforted, and were to maintain that large numbers of industrious people in the East . . . ought to club their savings and cut a wagon-road to his house, load up his corn, and cart it off as far East as may be necessary to secure him a fair price for it, we should simply laugh and walk off.[16]

If there were high tariffs that encouraged the manufacturer at the expense of the farmer, so be it. "If we decide for manufacturers as at present, why farmers must grin and bear it."[17] It is not surprising that the farmer might express some opposition to eastern and urban interests.

The conflict between East and West and between farmer and merchant is partly explained by the way in which the boom of 1881–85 in Kansas was financed before it collapsed. The principal means of financing growth of towns, as well as of the farming community, were mortgages, municipal bonds, and railroad securities.[18] These were sold almost exclusively to eastern companies or individuals, and as far as the farmers were concerned the railroads also represented the East. As we saw in chapter 3, towns and counties borrowed heavily, and then, when the downturn came, found themselves with a debt they could not pay. Eastern bondholders were furious at the attempts of municipalities to escape their obligations to pay off bonds.[19] But after all, while one *might* seize a farmer's mule and plow and drive him off his land, one could hardly appropriate a municipality for repudiating its debt. Eastern moneylenders lobbied Congress to prevent the western farmer—for the farmer, not the town merchant, was seen as the problem—from repudiating his debt. One eastern politician went so far as to say that no more states should be admitted to the Union "until we discipline Kansas." There were those in the state who were equally eager to get the farmer back in his traces, because they were afraid the farmer was scaring capital away from the state. People wanted to make money, and some had done quite well during the boom.

A small Nebraska newspaper carried this ditty:

Mary had a little lot, and thought she'd better sell,
She placed it on the market, and the lot did very well.
It sold four times within a week, and every time it went,

The lucky man who bought it cleared ninety nine percent.
"What makes town lots go flying so?" the eager buyers cry.
"Our town is on the boom you know," the agents do reply.[20]

Charles Harger, writing his account of what happened, said, "and in the summer of 1885 began the 'boom.'" It was as if "a wave of insanity swept over the West. It seemed plausible then that every town would be a commercial metropolis or a great railway centre—or both. . . . It was not joking . . . never were men more serious."[21]

James C. Malin, writing about the boom in the little town of Kingsley, Kansas, and the subsequent collapse, noted how enthusiasm for growth and progress completely dominated all public discussion.[22] Newspapers never tired of reminding their readers that they lived in the land of milk and honey. Here is the Kingsley *Mercury* on the subject:

> Oh hear the boom,
>   the rumbling boom!
> What a shower of golden wheels to dissipate the gloom.
> Children of the eastern land, where your farms are spoiled; leave the barren sand where your fathers toiled. Leave the rivers and hills, leave your spades and hoes; leave your rough and rocky hills where no harvest grows. Hither come and upward grow. Here your dimes invest, and you'll never want from the Golden West. Here you may in every truth, in a country where from your breast will swell with healthy breath, and "Ring a Chestnut Bell on the form of Death."[23]

In the face of enthusiasm such as this, no scheme seemed too fantastic for town fathers, who were remarkably willing to spend the community's monies in the face of naysayers. In 1881, John Limerick arrived in Alma, Kansas, from Illinois with money in his pockets and credits on an eastern bank.[24] No one seemed concerned with anything other than the fact that he was willing to invest in the town, as evidenced by the fact that he promptly opened the firm of J. F. Limerick & Company, Bankers. He listened to old settlers tell about a previous hoax in which a number of townspeople had been bilked out of their money in a scheme to drill for oil. He was especially interested in the fact that before the drilling had stopped at 585 feet, the drill bit had passed through several seams of coal. Limerick acquired property east of town and began drilling. Ignoring the findings of a state geologist who said that the layers of coal beneath the area were not worth mining, and the recollections of some citizens that in the drilling for oil the shaft had not passed through any substantial amounts of coal, the majority of the town readied for a boom, "with a Capital B," as the local newspaper announced.[25]

The *Enterprise* kept its readers apprised of progress. The were told the drill had reached a depth of 550 feet, passing through a vein of coal 18 inches thick at 400 feet, and that it would reach deeper into the earth in its explorations.[26] Limerick, now the mayor, was returned to office in the April elections of 1887, and at his urging the town endorsed the issuance of $9,000 worth of bonds for the future "coal mine." In exchange, the city received stock worth $3,000 in three different companies headed by Limerick. In May the paper ran an entire issue devoted to Alma's growth and future prospects. It was not just coal that lay buried under Waubaunsee County, but silver, oil, salt, stone, cement, water, and most probably, natural gas. Gold was not mentioned. With the Limerick drill at 800 feet and proceeding, the town was wild with speculation about the glimmering future. The paper proclaimed Alma to be "A Sparkling Diamond Nestling on the Bosom of Beautiful Waubaunsee County, the Golden Agricultural Belt of Kansas," whose "Boom Reverberates Over Hill, Dale, and Valley."[27]

Alma did experience a modest boom. Stone was shipped from the local quarry by the Rock Island Railroad, and the business district was lighted during the evenings with kerosene street lamps. Boardwalks were ordered to keep customers out of the mud, and a new jail was built. Mayor Limerick was again reelected. To show his gratitude, he gave the town a 16-acre parcel of land to use as a city park; it came from his parcel of 160 acres. The city was to maintain the park and provide an easement through it to the Limerick cement works on the east side. The city accepted the land, and a new bond was passed to make general improvements to the city and the park.

Limerick continued to report on the "vast" amounts of coal that were supposedly being found by his company. At the beginning of 1889 he held a large party for the community to celebrate the opening of his new bank building and the Limerick General Merchandise Store. That month he also announced the Park Valley Development, where homes would be built on Limerick's land surrounding the city park. The citizens of Alma were asked to issue bonds in the amount of $25,000 for "general improvements" (the

opening of Limerick's coal mine). A special election was set for
April 1, 1889, and the *Enterprise* urged the citizens to seize the opportunity for prosperity.

> The time is now here when the people of Alma have it in their
> own hands to make their future one of wealth and prosperity and
> greatness, or to crush out every sentiment that . . . (is opposed) to
> the establishment of a city of unlimited wealth, prosperity, and
> population. . . . The finds of four good veins of coal are useless
> without further development. . . . Mayor Limerick is willing to
> guarantee our people that work will be commenced at once in the
> sinking of a shaft and that it will be carried to a successful comple-
> tion. . . . Vote the bonds![28]

The citizens of Alma heeded the paper's call for prosperity and
voted the bonds, but trouble was not long in coming. A rival to the
town's two newspapers—the *Enterprise* and the *News*, which had
served as outlets for Limerick and the city council—was introduced
to the community. The *Signal* began to ask what proved to be embarrassing questions about the disposition of the bond money, and
challenged the idea that all of it should be spent for the coal mine.
In May 1890, when the men working for the coal mine complained
that they had not been paid for several weeks, or had been paid in
script good only at the company store, the *Signal* ran stories ques-
tioning the integrity of those people in whom the town had placed
so much of their trust. Then, when people found out that Limerick
and the city council were going to ask for an additional $8,000 in
bond money for the mine, both the *Enterprise* and the *Signal* began
to speak of the "inflated" evaluation of the mine, and urged that a
special bond election not be called.

In the fall of 1890, the Limerick enterprises began collapsing on
one another, and Alma's "boom" was truly over. The Alma Coal
Company had turned over all of its assets to a new company, the
Park Valley Coal Company, of which Limerick was the president,
with the sole purpose of trying to circumvent an attachment order
for $10,000 from a Massachusetts bank. The bondsmen who had
been pursuing the county treasurer's personal assets to cover the
missing $24,000 tried to collect from Limerick, as he held the notes
on all of the treasurer's personal property. Limerick went East to try
and raise money to keep both the bank and the coal company
going, but was unsuccessful. By November both were out of business. With the town's treasury depleted, one of the banks closed,

and the coal company out of business, the *Signal* hooted, "King Boodle is dead!"[29] Limerick did not run for a sixth term as mayor, and a new city council and mayor were elected in 1891. The new leaders' hopes that Alma could recover from her setbacks were dashed when they found that literally all of the city funds which had been placed in Limerick's care were missing. He had no assets, and left town for "parts unknown," according to the *Signal*. The new councilmen also found that interest on city bonds had not been paid, and that they owed $2,600 to the Guaranty Savings Bank of Manchester, New Hampshire. In the decade that followed, Alma would try to find ways to pay its debt, and was constantly beseiged by eastern banks to settle. It was not until 1904 that Alma was able to negotiate with the bondholders to reduce the debt from $46,000 to $29,000, which they finally "paid" by passing another bond issue.

The story of Alma is typical. A probusiness group within a community would urge a town, and often the surrounding countryside, to pass a bond for the expansion of a business, or set of businesses, that were supposed to provide employment and assure a rise in the value of people's vacant lots. As long as the boom proceeded apace, discouraging words were seldom heard. In fact, the usual practice was to try and discredit and shout down those who questioned the practice of booming a town before the countryside had grown up around it.[30] In the town of Kingsley, which also went through the cycle of boom and bust, farmers who believed that efforts should go to developing agriculture were warned off with these words:

> Oh, kickers all,
> Both great and small,
>   No longer stand aloof,
> If you can't join the throng,
> And help boom things along
>   You'd better "come off" the roof.[31]

The town was to grow: build packing houses, find coal and oil, expand! In Kingsley, with a packing plant only in the planning stages, the *Banner-Graphic* carried these headlines: "Oh, Ye Gods and little fishes, read, read, and reflect. Business barometer booming— Buildings being builded. Fair fare forging forward finely."[32] The solution to all problems was growth; the efforts of merchants, manufacturers, and capitalists were seen as worthy. Those who worried about the decline in agriculture were reminded that those who had predicted that "Kansas would go to their eternal bow-wows because of a little drought in the months of June and July are beginning to find out that they missed their bearings."[33] The businessman was seen to be the driving and vital force in the emerging society. The probusiness newspaper in Kingsley said that "our capitalists" would move the town and civilization forward, and the concentration of capital was encouraged—something most farmers argued against because of their fear of the railroads. Trusts "benefit labor materially, and inaugurate a radical change in the advancement of the mutual interests of labor and capital." If there were to be a civilization in the prairie wilderness, it would be a result of the capitalists' efforts.

> Employees will have homes of their own, the land to be donated and the residence to be built by the company, to be paid for by a certain retained percentage of the wages. Such, at least, is the plan to be adopted by the establishments to be located here, as we comprehend the idea, and certainly if such a revolution is to be brought about, it will do more to correct the differences theretofore existing between capital and labor than anything else, because there is nothing so potent as the influence of the possession of a home.[34]

The idea that capital, in the guise of the soldier-entrepreneur, would solve the problems of America, was not unique to Kansas, but it was unacceptable to her farmers. It would be the Alliance and then the Populist party that would articulate the ideology of the farmer, and the Republican party that would serve as the voice of the capitalist in Kansas.

Voices in Contrast: Alliancemen and Republicans

The Alliance and Populists' sharp critique of American society in general and conditions in Kansas in particular drew the attention and barbs of the dominant political parties. Nowhere are the ideas of the Populists and their followers more clearly articulated than in the "stump" speeches given by fiery orators like Mary Elizabeth Lease, Annie Diggs, and Jerry Simpson. These speeches were a way of educating the faithful, reaffirming their commitment to common ideas, and assuring one another that power did, indeed, lie with the people.[35] There were some important differences between the speakers in terms of what they offered as solutions and political strategies, which I will discuss in the following chapter. Here, though, I wish to look at common themes, and common responses

The Populist congressman Jeremiah "Sockless Jerry" Simpson, among the most popular of the stump speakers, is shown here in a political debate with his opponent, Chester I. Long, at Harper, Kansas, in 1892. Courtesy Kansas State Historical Society.

to the ideas of these speakers. Annie Diggs, in writing about the emergence of the Alliance and Populism, was to later note that what distinguished the movement was its desire to extend democracy into all spheres of life, particularly the economic sphere.

> For the first time in the life of the great Republic there was a political organization which grappled directly and fundamentally with the gross injustice which marked the dealings between Exploiters and Exploited in the realm of industrialism. It marked the beginning of an entire change of things Governmental in relation to the Server and the Served.[36]

Its function was, as O. Gene Clanton remarked in *Kansas Populism,* to "protect the weak from the oppressions of the strong."[37] In a speech that was to carry him to the state capital in Topeka as governor, Lorenzo Lewelling said, "We demand no paternalism at the hands of government, but we do demand protection from corporate vultures and legalized beasts of prey. We ask in God's name that the government shall be so administered that the humblest citizen shall have an equal chance."[38]

Inequality existed in the economic sphere, argued the Populists, because of class legislation, which allowed the country's wealth to concentrate in the hands of the few. Ignatius Donnelly, in *Caesar's Column,* a book widely quoted by Populist speakers in Kansas, said that there was a direct relationship between concentration of wealth and a nation's collapse.

> When Egypt went down 2 percent. of her population owned 97 percent. of her wealth. . . .
> When Babylon went down 2 percent. of her population owned all the wealth. . . .
> When Rome went down 1,800 men owned all the known world.[39]

Populist speakers hammered away at the notion that America had become a class-divided society during the Civil War and that these distinctions were being maintained by the national government. On one side were gold, the bankers, "the money powers," "the gigantic octopus" of Wall Street, "conscienceless capital," "bondholders," "monopolists," "corporate vultures." On the other side stood "the people," "the toilers," "the horny-handed sons of labor." Mary Elizabeth Lease emphasized the link between concentration of wealth, politics, and the welfare of the people.

> Kansas suffers from two great robbers: the Santa Fe railroads and the loan companies. The common people are robbed to enrich their masters. There are over 30,000 millionaires in the United States. Go home and figure how many paupers you must make in making one millionaire. There are over thirty men in the United States whose aggregate wealth is over 1.5 billions of dollars. There are 1/2 million tramps; that is men looking for work here, too. There are 60,000 ex-soldiers of the Union in poor houses, but no bondholders. It would have been better if Congress had voted pensions to these 60,000 paupers who wore the blue and dyed it red with their blood in the country's defense than to have voted to make the bondholder's bonds payable, interest and principal, in gold and non-taxable. . . . [We want] money, land, and transportation.[40]

The Republican opponents of the Populists were made up of the small-town boosters and optimists, who claimed that people like Lease were wreckers, against progress, negative, and giving the state a bad name. The *Wellington Monitor* reported:

> At the opera house meeting last Monday night, a miserable caricature upon womanhood, hideously ugly in feature and foul of

tongue, made an ostensible political speech, but which consisted mainly of the rankest kind of personal abuse of people in this city. . . . All we know about her is that she is hired by this great reform business, spouting foul-minded vulgarity at $10 a night. No doubt the petticoated smut-mill earns her money. . . . Her venomous tongue is the only thing marketable about the old harpy, and we supposed she is justified in selling it where it commands the highest price. In about a month the lantern-jawed, goggle-eyed nightmare will be out of a job.[41]

Lease gave as good as she got and was to have the last laugh, at least in 1890, when the Alliance/Populist ticket swept to victory in the state.

Coupled with the belief that the government was in the hands of the monopolists, or at least acting in their direct interests, was the belief in a conspiracy. A favored reference was the "Crime of 1873," which demonstrated to Populists the power of bondholders and banks. Mrs. S. E. V. Emery's *Seven Financial Conspiracies Which Have Enslaved the American People* served as a movement bible on this topic.

But we have not yet completed the enumeration of crimes perpetrated against the people of the country through this infernal system of legalized robbery. Having purchased their bonds with government money, depreciated from 38 to 60 percent . . . and having exempted them from taxation, with advanced interest payable in gold, it would seem that the climax of audacity had been reached. But who can fathom the greed of the money shark, or set bounds to the voracity of the civilized brigand?[42]

Society was divided into two groups: a class which produced nothing for the society, parasites who fed off of the rest, and a class made up of producers—farmers, workers, and honest capitalists. The problem was not capitalism but bad capitalists. Labor could not be treated as a mere commodity but had to be seen as the true source of all value. Speaking against the industrialists who would define men as simple working machines to be hired and dismissed as the market dictated, Henry Demarest Lloyd added, "The new theory that though the workingman is not a thing, his labor is a thing, marks but a slight advance on the old. It means that the labor can be bought and sold regardless of the man behind it."[43]

The Populists stood for the producer, for justice. As Ignatius Donnelly said, they were for "stopping the stealing, and permitting industry to keep the fruits of its own toil. How beautiful it is when it means plenty, prosperity, happiness, a clear mind, a serene heart, a comfortable home."[44] The Populists would purify America. Principle would triumph over party. The fact that Kansas Populists wished to redeem the political system was clearly revealed in the attacks they directed in 1890 against a United States senator from Kansas, John Ignalls. Ingalls thought of himself as a political realist and as early as 1878 had commented, without apparent concern, that the "poor are growing poorer and the rich richer, and by the end of this century the middle class will have entirely disappeared."[45] He had also proclaimed that a politics free of corruption was "an irridescent dream." He was happy to assert that "Men Are Not Created Equal" and was opposed to virtually every reform theory. As for socialism, with which he equated Populism, it "is the final refuge of those who have failed in the struggle for life. It is the prescription of those who were born tired."[46] It was the special task of Annie Diggs, while on the Populist speakers' circuit, to point out to the crowds what Ingalls had said. Her attacks were greeted, at least among Populists, with great shouts and applause. On the other hand, the *Walnut Valley Times*, a Republican paper in Eldorado, tried to dismiss her with a bit of doggerel headed "Dig at Diggs":

> I heard the voice of Anna Diggs
> Across the city park;
> It scared the geese and pigs
> And made the watch dog bark.[47]

The general thrust of farmer ideology, then, was similar to that of the Social-Gospel movement as it related to a demand for justice, equality, and a purified body politic. Farmers would be able to mobilize on this basis, and would begin to develop a distinctive class-consciousness. This language would not, however, allow for long-term mobilization, or the full development of the class. Peter Argersinger has suggested that one could describe the politics of the Alliance as "pentecostal." "The situation of being permanently underprivileged was to be replaced with a putative society in the Kingdom of God where those who followed the primal mandate—'Replenish the earth and subdue it'—would be the elite."[48] The images and ideas which people used were often biblical. The farmer was to be a modern Joshua, and march, blowing his horn, around the citadels of power until the walls came down. When the walls of privilege remained in place, two things could and did happen. Some stayed the course, while others abandoned the movement for what they regarded as more realistic options. In short, within the Alliance/Populist movement, pentecostal rhetoric turned people away from a sustained political struggle, and sometimes caused them to adopt strategies for change that limited the movement's potential for success. The ideology of the movement contained within it tendencies that caused people to shift their attention when the dramatic changes they hoped for were not forthcoming.

Because the Alliance placed such faith in the political system, albeit a purified one, socialist ideas about developing alternative centers of powers, or destroying the political system, did not attract its members. Whatever the problem, farmers kept turning to the political system, and often to established political leaders, for solutions. When a Farmers' Alliance was formed in Washington, Kansas, in 1887, those assembled noted that "farmers are oppressed by subsidies to monopolies, by selfish and dishonest officials, by railroad extortions and discriminations, and other privileged classes." They also complained that the county officers received "too high salaries," and that the governor's appointment of three members to the board of railroad commissioners was subject to the influence of the railroads. Their idea of how to solve these problems is instructive. "First . . . we petition our members in the legislature through the county alliance to inquire into all laws affecting the interest of the farming classes." "We furthermore ask the legislature to enact such laws in regard to railroad rates as will give the several companies a just and reasonable profit and allow them not to exact exorbitant charges on freight."[49] In short, for every problem, there was a legislative solution; the state legislature could deal with the issues raised. Later, of course, farmers would find the state legislature unwilling or unable to deal with some of their most pressing concerns, such as monetary inflation. Then they turned to a third party as a means of challenging the system and also expressing optimism in it.

The Republicans would continue to push what amounted to one issue: Would people vote for anarchy and lawlessness or would they support business? Perhaps there is no better expression and summary of Republican sentiment than the editorial that made William Allen White of Emporia, Kansas, a national figure. Populists of the town and countryside attacked White on the streets of Emporia one day in 1896 for his unwavering support of the Republicans and his constant attack on Populists. Returning to his office, he wrote in the heat of anger an editorial entitled, "What's the Matter with Kansas?" So popular was this piece with Republicans that their national committee reprinted it and sent tens of thousands of copies across the land. White began by noting that for eight years Kansas had been losing people and money while the nation as a whole had grown rich. Why, he asked, did Kansas have no large cities, no big industries, no magnates of industry? What was the matter with Kansas? His partial answer was:

> We all know; yet here we are again. We have an old mossback Jacksonian who snorts and howls because there is a bathtub in the State House. . . . We have another shabby, wild-eyed, rattle-brained fanatic who has said openly in a dozen speeches that "the rights of the user are paramount to the rights of the owner"; we are running him for Chief Justice, so that capital will come tumbling over itself to get into the state. . . . Then, for fear some hint that the state had become respectable might percolate through the civilized portions of the nation we have decided to send three of four harpies out lecturing, telling the people that Kansas is raising hell and letting the corn go to weed. . . .
>
> Oh, this is a state to be proud of! . . . What we need is not more money, but less capital, fewer white shirts and brains, fewer men with business judgment, and more of those fellows who boast that they are "just ordinary clodhoppers, but they know more in a minute about finance than John Sherman"; we need more men who are "posted," who can bellow about the crime of '73, who hate prosperity, and who think, because a man believes in honor, he is a tool of Wall Street. We have had a few of them—some hundred fifty thousand—but we need more.
>
> We need several thousand gibbering idiots to scream about the "Great Red Dragon" of Lombard Street. We don't need population, we don't need wealth, we don't need well-dressed men on the streets, we don't need cities on the fertile prairies; you bet we don't! What we are after is the money power. Because we have become poorer and ornerier and meaner than a spavined, distempered mule, we, the people of Kansas, propose to kick; we don't care to build up, we wish to tear down.[50]

Intemperate as White's remarks were, they paralleled the sentiments of those who saw the Alliance and the Populist party as direct threats to capital.

When the Republicans suffered their first defeat at the hands of the Alliance, they gathered to discuss how they might turn back the threat they defined as anarchy and ruin. The Kansas Day Club met annually, beginning in 1892, to offer explanation, self-congratulation, and the prospect of future victory to the Republican faithful. The short speeches were preserved and show how clearly the Republicans believed that *they* were the party of principle and integrity; that *they* represented moral, as opposed to class, politics; and above all, that *they* stood for progress.[51]

Charles Harbaugh of Erie, Kansas, claimed that the Populists had brought about the state's economic ruin. "In 1890 there went up a howl from every Populist in Kansas, from Senator Peffer down to the lowest man in rank in the party, that Kansas was bankrupt and that her people could never pay their debts. This most damnable and unpardonable lie was heard by investors in the East who held Kansas farm mortgages." Though they had been eager to loan money before, Harbaugh said, "these investors instructed their Western agents to withdraw their money from Kansas."[52]

The problems of Kansas, said W. Y. Morgan, from Hutchinson, can be reduced to "those three evils, those blights, those horrors, those nightmares, those jimjams, those delirious tremens: droughts, hot winds, and Populists."[53] The farmers were seen as reacting blindly to an economic downturn. First, according to Chester Long of Medicine Lodge, "Everyone was becoming rich, and all were on the high road to financial prosperity. Then God took a hand. The rains did not descend and the floods did not come, but the hot winds blew and beat upon the corn, and it withered and died." The mortgage came due, and was defaulted. Now, people "were not becoming wealthy; they were discouraged." So, they organized, and met secretly. "They felt worse after each meeting." And the Populists seized the opportunity to argue for legislation for just one class. Commented Long, "In olden times the blind were not selected to lead the blind. It is different now. The farmer should legislate for the farmer . . . , the dish-washer for the dish-washer, and the hotel porter for the hotel porter."[54]

The idea that the Alliance and Populists stood for one class, while the Republicans represented all classes, was worked heavily by the Republican party. Edward Greer of Winfield said that the Alliance represented a "class that would enslave thought and stifle discussion."[55] He apparently found acceptable his party's habit of branding all who dissented from their platform as demagogues and traitors to the memory of the Grand Army of the Republic. Bristow of Salina said that class legislation was not necessary because there were no classes. "The triumph of individualism has destroyed class distinction. . . . The progress of the race is no longer in the hands of a few individuals of a favored class. Any man, regardless of his race or condition of birth, has the right to cherish the loftiest ambitions and an opportunity to attain to the highest success."[56] And damn the men and political parties who would say it is otherwise. Because in the United States there were "always two great political parties. The one is composed of the most aggressive and progressive citizenship; men of conviction. . . . The other party is composed of that class of citizens who are opposed to that which has been done. The one is the positive element of society; the other the negative."[57] The choice offered Kansans, then, was a simple one, according to J. B. Tomlinson of Minneapolis. Kansans can support the Populists or Kansas "can put . . . [themselves] in a position where . . . [they] can fight anarchy and socialism to death. . . . Anarchy and socialism are today the most dangerous evils in Kansas. . . . When THEY have been crushed out, it will be time enough to devote our attention to less important matters."[58] To vote for the Alliance was treason, and J. S. West of Fort Scott said, "We must make treason as bad as selling beer or not paying a debt, anarchy as atrocious as the rockpile."[59] "Republicanism," claimed Nelson of Lindsborg, "is synonymous with patriotism."[60] The question, according to T. B. Wall of Wichita was "whether Kansas is to be Republican or Cossack."[61]

The Alliance and Populists were described in the same way that reformers throughout the country were described: as dangerous and ignorant men and women, as "crack-brained" charlatans and "chimerical theorist[s]."[62] Henry Allen of Ottawa had this observation to make: "When the reformer made his appearance in Kansas we did not take him seriously. . . . We overlooked the metaphysical truth that men, by dint of mere repetition of sonorous nonsense, may finally come to accept it as a serious philosophy."[63] The Populist leaders were described as men who simply wanted a share of the political spoils and did not stand for principle, as the Republicans supposedly did. James Troutman of Topeka summed up his view of the party and its leaders.

> According to our orthodox creed, a party conceived in iniquity, born in sin, rocked in the cradle of superstition and perfidy and nurtured in ignorance and hypocrisy must be of few days and full

of trouble. Aside from its contempt for the constitution and laws of the state, it has lived a life of duplicity and falsehood. Proclaiming itself to be a party organized in the interests of labor, it has crucified upon the altar of personal ambition and aggrandizement the distinctive claims of every form of industrial toil, and elevated to exalted places a class of nondescripts having no visible means of support. This party, organized, as it maintains, to subserve the interest of the toiling masses, is dominated by lawyers without clients, by doctors without patients, by preachers without pulpits, by teachers without schools, by soldiers without courage, by editors without papers, by bankers without money, by financiers without credit, by moralists without morals, by farmers without farms, by women without husbands, and by statesmen out of a job.[64]

It is hardly my intention to suggest that the Republican analysis of the farmers' plight and of the origins and purposes of the Alliance and Populist party was a correct one. Nevertheless, the ideological low road that Kansas Republicans chose to follow connected with the broad highway of antireform sentiment in the two dominant national parties, and with their probusiness, antilabor, and antifarmer sentiment. The farmer, then, was confronted with the necessity of struggling, simultaneously, on three different fronts: he needed to legitimate his ideology, argue for a modified economic system, and capture political power. All of these struggles were bound together; failure on any front would lessen the chances for success in other areas. Thus, long-term mobilization could be hindered by the Republicans undercutting the Populists politically through selective endorsement of their ideas. The Populists could be checked, ideologically, if they were placed in the position of having to argue that they were not socialistic, that they were really procapitalist. If, then, the Republicans could pose as economic saviors, they would draw votes away from the Populists, which is just what they did. But the dominant parties would not have responded at either the state or national level were if not for the fact that thousands of farmers organized to challenge their power and their received wisdom. Farmers, acting autonomously, generated a system crisis that the established political parties had to deal with or lose their grip on power. *Because* farmers mobilized, class contradictions became embedded in the legal-political system of Kansas and the nation. A key to mobilization and development of farmer autonomy lay in the creation of a distinctive movement culture.

Summary

For people to march against the oppressors, they must believe they are oppressed. They must possess a primitive sense of justice and fair play and believe these to have been violated. Language provides a means for people to analyze their troubles, as well as speculate about how they might be overcome. It provides both visions of the future as well as an imagined past which will unify people. Language is central in drawing people together and in affecting their structual capacities to act as a class, for a uniform language can cut across racial and cultural boundaries. Likewise language shapes organizational capacities—the ability of people to form class-dominated parties or unions to carry out their political agenda, to act in the name of the class. Thus, the potential for a group to realize itself as a class is determined not just by one's location in the economic order but by the very vocabulary or ideology with which one makes sense of the world.

Portions of a class language are emergent; they are derived from people's involvement in an organization or in challenges to the political system. But people also draw on their everyday experiences and their own social histories to understand the turbulence of an era. Kansas farmers employed a Jeffersonian language to question the emergence of monopolies and changes in the nature and meaning of work. Because of past experience, they argued for a cooperative commonwealth of all producers, for democracy in the marketplace, for harmony between capitalist and worker. This language was refined in the Alliance and in the Populist party, but it provided the starting point for mobilization in a period when none of the established powers seemed to care what happened to the farmer.

Workers in Kansas also argued for cooperation between capitalists and workers, but their experience with the world was such that their demands focused on restrictive immigration, and the prohibition of convict labor, to protect their jobs. Like the farmers, they wanted government regulation, although they were far less concerned with the issue of railroad legislation, the subtreasury scheme, or monetary inflation. The potential, then, for farmers and laborers to band together to fight for collective rights was inhibited by the fact that they held different class positions in society, and by the fact that they employed different languages to analyze their social conditions.

Farmer-worker liaisons were also made difficult by issues which cross-cut class as well as political party. In Kansas, for example, the issues of temperance, women's suffrage, and the tariff would fissure class. Temperance divided pietistic voters from those who were members of urban ethnic groups. Republican reformers lobbied for women's suffrage because they fully believed that women would vote for prohibition, and against the urban ethnic who struck against capitalism and progress. And, though farmers believed high tariffs raised the prices they had to pay for goods, many workers believed, along with the Republican party, that protectionism was the key to their prosperity. It was not easy for the Alliance and Populist party to choose a path that would lead them through this tangle.

Finally, workers, farmers, and the probusiness classes all made use of some of the same terms, or language, to describe the conditions facing American society. All stood for harmony, or claimed they did. All argued for prosperity and for a muting of the inequalities between the classes. Workers, and their leaders, as well as farmers, took pains to make it clear to potential recruits that they were not opposed to capitalism per se, or the system of government, only to rank inequality. Farmers and laborers took this position partly because, since the failure of Reconstruction, reformers of all sort were suspect, unless the reform took a decidedly nonrevolutionary cast. The social-gospel movement, which was part of the "progressive" ideology of the day, took an Enlightenment attitude toward political and economic problems—they were the fault of the individual and could only be solved by individual effort. If the worker, and by extension the farmer, had problems, then he should become sober, save, and work harder. If the worker would educate himself, clean up the ghettoes in which he lived, practice thrift, and not have too many children, then he would prosper. If the farmer could not make a living as a result of his toil, then it must be because he had made bad individual business decisions. The farmer could be helped when he stopped complaining and learned the law of supply and demand. What the "better" classes owed to the "lesser" ones was an *opportunity* to improve. Either one could work, or one could die.

Thus, even though farmers understood what was the matter with America, the language they used to describe and explain their troubles was embedded in an American language which delegitimated reform and third-party movements. They needed to fight a linguistic as well as political and economic battle. Of course, they did form an organization and party in the face of concerted opposition, which came primarily in Kansas from the probusiness village boomers. The businessmen of every hamlet seemed to believe that with just a little capital, and a railroad line or two, they could be the next Chicago or St. Louis. The towns were pushed ahead of the countrysides, bonds were floated, and the county was taxed, usually far above the assessed valuation, to encourage growth. In 1881, when farmers received the highest prices for their products since the close of the Civil War, people rushed to the state, and land values shot up along with land mortgages and town debt. This ephemeral prosperity disappeared with the long drought of 1887–89 and a collapse in the prices for farm products by 1891.

The farmers' response was to challenge the Republicans' control of the state, and the appropriation—direct and indirect—of their surplus labor. They wanted legislators who would vote for lower railroad rates, who would prevent foreclosures, and who would tax the bondholders. They directly challenged the progressive attitude of the town's businessmen and the Republican party, who saw in their challenge a threat to their economic welfare. The farmers mobilized and seized control of the state government. Surprised and alarmed, the Republicans fought back, claiming that they were the party of morality, that they represented integrity, that the opposition was made up of wild-eyed fanatics who would destroy the state and beggar both worker and businessman. The Alliance held firm to its language, which argued for a country of simple republican yeomen. As the Alliance shifted to the Populist party and directly involved itself in politics, it honed its vocabulary and focused on specific evils. The language was not, however, consistent on what needed to be done to make America something other than a land of Hamiltonian salesmen. The language of the movement inhibited the development of both structural and organizational capacities; in short, it inhibited the development of class and class consciousness. Alliance leaders did not always speak with one voice.

Part Four

THE MOVEMENT FORMING: ADAPTATION AND RESPONSE

6

Creation of a Movement Culture

The Populist orator Mary Elizabeth Lease, who is reported to have told Kansas farmers in 1890 that what they needed to do was "raise less corn and more hell." Courtesy Kansas State Historical Society.

It was July 17, 1889. The president of the Beaver Valley Alliance rapped his gavel on the table which served as the teacher's desk during the daylight hours, and called the meeting to order. He asked all of those who were nonmembers to leave, and said, "Brother Doorkeeper, please secure the door and admit no one during the opening ceremony." About twenty men, some fathers and sons, bowed their heads, and joined the order's chaplain in "invoking the blessing of Almighty God."

Knowing that a prospective brother was standing outside the

schoolhouse, the president then said, "Brother Secretary, is there any candidate for initiation?" In a voice loud enough to be heard on the other side of the door, the secretary informed him there was. The candidate, who had been kept company by the steward, then rapped loudly on the flimsy door.

> Doorkeeper: "There is an alarm at the door, Brother President."
> President: "Seek the cause and report."
> Doorkeeper: "A candidate seeking admission to our order."
> President: "Admit him."

Having been duly admitted, the candidate was informed that he must take on a solemn and secret obligation, though the president assured him that it would "not conflict with the freedom of your political or religious views." His obligation having been spelled out, the president went on to enumerate the goals and purposes of the Alliance.

> We constitute a common brotherhood, bound together for our collective and individual benefit. Our aims are high, our purposes noble. We aim to elevate man by blending together more intimately the ties of brotherhood and humanity in his social life, thus dissolving prejudice and selfishness in the sunlight of human love. We aim, by cultivating the mind, to reach a higher degree of intelligence, thereby adding to the pleasures and relieving the cares and anxieties of life. . . . Our purpose is to exert an influence in opposition to the glaring and shameful vices which degrade mankind, lower him in the scale of human existence and bring despair and woe to the dearest creatures he has on earth. *We are allied together to render the lives of farmers and laborers more attractive, country life less lonely and more social, and to better our financial condition.*[1]

If farmers were to assert themselves as a class, they would have to organize.[2] Class organizations are not, however, created out of whole cloth. There must be a cultural tradition of shared experience and expectation to draw on, and the distinctiveness of this tradition must be nurtured. In other words, as Antonio Grasmci put it, if a class hopes to achieve dominance, it must offer a counter-ideology.[3]

A common vision is essential if a class is to succeed as a class. This vision provides solidarity in the face of defeat and provides for commitment to long-range goals. Goodwyn theorized that the first steps in the growth of the farmers' movement were the creation of an alternative worldview, a new way to look at industrial America, and the creation of a culture in which people who had been shut out of the political arena could learn to practice democratic politics.[4] For him, learning and practice took place in the Alliance cooperatives. If we were to rely solely on quotations such as the one above from the ritual of initiation into the Alliance, we might justifiably conclude that it was the vision of a cooperative commonwealth which brought farmers together and sustained them. This is certainly partly true. But farmers were also interested in obtaining specific resources with which to address their economic concerns.

I have argued that a sense of injustice is essential for mobilization and that this feeling grows out of the actual lived experience of the actors. The Alliance fostered a feeling of solidarity among farmers which was essential for initial mobilization. I also argued that a movement must hold out to potential recruits the possibility of achieving specific goals. Both selective incentives and a sense of community are important for success. As we will see here, though, the movement culture made use of an ideology which limited the possibility of long-term success. That is, the Alliance stood for a purified system of politics, and many of its followers believed that all they hoped for could be accomplished with their votes. They simply would vote into office men of conscience who would act for the farmer. They did, in fact, just what Piven and Cloward, if they had been acting as the farmers' advisors, would have suggested they do—concentrate on wringing as much as possible from the system, and give less attention to the creation of an organizational framework and structure.[5] But it would be the lack of an organizational structure that would prove to be the undoing of the farmers' movement, when the material gains they sought were not immediately forthcoming.

Organizationally, the movement would be plagued by the fact that when the Alliance was founded, strong emphasis was placed on the creation of a unique and distinct culture that was supposed to elevate principle above party. Some were drawn to the movement by this emphasis. However, when the Alliance shed its apolitical skin many recruits were alarmed by the transformation. Moreover, attention was not given to the development of an organization which could position itself for a long struggle. From the speeches and writings of those involved, one has to assume that they saw victory close at hand.

It was rational for a farmer to join a movement and to cast his lot with it, if the entry costs (both material and psychological) were low and if results were forthcoming. It was equally rational to abandon the cause and to vote for the Republicans, or even the Democrats, if change did not occur and these parties had adopted portions of the Populists' platform. Individual rational actions, however, produced a collective irrationality, because they limited the possibility of farmers becoming an autonomous and hegemonic class.

The agenda of the Alliance was extremely complex, and the complexities would come to light. During a period of rapid mobilization, actors with very diverse interests, both members and leaders, came together. As there was little or no debate within the suballiances, people did not have time to develop a uniform ideological perspective. Once the organization became a fully functioning political party, the different interests (suffrage, temperance, the desire for political office and patronage) were highlighted, and without a strong, centralized, organizational structure the movement faltered.

Kansas farmers, not unlike those described by Schwartz in the Southern Alliance, also found it difficult to learn from past mistakes, although for different reasons.[6] In the South an entrenched oligarchy made such learning difficult, while in Kansas the speed of movement formation and the immediate focus on politics made it difficult. Donna A. Barnes has suggested that with the Texas Alliance there was a clear progression from one strategy to the next, e.g., from economic cooperative, to the jute boycott, to the subtreasury scheme.[7] In Kansas, however, *the* strategy was always "vote the rascals" out. This was an effective strategy for one election, but it resulted in the almost immediate mobilization of a powerful elite against the movement. The pro-business Republican party, supported by national climate that left little room for new experiments, was soon back in power. I do not wish to imply that the outcome of this struggle was preordained. Rational actors, acting in concert, tried to offer America a choice; but mistakes were made that limited Kansas farmers' potential impact.

The pageantry of the Alliance was memorable and moving. Long, winding parades of farmers covered the dusty roads on the way to picnics, where the farmers raised their voices in new songs that spoke of the virtues of the agrarian classes. Torchlight parades, picnics, speeches, and lectures were all means of creating solidarity.[8] However, many farmers came to the Alliance already politicized, already knowing what their troubles were. They turned to the Alliance because they expected it to do something concrete, political or economic, about their individual plight. In this chapter, then, we will consider what farmers learned in the Alliance, just how distinctive that body of knowledge was, and whether the Alliance was responsible for politicizing its members. We will also carefully examine the rhetoric of Alliance leaders: what they saw as solutions to the farmers' problems, and whether expectations of leaders and followers were the same.

From Picnics to Politics

Farmers began to mobilize throughout the United States in 1873. This was the era of the Grange and the first concerted attempt by farmers to bring the railroads to heel. In 1873 *The Kansas Farmer,* a newspaper which would serve to publicize the farmers' plight and lobby for just laws and Alliance tickets, pondered the question "What Do Farmers Need?" "The editor noted that "Farmers are an abused class of men," and went on to add that this was a fact "beyond the pale of argument." But he also recognized that two questions had not been satisfactorily answered, "Who is it that is abusing them? What are the ills they complain of?" The problem was a lack of agreement. "One farmer says it is the railroads; another, that it is thieves in office; another, that it is high taxes; a fourth, that there are too many consumers; a fifth thinks there are too many producers; a sixth says it is 'rings'; a seventh, middlemen; the eighth, a lack of capital; the ninth, protection to manufacturers and none to agricultural products; a tenth thinks it is too much grain and not enough cattle, sheep, and hogs." The editor himself felt that the problem was the railroads that "charge too much for transporting our produce." But what to do about this? The answer was "simple and the remedy of easy accomplishment, if farmers desire it. Elect men to office whom you know will legislate rationally in your interests, and who will enforce laws so made."[9] He put out a call for a state convention to be held on March 26, 1873, so that farmers could come together and find a means of communicating with one another.

Several hundred did so and formed the "Farmers Cooperative Association of the State of Kansas," which was "enlarged so as to include Farmers' Unions, Granges, and other similar organizations."[10] Those who met discussed issues of supply and demand, and noted that "All classes, whether they be mechanics, engineers, shoemakers, or boot-blacks, combine and fix the price for their different products or labor." Why not, then, farmers? They were urged to combine at the state and national levels in order to make it possible to set prices and to pass laws that would benefit the farmer. Though they did not urge support for any particular party, they did argue that farmers should support only those candidates who would act on their behalf. They also resolved that the general system of taxation was unjust, that protective tariffs were unnecessary, that bonds and notes should be taxed along with farmers' property, and demanded that "the Legislature . . . pass a law limiting railroad freights and fares to a just and fair sum."[11]

At this stage, farmers seemed to agree that economic conditions could be improved by favorable legislation. They had faith in the system of politics and believed that local legislators and national parties would respond when the farmer made his needs clear. The duty of farmers was to come together to discuss their problems, educate themselves, and present "facts" to politicians. They tried very hard to keep their effort social and nonpartisan.

Jonathan Periam, writing in 1874 at the beginning of the farmers' movement, said that one of the keys to success was that the farmers' clubs must be social. "If we could have Clubs throughout the length and breadth of the land, conducted on true social principles, so that the farmers of each neighborhood might meet together, both men and women, at stated times, especially during the winter months, and discuss matters of general interest (eschewing politics, or course), it would go a great way to elevating the *status* of the fraternity." He suggested that "individual leaders in each neighborhood inaugurate the movement." The clubs would discuss the information gathered by their members. "It is the duty," said Periam, "of every farmer in the land to collect facts." These facts were to deal with ordinary matters, such as how to prune fruit trees, as well as new ideas—how to deal with the problem of low prices for commodities. Periam also suggested that farmers hold debates to enliven their meetings, organize Fourth of July picnics, and engage in cooperative buying and selling. Above all, farmers were to help one another, because "Farmers, from their isolation and peculiar position, have constantly felt the necessity of mutual assistance." Husking bees, and what he referred to as "other frolics of like nature," were strongly recommended.[12]

Farmers' unions, clubs, and the Grange grew very rapidly in 1873 and 1874.[13] In 1873, Kansas farmers did not run an independent ticket, as they did in states such as Illinois under the label of Independent Reform. To the extent that farmers did support an independent ticket, they did so when the Greenbackers came on the political scene in 1874. The Greenback party's platform was essentially a duplicate of that proposed by the farmers in their 1872 convention in Topeka, with an added emphasis on fiat money. They captured few votes in either 1874 or 1876, because the Democrats adopted their plank on the money question, and the Republicans pushed their proposal on an expansion of public lands for homesteaders. It was not until 1878, with a broadening and radicalization of their platform, that the Greenback party received enough votes, about 19 percent, to attract much attention. The fortunes of "farmers'" parties, then, waxed and waned in the 1870s and had no political effect at the beginning of the 1880s.

W. A. Peffer, editor of the *Kansas Farmer,* and later the Populist's United States senator from Kansas, gave his reasons in 1891 why the Grange faded from the scene and was ineffective in acting on the farmers' behalf. In a word, "it lacked discipline." [14] It lacked discipline because, when it was founded, it attracted people from a wide variety of classes. "In New York and Boston, and in other large cities, lawyers, bankers, loan agents, indeed, all classes of professional men, were members of the Grange; in some instances even stock gamblers posed as grangers." In 1874, the Grange met in St. Louis determined to rid themselves of "every person who was not either practically engaged in the work of farming, or was so closely connected with that sort of work as to be [for] all intents and purposes a farmer." The unintended result was that the class base became so narrow, that "the order . . . ceased to be strong, either socially or politically." [15] Though its emphasis on the social was important in drawing farmers together, in getting them to think of themselves as a group of people with common values and economic interests, a failure to move beyond this level doomed the Grange. A movement must transcend the social-psychological conditions that give rise to it, if it is to become a class organization.

The membership of the Grange began a slow downward drift that continued through the 1880s. [16] However, the call for farmers to organize went out again in 1888, after a year of long drought and worsening economic conditions. The Alliance was first heard of in Kansas in 1888, when the Southern Farmers' Alliance was organized in Cowley County. "It was brought to Kansas by the Vincent brothers, publishers of the *Non-Conformist* at Winfield. They went to Texas, were initiated, and returned to organize."[17] This early identification of the Alliance with the South would be used by the Republican political machine in the ensuing years to condemn the organization as a Confederate plot. The southern influence was short-lived, for in the summer of 1888 a State Farmers' Alliance, a part of the Northern Alliance, was formed, and literally all of the Kansas alliances belonged to that organization. The Alliance grew quickly, most of its growth being concentrated in a two-year period, 1890–91. Even more significantly, by 1890 the Alliance had become the People's, or the Populist, party in Kansas. Rapid as this shift to politics was, the resurgence did not begin with that emphasis.

In the *Kansas Farmer,* Peffer publicized the doings of farmer clubs and organizations throughout the state. At the beginning of 1888, he reported that twelve families in Lakin had formed a club. Meetings were held every third Saturday at 10 A.M. in the winter, and at 2 P.M. during the summer. It was the responsibility of the hosts to serve dinner or supper, and it was the responsibility and privilege of the hosts to invite outsiders and introduce them to the club. It cost $1 for a family to join, and "ladies are invited to take an active part. Clubs of this type offer a way to unite the neighborhood, and give a chance to meet with fellow farmers to share experiences and socialize."[18]

In February, B. F. Sinderman wrote to Peffer asking if he would provide farmers with some suggestions on how to organize. Before doing that, Peffer provided the reasons for organization. "Farmers must become better acquainted with one another, with the general business of farming, and with the affairs of the business world, or they will soon become mere hewers of wood and drawers of water for wealthy corporations." Peffer then provided the initial blueprint for organizing, which made it clear that they were to call on friends and neighbors to get started. Interpersonal networks were thus the means of recruitment, and a means of diffusion.

> Let any one person, no matter who, that wants to see a Farmers' Club organized in his neighborhood, call upon a neighbor and they two go to a third and the three talk over the subject and agree upon a general meeting of the neighbors at some convenient place on a certain evening, and then each one agree to inform as many people as he can of the meeting and of the subject. Be sure to invite women and young people of both sexes. Let it be understood that at this first meeting there will be some good music, and see that people are not disappointed. One active young

man or young woman put in charge of that matter will do the necessary work and prepare for at least two songs, one at the beginning, and the other at the end of the meeting.

If the meeting is to be held at a school house or any other public building where there are no conveniences for lighting, let each one of the three persons first above mentioned take with him a lamp and oil, and see that the house is lighted and warmed early—*early,* please, so that when other persons get within range of the building they will see the light in the windows.

Peffer recommended that the people then organize themselves as a formal club and adopt bylaws. Everything should be kept as simple as possible, and they should introduce the "honest, earnest pure spirit of the home" into the organization, just as they should into all political activities. "Let everybody help," he concluded, "cast none aside." [19]

The call to meet, and reports of meetings, would for the next few months emphasize the aspect of sociability. The Stevens County Alliance noted in forming that "Its objects are the development of the resources of the county and promotion of friendship, benevolence, and charity." As July 1889 neared, county alliances began to make plans for a day of celebration and a show of strength. The Delaware Farmers' Alliance of Jefferson County sent a notice to the paper that they would have a "grand celebration. Everybody cordially invited. We expect most of the suballiances of our county to be fully represented, many having promised to come in procession with a grand marshall and banners." [20]

Those gathered at a town's picnic area would first see clouds of dust on the horizon, and then catch a glimpse of the colored banners fluttering in the breeze. Winding into town on wagons loaded with food for a day of celebration, with as many people as could be squeezed on, the farmers came. Those waiting in Augusta, Kansas, saw wagons roll by with banners bearing these mottoes: "United We Stand, Divided We Fall," "In Union, Strength," with a large sheaf of wheat in gold against a blue background, and "Truth Is Our Anchor," with a large gilt anchor in the center. There was also a banner bearing the device "Death to Monopolies," another asking that "God Bless Our Efforts in Liberty, Union and Brotherly Love," and a small one bringing up the rear, "The Farmer Is all." [21]

In other towns, they came in elaborately decorated wagons, and "By their very presence they made it a cheering, good-natured, color-flecked pageant. They rode on hayracks covered with patriotic bunting, and they were dressed in white and in yellow at the ratio of sixteen to one, to symbolize their financial creed."[22] The parades were elaborately structured events, and drew crowds of thousands. In Medicine Lodge, Kansas, the wagons wound their way through town toward the picnic grounds on the far side. "This included about 450 vehicles, and took an hour and five minutes to pass the Post Office. Flags, mottoes, banners, even a 'Bloody Shirt' or two were waved aloft, and the wagons were interspersed with marching singers, bands, a fife and drum corps. There was even a wagonload of children caustically labelled 'overproduction'!"[23]

Before the speaker took the rostrum, there might be a local quartet, or some young woman would have been chosen to sing the "Farmers' Song."

> Oh, the farmer comes to town with his wagon broken down,
>   but the farmer is the man who feeds them all.
> If you'll only look and see, I think you will agree
>   that the farmer is the man who feeds them all.
>
> The farmer is the man, the farmer is the man,
>   Lives on credit till the fall.
> Then they take him by the hand
>   and they lead him from the land,
> And the merchant is the man who gets it all.
>
> When the lawyer hangs around
> While the butcher cuts a pound,
> Oh, the farmer is the man who feeds them all.
> When the preacher and the cook
> Go strolling by the brook,
> Oh, the farmer is the man who feeds them all.
>
> When the banker says he's broke
> And the merchant's up in smoke,
> They forget that it's the farmer
>   feeds them all.
>
> It would put them to the test
> If the farmer took a rest;
> Then they'd know that it's the farmer
>   feeds them all.
>
> The farmer is the man,
> The farmer is the man,

Lives on credit till the fall—
With the interest rate so high
It's a wonder he don't die,
For the mortgage man's the one
　　who gets it all.[24]

During the summer of 1889, farmers continued to come together in the thousands, sometimes in weekend encampments, to
discuss their common plight. "The alliance rally and basket dinner
of Northeast Kansas will be held at Valley Falls, Jefferson County,
Kansas on October 11, 1889. Eminent speakers from abroad already engaged. There will be well-filled baskets, enough to feed a
great multitude (in new and ancient form), so let all the world and
part of Europe be present."[25] The newspaper, whether it was a
local Republican paper or the *Kansas Farmer,* usually commented
on the deportment of those who gathered. "There was the least
obscenity, vulgarity and profanity ever known on such an occasion
in any section I think; and not the least sign of the presence of that
which will intoxicate, came under our notice throughout the entire
day."[26] The positive contribution of women, not just in terms of
being "neatly and appropriately attired," or having properly prepared the picnic site,[27] was noted. Great stock was placed in the fact
that the Alliance was a family affair.

In 1889, the issue of temperance was favorably discussed in the
encampments, and women took a leading role in doing so. "Mr.
Bowman's little girl gave a temperance recitation which was highly
applauded," at a meeting in Osborne County.[28] Had the speech
been given to an ethnic assembly of workers, it is unlikely that any
applause would have been heard. The Kansas State Grange, whose
membership overlapped with that of the Alliance in many communities, issued a report in 1889 on "Woman's Work in the Grange,"
which said that "it was time for women to more fully exemplify a
proper appreciation of the grange, and become something more
than 'ornamental wall-flowers' in its work and deliberations." They
were urged to make haste and engage in self-improvement, because "the hand that rocks the cradle rules the world."[29] This was a
period in our history in which many women became involved in
politics and community affairs in order to "clean up" the world.

The *Kansas Farmer* began to run a column entitled "The Home
Circle," which served as an open advice-column for women. The
paper also reprinted instructive speeches and articles. One, which
had been given at the Shawnee County Farmers' Institute, stressed

the political equality of the sexes and demanded full suffrage. "We now have school suffrage in sixteen States, municipal suffrage in Kansas, and, best of all, *full suffrage* in Wyoming Territory, where, after twenty years' experience, equal franchise has just been submitted to both men and women, and has been incorporated in the new constitution. We wish Kansas would lead off in the same direction." If women had the vote, then the troubles of the nation could be settled by peaceful arbitration. The war between the states would not have broken out. "Could a mother have the casting vote as between war and peaceful arbitration, all national difficulties would be amicably settled. . . . Woman's presence is as much needed in our halls of legislation as in the halls of family residence."[30] The issue of suffrage would, however, prove to be divisive within the Populist party, and would drive a wedge between those committed to full reform and those, such as the Democrats, with whom the Populists fused, who had much narrower goals.

A woman, identifying herself as "Englishwoman," wrote to the "The Home Circle," asking about women becoming members of the Alliance. Said editor Peffer, "I would advise every woman in Kansas that is eligible to join the Alliance. Attend when you can conveniently: take part in the proceedings, if nothing but to ask a question. Hold office in the Union if you can get one, and take every opportunity for self-improvement." She was also told that "The work a Christian woman can do outside of her home is only limited by the ability she has of getting away from home, and only governed by the laws of Christ." A woman writing in response to "Englishwoman" said that she was a member of the Farmers' Alliance and Industrial Union, and urged her to join. "I have never been," she said, "an advocate of woman's rights, but there are rights which some women have not the privilege of enjoying that might tend to elevate and bring them into a common sisterhood, where their influence might be retained for good. But those of us that have these privileges, let us not forget the sacred trust which is imposed on us, and ever stand ready and willing to lend a helping hand, although we are the weaker sex."[31] "Milly," from Barnard, Kansas, also wrote to "Englishwoman," telling her to join, and noting that "Our Alliance, a few weeks ago, passed resolutions favoring woman suffrage and prohibition."[32] The Alliance thus included among its members both women and men who stood for prohibition and suffrage, issues they saw as above politics, although the success of both was to be accomplished *through* politics. Since a number of women and men in the Alliance stood for reform in general, when the Alliance shifted rapidly to politics, and when the Populist party first refused to take a stand on these two issues, the potential for schisms within the nascent organization increased. The movement would be less than a year old, in fact, before people began to experience uneasiness about its political nature.

One of the first political acts of the Alliance was taken in the late summer of 1889. The organization made it clear who could, and who could not, be members. Those who could not were:

1. Merchants, merchant's clerks, or anyone else who owns an interest in a dry goods store, hardware, furniture, drug or other mercantile business, unless said member is selected to take charge of a co-operative farmers' and laborers' union store.

2. No lawyer who has a license to practice in a county, district, or supreme court.

3. No one who owns any stock or shares in a state, National or banking association.[33]

The Alliance saw itself as a group with potential political power, if farmers simply voted together. In October 1889, about 1,500 Alliancemen and their families met in Jefferson County. The paper reported that "They passed and repassed through the principal streets in a long procession—so long that observers had no difficulty in seeing that when farmers move the whole country is in motion. That procession was worth a hundred political conventions. If all those farmers vote solidly against a bad candidate he will be elected to stay at home—sure."[34]

In some locales farmers did band together for purposes of directly influencing the election. This was done by selecting a group of favorably disposed men from the regular parties and urging that farmers vote for them. "Cowley county," the *Kansas Farmer* informed its readers, "has demonstrated that when the farmers get together in earnest they can accomplish any legitimate object. The election last week was highly successful, and the candidates on the People's Ticket were elected. It was not a party success, but a farmers' alliance Victory."[35]

The Cowley County model, as some called it, was to prove infectious. With the beginning of 1890, farmers held celebrations in anticipation of increasing their political power. On a cold January day, "One of the largest and most enthusiastic conventions of the Farmers' Alliance ever held in this county convened at the courthouse in Holton, January 9 for the purpose of electing officers and transaction of business; fully 100 had to stand, after every seat was taken.

The meeting was very harmonious and everybody seemed enthusiastic. The meeting was addressed by Bro. A. W. Hays of Topeka who spoke on 'State Exchange.' The speaker handled the subject well and will result in much good."[36] The Kiowa Alliance met in Brenham, and "exercises included addresses, essays, music, declamations, dinner, etc. Three little girls delivered the address of welcome. Organizer Thompson is doing good work in that part of the state."[37] Over 1,000 gathered in Alton, Kansas, with some traveling twenty miles to be at the meeting. "A long procession was formed, headed by a brass band composed of farmers exclusively, moving through the principal streets," and halting at the town's ice rink.[38] After afternoons of long speeches, farmers and their families often sat down to an oyster supper.

The farmers were moving forward on two simultaneous fronts— the political and economic—though the political seemed to receive the greatest emphasis. As soon as the alliance came into existence, there were attempts to establish economic cooperatives and mutual benefit societies, although these were few in number. In Cheyenne County, members of the Beaver Township Alliance filed the report of their first year's activity (1889) and noted that committees had been formed to deal with the purchase of coal, lumber, implements, general merchandise, and with the sale of grain and cattle. President Cady approvingly commented, "The farmers of the county have come to know each other better, have had their own social entertainments, and have been greatly benefitted financially. They have not been like enemies to each other, but warm friends, ready to help one another. This is one of the best results of the organization. We have not been obliged to pay our merchants $8 and $10 for coal, or $35 to $40 per thousand for lumber."[39] The normal pattern was for farmers to find a local merchant who was willing to be identified as "The Alliance Store," and purchase directly from him at lower prices, or to bulk their purchases for coal or flour, rather than to set up stores of their own. Farmers in St. Francis were told, "Remember that Brenaman's Pioneer store is the headquarters of all alliance people and is where they buy their supplies."[40] They also formed cooperatives to sell their grain and animals, as an announcement in a local paper indicates.

Attention Farmers

The Selden Farmers' Alliance is ready to ship your hogs or grain. All those having anything of the kind to sell must report the same to the selling agent, or at a meeting of the Alliance, and

when enough is reported to make up a car load, a day will be set
for delivery. Those not belonging to the order can put their stock
in by signing an application for membership and file same with a
fee of 50 cents with the agent.

                              G. H. Ottaway, Selling agt.[41]

Such organizations had varying degrees of success, but one co-
operative endeavor that flourished, and lives today as the Farmers'
Insurance Group, was the McPherson County Farmers Fire Relief
Association, which was the "official" insurance company for the
Alliance.

The move to politics was greeted by Alliance supporters with decidedly mixed feelings. The shift would erode the integrity of the
suballiances, and because of this would affect the organizational capacities of the farming class. A. P. Reardon wrote to the *Kansas
Farmer* in the spring of 1890, explaining why the Alliance should
stay out of politics. His words are worth quoting at length.

> Last fall [our alliance] made the error of going into politics, and
> while we had good attendance prior to the election and enthusi-
> astic meetings, since then . . . we were unable to ever get enough
> together to constitute a quorum for the transaction of business,
> and I have recently learned that every subordinate Alliance that
> went into politics in our county lost one or more of its members by
> so doing. Sixteen years ago there were in Jefferson county thirty-
> four subordinate Granges, with just as much enthusiasm then as
> there is in our thirty-five subordinate Alliances of today; their
> aims, objects and purposes were for the improvement of agricul-
> ture and the elevation of the farmer, just as the objects of the Al-
> liance are today. We nominated men of both parties that were
> members of the Grange and elected them to office; we lost their
> influence as members for all time to come, for they never came
> back; and we lost the influence of their friends. Party prejudices
> got into our ranks, dissolving our membership. . . . [W]e should
> in our Alliances, discuss and dissect these national issues until we
> can gain a knowledge that will bring us nearer together; then as
> good Democrats, Republicans, and Prohibitionists attend our pri-
> maries, nominate good men in each party, tell them plainly the
> issue upon which you elect them, give them to understand that
> they are elected as the servants of the people; tell them in a purely
> business manner just what you want and expect of them; in that
> way we can maintain our organization, use it as a source of en-
> lightenment for the membership. . . , wield a power for good and
> command the respect of our fellow citizens.[42]

Reardon was not alone in his view that the move to politics was unwise. The readers of the *Weekly Review* were informed that, "During the meeting of the Farmers' Alliance held at our city on the 23rd, a resolution was offered by some political crank from near Bird City, that the alliance enter the political arena this fall [1890] and work it to the full extent of the order." The editor went so far as to assure townspeople that "A majority of the Alliance people of this county are opposed to taking up politics and making it an issue of the order."[43]

Others, too, recognized the danger of shifting to politics, but argued that the very principles of the Alliance demanded it. That is, people needed to lay party prejudices aside and vote an Alliance ticket. An Allianceman, identifying himself as "C. C.," wrote to the *People's Advocate* asking that people give him their attention. He asked rhetorically, "Can a man be a democrat or a republican and be a farmers alliance man?" His answer was, "I think not." In his view, Alliancemen had important responsibilities.

> We have a code of principles upon which our order is founded and those principles in their very nature are political because it will require the action of our legislative laws to make them of any use to the masses of the people, and they can only reach the law-making mill through the political machinery of the government. And it is the duty of every alliance man to use all the means in his power to crowd those principles forward. Now how is this to be done? By voting the democrat or republican ticket? I say not. . . .[44]

The Alliance did shift to politics, and rapidly. First, on March 5, a convention in Emporia brought together the Farmers' Alliance, the Farmers' Mutual Benefit Association, the Industrial Union, the Grange, and the Knights of Labor. The convention adopted planks from two earlier conventions, held by the Cowley County and Jefferson County Alliances, which among other things called for additional land for homesteading, a tax on bonds, support of labor, a graduated income tax, repeal of the tariff, and legislation controlling monopolies. B. H. Clover, president of the Kansas Farmers' Alliance, issued a call to all alliances in the state, asking that county representatives be sent to a mass meeting to be held in Topeka on March 25. The sessions were held behind closed doors, and newspaper reporters could get their information only from materials handed out by the Alliance. One of the first items of business was passing a resolution declaring against Senator John Ingalls, who "in his eighteen years service for Kansas had never championed any measure which was for the interest of the agricultural [classes]."[45] Many opposed the resolution, claiming rightfully that they had not known it would appear on the agenda, and were not sure that it represented the views of those in their organizations.

Those assembled sent notice to the Congress of the United States that conditions in Kansas were difficult. "The agricultural interests of Kansas are suffering great depression, although corn is stacked at railroad stations like cord-wood."[46] They demanded that Congress allow free trade with Mexico and remove the tariff on silver, which had provoked retaliatory measures by the government of Mexico against Kansas meat and grain.[47] They also passed a set of resolutions similar to those adopted by the Jefferson and Cowley county alliances, and added some of their own: a reduction in the value of mortgages proportionate to a reduction in the value of farm land and prices; direct election of United States senators and railroad commissioners; and low-interest loans to farmers.

Most of the ideas and resolutions advanced at this major organizational meeting centered around the needs of farmers, although overtures were made to laborers. "[W]e most earnestly invite the Knights of Labor, trade unions and trade assemblies of all the incorporated cities of the State to unite with us in helping to secure the demands herein set forth."[48] A proposition was put forward that would have made the Alliance a formal political organization, but it was voted down, and the assembly adopted another resolution in its place: "Resolved, That we will no longer divide on party lines and will only cast our votes for candidates of the people, for the people and by the people."[49] Another convention was called for June 12, 1890, in order to deal with the practical aspects of casting votes for representatives of the people. On that day, ninety delegates arrived in Topeka (forty-one were representatives of the Alliance, seven were from the Grange, twenty-eight were Knights of Labor, ten were from the Farmers' Mutual Benefit Association, and the Single Tax club had four representatives).

A resolution to place a full state and congressional ticket in the field in the fall of 1890 was unanimously adopted and the group formally adopted the name of the People's Party. The Alliance threw its support behind the new organization and disappeared into it; though it continued to exist as a formal organization, it ceased to function as an independent entity.

Neither those in the Alliance, nor opposition newspapers, seemed to make a distinction between the Alliance and the People's party, or the Populists. Picnics now became political rallies featuring speakers and candidates who spoke of the need to vote together. "Sockless" Jerry Simpson, the Populist candidate for Congress from the Seventh District, addressed a large crowd on September 27 in Medicine Lodge. This "was by far the largest gathering ever held in Barber County. Over five hundred teams and a large number of persons on horseback formed in procession and marched through Main street to the beautiful grove on the outskirts of town. . . . Old politicians stood aghast. . . . The People's Party is awake to [the farmers'] interests. Our Alliance is steadily growing; additions nearly every meeting."[50]

It was not just old politicians, however, who stood aghast. Some Alliance members still hoped that they could achieve reform through the Democratic or Republican parties, and even after the Alliance fielded its own slates of candidates, there were still those who claimed it was *not* a political movement—at least not like the regular parties. A man identifying himself only as "R" wrote to the local newspaper in Osborne trying to explain his position as a member of the Alliance. It was the goal of the Alliance to elect people, without regard for their political allegiance, who would then

> use their influence for reform and erase the party corruption. Thus it will not be "Democratic," as the Republican organs claim. A great part of us have as much aversion to the appelation, "Democrat," as the rankest Republican. Many of our elected members are ex-Republicans. Therefore it is not Democratic any more than Republican. We have accepted what is good from both, and rejected what is not good. We have received aid from the Democrats, but they were the more willing for reform from corruption. We will continue to send true principled, patriotic men to legislate, not only in this "off year," but in years to come.[51]

"R" was correct that the ranks of the Alliance contained a number of Republicans, as well as some Democrats. Few, though, seemed to be impressed with the logic that the Alliance was nonpartisan, because in literally every town and county an Alliance ticket directly threatened Republican control. Village newspapers were quick to argue that an Alliance ticket was simply a scheme to slide the Democrats into office, and that the Democrats were secretly, and openly in some cases, supporting the Alliance ticket as a way of embarrassing the Republicans at the polls.

The Alliance is holding conventions all over the eastern part of
the state and in almost every instance they nominate democrats
and denounce Ingalls. We ask our readers what does this mean.
Does it look like the work of democrats or republicans? The
democrats being in the minority have the world to gain and
nothing to lose, and by advocating Alliance or any other measure
that will divide the republican party and put them in control is
what they want.[52]

One dropout from the Alliance wrote to the paper in St. Francis,
saying "The members of that party claim it to be one of reform but
it is simply a party headed by Democratic office-seekers whose sole
objects are the spoils of office and the destruction of the Republican Party." He no longer supported the organization because membership was restricted solely to the farming classes and women and
children were allowed to vote. "They claim to be a party founded
upon the principles of justice between man and man, and while
denying the right of membership to the legal voters of towns and
cities, admit minors and women to membership, giving them the
same voice in nominating candidates as a legal voter."[53] Whether or
not we regard this man's reasons as compelling, they do signal the
fact that the movement was hardly of a piece on the question of politics. The movement gathered together people of amazingly diverse
backgrounds. There were those who were interested in reform in
general and wanted prohibition and suffrage pushed forward at
the same time, as well as those who were interested in specific economic benefits. There were Republicans who had not wanted to
abandon their party, and then saw the Alliance move to politics as
threatening the progressive reform tradition they believed the Republicans stood for. If the movement could have achieved rapid
success, these tensions would have been far less important. Speed
of movement formation and diversity undercut the organization's
potential.

The movement began, then, as an explosion. In a year's time, alliances were formed where none had existed before. Exchanges
were set up in some communities, and people gathered in schoolhouses and one another's homes to discuss their economic plight.
People believed, as Senator Peffer said, that "Agriculture is de-
pressed, labor is profitless, discontent broods like a cloud over the
land. The homes of the people are encumbered by an indebtedness
which it is impossible to pay under existing conditions."[54] People

also came to believe that they could elect politicians who would support the demands of the farmer. Had not the massive rallies, the picnics and caravans drawing literally thousands of people shown them that the farmer was on the move? The pageantry "spoke" of solidarity and the possibility of triumph.

The move to politics occurred at the same time that the organizational structure was evolving. Powerful elites were mobilized against the Alliance and the Populists while the movement was still building and consolidating its strength. Time for learning was also abbreviated, but learning did take place: about solidarity, union, and the strength of the vote. They did not learn how to confront the system beyond the ballot box. They did not learn, or imagine, what they might do if they failed to bring about the changes they so desperately desired. Let us focus in more detail on what was learned at rallies and meetings, and how information was spread.

Learning and the Process of Diffusion

Alliance Lecturers

It is not clear how many lecturers or state-wide organizers there were for the state of Kansas, though the numbers could not have been great. The *Kansas Farmer,* which took pains to keep track of Alliance doings, listed only one state lecturer for 1889–90. We know there were more, because local newspapers reported on their efforts. However, it is clear from newspaper accounts, as well as from the memories of one lecturer, that they were assigned to cover entire congressional districts, which could mean upwards of thirty counties.[55] I could find no indication that there were any lecturers assigned to the western part of the state. The people who did speak there were usually identified with the Populist cause, and addressed large crowds, not individual alliances. Furthermore, their speeches were made after the initial organizing efforts. In short, there may have been no more than three or four men whose job it was to organize local alliances and educate the members to the purposes and goals of the state organization. This suggests that we cannot place great stock in the assumption, as Goodwyn does, that the local alliance served as *the* cradle of democracy, where people gathered to debate complicated issues and develop insurgent strategies.[56]

What, then, did they talk about? We are fortunate to have the actual speeches and suggestions for organizing left by one of the most active of the Alliance lecturers for Kansas, S. M. Scott. Scott's first piece of advice to prospective organizers was that they avoid controversy. The consequence, of course, was that differences in ideology were actively suppressed.

> There is one great mistake that would-be organizers make and that is undertaking to convince the farmers of the benefits of our great order by meeting them in their homes, presenting the subject to them and allowing yourself to be engaged in an argument. There is no such thing as convincing a person against his will, for they will be of the same opinion still. In consequence of this being a universal fact, to be a successful organizer it is strictly necessary to avoid all controversy . . . , to speak the truth at all times, and have the documents to prove what you say.[57]

Scott's speeches were a mix of facts concerning rates of interest, problems with the railroad, and the concentration of wealth in the United States. These talks, which often lasted for more than two hours, were also liberally interspersed with "entertaining" stories designed to illustrate the point under discussion. As to why farmers should not trust politicians, they were offered this homily:

> As a rule, when the time comes for the campaign to open, Mr. Politician steps out and sniffs the political atmosphere. His most fruitful field heretofore has been the farm. He comes to our houses about 10 A.M., where you are in the field. [He] always drives to your house, provided he is sure your little boy is large enough to send for his papa. The first step necessary is to brag on your small boy and make his mama think, if possible, that it is not all put on, but in nine cases out of ten this is his hardest task.
>
> The little boy and girl are soon captured by his "ta tas" and "lu lues," mixed well with high colored candy, with more color than candy. . . . In many cases this could be aptly compared to the donor, more clothes and fine talk than common sense.
>
> This puts me in mind of the story of Pat and the Dutchman. They were traveling together and Pat ran out of food, but August had another square meal of sausage. Pat made a proposition to him that he thought [August] ought to give a poor man a chance for life, and he believed it would be fair for each of them to take hold of the sausage and take a pull. The fellow who got it would be the lucky man. So they got ready to pull and Pat said, "Air you reddy?" August could not say, "yes," but had to say "yaw," so away went his sausage.

Now, the sausage was August's and he had thought, through sympathy, that he would give Pat a chance. But just that moment this favored son of Erin got the chance and took all the poor man had.

The whole trouble had been "lo these many years," that the farmers have had the power to send men who would work for them, but just because these dudes came around and made them some fine promises, we have said "yaw, yaw, yaw," to everything, and we have always lost the sausage. It is time that we look these matters squarely in the face. It is time that there was a school started to educate the people in the science of economical govern-ment. And this is what we have to offer you in the Alliance.[58]

Scott would often go into great detail in his speeches to make a point, drawing, as did other Alliance and Populist speakers, on published government reports or the remarks of elected officials. On the question of railroads, Scott said, "We should study their his-tory with intense interest, not with prejudice and malice, but with a view to justice and equity." He asked his audience a number of rhe-torical questions such as: "Why is it then that the railroads are allowed to issue watered stock?" "Why are they allowed to set rates which ruin the farmer?" "Most emphatically," he said, "our law makers" are to blame. He then presented his listeners with a de-tailed set of figures from the Railroad Commissioners' Report, to make the point that the railroads were making astonishing rates of profit, at the same time the farmer was suffering. He urged people to "view these great questions from a non-partisan standpoint" and demand justice: "That the freight and passenger rates be so ad-justed as to pay a reasonable interest on actual investment or we shall demand that in the near future all transportation be owned and controlled by the government. We would say this only as a way of evening up." He told his audience in Gaylord that he would like to go on and tell them about other problems, but knew they must be growing weary. He reports that there were cries from the house, "go on, go on." At this time he had spoken for one hour and thirty minutes. He went on.

He warmed to the topic of the beef trust, and how it acted in col-lusion with the railroads to cheat the honest yeoman. Again, this was possible because "our law makers have granted to these men power to control the whole cattle industry of this country." He said that he could not give a full report of the "dressed beef combina-tion . . . , only enough to prove the necessity of laying aside all party prejudice and joining hands in the effort to wrest from their grasp the control of the cattle and beef industry of this country." Scott, like his audience, was particularly incensed that the large shippers and packers of beef were able to get rebates from the railroad when the individual farmer could not, so that shippers and packers reaped millions in profits that "belonged" to the farmer.

Scott offered his audience a specific analysis of just how much they had lost:

> During the eleven years spoken of before, of the cattle marketed in Chicago there were 13,973,175 slaughtered in that city. Counting three-fourths of these as shipped east in refrigerator cars, we have 3,493,293 carcasses, at an average of 500 lbs., making 1,746,465,000 lbs. of beef equal to 58,223 carcasses, with a rebate on the same of $15 per car amounts to $873,355. Add to this $15,665,400, which is the amount of the rebate west of Chicago: $16,538,795.85. This is only a fair estimate of the rebate allowed for these firms. Add to this $7.13 profit on a steer. $13,973,175 at $7.13 amounts to the enormous sum of $100,288,737.75; rebate on cars, $14,655,400.85; rebate east on cars, $873,355; results in a net profit of $116,737,533.60 in eleven years.[59]

Even if Scott's listeners did not follow his precise arithmetic, they did follow his general logic: those in office should be voted out and replaced with men who would support the farmers' cause. It seems remarkable that people, even those with stout constitutions, could sit through two and three hours of detailed lecturing on the evils of monopolies. Yet they did so with apparent enthusiasm. Their enthusiasm was no doubt related to their pleasure in hearing lecturers speak, as the politicians never had, about facts and issues they felt they understood, because they were repeated over and over. The Crime of 1873, Crédit Mobilier, a shrinking currency supply which favored bondholders, the concentration of wealth in the hands of the few, a government that operated at the behest of corporations all got their due, and more. Knowledge about these matters must have been felt as power by those who listened. People were also reading the same materials to which lecturers referred: Ignatius Donnelly's *The Golden Bottle* or *Caesar's Column;* Sarah Emery's *Imperialism in America,* or her even more famous *Seven Financial Conspiracies Which have Enslaved the American People;* Emory Allen's *Labor and Capital;* William Hope Harvey's *Coin's Financial School, Coin on Money, Trusts and Imperialism,* or his *Tale of Two Cities;*

Henry Demarest Lloyd's *Man the Social Creator;* or, perhaps Tom Watson's *The People's Party Campaign Book.* There was a great deal of intertextual referencing in these works, and reference to the same issues. Stump speakers often took their themes and facts directly from these materials. Diffusion of information, and the culture of the movement, was spread through meetings, speeches, and the literature that people read. There was, apparently, little opportunity to debate proposed solutions or to formulate a complex ideology. Alliance lecturers and literature would pose Manichean alternatives that left little room for political compromise, and made fusion highly problematic.

The Reform Press

The growth of farmer newspapers was rapid and paralleled the growth in the Alliance. There were at least 150 such newspapers, perhaps as many as 250. Like many editors of the day, farmer editors bought their printing plates from Kansas City, with much of the news already set. A local editor would get a paper laid out with serialized stories and national and state news already in place. The editor would then fill in the blanks with advertisements for local stores, and news and gossip of the town. In the reform newspapers, a column was usually given over to the Alliance. It might be written by the editor or by someone designated by the local alliance. Thus, people got a mix of standard national news and local news that reported specifically on Alliance activities.

There was, as Barr tells us, "a perfect avalanche of literature, most of it in convenient pamphlet form selling for twenty-five to fifty cents each." These pamphlets and newspapers dealt with the "questions of money, poverty, wealth, strikes, panics, monopoly, political graft, railroads, . . . single tax, mortgages, interests . . . from every possible angle, and arrays of figures were produced." "Pamphlets were sold by the tens of thousands. The alliance was sowing the ground of Kansas to dragons' teeth." [60]

One major means of communicating political sentiment in the late nineteenth and early twentieth century was the political cartoon. These cartoons were enormously complicated allegories. Each figure in the cartoon would have a name, and the characters would usually be involved in some activity that was also labeled. In addition, in case people did not get the point, there was an explanatory paragraph at the bottom of the cartoon, clarifying and some-times amplifying the point. Nineteenth-century cartoons differ from today's cartoon partly because we now have a national political language with common symbols, so that political issues can often be reduced to a few words or images. But the complexity of nineteenth-century cartoons was also an end in itself, a style as florid as the style of popular orators. The richness of Alliance and Populist cartoons provides us with a summary of what people felt was important, as well as some understanding of what they learned while reading and reflecting and of their pleasure in that learning.

My examples come from the *Osborne County News*, published in Osborne, Kansas, one of the counties organized by lecturer S. M. Scott. One of the first cartoons to appear in the paper shows a file of male voters approaching a ballot box, so labeled. Each voter carries a piece of paper in his hand, "People's ticket." (Prior to the Australian or secret ballot, people would fill out a ticket or slate ahead of time and then take it to a polling place, deposit it, and have their name checked off.) The voters in this line were tagged: "One of the Old Guard," "Ex-Republican Allianceman," "Southern White Allianceman," "Colored Allianceman," "Knight of Labor," "A.F. of L.," with others following behind with shovels and toolboxes in hand. All were watched over by Liberty and the American Eagle.[61] In unity would lie strenth.

The idea that the Alliance was a nonpartisan political organization was stressed in many cartoons. In one, composed of two panels, voters designated as "independent" are casting their ballots for "The People's Ticket." A footnote says: "The Graduate of the Alliance School Thinks for Himself." In the right-hand panel, a group of men (no women appear in any of the cartoons, with the exception of Liberty, who watches over all) are seated in straight-backed chairs giving their attention to an Alliance "school teacher." He is pointing to a blackboard crowded with these messages: "Tariff: The solution of this question depends on low rates of interest;" "The Silver Question: Silver demonetized by a conspiracy in 1873;" "Gold Basis: The speculator's advantage." The apparent lesson for the day involved the question of fiat money: "15 cents worth of copper or 412 1/2 grains of silver, or any value of anything, plus the *real* (fiat) money of *the people* = $1.00." The paragraph appended to the bottom read, "The alliance is a non-partisan, educational organization, and the result of its course of education is the nation's hope. The party affiliation of its individual members is purely a personal affair, voluntary and free of coercion. In the alliance the majority has no right to dictate political action to the minority, or to commit the organization to any particular party, whether it be republican, democratic, or people's. But every true allianceman will act with the party that endorses its principles and vote for men who are known to be in sympathy with its object."[62] Thus, in one "reading" we get a conspiracy theory, the idea that an educated farmer will vote for the People's ticket, and the view that the federal government must act to right matters.

If the federal government was seen as the ultimate solution, why did farmers fight so vigorously to win local and state races? The answer is simple. People supposed that the state legislature could change the composition of the railroad commission or fix transportation rates. The state legislatures could change laws relating to mortgages, the valuation of property, and what did, and did not, get taxed in the state. But even more importantly, the legislature chose the men who would represent Kansas in the United States Senate. Control of the legislature, then, was essential for controlling the political-economic environment at the national as well as at the local and state levels.

Cartoonists, as well as those who hoped to preserve the integrity of the Alliance and its demands, struggled with the problem of becoming actively involved in politics. One illustration featured two street urchins, one symbolizing the Democratic press and clutching a sheet labeled "slanders and misstatements," the other symbolizing the Republican press and holding a sheet of 'libels." These two miscreants are reading a notice of the upcoming convention in St. Louis in which delegates were urged to not commit the Alliance to any political party. They are flanked by an Allianceman and a Congressman Cox from Tennessee. The Allianceman says, "Why, bless your soul. We never expected the two old parties to endorse our principles. We take this course to satisfy such of our members as yet fondly dream of 'reform within the party.'" The Democratic politician, on the other hand, says, "The Democratic Party is never going to endorse the Ocala Platform, nor will the Republican Party. The People's Party, so called, has already endorsed the Ocala demands, so that resolution is virtually a declaration for the People's Party."

Readers were told in the accompanying explanation that they

must stick to their principles and not be fooled by wily politicians, or those who pretend to be reformers.[63] The so-called reformed politician, or Democrat who promised to deal with the farmers' demands, is portrayed as a reformed drunk, saying, "Please donate a small sum to relieve the needs of a reformed inebriate." An obviously sober, stiff-backed Allianceman answers, "The smell of your breath gives the lie to your words."[64] Little Red Riding Hood, with "Alliance" emblazoned across her apron, is seen approaching a large "Democratic Tiger," snuggled down in what is supposed to be grandmother's bed. "'Oh, Grannie Dear! What Great Big Teeth You've Got!' 'The Better to Eat you up!,' said the Great Brute." The caption tells us that, "In the original story, the tradition runs to the effect that the child's father, a Hardy Farmer, arrived just in time to kill the monster, and save her life."[65] In short, one should not trust those from the regular parties. By implication, fusion with Republicans or Democrats is unthinkable. Yet fusion took place in Kansas, and it is one of the reasons that many Alliancemen left the organization, and/or the People's party.

Cartoons posed the people, represented by Hercules in a loincloth, against the snakes of trusts, watered stock, combines, and usury.[66] The people were also often represented as Liberty, in a diaphanous gown, wooed by the western Republicans, in the guise of a wolf: "Drop that nonsensical silver flirtation and be my bride. You will ruin the G.O.P. and yourself if you persist in your headstrong course. It's only a democratic scheme to bust up us republicans." Or Liberty would be portrayed stalking past the Democratic tiger, who tells her, "Hop into the ring with me, birdie, and quit your 'hollering' for silver. You will ruin the democratic party if you persist in your foolish course. It's only a republican scheme to bust up us democrats."[67] For Alliancemen and Populists, in the South and in the cities, the Democrats were the threat, as the Republicans were in the West and the North. The message, repeated often, was that the people must not divide along regional or party lines. The farmer and city worker were seen standing at a crossroads. One path leads to "Civil liberty. The government of the people, by the people and for the people." The sign which points down this road is headed, "Alliance principles and People's Party. Protection for Labor and People's Party." The other road leads to "Wall Street and the Republican and Democratic Camps." Another sign pointing the way says "Gold Bug Conspiracy, Protectionism and Bayonets, G.O.P.

and D.P."[68] The people would have to choose. They would receive help in making this choice from the Alliance and Populist speakers who covered the state, amplifying and reiterating these themes.

Alliance and Populist Speakers

Alliance speakers and lecturers had significantly different jobs in Kansas. Lecturers traveled from one location to another actually setting up suballiances and county alliances. They were paid for their efforts by receiving a portion of each new member's dues. Alliance speakers, on the other hand, had a task that was primarily inspirational. They addressed large rallies and were not faced with the kind of organizational tasks assigned to lecturers. Speakers, too, were paid, but this was usually a flat fee.

The main speakers for the Alliance and the Populist party in Kansas were Annie L. Diggs, Mary Elizabeth Lease, Lorenzo D. Lewelling, who would become the first Populist governor, William A. Peffer, who would become Senator Peffer after running as a Populist, and Jerry Simpson, United States congressman. Among them, they gave hundreds of speeches in the eastern and central areas of the state. Few ventured into western Kansas. Lease, for example, gave ninety speeches between March 15 and October 28 in 1890, while Peffer gave ninety-three between February 16 and November 1 in the same year.[69] All speakers urged farmers to unite and demanded on their behalf legislation against the railroads and monopolies, as well as an expanded currency. Some of them, Lease for example, understood that silver alone would not solve the farmer's troubles, and that a subtreasury scheme was called for. This was not emphasized by other speakers. As for economic cooperation, that was seldom spoken of, at least as it related to the question of forming Alliance cooperatives. These speakers spoke in biblical terms of a final conflict between the forces of good and evil, and believed they would emerge triumphant, with the legislature controlled by the people and laws that would benefit the true producers of wealth. Their speeches were meant to arouse enthusiasm, not to delineate a clearly articulated strategy. Voting was the way to claim the temple. None of the speakers articulated strategies that could carry the movement beyond defeat, and there were no lessons to be learned, as there had been in the South, from past defeats.

Annie Diggs, whose job it was to vilify the opposition, often quoted establishment politicians to make her points. Standing before an enthusiastic crowd in an Osborne opera house, she said that America was being subjected to a "financial conspiracy." She then quoted Senator Plumb, who had said on the floor of Congress that "financial conspiracies breed great revolutions," and that "unwise and wicked legislation is the cause of the present financial depression." She also quoted Senator Ingalls and attacked his war record: "John J. Ingalls never smelled gunpowder in all his cowardly life. His war record is confined to court marshalling a chicken thief." This was greeted by great shouts and applause from the audience.[70]

Diggs took issue with the notion that the Alliance should open small cooperative stores. She said that while cooperation was valued, "under present conditions failure and disappointment will be the rule." She compared Kansas to England, and said that the reason cooperative endeavors had succeeded in England was because those in the laboring classes lived in close proximity to one another. As for American farmers, "They are scattered as to location, the supervision must be delegated to agents, they cannot convene at brief notice as do the laborers of England, without inconvenience, and more than this they would be at the mercy of the transportation agencies." She asked what would happen if farmers could overcome all of these unfavorable conditions? "There would simply be a withdrawal of a number of farmers from their industry who would become merchants and tradesmen." Who wanted the development of another class of industrialists? And, though she agreed that farmers should seek fair treatment and fair prices, she believed they should not do so at the expense of the village merchant. She urged farmers to do nothing that would split their ranks or alienate potential supporters.

> The contest now on is between the industrial classes, of which the agricultural class is but a section, and the moneyed powers which have been favored by all manner of class legislation for many years. The contest will be severe and there should be no division in the ranks. The small merchant and the smaller grocer are alike with the farmer the victims of an unwholesome concurrence of tendencies. It is no flowery bed of ease to be in the struggle of trade. An overwhelmingly large percent of retail dealers fail in business; this means distress to families such as nothing short of foreclosure on the farm can bring to the farmer's family.[71]

Though Diggs might argue against alienating the small merchant, the fact was they had been excluded from membership in the Alliance. It would not just be small-town merchants, however, who would mobilize against the Alliance and the People's party. Many of the jibes of Populist speakers were aimed at the Republican elite within the state, and against the national "money interests."

Mary Elizabeth Lease was, perhaps, the most masterful of the stump speakers. Referred to as the "People's Joan of Arc," she wove together biblical imagery, data, and insults. According to the *Kansas City Star*, "Her voice is strong, deep, and a pure sweet contralto and no hoarseness or effort attends the performance. Her tall figure was neatly clad in black and white dress trimmed in black velvet and no ornaments of gold or gems lent their barbaric aid to the makeup."[72]

> Ladies and gentlemen: This is a nation of inconsistencies. The Puritans fleeing from oppression became in turn oppressors. We fought England for our liberty and put chains on four million blacks. We wiped out slavery and by our tariff laws and national banks began a system of white wage slavery worse than the first. Wall Street owns the country. It is no longer a government of the people, for the people, by the people, but a government of Wall Street, for Wall Street, and by Wall Street. Great common people of the country are slaves, and monopoly is the master. . . . The parties lie to us and the political speakers mislead us.[73]

She continually emphasized that the nation's wealth had been concentrating in the hands of a few since the Civil War, aided and abetted by the politicians. The implication, of course, was that the Alliance would purify and redeem the political order and bring about a fair distribution of people's efforts.

> Capital (that should be the servant of labor, because labor produces every dollar of capital) has become a tyrannical and avaricious monster. The burdens of the nation are placed upon the toiler. He sows unceasingly, yet reaps no harvest. . . . The old-world vampire, "Land Monopoly," fattens upon the blood of the people. . . . The land, which is the heritage of the people and the source of all wealth, has passed into the hands of a few who toil not, neither do they spin, and the rough-handed, kingly-hearted, sons of toil—chieftans fit to guard the ark and covenant of liberty—are compelled to compromise with the silk-hatted dude and the soft-handed son of idleness, for permission to exist. . . . The wealth created by the common toil of the people has been transferred by legislation into the hands of a few, less than two percent

of the people owning forty-five percent of the wealth of all. . . .
The moral conscience has been quickened, the heart of the nation
aroused, and we are asking, in all earnestness, "with malice toward none and charity for all," which of the political parties can
best solve the problems of the day? And we answer unhesitatingly,
that party which is most in accord with the teaching of Christ and
in harmony with that safeguard of human liberty, [and] the constitution of the United States. . . . The Populists are in line with
the constitution."[74]

In one of her most famous speeches (in the Lease-Brumbaugh
debate held in Concordia, Kansas) she spoke for over two hours
with no apparent loss of attention or enthusiasm on the part of her
audience. She explained, using detailed facts and quotations from
prominent politicians, how capital had triumphed as a result of the
war, and how capital, through manipulation of the currency, managed to control labor. She then took aim at the Republicans' claim
that to loan money to the farmer would be unconstitutional:

> What, the government loan money to farmers? Why not loan it to
> the farmers, friends, as well as to the bankers? Why not loan it to
> the farmers as well as to the railroads of the nation? Why not loan
> it to the farmers on the sub-treasury plan; upon the corn and
> wheat and oats of the country as well as to loan it to the bonded
> whiskey men of this nation upon whiskey? [At this point the
> paper reports that there was considerable applause.] Surely if the
> government can loan money to the bonded whiskey men upon
> corn juice it ought to be willing to loan it upon corn.[75]

The farmer might well wonder why not.

In her speeches, Lease pushed for laws for the common man
rather than for the corporations. She also, unlike the other speakers, argued against free silver, and for the subtreasury scheme,
though her differences with her colleagues were not made explicit
in her talks. She later would brook no compromise on the issue of
fusion. She was emphatically opposed to the Populist party's fusion
with the Democrats in the state. And though she kept her own
counsel on the subject, she was also angry that the Populists failed
to support temperance and suffrage, two important concerns of
hers.[76] (Though they did support suffrage in 1894, at her urging,
she later turned her back on Bryan and the Populists, and, once

again, supported the Republican party and the progressivism of McKinley and Roosevelt.)

Lorenzo Lewelling, who was elected governor of Kansas in 1892 on a fusion ticket of Democrats and Populists, emphasized in his speeches the theme of a common brotherhood of the producing classes. He favored a reduction in the tariff and argued for an expansion of the monetary supply through the free coinage of silver. Lewelling seems to have been the only speaker who understood that the struggle might be a long one, though even he did not develop long-term strategies. In speaking of the people's struggle with the plutocracy, he said it "will demand the most persistent effort."

> It will demand the most unswerving fidelity. It will demand the most dauntless courage. It will demand the most sublime devotion of the best citizens of our commonwealth. It took the plebeians of Rome 200 years to extort their legal and moral rights from the rich and merciless aristocracy. But the people prevailed. . . . Let us emulate the plebeians and with the acceleration of human progress in these modern times we shall achieve greater results.

Like other Alliance and Populist speakers, he made an effort to dissociate the movement from reckless reform. "Oh, no my fellow citizens, the farmers and laborers of this country are not anarchists. They are earnestly seeking to avert the experiences of the old world and subdue the spirit of anarchy with the milk of human kindness."[77]

Lewelling's vision of what Populism had to offer was captured in his inaugural address of 1893. He first noted that the state itself must be morally transformed, for it had produced and sanctioned misery; then a new future would beckon:

> I have a dream of the future. I have an enduring faith in the evolution of human government. And in the beautiful visions of a coming time I behold the abolition of poverty. A time is coming when the withered hand of want shall not be outstretched for charity, when liberty, equality and justice shall have permanent abiding places in this republic.[78]

Some of the Populist politicians would continue to believe that the movement of which they were a part should stand above politics. If it had to become involved in legislative activities, it should be for a short time, only until the American dream and democratic ideals were realized. This millennial optimism is but one reason so little emphasis was placed on the need to form organizations that would act in the long-term interests of the people.

Judge W. A. Peffer, editor of the main Alliance newspaper, and the man who would replace Ingalls as United States senator, hit on all of the standard themes in his speeches and writings. He argued that money had concentrated in the hands of a few because of government legislation, and that a party composed of the people could make things right. However this primary solution for practically all of the problems of farmers and laborers was an expanded currency. His proposals could have been taken directly from the earlier programs of the Greenbackers.

Peffer, also known as "Whiskers" Peffer because of his shaggy, waist-length beard, addressed the citizens of Lyons, Kansas, on June 7, 1890. The paper reported that seats had been arranged in the shade of the courthouse park, and that Peffer's speech had been preceded by a long parade. After families ate their picnic lunches, Peffer spoke for over an hour and half. He began by noting that we had fought a war against slavery, only to find that the farmer and worker were now slaves to capital. He presented a list of seventy persons whose average wealth was claimed to be $37 million, and another thirty whose average wealth was supposed to be $300 thousand. He cited the oft-quoted figure that "sixty thousand people own about one-fifth of the wealth of the nation." The wealth of the average citizen was put at $960. These figures could be changed, he claimed, if the "caucuses of the parties in power," were replaced with representatives of the people. Then, the government could expand the monetary supply and loan money at low interest.[79] If the government controlled the supply of money.

> It would dethrone the money power and make panics impossible. . . .
> It would add twenty-five percent to the value of all commodities in general use,—farm products and manufactured goods more particularly. . . .
> It would aid poor people to obtain homes on public lands. . . .
> It would afford a ready means of relief to farmers who wish to hold their crops a few months; elevator and warehouse receipts would secure money at low rates on short time.[80]

The last point, which was buried in one of Peffer's written works, clearly implied a subtreasury scheme, although expanded money and the free coinage of silver figured prominently in his speeches. It has been suggested that the Alliance was destroyed by the adoption of free silver as a major plank in its platform.[81] When the Alliance movement became the Populist party, its principles were reduced to this one issue, which would not have altered the capitalist system and which would not, as Lease and others recognized, change the monetary system of the United States. (The use of any specie, and one pegged at a fixed ratio, e.g., 16 to 1, would not have led to an expansion in currency and would not have weakened the power of bondholders.) The argument for the free coinage of silver was certainly a simplification of complex monetary arguments, but silver seems, at least in the speeches of these orators, to stand as a symbol: for control by the people, for an expanded monetary supply, for improved prices for agriculture products, for a direct challenge to the established political parties. There is no direct evidence that Kansas farmers found the subtreasury scheme an important issue. The problem became a strategic one: with the movement reduced, symbolically, to this issue, it could be undercut by dominant parties promising to adopt a silver plank. The Populists, then, adopted two strategies in order to achieve political dominance. First, they fused with the Democrats, but this actually weakened their base among farmers. Second, they adopted silver as a strategy but had the issue "stolen" from them by the national Democratic party. Why did they adopt the strategies they did, especially ones that alienated the very class they were supposed to represent? The major problem was that learning was made difficult.

The speeches of Alliance and Populist orators seem to indicate not just that they held different opinions about what might be done, or that they oversimplified issues, but that there was no controlling organization or center of learning. Although there was a great deal of reference to similar texts and facts, at no point is there any clear evidence that movement speakers sat down together and agreed on common themes or strategies. If they had a political strategy at the movement's inception, it was one designed for the short term, just until they had won. It was not a strategy designed to coalesce people for a sustained struggle.

Thus, when Alliancemen and Populists were elected, there was often vacillation over how problems were to be solved, or which ones were the most important. Acting in their short-term interests, they made mistakes. This is not surprising, but it does deserve comment. People do what they think is best in the immediate circumstances;

they act rationally, but rational actions do not always produce the desired long-term outcome—in this case, control by farmers of the political and economic system. The Populist congressman from Kansas, Jerry Simpson, serves as a good example of how difficult it was to translate principles into political payoffs.

Jerry Simpson, sometimes referred to as the "Sockless Socrates" of Kansas, or simply "Sockless" Jerry, was described by one writer as having "a Lincolnesque personality, a homespun political style, a quaint expression, and a folk wit."[82] His "Sockless" sobriquet was earned during a debate when he referred to his Republican opponent's silk socks, and claimed that he had no socks at all.

Simpson had long been involved in reform movements. He first supported the Greenback party, then the ideas of Henry George, Union Labor, the Alliance, and the Populist party. As an Alliance and a Populist leader, he stitched together ideas from all of these groups. He spoke out in favor of land, labor, and transportation (the central demands from the St. Louis platform of the Alliance) and added to these ideas about the need for pensions for Union soldiers and for women's suffrage, though, like Lease, he too would go along with the Populists' decision to avoid the latter issue. His labor sympathies were evident from the fact that he supported restrictive immigration policies and would have banned Oriental and convict labor.[83] These were not, however, issues of importance to the Populist party or to most Kansas farmers.

Karel Bicha, in fact, has labeled Simpson a "Populist without principle," because, once elected, he concentrated his efforts on protectionism and militarism, rather than on issues that would have made a difference to Kansans. It is not my intention to justify Simpson's congressional record, though it is worth pointing out that he, along with other Populists, had a difficult time in gaining legitimacy in the House. He may, in fact, have been trying to curry favor with members of the two major parties, without whose support he had no hope of effecting monetary reform. Contrary to Bicha's claims, he did focus on the issue of silver, and introduced resolutions from Kansas citizens on regulating speculation in farm products and on monopolies, though he never dealt with the issue of the railroads— a favorite Kansas topic. In fact, on the question of the free coinage of silver, and the need for the federal government to control all currency, he was untiring. A reading of the *Congressional Record* for the period 1892–94 makes it clear that he was involved in a major effort to first educate his colleagues in the House as to what a gold standard was doing to farmers and laborers, and then to get them to vote for reform.

The thrust of Simpson's position can be seen in his comments to the House on February 15, 1894:

> The people's interest is to have a currency going out to them with which to do business and to carry on their exchanges at the least possible cost, while the bankers' interest is to have the cost of the currency as large as possible, that cost flowing into their own pockets. . . . We are in the worst financial condition of any country in the world. That is the result of the bankers' system of finance. . . . The attempt to bring this country to a gold basis has made of us a debtor nation, putting 80 percent of the people in bondage to the balance, who are the creditor class. . . . I will oppose any measure that hands over to a private corporation the privilege of issuing the currency of the country, because I believe the moneyed monopoly is the worst of all monopolies in the world.[84]

The problem that Simpson and the Populists would have was that a focus on these limited issues would subject them to the charge by the state's Republican party that they were not attending to the most particular interests of the farming class or the laborers. As we will see in the next chapter, the Kansas Populist party was not a well-organized group, able to articulate a clear set of proposals, translate the ideas of leaders to followers, or provide for the extended debate, discussion, and learning that would have allowed representative leaders to develop within the movement. Learning and the development of strategy were not given enough time in Kansas.

Summary

The first step toward farmer insurgency occurred in Kansas during the 1873–74 period, as the national depression deepened and the skies were darkened by the clouds of grasshoppers that destroyed the crops and hopes of thousands. Farmers were urged to organize to gain political and economic strength, and to overcome the loneliness and isolation of pioneer life. They were told to vote for candidates who would look out for their interests, who would pass legislation controlling the railroads, and who would vote to provide relief in the form of direct economic aid. Many candidates claimed to be the farmer's friend and said that their party would solve his problems. Kansas farmers seemed to have believed in the political system and its institutions. They believed that their calls would be heeded and their way of life protected, if they simply voted for the right people. Their organizational efforts, to the extent that they existed, often took the form of founding farmers' clubs for the purposes of becoming better informed about scientific agriculture, meeting with their friends, and talking about which candidates might best represent them. A strong, centralized organization that could act in their political and economic interests was not formed; and with the close of the decade, and the beginning of the boom in the 1880s, people's interest in farmers' clubs dwindled.

As the economic crises of 1887–89 unfolded, farmers once again mobilized on their own behalf. They began, however, where the movement of 1873–74 left off. That is, they emphasized the need for acting in concert to achieve a commonwealth of producers. They spoke of justice and fair play for all. Their initial efforts were channeled through and shaped by the Farmers' Alliance. It was an overnight phenomenon: in 1888 there were no organizations, but by 1889 the state Alliance was claiming hundreds of new county alliances and suballiances, and thousands of new members. In the summer of 1889, Alliancemen and women met in massive weekend encampments. Farmers would sometimes ride in from miles away, their wagons gaily decorated, with fluttering banners, to pledge their allegiance to a common cause. They saw strength in the physical and psychological unity that was demonstrated at these meetings, and they began to talk about how they could translate this unity into political power for the benefit of all people.

Amidst the pageantry and fellowship were differences that were initially ignored. Some spoke of the need for reform in general: the need to give women the vote, and to enforce the prohibition amendment. Others talked about the need to uphold the principles of the Alliance, and others about the more practical aspects of how to make these principles a reality. There was a vague consensus that the Alliance was a nonpartisan organization, and should stay one. This was because the summer encampments drew together farmers who were Republicans, Democrats, Prohibitionists, former Greenbackers, and members of the Union Labor party. If there was a message that came out of the 1889 meetings it was, "Vote for those who will uphold the farmers' interest." Thus, reform would come from within the dominant parties.

As the farmers began the odyssey toward solving their problems, they would be lured by the siren song of politics. Though they had proclaimed themselves apolitical, they had already taken a major political position in 1889: they had excluded all nonfarmers from the ranks of the Alliance. In many communities, they also returned home from the summer encampments of 1889 to run "farmer" tickets. By the summer of 1890, the Alliance had become the People's party, and Alliance/People's tickets were being pushed across the state, with candidates for all of the major offices, as well as for local ones. Even though the Alliance was now a "party," there were still members who proclaimed that it stood above politics, that its purpose and function was to redeem the old parties, and to purify the legislative halls of corruption. The Alliance called for principles above politics at the same time that it urged farmers of all political parties to vote for its tickets. This was not an act of hypocrisy; many in the Alliance truly believed that what they were doing was "nonpolitical," although they understood that they had to participate in politics in order to achieve their economic and political goals. It is just that they thought these goals were ones shared by all good Americans.

The claim that the Alliance was not political was met with considerable skepticism by the dominant parties, particularly the Republican. Republican party leaders saw the Alliance as a direct threat to their control, and argued that the movement was simply the Democratic party in an unfamiliar set of clothes. The idea that the Alliance might lead to the disintegration of the Republican party was greeted by some of the Alliance faithful with considerable alarm. Almost as soon as the Alliance had become a party, less than a year after its inception, some people left it precisely because it had become a party. There seems to be little evidence that the Kansas Alliance ever possessed the mechanisms for debating and articulating policy. The shift to politics seems to have occurred with little understanding of what it would mean to the membership, or of how such a move could be explained. This was more of a spontaneous uprising than a carefully planned development. It was certainly logical for people to talk about voting for farmers' candidates, and it was reasonable to draw up lists of such candidates. It was just as natural, at least, for most Alliance followers, to vote for those running for office under the label of the People's party. The very logic built into movement principles—that the only way to achieve economic justice is to redeem the political order and vote out legislators who support monopolists—dictated the shift to politics.

Alliance lecturers, such as Scott, made it clear that debate was to be avoided while suballiances were organized. The task of the few lecturers who covered the state was to concentrate on ideas that would get the farmers to see themselves as members of a distinct group who should act together. This effort was aided by the fact that many people read the same books, pamphlets, and newspapers, reiterating the same themes: there was a growing concentration of wealth, monopolies were enriched at the expense of the people, and all of this was made possible by legislators and a federal government that acted at the behest of the "money power." The solution was to vote corrupt politicians out of office.

The major Alliance/Populist speakers such as Annie Diggs, Mary Elizabeth Lease, Lorenzo Lewelling, W. A. Peffer, and Jerry Simpson also posed the people against the trusts. And their solutions, too, were to vote for the people's candidates. Among themselves, however, there were differences as to what the central issues were. Diggs, for example, argued against the formation of economic cooperatives, which never figured prominently in the efforts of the Kansas Alliance. Lease did not see the free coinage of silver as a panacea for the farmers and argued, instead, for the subtreasury scheme of the Southern Alliance. Peffer and Simpson, on the other hand, seemed to believe that free coinage was the solution. All would support the central demands of the St. Louis platform— land, labor, and money—but Simpson would, as a result of his former affiliation with the Greenbackers and Union Labor, argue for restrictive immigration and a prohibition on the use of Chinese and convict labor. These were issues of concern to some Kansas workingmen but not items high on the Kansas farmers' agenda. And, finally, Lease wanted suffrage for women and the enforcement of prohibition, while other Populists argued against being "sidetracked." It is probably reasonable to argue that these speakers reflected differences among Alliance followers, though these differences were not significant at the initial stages of movement formation.

At the inception of the movement, the emphasis was on the creation of a commonwealth of love and charity. Much of the rhetoric of Alliance publications and speakers centered around the issue of what had gone wrong, and what might be done to make it right. The solution was made simple: the people must act in concert to save the democratic experiment. Principles would triumph over narrow class interest and partisan politics. Differences between speakers for the Alliance and farmers were papered over. The rapid shift to politics, however, gave these differences a new importance. Furthermore, people seemed to view their participation in politics as a short-term venture. They believed they would triumph: their speakers, friends, and the numbers present during the summer encampments gave them every reason to assume the solution to their troubles was within reach. No one was thinking about what to do if they failed. In my view, those who allied themselves with the movement did so because they made a rational calculation that it could change the economic and political environment, and, like rational actors, they abandoned the movement when it failed to do so. Movement formation was so rapid, and captured such a diverse group of actors, that the learning necessary for the creation of a counterideology did not take place.

7

Movement Formation, or "I Wore the Wrong Hat"

"I wore the wrong hat." Permission of the Joseph J. Pennell Collection, Kansas Collection, University of Kansas Libraries.

S. M. Scott, the Alliance lecturer for the Seventh Congressional District in Kansas, took for himself the title "Champion Organizer of the Northwest," because he had organized almost ninety alliances in a period of sixty days. However, in one attempt he was unsuccessful, and his list of appointments carried this cryptic message: "March 19, Bloom Valley, Meeting Failed. Used wrong hat." He later explained that he had two outfits that he wore to organizational meetings. He chose either a work shirt and old hat, or a white shirt and bowler. In reference to March 19, he said, "This day I started south thinking I would call a meeting in a German neighborhood. We went to the school house as per appointment. I took my seat next to the wall. I supposed if ever I needed my old cap and common shirt I would need them this evening, on account of our audience." He guessed wrong, however, for the leader of the assembled farmers was quite miffed that the man who had been sent to organize them was unsuitably dressed. According to Scott, the German refused to believe, at least momentarily, that Scott was indeed Scott. "[I]s dis Scott, ve will not have a tinks to do mit you . . . I bin bit mit every ting dot come along dese mony years, and now you bets you don't bites me. . . ." Scott finally gave up and concluded, it was "a mistake to wear the old cap. This was the first and last meeting I ever called for the purpose of organizing which failed."[1]

Other organizers, however, were far less successful than Scott. They saw the task of organizing farmers as a very difficult one. Tom Watson, reflecting on the collapse of the agrarian crusade at the end of the nineteenth century, noted:

> One of the peculiarities of the agricultural situation of all the countries is the lack of unity among the farmers. It is almost impossible to organize them. The reason for this is found in the nature of farm life itself. Agriculture tends to develop individuality. In mechanical pursuits, and in other industries incident to city life, men are inclined to move in groups. The host of urban workers march in companies and battalions. Therefore, organization is easy. But each farm is a separate kingdom, however small. Each farmer develops self-reliance, and glories in being his own boss.[2]

While Watson may have been wrong about the ease with which one could get urban workers to march to the same tune, he was surely right about farmers: keeping them together posed special difficulties. In his view, the farmer who set about the task of organizing other farmers had a job equal to all of the twelve labors of Hercules. The central reason was the farmer's individuality.

> Each farmer is so set in his own way, so full of self-reliance and sense of manly independence that he hates like blazes to make the least surrender for the good of his class. He has always bought as he pleased, and planted what he pleased, and bossed himself generally. Therefore, he cannot bear the idea of bending his stiff neck to the yoke of organization which will, in the least, interfere with that glorious independence of his.

Apparently, he would rather go to industrial Hades, if permitted to take his own time and methods in doing so, than to be
lead into the Promised Land of Prosperity by a Moses who *may*
find it necessary to substitute the will of the class for that of the
individual.[3]

One of the important questions raised by Watson's observations is,
What are the conditions under which people will suppress individualistic interests for those of the larger collective? Are there instances in the growth and transformation of the Kansas Alliance
and Populist party which would suggest that the people acted as a
class, rather than as individuals? Before examining data on the
Kansas Alliance, I shall review some of my central theoretical propo-
sitions relating to movement formation, the development of soli-
dary, and the evolution of strategy.

Theoretical Issues

When people mobilize to protect cherished values, they often look
to friends and neighbors to determine whether they are doing the
right thing. It is the rare individual who will act in the face of community disapproval. On the other hand, should acquaintances take
up a cause, an individual is more likely to join with them than not.
Solidarity, or social networks, then, operate to pull people into social movements. Solidarity is also emergent; it can (and must, if the
organization is to be successful) develop out of participation in the
movement itself. Through interaction, people come to share knowledge about collective goals and purposes.

Closely knit groups, as was suggested, have a democratic structure. That is, there is not a centralized bureaucracy which makes
decisions for the collective; rather, through discussion and action,
people agree on collective goals and how to achieve them. In such
organizations, people are highly motivated precisely because they
know the group is acting in both their individual *and* collective interests. But a closely knit group is usually small, which means that
the group lacks the material resources necessary to bring about
major changes in the political and economic order.

As a movement shifts from a local to a regional or national level,
it might represent a simple accretion of communally based networks, instead of an organization in which there was interaction
among these groups. The movement could remain a collection of
discrete groups if learning did not accompany growth. For a social

movement to maintain a democratic structure as it increased in size, and as it shifted its focus from local to national issues, it would have to ensure the education of its members. This is just what Schwartz and Goodwyn assumed happened with the Alliance; e.g., movement formation was a slow, logical progression.[4] First, farmers came together to deal with their economic plight; they then formed economic cooperatives; only later did they turn to politics. However, the evidence I shall present for Kansas shows a different model. In Kansas, movement formation was rapid, and in some counties there were no economic cooperatives associated with the alliances. Moreover, the creation of the alliances and the shift to politics occurred simultaneously in most cases.

If speed of mobilization is rapid, and the movement is large, then there is a diversity of interest captured in the makeup of the original movement. I believe that the diversity of class interests represented in the composition of the Farmers' Alliance has not received sufficient attention, and that it is this diversity which explains why the movement became bureaucratic, or tended toward oligarchy. Furthermore, it is both diversity of interest, as well as the concomitant lack of motivation to act on behalf of the entire collective, that explains the rapid withering of the movement once goals were not achieved. I am arguing that farmers joined the Alliance and voted for a farmers' ticket precisely because they believed it was in their *individual* interests to do so. Though they may have come into the organization at their neighbors' urgings, the shift to politics occurred so rapidly that they literally did not have time to learn how or why they should operate as a class. The investment represented by membership in the Alliance was simply *not* high, whether measured in psychological or economic terms. An economic sacrifice was not required to join, because they were not forming cooperatives. Casting a vote for a legislator who would supposedly uphold the interests of the farmer was also a low-cost gesture. Therefore, when the results that farmers demanded were not forthcoming, there was little to hold them in the Alliance, or the Populist party. As rational actors, they could pick and choose among the political parties that promised them relief.

Oligarchy, then, was a characteristic of the organization and was brought on because of the speed of mobilization and the rapid growth in organizational size. I have argued that bureaucracy is a logical outcome of organizational size if the goals and values of movement actors are not similar. I have also argued that goals and values cannot be similar unless there are definite mechanisms for learning—for understanding why the group must vote and act in a particular way and why defeat occurred. It follows that there is a tendency toward oligarchy in social movements. Oligarchy is not the exception; it is the rule. However, the tendency toward oligarchy need not be seen in an entirely negative light.

For a group to achieve power or success, large numbers of people must be mobilized over extended periods of time. Success is seldom instantaneous, which means that some group of people, usually a bureaucratic staff, must act in the collective's name during setbacks or lulls in the drive for power. It must find ways to cut through the diversity of interests represented by the membership to find programs and ideas around which the group can rally. It is normally the leadership which develops new strategy and methods of creative escalation, for there must be a sense of going forward. This group also, in the absence of active community-based collectives, must interpret for the membership twists and turns in the movement's fortunes. A centralized bureaucracy is also in a better position than the group as a whole to seize opportunities, to respond to system crises. This is especially true in American society, where success depends on the ability to influence the dominant political parties, either by getting them to make direct concessions in terms of real material resources, or getting them to pass legislation in exchange for votes. It is often votes, then, which serve as the bargaining chips in our political-economic system, and for votes to be effective in this way hundreds of thousands of people must act in concert. The ideal situation, as it relates to oligarchy, is to have a group of people who clearly represent the interests of the collective and who act in the long-term class interests of that collective. But oligarchs can become separated from the people they are supposed to represent, and then confusion is the result. Ideally, leaders will rise from the ranks of the movement, contribute toward the education and motivation of the members, and be poised to act in the interests of the class. The ideal is seldom realized.

From the inception of the Kansas Alliance and Populist party, there were differences among members as well as leaders over the overall goals and purposes of the movement. Was this a general reform movement, one that should aim at changing the moral character of American society, or should it simply focus on limited economic and political reforms for farmers? Could change be affected through the dominant parties, or should farmers and laborers form a new, national party? Those who came to occupy the central leadership positions in the Alliance and Populist party were not of one mind on these questions, and neither were the members. Furthermore, many of the leaders came to the Alliance and Populist party from long careers in third-party movements. One consequence was that these leaders saw a shift to politics as inevitable, and the formation of a new party as appropriate. Obviously, some other members felt this way, too; still others would see it as the worst form of treachery. The point is simply that at the state level the leadership did not come from the ranks of the members, and there were differences from the outset concerning appropriate strategies. The problem was that there was not a well-developed organizational structure for mediating differences of opinion or communicating plans. The movement grew too rapidly for that. I am not suggesting that the leaders of the Alliance and Populist party acted without regard for Kansas farmers. They did what they thought was right; unfortunately, not all members of the movement were in agreement. People's commitment to the movement, then, changed as it unfolded. Let us now examine the process of movement formation.

Micromobilization

Our champion organizer, S. M. Scott, provided a list of his appointments for the year 1889, specifying through whom or how a meeting was called. He had become an organizer on December 14, 1888, after passing an examination for that purpose at the state headquarters of the Alliance in Topeka. He decided to focus his efforts on Osborne and Smith counties, which lay about 150 miles to the west of the state capitol. He wrote to "Brother Peters," who assured him that farmers in the area were enthusiastic and desired to form an alliance. They had, according to his report, been reading Peffer's the *Kansas Farmer*. So, Scott traveled to Willowdale, where, on January 4, 1889, he successfully organized his first suballiance. From there, he traveled to Medicine Creek, and called a meeting upon arrival. Apparently, he had sent ahead a poster, which read:

STOP AND READ

Farmers,
There will be a free lecture on the aims and objects of the Farmers' Alliance and Co-Operative Union of Kansas at the Willowdale School.

Come one, come all over sixteen years of age and hear a lecture you cannot afford to miss. The unparalleled growth of this order warrants us in saying that before another year rolls around we can boast of the strongest organization in America.

Ladies are especially invited. Don't forget the date.

S. M. Scott
Organizer of Farmers' Alliance
Co-Operative Union of Kansas

Scott sent word from one community to another via a farmer who attended an organizational meeting, or went to another town because a person had heard of his efforts and asked him to come. He went to the homes of farmers, the township schoolhouses, and occasionally held a mass meeting, which would further attract people. He went to Pleasant View, Cook Stove, Crystal Plains, White Rock, and several other places as the result of a large meeting he held at Smith Center. Those in attendance from outlying communities to which he had not yet ventured issued invitations. In short, most of Scott's organizing activities were determined by personal networks: people heard of him, or heard of his activities, and then invited him to make a presentation. The person who made the contact would be urged to get in touch with his friends and neighbors to make the meeting a large and friendly one.[5]

Scott was not alone in his efforts. In Cheyenne County, I. N. Taylor, who became a state lecturer at the same time as Scott, was busy mobilizing the farmers. Prior to 1889, there were no Alliance organizations in the state, but by July 17 of that year the Beaver Township Alliance had been formed and, according to the *Cheyenne County Herald*, "This association is becoming very powerful in our county and making their influence felt."[6] With the onset of the new year, several organizations were formed in a very short period of time. On January 17, "the farmers of Logan Township formed a lodge with twenty-nine members and ordered a charter from the State Alliance." The first week of February, Taylor formed two new groups, the Gurney and Lulie Alliances. And, he had organized three more (Red Top, Hackberry, and Prairie View Alliance) in the last week of the month.[7] Throughout the months of January and February, I. N. Taylor was extremely busy, and if the local newspapers were correct, he established new suballiances within almost every township of the county.

If the Kansas Alliance organization was at all similar to that of Texas, men such as Taylor and Scott were paid a fee, which constituted their salary, for forming the groups.[8] In Texas, in 1884 for instance, lecturers/organizers were paid $5.25 for each suballiance they formed. They were paid from fees collected by the Grand State Alliance. In 1882, a member of a suballiance would pay quarterly dues of 30 cents, of which 5 went to the county alliance, and 10 to the suballiance for its own organizing activities, with the remaining 15 cents going to the state Alliance.[9] Under these conditions, i.e., rapid formation of groups, with organizers paid by the number they had formed, it is probable that people had varying degrees of attachment to these organizations and the goals for which they stood. Ease in joining the organization may, in fact, have weakened it in the long run.

An alliance was far easier to form, and less costly to join, than was the Grange. For one dollar, a group of men could start a suballiance, and dues were normally 25 cents a month for men, with fees waived for women. Neither did an alliance member have to pay for regalia, or for the rental of a building, or have to assume the debt on a Grange building.

Scott advised lecturers, "Never give your audience a chance to make remarks, as they have no doubt heard one another time and again, only to be farther apart each time they meet." Basically, an organizer was to have his say, allow people to ask questions, and then provide a recess. "Tell them, however, that this is for the purpose of having them place their names on a paper to become members." He added, "Always have a temporary secretary appointed before recess and tell them that he will be at the desk to receive names." He said that one ought to keep an eye on the secretary, and copy the names he recorded on a separate sheet of paper. As soon as five or seven names were recorded, "announce at once that you have enough names to organize." He intimated that one should never let the audience know how many people had signed up, and that one should take from the secretary individual sign-up sheets just as soon as they had a few names on them. It was also a good idea to say that "it is so much better for them to [sign] then than any time in the future. . . ." The house should then be called to order.

> While this is being done have those come forward and pay their money, providing there are any that have any money to pay. If you have five names who want an order, never let them go with-

out it if they have not one cent to pay. Of course, make it a matter of business never to pay for anyone unless they agree to make you perfectly safe. They will think more of you for this.

When this is done thank those present for their attention, hoping to meet them in the future as alliance brothers and sisters. It will be safe at this time to excuse them. If they seem reluctant about going, you have a pretty good show to get the whole house.

Branch off on some story. Get them in real good humor by telling them you will give them another slice. By this time you can give another invitation to join. If there [are] not very [many] holding back [at] this time, there are nine chances to one you will get them all. Excuse those who have not seen fit to join and proceed at once with your work as per instructions from the state president. Have this work perfectly so that you will give it the same everywhere. The brethren will follow you from place to place and they will notice any little mistake you may make.[10]

According to Scott's accounts, he was quite successful in getting the majority of his audiences to sign up. At Star, "Those from a distance were finally excused and we proceeded with twenty-six new recruits."[11] At Banner, Scott occupied a buggy while the crowd formed a square around it. "I proceeded to tell them what I knew about the order and invited twenty-four of the thirty."[12] He provides us with one of the reasons why those in attendance joined. "The next Monday night we went to Leesburg [and] arrived at the schoolhouse and found several brethren, but a very few were unconverted. . . . Those who had come out were already convinced of the necessity of cooperation. Thirteen members joined."[13] At such meetings, those assembled would choose a president, secretary, and lecturer.[14]

Scott apparently was successful in signing up most of those who came to hear him. He tried to keep dissent to a minimum, and proceeded to move with alacrity through the stages necessary for setting up the organization. There is no indication from his records that he talked to those present about the need for long-term efforts, or about how the local suballiance was to link up with the activities of the state organization. People were simply urged to stick together, and to vote for those who would uphold the farmers' interests. Scott's members, then, probably represented a mix of people: Republicans, Democrats, Prohibitionists, and successful farmers, as well as the unsuccessful. The Alliance also counted among its members those who would not be able to affect the outcome of a statewide or national vote—women and men under the age of twenty-one. (Women could, as of 1887, vote in municipal elections. They did not win full voting rights in Kansas until 1912, eight years before the rest of the nation.)

But who joined the Alliance was determined by more than sheer chance. People were urged to bring their friends and neighbors to organizational meetings, and it appears that this worked. I was able to secure the complete membership listing for an alliance in Jewell County, Kansas (Lone Tree Suballiance), and I plotted on a township map the location of members and nonmembers. First, those who belonged to the Alliance tended to live next to one another, and on roads that led to one another's houses. The men who formed the original Alliance were most likely to recruit their immediate neighbors. There is, of course, nothing startling in this, but it does reveal that social factors played an important role in determining who would, and who would not, join the Alliance in the township of Odessa. Further, there was a tendency for members to cluster around the United Brethren Church, in the northwest quarter of the township. It was, apparently, not only the meeting place for the Alliance but also the central place of worship for many of those in this particular order. Though the records of the United Brethren Church are not complete, there are clear indications that many of the Alliance members were also church members, some playing an important role there. In addition, the Odessa cemetery, located close to the church, records the burial of several members of the Alliance.[15] My materials suggest not only that social networks were important in determining who joined but that, contrary to what others have implied or found, economic factors were not primary within a given county in determining who enlisted in the Alliance cause.[16] Let us look more closely at the social characteristics of the members.

Social Characteristics of Alliance Members

The data on who did and who did not join the Alliance are scant. To my knowledge, the only systematic comparison is Dibbern's, of Alliance and non-Alliance farmers in Marshall County, South Dakota. Dibbern found that 40.3 percent of the farm owners and 51.2 percent of the landless farmers joined the Alliance.[17] What distinguished the joiners from the nonjoiners was that Alliancemen were more commercial and entrepreneurial.[18] Because of their desire

Table 7.1   Comparison of Alliance and Non-Alliance Farmers, Jewell County, 1885

Social characteristics	Alliance Members* (N=26)	Non-Alliance Members (N=26)
Average age	32.54	42.19
Married	88.5%	96.00%
Average household size	4.7	4.7
Occupations		
Farmer	24	26
Carpenter	2	0
Fought in Union army	15.4%	19.2%
Native-born	96%	96%
From Illinois, Ohio, Iowa, or Indiana	92%	92%
Farm status		
Renter	2	1
Owner	24	25
Average farm size (acres)	154	171
Average total farm value	$1,129.20	$1,622.00
	(S=603.63)	(S=1,442.03)
Average wages paid out for farm labor	$47.06	$37.81

Note: Though the membership data on Alliancemen are from 1890–91, the 1885 agricultural census of Kansas is used for purposes of comparison because the U.S. Census records for 1890 have been destroyed.

*The N of 26 represents the total number of Alliancemen for the county, a number drawn from the record book in the possession of the Kansas State Historical Society. Thus, out of the 106 farmers in the county, 24.5% belonged to the Alliance. A random sample of non-Alliance farmers was drawn for purposes of comparison.

for expansion and growth, they often carried greater debt loads than did their non-Alliance neighbors. I found no meaningful distinctions to be made between Alliance and non-Alliance farmers in Kansas, except at the macro or regional level.

Alliances were concentrated in the central sector of the state. Of the known alliances, 72 percent were concentrated there, with only eight percent in the western sector, and 20 percent in the eastern.[19] It was the central sector of the state, as noted earlier, that experienced wide variations in amounts of rainfall and was hardest hit by the cycle of boom and bust. There were counties in which the population turnover exceeded 50 percent between 1880 and 1890.[20] The effect on social institutions was devastating. Lyceums, debating societies, and reading groups were formed, died out, and formed

Table 7.2   Comparison of Alliance and Non-Alliance Farmers for
Haven Township, Reno County, 1890

Social characteristics	Alliance Members	Non-Alliance*
Average age (*N*=33)**	44	45
Married (*N*=33)	92%	92%
Average household size (*N*=33)	6.4	5.1
Occupations: (*N*=33)		
Farmer	28	27
Carpenter	2	3
Other (doctor, blacksmith, merchant)	3	3
Fought in Union Army (*N*=33)	33.3%	12.2%
From Illinois, Ohio, Iowa, or Indiana (*N*=33)	75.7%	72.7%
Farm status (*N*=31).		
Rent	1	5
Own	30	26
Average farm size, acres (*N*=33)	160	160
Average total farm value (*N*=30)	$4,270	$3,269
Average yearly wages paid out for farm labor (*N*=33)	$ 215	$ 184

Source: The information on farmers and nonfarmers comes from the agricultural
census of 1885 for Kansas.

*A random sample of non-Alliance farmers was drawn for purposes of com-
parison. Note: The total number of farmers in Haven Township is 249, of whom
38 were listed as Alliance members. I could not, therefore, find any data for five of
those listed as belonging to the Alliance. The total percentage of farmers in Haven
Township who claimed membership in the Alliance was 15.3 percent.

**This figure represents the number for whom information was available.

once again with new participants. In settings such as this, the Alliance may well have provided stability, and might have been attractive to farmers for noneconomic as well as economic reasons.[21]

I will later show that it is extremely difficult to explain Alliance
membership or voting patterns on a county-by-county basis when
considering only such things as level of indebtedness or number of
tenant farmers.[22] There are no other readily apparent socioeconomic distinctions between members and nonmembers. Using the
membership listing for the Lone Tree suballiance, I compared Alliancemen to their neighbors. As table 7.1 shows, the differences
between these two groups are not readily apparent. We find the
same ownership status, the same approximate value of farms, the

same amount paid out for hired labor, and the same household composition. The only truly noteworthy difference is that Alliance members are almost ten years younger, and, as a result, less likely to be married. I also pieced together the Alliance membership for two other townships in Kansas—Greeley in Sedgwick County, and Haven in Reno. Though the numbers are so small as to make any comparisons questionable, what is, again, most obvious from tables

Table 7.3 Comparison of Alliance and Non-Alliance Farmers for Greeley Township, Sedgwick County, 1890

Social characteristics	Alliance Members	Non-Alliance*
Average age (N=13)**	49	40
Married (N=13)	92%	100%
Average household size (N=13)	4.3	6.4
Occupation: (N=13)		
Farmer	10	12
Carpenter	—	1
Other (merchant, real estate)	3	—
Fought in Union Army (N=13)	38.4%	38.4%
Native born (N=13)	100%	69.2%
Farm status (N=13)		
Rent	0	0
Own	13	13
Average farm size, acres (N=13)	160	160
Average total farm value (N=5)***	$8,152	$4,154
Average yearly wages paid out for farm labor (N=5)****	$ 415	$ 170

Source: The information on farmers and nonfarmers comes from the agricultural census of 1885 for Kansas.

Note: The total number of farmers in Greeley Township was 164, of whom 22 were identified as Alliance members. No data could be found on 9 of those who belonged to the Alliance. The total percentage of farmers in Greeley Township who claimed membership in the Alliance was 13.4%.

*A random sample of non-Alliance farmers was drawn for purposes of comparison.

**This figure represents the number for whom information was available.

***This figure is skewed by virtue of the fact that one owner listed the value of his farm as $20,070.

****This figure, too, is unrepresentative because the same farmer who listed a high value for his farm paid out $1,500 in wages.

7.2 and 7.3 is that there is little apparent difference between these two groups. One cannot conclude, at least on the basis of my findings, that socioeconomic conditions explain Alliance membership. This should suggest that economic reasons alone did not provide the necessary motivation for initial mobilization. Those who flocked to the Alliance spoke about the need to redeem society as a whole. This means, as Malin has suggested, that when people cast their votes for an Alliance ballot in 1890, they were doing so for a complex of reasons: to challenge the entrenched Republican political machine, to protest against railroads and monopolies, to object against changed patterns of work and ways of relating to people.[23] This further implies that one cannot simply count votes to determine what the strength of support among farmers was for the Alliance, because there were undoubtedly nonfarmers interested in the general question of reform who voted for the ticket.

Organizational Size and Strength

Though they did not win the race for governor in 1890, the People's party, running on a separate ticket, polled over 100,000 votes, compared to 115,000 for the Republicans and 71,000 for the Democrats. Clearly the Alliance had been successful in mobilizing votes for this election, though their hold on these voters would prove tenuous. What might the real strength of this movement have been?

Schwartz looked carefully at the claims of Hicks and Woodward that the strength of the Southern Alliance lay in the range of between one and three million members. His calculations revealed, however, "that the maximum size of the Alliance in 1890 was not more than 964,000, less than one-third the Hicks-Woodward maximum. Moreover, it is likely that the Alliance never attained a membership of 900,000."[24] Overall, this still means that the Alliance successfully organized about 25 percent of the men of the rural South and as high as 50 percent of the farmers in Texas. Like Schwartz, we must take a careful look at just how many Alliancemen there really were in a state like Kansas.

One problem, even with Schwartz's lower estimate, is that he takes for his estimates membership figures published by the Alliance, because actual records are not available. It would not have been unusual for the Alliance to inflate membership figures in the hope of showing it was a powerful force to be reckoned with. To show the strength of the movement, Hicks cites two accounts from

Table 7.4   Estimates of Number of Suballiances and Total Membership of the
Kansas Alliance, April 1889–March 1891

	No. of Suballiances	No. of Members
April 1889	700[a]	21,000[f]
August 1889		25,000[g]
December 1889	840[b]	25,000[h]
February 1890	800[c]	24,000[i]
May 1890	2,000[d]	100,000[j]
October 1890	2,886[e]	145,000[k]
March 1891		100,000[l]

Source: Stanley Parsons et al., "The Role of Cooperatives in the Development of
the Movement Culture of Populism," *Journal of American History* 69:881.

[a] Winfield *Non-Conformist*, April 11, 1889.

[b] *Burr Oak Herald*, December 12, 1889, listed as December 2, 1889, by Parsons et al.

[c] Possibly *Burr Oak Herald*, February 6, 1890, which says "over 800 organizations."
This apparently accounts for the "loss" in number of alliances from 840 to 800.

[d] Argersinger (1974:35), who cites Kansas newspapers that in turn cite the
Alliance.

[e] This figure may come from the *Annals of Kansas* (1954:110), which also lists a
membership of 140,000 for this period. No reference given by Parsons contains
this figure.

[f] There is no apparent source for this figure. It appears as though it, as well as the
figures for December 1889, and February, 1890, have been arrived at by assuming an average membership of 30 for each suballiance. (This would not be unreasonable, though no justification or explanation is given.)

[g] Probably McMath (1976:80) who cites data from the secretary of the Kansas
Alliance.

[h] Apparently an estimate, or based on McMath.

[i] Apparently an estimate which assumes 30 members per suballiance.

[j] McMath, citing Alliance data.

[k] *Western Advocate*, November 20, 1890, citing President L. L. Polk of the Alliance.

[l] Apparently an estimate.

Alliance newspapers.[25] One refers to "a procession four miles long
[that] entered town singing and playing, and left the same way,"
and in the small town of Winfield, Kansas, the local paper reported
that "when the head of the procession was under the equator, the
tail was coming around the North Pole." Clearly the size of rallies
was impressive, as was the growth in number of Alliance chapters,
but we need greater specificity.

There is a problem of intertextual referencing that must be dealt
with in determining Alliance strength. Often authors cite several

secondary sources to gain closure on the question of the size of the organization, but when we trace the references in the secondary sources we find they are often to Alliance materials. One of the best efforts to try and determine the number of suballiances in Kansas and the size of their membership is that of Parsons and his colleagues.[26] It is instructive to follow through, step by step, the sources from which Parsons et al. derive the figures presented in table 7.4.

Parsons' first reference is to the April 11, 1889, issue of *The American Nonconformist*. (The actual title is probably the *Winfield Non-Conformist and Kansas Industrial Liberator*.) In a brief, celebratory piece, the estimated membership for Wheels and Alliances in twenty-two states is given. That for Kansas was listed as "over 700 alliances." There is no source listed for the information other than the editor's knowledge, nor is a figure given for membership. Parsons' next reference is a bit more complicated and refers to two different pages in McMath's *Populist Vanguard*.[27] McMath, citing the secretary of the Kansas Alliance, says that in August 1889 there were 25,000 members, and that by the end of 1890 there were 100,000. (The figure of 100,000 is taken by McMath from *Appleton's Annual Cyclopedia*, which got its figure from the secretary of the national Alliance.)[28]

Parsons' next source is given as the *Burr Oak Herald*, December 2, 1889. This is probably a misprint, as there are no data on the Alliance in the December 2 issue of the paper. On December 12, 1889, providing no source, the *Herald* reports, "there are 840 farmer's alliances already organized in Kansas." No information about membership is given. The *Burr Oak Herald* of February 6, 1890, which is also listed as a reference, says, "The Farmer's alliance claims over eight hundred organizations in Kansas." Next is Argersinger, who says that by the late spring of 1890, "the Alliance claimed 100,000 members in nearly 2,000 local suballiances."[29] His references are to three different Kansas newspapers, one of which is the same source, the *Kansas Farmer*, used by McMath. Argersinger makes it clear that he is dealing with the claims of the Alliance, not hard facts.

Parsons' last reference is to the *Western Advocate* of November 27, 1890 and March 5, 1891. (The name changed to the *Mankato Western Advocate* in January of 1891, and I find no information on the Alliance in the March 1891 edition of that paper.) On November 20 (not the 27th as Parsons' footnote indicates), the following statement, which was based on comments made by L. L. Polk, president of the National Farmers' Alliance and Industrial Union, was given. Polk said, "The enthusiasm displayed by the farmers in joining the organization is demonstrated by the fact that in December, 1889, when the Alliance was organized in the state of Kansas, the scattering of alliances contained only 35,000 members, and today it has over 145,000." We can see where Parsons and his colleagues got the figure of 145,000 for October of 1890, but why did they not use Polk's figure of 35,000 for December 1889, instead of substituting 25,000? Nor is it clear just who was a member. Parsons has apparently assumed, and not unreasonably as I will try to demonstrate, that there is an average of 30 members in each suballiance. One must consider, though, just who is a member.

There is one known record book for Kansas, that of the Lone Tree Alliance in Jewell County. This record book is instructive for several reasons. First, it lists as members several young men under the age of twenty-one (one who is only fourteen) and as the manuscript census records reveal, many sons of farmers were listed as members. Second, the Alliance had a women's branch, and the names of a number of women, who were usually, though not necessarily, the wives of farmers, were listed as regular members. If one substracts from the total number of members those who were ineligible to vote in state and national elections, then the total reported membership of the Lone Tree Alliance is cut almost in half. It seems likely, though, that when the Alliance reported its strength it counted all those on the membership roles and not just those who could affect the results of an election. Scott makes it clear from his account that women were counted, though they do not seem to have made up a significant portion of the membership of the alliance for which he was responsible.

Scott indicates that when he formed an alliance at Natoma there were "twenty seven members, [and] twenty six voters." As for Cedar Forks, where he arrived at dusk, "This proved to be the largest organization I ever started, consisting of forty-eight male members. There were three ladies [who] came, but the men frightened them out."[30] Some deflation of the total membership figures is required if we wish to get a better idea of how effective the Alliance was in turning members into voters.

If one took at face value the statement of the president of the Kansas Alliance, B. H. Clover, about the size of the membership (70,000) and number of suballiances (1,800), as of March 1890, there would be an average of 38.8 members for each suballiance.[31]

If one accepted another published figure—"There were 2,886 Alliance organizations with 140,000 members"—then there would be an average of 49.2 members per suballiance.[32] This would include all of those listed on rosters as members. Now, when county conventions were called, each suballiance was entitled to send one representative for each ten members. Because these were often conventions designed to pick election slates, and because they also involved the selection of delegates to the state convention, it is likely that those who attended were males over the age of twenty-one. The *Cheyenne County Rustler* reported, "Dispatch from Anthony. The convention of the Farmers' Alliance met here to nominate a county ticket. Thirty-nine alliances were represented by one hundred and one delegates."[33] If we assume that each delegate represents ten members, then there were 1,010 members in the county, which would result in a figure of 28.5 members for each suballiance. (This figure is similar to that for the Alliance in Odessa reported in table 7.1.)

The data from Scott's accounts of his recruiting activities are somewhat contradictory. At one point he proudly says of a meeting in Osborne, "There were twenty-eight sub-Alliances reported . . . with [a] little over 1100 members." This would yield an average of almost 40 members per suballiance. However, if we deal with the actual figures he gives for each suballiance he formed, the average is only 18.9, which includes everybody.[34]

There are a number of factors that would suggest a figure of approximately 30, and certainly no more, for the average suballiance. First, meetings were held in small, one-room schoolhouses, or sometimes in people's parlors. In addition, by virtue of the fact that meetings tended to be held in the township's schoolhouses, there was a limit to the number of people who could get to and from a late night meeting.[35] As will be recalled, we plotted the membership of all of those who were Alliance members in Odessa Township, and found that practically all Alliance members lived within 2.5 miles of the meeting site—in this case the United Brethren Church. If each farmer owned 160 acres of land, then, theoretically at least, only 72 farmers would be within easy distance of the meeting site. This suggests that if the Alliance was able to mobilize half of all farmers (and the Alliance never successfully captured on its own more than 40 percent of the statewide vote), the maximum meeting size would be 36. Dibbern, who had the complete listing of Alliancemen in one South Dakota county, found the maximum mo-

Table 7.5   Sources of Populist Support in the Election of 1890

	1888	1890		
		Expected	Actual	Loss
Republicans	180,841	160,948	115,024	45,924
Democrats	107,582	95,748	71,357	23,391
Union Labor	36,291			
Alliance/Pop.			108,179	

Source: Hein and Sullivant, *Kansas Votes.*

bilization rate to be 44 percent.[36] In the case of the townships which we report (tables 7.1, 2, 3), the rates of mobilization were 24.5, 13.4, and 15.3 percent. Parsons' figures must be deflated (table 7.4). Even if we accepted the figure of 2,000 suballiances, which comes from an Alliance source, and then assume an average size of 30, the membership is closer to 60,000 than to the 100,000 reported. This makes a difference because there is a supposed relationship between size and power, and we are concerned with the Alliance's ability to translate sheer numbers, whatever they might have been, into political power. Did the Alliance have the power to motivate voters?

In 1890, after a period of intense organizing and numerous speeches by Lease, Diggs, Simpson, and Peffer, the Alliance/Populist ticket polled over 100,000 votes in the race for the governor's office.[37] The Republicans garnered 115,024 votes, and the Democrats 71,357. (Union Labor had been absorbed by the Alliance/Populist ticket.) The total vote had, however, dropped considerably from 1888, a year in which there was a presidential election and 92 percent of the eligible voters went to the polls.[38] If we reduce the expected Republican and Democratic votes to reflect the decline in voter participation (only 72 percent of the eligible voters cast ballots), we can gain a better idea of where the Alliance/Populist Ticket got its support.

It is clear that the Republicans were the big losers between 1888 and 1890. The Alliance/Populist vote, then, represented 45,924 disaffected Republicans, 23,391 Democrats, all of the Union Labor vote, and a few Prohibitionists.[39] The Populists were, as Clanton said, "jubilant."[40] They had swept to victory in local races, and dominated in the House of the state legislature. Republicans maintained complete control (38 to 1) of the Senate, and elected the governor. The Republicans were alarmed by this turn of events, but they remained undaunted. Even though they lost the governorship in 1892, their vote total shot up to 158,075, a gain of 43,051. It was only by fusing with the Democrats that the People's ticket slipped to victory, with 4,000 more votes than the Republicans. I will analyze voting shifts in some detail in the next chapter. The points to make here are that the Alliance's coalition was diverse, and that the coalition was not sufficient to capture control of the state's political apparatus. The pressures for fusion with the Democrats would be great. But as I have repeatedly emphasized, this strategy was not likely to meet with sympathy from those Kansans who saw the Democratic party stained by its link with the Confederacy and contaminated by contact with urban political machines. Furthermore, there were those who cast their lot with the Alliance/Populist movement in 1890 because they saw it as a way of reforming the Republican and Democratic parties, not because they wished to distance themselves permanently from those organizations. As I will show in the next chapter, there is strong evidence to suggest that some Alliance supporters had begun to drift back to the Republican party by 1892. What concerns us here is why fusion would be seen as an appropriate strategy, and whether there were mechanisms for communicating between leaders and followers in the rush to transform the social order. One of the keys to answering these questions lies in an analysis of the evolution of the organization.

Organizational Development

Number of Cooperatives and Members

Schwartz made the case that the Southern Alliance was dominated by the Alliance Exchange, or cooperatives, both in terms of ideology and in terms of real activities.[41] Goodwyn, though he draws almost exclusively on data from Texas, also argues that cooperatives loomed larged in shaping the movement.[42] Parsons, however, directly challenged Goodwyn's assumption that Alliance cooperatives played an important role on the Great Plains.[43] Drawing on a sample from the *Mercantile Agency Reference Book* (which eventually became the Dun and Bradstreet credit reports) for the years 1885, 1887, 1889, and 1891, Parsons and his colleagues found that there were about 18 cooperatives in 1885, 30 in 1887, 32 in 1890, and over 70 in 1891.[44]

Table 7.6   Cooperatives and Farmers' Alliance Organization: Kansas, 1887–1900

Year	No. of Charters	(% of Total)
1887	0	
1888	0	
1889	0	
1890	101	(51.0)
1891	54	(26.3)
1892	19	(9.6)
1893	10	(5.0)
1894	7	(3.5)
1895	9	(4.6)
1896	0	
1897	0	
1898	0	
1899	0	
1900	0	
$N =$	198	

Source: Jennie Small Owen and Kirke Mechem, *The Annals of Kansas, 1886–1910,* vol. 1, pp. 49, 71, 85, 114, 128, 145, 161, 187, 202, 225, 258–59, 282, 298, 331.

Drawing on the articles of incorporation for all of those cooperatives and alliances which were filed with the Kansas secretary of state, as required by law, for the years 1887–1900, I found *no* Alliance cooperatives formed prior to 1890. (These differences between my data and Parsons' may be due to ambiguity in what constitutes a Farmers' Alliance, as opposed to an economic cooperative that had an Alliance affiliation.) In fact, it is not until 1890 that I find *any* Alliance cooperatives, as table 7.6 indicates. If one looks only at 1890 and the year following, 1891, 77 percent of all Alliance cooperatives were formed quite late in the movement's development. This means that one cannot argue that it was the exchanges which educated farmers and then pushed them into political action, because the formation of suballiances, cooperatives, and the move to politics occurred almost simultaneously.

One might well ask at this point whether some other organization served to educate the farmers prior to their involvement in Alliance activities. Did the Alliance, for example, replace the Grange, or draw on the early efforts of that organization? If it did, then one ought to find strong Alliance activity in the same regions where one found strong Grange activity. But the opposite appears to be the case. As can be seen from table 7.7, Grange activity—as defined by

Table 7.7   Pattern of Growth in Granges of the Patrons of Husbandry for Kansas, 1883–1910

Year	No. of Granges	No. of Members
1883	65	3006
1886	39	2040
1889	49	2009
1892	33	2009
1895	36	1927
1897	39	1804
1905	69	4337
1910	116	8256

Source: Adapted from J. Harold Smith, "History of the Grange in Kansas, 1883–1897," pp. 40, 42–43.

number of members—declines precipitiously during the period 1883–97, the biggest drop occurring between 1883 and 1886, while the Alliance did not begin organizing until well into 1889, which means that Alliance activity is not the explanation for a decline in Grange membership. (Probably farmers simply saw the Grange in an entirely different light, because it did not aim at changing their political and economic position.) Even more telling is the fact that Kansas Granges were concentrated in the eastern counties of the state, which is also where the most prosperous farmers lived.[45] The Alliances, on the other hand, were located in the less prosperous, central counties of the state, which had few Granges. Generally, then, Granges represented more prosperous farmers, which may be one reason why, as farmers' prosperity increased in the early 1900s, Grange membership again increased.[46] In any case, it is clear that Alliance cooperatives came late on the scene, and their creation is concentrated in a two-year period, 1890–91, which implies that people's opportunities to learn movement ideology were hindered. Membership activity was also concentrated into a brief time-span.

As table 7.4 indicated, prior to the year 1890 there were few Alliance members, compared to the number for late 1890 and the beginning of 1891. Even though these membership figures are suspect—as they undoubtedly represent the *maximum* numbers—it is evident that the Alliance cooperatives and suballiances were created at the same time.

Can we conclude that organizational development paralleled this spurt? That is, was there also a growth in the organizational complexity of the movement? To answer the question before I present the evidence, it appears that organizational development, particularly at the local level, was attenuated, and the organizational growth that did accompany the movement did not occur until after 1890, when the first Alliance/Populist ticket was fielded. This means that when the Populists fused with the Democrats for the election of 1892, the Populists were not relying on their own well-developed system for communicating between leaders and followers.

Organizational Complexity

W. F. Rightmire, who played a major role in the reform movements of Kansas, explained how the Alliance became the People's party. Speaking of the St. Louis meeting of 1892, which created the National People's party, he noted that, "A platform embodying all of the planks of the Alliance platform, and a plank presented by the ex-Confederate delegates from Texas demanding a service pension for every honorably discharged Union soldier, was unanimously adopted." In his view, this meant that people's interest in the Alliance was simply transfered to the new party. "The Alliance organizations perished through the neglect of their members to attend upon the meetings of their suballiances."[47] Indeed, they perished, but this may have had less to do with a wholesale transfer of allegiance than it did with the fact that the Alliance organization was never well developed at the local level. Besides, once the People's party was created, many of those who had initially supported the Alliance once again returned to the Republican fold.

Rightmire's account of how and by whom the Alliance was created is intriguing. It was never challenged by others involved in the movement. Basically, Rightmire argued that, from its birth, the Kansas Alliance was under the control of leaders who were interested in the broad question of reform, and not just legislation for farmers. Furthermore, he said, "The Kansas organization was planted, by a few persons, for a distinct political purpose."[48] Supposedly, in 1888, members of a disbanded secret society, the Videttes, and Union Labor representatives met in Wichita to form a new organization, the State Reform Association, of which he was the president. The group decided that in order to achieve their political goals they would select some existing organization for their own purposes. "[I]t was ascertained that the declarations of the secret Farmers' Alliance of the South embodied every tenet of the platform on which the Union Labor party had waged its campaign that year."[49] They sent three members of their executive committee to Texas, and they returned home to Cowley County, to found the first Alliance in Kansas. His description of what they did next is worth quoting at length:

> The members of this executive committee [of the State Reform Association] constituted themselves recruiting officers to enlist organizers to spread the organization over the state. Selecting, if possible, some Republican farmer in each county who had been honored by elections to two terms in the state house of representatives, and then retired, and who had become dissatisfied because his ambition and self-esteemed qualifications of statesmanship received no further recognition at the hands of the nominating conventions of his party, he was engaged to "organize the farmers of his county in the order, so that if the order should conclude to take political action, he, as the founder of the order in his county, could have any place he desired as the reward for his faithful services at the hands of his brothers in the order."[50]

Few men so chosen failed to answer the call, according to Rightmire, and the work of the organization progressed rapidly.

A call was then issued for a meeting to be held in November 1889, to perfect a state organization of the Alliance. Rightmire and his forces sent out a call "through the Vidette channels for all of its former members to be present" at this organizing meeting. "This call was obeyed, the program of the Reform Association adopted in detail, and its choice elected as the officers of the state Alliance."[51] It was not just the Reform Association's platform that was accepted, for all of the elected officers of the state Alliance were officers in the Reform Association. The first president of the state Alliance, Benjamin H. Clover of Cowley County, was an old Greenbacker. "He placed himself under the guidance of the members of the executive committee of the Reform Association, and actions advised by its president . . . always received his approval and hearty cooperation."[52]

There is surely some puffery in Rightmire's account of both his own and his organization's control over the fortunes of the Alliance. However, his remarks, coupled with Scott's on how the local suballiances were established, do indicate that there was apparently little discussion within local suballiances about such issues as whether or not to become a political party, and certainly few

mechanisms for communicating between the local community organizations and those at the state level. Also, both writers make the
important point that the state organization was established prior to
most of the local suballiances, and as a result set the agenda for the
local organizations. There was an organizational split, then, between local groups, which might have had their own agendas, and
the state-level organization, which seemed bent on capturing political power instead of educating members. Such aims for state-level
organizations need not have been mutually exclusive. The point is
that leaders within the movement seemed to believe that early and
direct involvement in politics was more important than building
strong grass-roots suballiances which would be in a position to com-
municate member desires and translate leader strategy. The spontaneous nature of the movement created the structural flaw. There
was no real organizational means for reconciling diverse interests
or for dealing with failure. Furthermore, the state-level leaders did
not come out of the Alliance movement itself; often they were
people who had been deeply involved in prior reform movements
and carried these agendas with them into the Alliance and Populist
party. The problem of oligarchy seems to have been a real one for
Kansans.

Oligarchy

One way to gain some perspective on whether Alliance leaders
were an elite, or oligarchic, group, is to compare them to the people
they represented. The organizer, Scott, listed all of those who were
elected as either president, secretary, or lecturer of the suballiances
in Osborne County. I compared these Alliance leaders with a sample
of farmers from the same county. As table 7.8 shows, there are few
differences between these two groups. There was a very slight tendency for Alliance leaders to cultivate more acres, to have smaller
families, and to be exclusively involved in farming.

If suballiance leaders were to be representative of their local
communities, what about those at the next level of leadership, i.e.,
those who were elected to the Kansas House of Representatives as
a result of the great mobilization in 1890? As table 7.9 shows, a significant number (47 percent) of Alliancemen elected to the Kansas
House of Representatives had some sort of previous political experience, which would suggest that they had been in their communities for some time. In addition, in an age when not many could

Table 7.8   Comparison of the Suballiance Leaders of Osborne County with
Other Farmers, 1890

	Alliance Leaders[a] (N=34)	Other Farmers[b] (N=133)
Average age	46	44.5
Household size	4.44	5.13
Total acres	276	260
Acres cultivated	131	104
Value of land	$2,458	$2,340
Value of implements	$ 77	$ 53
Occupation:		
Farmer[c]	94%	89%
Nonfarmer[d]	6%	11%
Nativity		
U.S. Native	97%	81%
Foreign-born	3%	19%

Source: The list of Alliance leaders—defined as president, secretary, and/or
lecturer of a suballiance—comes from S. M. Scott, *The Champion Organizer of the
Northwest.*

[a] Scott lists 128 Alliance leaders for the twenty-two townships of Osborne County.
   Using the 1895 agricultural census for Kansas and the 1900 plat books for
   Osborne County, I was able to identify and secure complete information for 34 of
   these leaders.
[b] The 1895 agricultural census for Kansas was used to draw a 10 percent sample
   of farmers from each of the townships in which I found Alliance leaders.
[c] None of those Alliance leaders who listed their occupation as farmer were
   tenants, and only 5 out of the 119 "other farmers" were listed as tenants.
[d] Only two Alliance leaders listed an occupation other than farmer: engineer and
   farmer/laborer.

boast of any education at all, 34 percent of these men reported that
they had some college education. Nor were all of them simple
farmers; only 35.6 percent claimed farming as their sole occupation, while another 10 percent had previously been teachers or lawyers. They were native-born Americans, rather than immigrants
(87 percent) and the majority (58.5 percent) had been Republicans. In some ways, this group stood above their fellow Kansans,
though their position was hardly as lofty as that of their Republican
brethren.

One way to gain some perspective on the extent to which Alliance
legislators were an elite, is to compare them to a group of Republican legislators. As can be seen from table 7.10, 97 percent of the
Republican legislators report having completed at least a grade-

school education, and 45 percent had some college. Even more significant is the fact that only 3 percent of the Republicans failed to provide information on their educational backgrounds, where the figure for Alliance/Populists is 43 percent. Although 47 percent of Alliance-Populist legislators had some previous political experi-

Table 7.9   Populist Members of the Kansas House of Representatives, 1891

1. Level of education ($N=98$)	
Common or grade school education	23%
Some college education	34%
No information	43%
2. Previous political experience ($N=98$)	
Some previous experience (county assessor, treasurer or auditor; delegate to congressional district or county convention; clerk or trustee of township, probate judge, etc.)	47%
No previous experience	31%
No information	21%
3. Occupations ($N=98$)	
Farmer	35.6%
Farmer/rancher/fee-lot owner	13.3%
Farmer and some other occupation (carpenter, contractor, real estate, mining)	11.2%
Teacher and farmer	10.2%
Became a farmer (was a teacher, builder, doctor, lawyer, railroad worker)	10.2%
Other (clergy, newspaper editor, salesman, lawyer)	7.1%
No information	12.2%
4. Nativity ($N=91$)	
Foreign-born	13.0%
Native-born	87.0%
5. Previous political affiliation ($N=106$)*	
Republican	58.5%
Democrat	17.9%
Greenback, Union Labor, or Union	10.4%
Prohibition	3.8%
Radical Republican	1.9%
Independent	4.7%
No information	2.8%
6. Age ($N=86$)	
Average age	48.2
Median age	46.5

*There is some double-reporting in this section, as some legislators, for instance, indicated they were previously a Republican and a Prohibitionist. Those who listed Greenback, and Union Labor, or Union were not double-counted but put into the same category. Source: W. W. Admire, *Admire's Political and Legislative Hand-Book for Kansas* (Topeka, Kansas: George W. Crane and Company, 1891), pp. 413–59.

Table 7.10   Republican Members of the Kansas House of Representatives, 1895

1. Level of Education ($N=91$)	
Common or grade school education	52%
Some college education	45%
No information	3%
2. Previous political experience ($N=91$)	
Some previous experience (county assessor, treasurer, auditor; delegate to conventions, etc.)	89%
No previous experience	11%
3. Occupation ($N=91$)	
Farmer	13%
Farmer/rancher/feed-lot owner	11%
Farmer and some other occupation (e.g., construction worker)	14%
Teacher and farmer	2%
Became a farmer	7%
Other	52%
Lawyer 18 (N)	
Merchant 7	
Editor 4	
Grain dealer 3	
Construction 3	
Physician 3	
Goverment position 3	
Banker 2	
Manufacturer 2	
Miner 2	
4. Nativity ($N=91$)	
Foreign-born	13%
Native-born	87%
5. Previous political affiliation ($N=91$)*	
Republican	97%
Greenback/Prohibition	1%
Populist	1%
Alliance	1%
6. Age of legislators ($N=89$)	
Average age	45.5
Median age	46.0

Source: George W. Crane, *Handbook of the Kansas Legislature, 1895* (Topeka, Kansas: Crane, 1894).

ence, this figure is far from the 89 percent for Republican legislators. Few Republicans (13 percent) listed their occupations as farmers, the majority (52 percent) of them holding such positions as lawyer, merchant, or doctor. Only two Republican legislators claimed any previous affiliation with the Populists or the Alliance. Clearly this group of Republican legislators was not a group of downtrodden insurgents.

We can conclude, then, that with the first wave of Alliance organizing activity, those elected to office were not a group significantly different from the people they represented. This situation would change somewhat as the decade progressed. Clanton, in an attempt to show that Populists were not the uneducated hayseeds that they were made out to be at the time, compared Populist and Republican legislators between 1891 and 1899, to show how well educated the Populists were. He also shows that, in 1891, 21 percent of the Populists were nonfarmers, whereas this figure grows to almost 35 percent by 1899. (Clanton's figure for 1891 differs from mine, because I define a "farmer" as someone whose sole occupation is farming. See the figures for 7.9.) He also develops a select list of Populist leaders in 1890 and 1896 and compares the two groups. Again, we find the group as a whole becoming more elite, and we also find that leaders differ significantly from Populist legislators. They tended to be better educated, to be nonfarmers, and to come out of a reform tradition. In 1890, for example, 65 percent of the Populist leaders were nonfarmers, a third of them had college degrees, and 41 percent of them had been formerly affiliated with a third party. By comparison, in 1896, 71 percent were nonfarmers, almost half were college graduates, and 44 percent had former third-party ties.[53] Those who held positions of leadership within the Alliance/Populist movement deserve closer scrutiny.

The Leadership

Those who came forward to speak on behalf of the farmer in 1890, and who ran for office, had various careers.[54] Prior to 1888, Mary Elizabeth Lease had lectured extensively on behalf of suffrage and temperance, as well as for the Irish National League. In 1888, she joined the ranks of the Union Labor party, and moved easily from there to the Populists in 1890. Her speeches, as we have seen, show that she was interested in broad-based social reform. Annie Diggs was a member of the Liberal League in Kansas, which championed sexual freedom for women and freedom from male oppression. She worked for the Women's Christian Temperance Movement and lectured for the Unitarians prior to her involvement in the Alliance. She argued for the moral improvement of individuals as a way of achieving progress for the human race.

The candidate for Congress from the Third Congressional District in 1890 was Ben Clover, former Republican, president of the state Alliance, and supporter of the doctrines of Union Labor. John

Davis, candidate in the fifth district, had been involved in reform movements for almost twenty years. John Grant Otis, running in the fourth district on the Alliance ticket, had left the Republican party in the mid-seventies to work, first, as a Granger, then as a Greenbacker and prohibitionist. One of the few farmers on the ticket, William Baker, from the sixth district, was a rancher and former Republican. He would be the only Populist elected to three terms in Congress, and was successful, according to Clanton, because he spoke to the needs of a diverse class base. "He spoke primarily from experience, emphasizing the particular difficulties that confronted farmers, ranchers, and small businessmen; it was the kind of approach that many people of the northwestern counties could well understand."[55]

"Sockless" Jerry Simpson, candidate from the volatile seventh district, revealed his Greenback or Union Labor sympathies in his campaign speeches, and continued to push for these ideas after his election to the U.S. House of Representatives. (He had run on the Independent ticket [a Greenback organization] for the state legislature in 1886.) After a Populist sweep of the House in the state legislature—they controlled 96 of the 125 seats—they were in a position to select William Peffer, editor of the *Farmer* as United States senator. Peffer was, however, opposed by many of those previously identified with third-party movements. They saw him as a conservative and Republican. In fact, Peffer would later move away from the Populist party, believing it had betrayed the interests of the farmers, and was found in 1898 running for governor on the Prohibition Party ticket. The leadership, then, was removed by both temperament and occupation from the farmers they represented.

Before the excitement over the election had cooled, there were calls to organize for 1892. Leaders of the Populists recognized that they could not exercise their mandate unless they controlled both houses of the legislature and elected the governor. Little of legislative note was accomplished then, in the session of 1891, because the Republicans had veto power. One issue did consume the energies of the Populist party; it was to prove particularly divisive. Leaders such as Diggs believed that the state should now pass a suffrage amendment. She was bitterly disappointed when Elder, the Populist speaker of the House, came out strongly against it. Though the House ultimately voted to support suffrage, the bill was defeated by the Senate. Prohibition, too, would be debated, and some Populists came out for resubmission, which some saw as a conces-

sion to the "whiskey interests." In any event, a difference in interests among leaders as well as members of the House eroded the
ability of the new organization to act in concert. The lack of coordi-
nation and agreement also suggests, of course, a lack of centralized
organization.

Beginning in 1891, there was a concerted attempt on the part of
those who had been involved in third-party movements, particularly Union Reform, to use the Kansas movement as the vehicle for
the creation of a national third party.[56] (This was finally achieved
in 1892, when the National People's party, dominated by former
Greenbackers, was formed.) Some felt that the creation of a separate party would consolidate the gains of 1890. Michael Senn, a former Greenbacker and Union Labor man, elected to the Kansas
House on the Alliance/Populist ticket in 1890, emphasized the need
to educate ignorant voters: "We must not forget that a large proportion of the people are ignorant, as well as biased by prejudice."
It was necessary to emancipate them from party prejudice if the
Populists were to retain their loyalty in forthcoming elections. He
noted that an individual "may have voted with us in the last election
on the principle that a change would be desirable, or because he is
inspired by the enthusiasm of the move; but in order to insure the
permanent support of this class, we must educate [them] until they
personally see the evils and injustice of the present monopoly system, as well as the justice, fairness and beneficent results of our
proposed remedies."[57] Not all Alliance members, however, wanted
to be educated to the benefits of a third party. Frank McGrath,
Clover's replacement as president of the state Alliance in 1890, was
less than enthusiastic about dissolving the Alliance into the Populist
party. As plans were being made in 1891 to call a convention in Cincinnati for the formation of a national party, McGrath made it clear
that he felt the Alliance should stay "in the middle of the road" and
avoid all political entanglements. The uproar from those who demanded a third party which would push for reforms for workers as
well as farmers was deafening. McGrath did not stand for reelection as state president and was replaced in October 1891 by someone thoroughly committed to a third party.

Leaders, then, felt that the way to achieve reform was through
the creation of a new, national party; they also assumed that this
new party would help to educate people to the evils of the day.
They took it for granted that those in the Alliance would willingly
shift their allegiance to the new organization because it would stand

for the ideals cherished by all right-thinking people. Whether the abrupt shift to a third party was a strategic mistake has been debated extensively.[58] It suffices to say here that *some* leaders saw no other alternatives. In 1891, for example, the Republicans staged a massive counteroffensive, and though their campaigns were based primarily on invective and assertions that they alone were the party of principle, they swept to victory in the local elections. (In some communities, Democrats and Republicans also came together to defeat Populist candidates.) Leaders were faced, then, with the problem of mobilizing for the 1892 elections, in which they wished, finally, to capture political power at all levels of state government. They had no other way of affecting actual laws and the social and economic conditions of Kansans. They had seen in the elections of 1891 that it was hard to mount a winning campaign based on the simple principles of justice and equality. Coalitions looked particularly attractive. J. B. Coons, a Populist state representative, said that the party was faced with a choice. It could either proceed with its educational and missionary work, or it could form a coalition with other parties. The only way to assure victory, he said, was through the formation of a fighting alliance. "The Republican Party has no desire or need of assistance from us in any shape. Besides, modern Republicanism is what we are fighting." He called for an alliance with the Democrats.[59]

The decision to fuse with the Democrats was not an easy one, and did not occur without a struggle among the leadership. Most of those clearly identified with the Alliance, and with the cause of the farmers, were opposed to fusion, as were those more "radical" elements of the leadership. Mary Lease declared in 1892, "there can be *no fusion*. We take warning from the past. The history of every fusion party has been destruction. Let us utterly and absolutely refuse to 'compromise with evil,' and go forth with the . . . hope of complete victory."[60] A growing number of Democrats, however, saw advantages to fusion, and there is strong evidence that they made initiatives to the Populist leadership. Eventually, under the leadership of John W. Briedenthal, chairman of the state's Populist party, a united slate was offered to the voters of Kansas. Democrats showed great flexibility when it came to joining with the Alliance, partly because the Republicans had decided in 1892 that the best way to beat the Populists was to offer a more "radical" program. As a consequence, the Republican state convention adopted a platform that included, among other things, a suffrage plank, some-

The bounty that the Kansas farmer raised often found no buyers. Here Mr. James Foreman sits with a load of corn in Junction City. Permission of the Joseph J. Pennell Collection, Kansas Collection of the University of Kansas Libraries.

thing that was anathema to many Democrats. Some Kansas voters were able to accept the state Republican party's shift to the left, but the majority cast their ballots for the fusion ticket. It must be noted, however, that even though the Populists captured six of the eight congressional seats and elected the governor, the total Republican vote had increased by more than 40,000 since 1890, and the combined Democratic/Populist vote had fallen by 15,000. Finally, as we will see, it was not at all clear that the "First People's Party Government on Earth," actually controlled the state legislature.

In the election of 1892, General Weaver captured the state's electoral votes for the national Populist ticket. As a presidential candidate he had attracted slightly over one million, or 9 percent, of the total votes. Though this was an impressive number, and he may have been responsible for putting Cleveland in the White House, it indicates that the national party and the state party had very different organizational strengths. At the national level, the party was disorganized, and its agenda was not as well focused as it was in Kansas. Many Kansas voters still saw the Populist party as an outgrowth of the Alliance, and supported it for that reason. The call for laborers and farmers to vote together at the national level to achieve reform was not successful, because they had not been mobilized on that basis, and because in other areas laborers and farmers saw it to be in their immediate interest to vote for one of the established parties. Workers were sometimes warned away from the Populist party by leaders who claimed that it was a party of farmers and small capitalists, and as such could not possibly represent their interests. There was no obvious bridge, then, between the state party and the national party; and there were no well-developed links that existed downwards, toward those embedded in the sub-alliances. The problem that the Populist party in Kansas faced, then, was the need to explain such things as the strategy of fusion to its members; however, the party had not nourished the organizational structures which would have made that possible.

The Populist party began the process of disintegration in Kansas almost as soon as it had achieved its first triumph. This was due in no small part to both the machinations and simple mistakes of the leadership. Movement members were often cast in the role of observers, and called on only when they were needed at the polling booth. The problems of the leadership, though, were considerable. Governor Lewelling was faced with what the press described as a "legislative war." The Populists controlled the Senate and were able to organize it with ease. In the House, however, the Republicans held sixty-five apparently valid certificates of election, while the Populists held fifty-eight, and the Democrats two. The result was that for a time there were two Houses, meeting separately, in each of which legislators and assistant sergeants-at-arms carried weapons. A compromise was engineered by Governor Lewelling, in which the Populists conceded to the Republicans. If Lewelling and state party chairman Briedenthal were guilty of mistakes, it was because of their desire "to maintain an effective Populist-Democratic coalition." As Clanton noted, "Both men were realistic enough to know that Democratic support was crucial if the party were to maintain itself in power. As part of that strategy, the administration and the Populist organization under Briedenthal's leadership tried to steer clear of the prohibition and woman suffrage issues, while at the same time attempting to strengthen the coalition by rewarding their Democratic supporters in the distribution of political offices."[61] Concessions to the Democrats opened the Populists to the charge that they were just another "patronage" party, and the failure initially to take a position on suffrage cost them part of the reform vote, just as it generated more dissension within the party.

Mary Lease would prove particularly difficult for the Populists.

Lewelling had appointed her chairman of the state board of charities, which gave her control over a number of patronage positions. When Lewelling tried to appoint Democrats who had helped the fusion ticket, Lease objected loudly and publicly. She was quoted in the press as referring to Lewelling as a "weak man" without a "backbone."[62] When Lewelling tried to remove her from her position, she countered with a bitter tirade, accusing him of trying to push her aside because she objected to his "office trading" and because she stood firm on the question of women's suffrage.[63] She further claimed the administration was in league with gamblers and in the pay of railroad companies. Lewelling would claim, not unjustifiably, that Lease was working behind the scenes with the Republicans to destroy the new party.[64] Nevertheless, the Lease revolt gave encouragement to other antifusion forces among the Populists.

As the campaign of 1894 neared, a combination of events threatened the delicate Democratic-Populist fusion in Kansas. First, there were many Populists who were opposed to the national candidacy of Cleveland, whose policies they saw as likely to worsen economic conditions. This led Populist leaders such as Lease and Diggs to propose more radical solutions to the farmers' plight, which distanced them from the Democrats who believed that the way to best the Republicans was to pose as another conservative party, one supporting business. Finally, the advocacy of a suffrage plank threatened the coalition between Populists and Democrats. At the party's convention in 1894, those who stood for moral reform were triumphant. Suffrage was adopted as an official plank within the Populist party, and Kansas voters were offered a chance to vote their consciences on the subject. Suffrage was turned down by a vote of 130,139 to 95,302, with the bulk of the opposition coming from working-class communities.[65] The Populists' stand on progressive issues cost them the election.

The conclusion that many seemed to draw from the Populists' defeat was the same as that drawn by the Republicans. In his inaugural address, the new Republican governor, Morrill, said there was little evidence that the people of Kansas had demanded any radical changes. He averred that one could not legislate the laws of the marketplace. All the legislature could and should do was to assist the invisible hand of the market in promoting commerce and industry.[66] Some of the Populist leaders also concluded that fundamental reforms would have to wait.

In place of these reforms they offered the free coinage of silver in the ratio of 16 to 1, not because they believed it was the panacea to all of the country's problems but because silver offered a way to maintain a bridge between themselves and the Democrats, without whom they could not win. It also allowed them to present themselves as interested in the same issues as the Republicans: progress and prosperity. The Populists came to assert that free coinage would lead to the expansion of business, and everyone—laborer, farmer, capitalist—would benefit. William Allen White of the *Emporia Gazette* wondered in print what had become of the old Alliance and the principles for which it stood. As for the Populists trying to rally people around the issue of free silver, he said, "There is nothing of the old alliance Puritan cry for reform in these men. Has not the whole fabric of the reform party, its heroes, its aspirations, its ambitions, its lofty desires fallen among thieves on the Jericho road?" "Where," he asked, "is the Alliance man with the courage to deny that his party that was going to reform the world has made a 'deal' that would have been hissed out of the first farmer's convention in the year of our Lord 1890?"[67] Where, indeed, was the Alliance man?

As we will see in the next chapter, a substantial proportion of the rural population continued to vote for a fusion ticket through 1896. However, many farmers cast their vote for the Republican party. Similarly, after 1890, an increasing part of the vote for the Populist party came from the middle-class areas of the towns, although the bulk of this vote would go to the Republicans. Under the influence of the Alliance, the party had argued for land, labor reform, cheaper transportation costs, and reduced rates of interest for the farmers. As a political party, it had two strategies. Initially, it concentrated on moral reforms—temperance and suffrage— which were sometimes of more interest to the leadership than they were to farmers or laborers. Then, particularly after the Populists were rousted by the Republicans in 1894, they became more of a middle-class business party. The leadership group which remained took pains to distance itself from radical reform. How much the party had changed is revealed by the fate of Senator Peffer. When the fusion ticket once again triumphed in 1896, it had the opportunity to select a U.S. senator. Peffer, for a variety of reasons, had almost no support among the Populists, though he had stood in the front ranks of the Alliance. An editorial in the Le Roy, Kansas, *Reporter,* explained why Peffer should not be selected. "Strong men have come to the front. Weak men have dropped to the rear. Black

sheep have been weeded out. Crazy and impracticable notions have
been dropped out of the profession and faith. Victory and a sense
of responsibility have made the party more conservative and imbued its leaders with broader and deeper ideas of statesmanship."[68]

Even though Bryan carried Kansas in 1896, and the Populists
elected Leedy governor, the epitaph of the farmers' movement was
already being written. In December of 1896, the *Marion Record*
reported:

> Six years ago the Farmers' Alliance had a membership of one
> hundred thousand in Kansas. Now it has less than one thousand.
> Every county had one or more Alliances. Now, the order is dead
> in all but six counties, and in these maintains an existence at a
> "poor dying rate." On its tombstone might well be written, "died
> of demagogism," or better, "killed by demagogues."[69]

Though we can understand this anger, the movement did not die
as a result of demagogues but came to grief because there never
was a strong community-based organization. Those men who were
elected to office in the first burst of enthusiasm found it extremely
difficult to get reelected, partly because of the Republican party's
attempts to regain control, and partly because they were fighting
a national mood which brooked few challenges to a probusiness
mentality. In addition, ethnic, religious, and economic differences
which could be ignored in the initial phase of organizing reasserted
themselves as the party and its candidates struggled from election
to election. It was neither corruption nor betrayal that spelled the
end of farmers' dreams; it was the lack of organizational discipline
and a leadership distanced from its grass-roots base. In the next
chapter I will explore more fully who supported the Alliance, and
then the Populist party, and the ways in which the Republican party
was able to derail the movement through the technique of selective
endorsement.

Summary

Those men and women who answered the call of the Alliance had a
complex agenda. They wanted an improvement in their economic
conditions and they wanted a reformed society. They longed for a
democratic society in which their labor would be rewarded and
their way of life esteemed, a country in which Jeffersonian values
would triumph over Hamiltonian ones. The solution appeared at

hand and simple to execute. They would join alliances, these alliances would select farmer legislators, who would lead the way into
the promised land.

Things were not to be that easy, for the very outpouring of their
sentiments, the strength they showed in their numbers, mobilized
the Republican party against them. As people grew battle-weary,
and changes were not forthcoming, their ties to the Alliance began
to weaken. The leaders of the Alliance and then the Populist party
tried to develop new strategies and agendas which would assure
them of a victory at the polls. Yet at each stage, the movement did
not become more solidified, nor did people become more determined. The opposite happened. Farmers were intelligent and strategic actors, and began to choose other options and parties that
promised to bring relief.

The main reasons why farmers failed to form themselves into a
class movement, and instead drifted away to other parties, had to
do with the speed of movement formation, and the problem of oligarchy. From its inception, the ranks of the Alliance were composed
of a diverse mix of people. Within specific counties, there was little to
distinguish the Alliance farmer from his non-Alliance counterpart
in Kansas. The only factor which seemed to explain who did, and
who did not, join the Alliance was propinquity: whether or not
people lived close to one another. In forming the suballiances, the
lecturers took care to temper dissent, which meant that there were
few opportunities provided to discuss strategy. In fact, the only
strategy which seemed to be offered upon formation of the suballiances was to decide whom to vote for. There is little evidence
that the formation of economic cooperatives, or economic cooperation, was a goal of Kansas farmers.

The Kansas alliances were formed almost overnight; most of
them came into existence between the spring of 1889 and the first
few months of 1890. The growth in economic cooperatives, of
which there appeared to be fewer than an average of one per
county, was also concentrated into this time period. By the summer
of 1890, however, the Kansas Populist party was a reality, and a
campaign was mounted to elect a separate slate of candidates,
rather than to work through the established parties, as many of
those who had signed up for the suballiances assumed would happen. The shift, then, from diffuse social movement to political
party was extremely rapid. This meant that there was little time for
people within the Alliance to learn movement dogma or discipline,

or how to continue to act as a cohesive body for an extended period of time.

The rush to politics had mixed results. In 1890, the farmers shocked the state Republican party by capturing a number of the local races as well as control of the House in the state legislature. Most of the Populist gain had come at the expense of the Republican party, a gain that did much to ensure a determined counterattack by the Republicans. It was also clear to leaders within the Populist party that control of the House alone was not sufficient to bring about changes in the economic and social circumstances of Kansas farmers. New strategies would have to be developed if they were to win in 1892. However, these strategies seem not to have been drawn from discussion among members, or adequately explained to members. There was great dissension over them, and one consequence was that even though the Populist ticket won in 1892, there was a substantial increase in the number of those voting Republican.

The leaders of the Alliance, the suballiances, and the Populist party represented different interests. At the local, suballiance level, those chosen to serve as president, treasurer, and secretary did not differ socially or economically from their neighbors. This leadership level did not, however, link up with the state level in any significant fashion. The leadership of the state Alliance was composed of a large number of former third-party men and women, although there was a small group committed almost exclusively to the farmers' cause and to working within the dominant parties to bring about change. When the Alliance was taken wholesale into the Populist party, the former third-party leaders came to dominate, and they set the agenda for what would happen in 1892, although even here there were differences of opinion among this group that would lead to ruptures within the organization in the ensuing years. The primary strategy agreed on for 1892 was fusion with the Democrats. Fusion was dangerous. In the first place, it drove from the party those members of the Alliance who believed that one could be both a member of the Alliance and a Democrat, or a Republican, or a Prohibitionist. Fusion was simply too bitter a pill for some to swallow. It also meant that those former third-party members, such as Lease, Diggs, and Otis, who stood for the moral reform of the entire society, had to suppress their desires to push for women's suffrage and temperance. This they did in 1892, but they would not be stilled in 1894, and managed to get the Populist party to support a suffrage plank. This had the partially intended consequence of driving a wedge between Democrats and Populists, but it also attracted some reform-minded voters to the Populists in 1894, because the Republicans did not take a stand on the issue.

The lessons drawn from the Populist defeat in 1894 differed for the leadership and for those who had voted for the Populist ticket. As the decade progressed, the leadership moved further from the original base of the movement and the issues that had motivated farmers to join the Alliance. For farmers, it was not clear how the Populist program addressed the issues of land, money, and transportation, because there were no organizational mechanisms for communicating the decisions of the leadership. Populist leaders apparently decided that 1894 showed that Kansans did not want a radical platform, and thus the party was transformed into one that each day more and more resembled the Republican party. Populist leaders began to argue that they, too, were for economic prosperity, and that their candidates were not wild-eyed fanatics but sensible businessmen and successful farmers. Silver was adopted, then, for two reasons. It allowed the Populists to argue that free coinage would expand all business activity, and it allowed them to deal with the sticky issue of fusion. By concentrating on silver, rather than moral reform, they intended to lessen the risk of alienating traditional, urban Democratic voters. The Populist message was not, however, one that most Kansas workers found compelling, as we will see shortly.

As the changes that Kansas farmers demanded seemed to recede from their grasp, they began to switch their allegiances, many casting their votes for the Republicans. The original speed of movement formation, coupled with a lack of organizational structure and discipline, meant that as the years passed other factors, which cross-cut class ties, reemerged. That is, people's original political affiliations, their ethnicity, their religion, the very things they had mobilized to protect, pulled them away from the Populist party.[70] A leadership isolated from its base made decisions intended to assure the party's success. Unfortunately, they made many strategic errors. Not, I would hasten to add, because they were corrupt politicians, but because they were reformers fighting a battle that had more fronts than they knew of, and because they imagined they had more resources and more commitment on the part of followers than they really had.

8
To the Polls

Democrats and Populists joined forces in 1896 to defeat their Republican opponents. In this parade down the main street of Leavenworth, Kansas, they have covered their wagons with flags to demonstrate their patriotism. Courtesy Kansas Collection of the University of Kansas Libraries.

In 1888, Kansas was proclaimed the banner state of the Republican party, for it had given President Harrison a greater margin of victory than any other state in the nation; the Republicans dominated all of the local and state races. Two years later, the elections of 1890 were referred to as "a Waterloo to the Republican party."[1] Republicans were shocked by the fact that close to 40 percent of the voters cast their lot that year with the Populists. In 1892, after fusing with the Democrats, the Populists captured the governor's office. The Republicans fought back, won many local races in 1894, and also placed their man in the governor's mansion. The Populists emerged as the winning party in 1896, but by 1898 the Republicans had reestablished their control and did not relinquish it, except for very brief intervals, in the decades that followed. The Populists, who were once so full of hope, and who once seemed on the verge of being the dominant power in the state, failed to hold the loyalty of voters. The Republicans were ultimately successful. The reason for this change had as much to do with local circumstances as with national conditions.

By my estimate, the Farmer's Alliance had about 60,000 members in 1890. The total vote for the Alliance/Populist ticket for governor in that year was 108,000, which means that the Alliance attracted a number of nonmembers to its cause. There were, of course, Alliance members who did not cast their ballots for the new party, choosing to stay, instead, with one more familiar to them. The majority of those who voted the Alliance/Populist ticket in 1890 came primarily from the rural areas of Kansas, and in particular from the middle third of the state—the area characterized by erratic rainfall, rapid population growth, and a high level of indebtedness. Throughout the decade of 1890–1900, the Populists would continue to attract the bulk of their support from rural areas, their base narrowing to those farmers living at the margins and those living in the middle third of the state. The more prosperous deserted to Republican ranks.

Kansas elections continued to be close. In 1892, for example, 4,000 votes out of the 325,000 cast would have been enough to throw the victory from the Populists to the Republicans.[2] This meant, first, that when the Populists were out of power the Republicans, in order to maintain power, "had" to make concessions to those represented by the Populists. In a probusiness, pro-Republican state, a Republican legislature adopted a number of laws designed to control monopolies (such as the railroad), to protect farmers against foreclosures by the banks, and to limit the worst abuses of workers by employers. Moreover, while the Populists were in power and pushing their agenda, it often could not be effected without the support or cooperation of Republicans.[3] The Republicans also practiced what I have called selective endorsement, as a means of trying to undercut the strength of the third party. They would adopt a particularly crucial plank from the platform of the People's party, such as a call for radical railroad legislation, as a way of telling Kansas farmers that they were willing to minister to their concerns. And when they were in power, they actually worked to pass such legislation.

Contradictions were therefore embedded in state policy because of the action of the political parties, which served as a mechanism for channeling and mitigating class conflict. Even the most "radical" of the parties, the Populists, represented diverse constituencies and had to try to craft political platforms that would represent the various interests of those constituencies. No party drew its support from homogeneous class groupings. For example, Germans who had not fought in the Civil War were likely to vote Democratic, while those who had were more likely to vote for the Republicans. Germans were good Democrats until fusion occurred; in 1894, when the Populists came out strongly for suffrage, the Germans veered away, returning to the fold only when that issue had been dropped. In short, cultural factors were to prove as important as economic issues in determining who voted for which party. This suggests that the organizational bases necessary for the creation and sustenance of class consciousness were attenuated.

The concerns of Kansas voters were undoubtedly unique, but they were also shaped by national issues. The class system of Kansas (including the organization and consciousness of classes) was structured by the larger political economy. For example, the state's Republicans were not helped when Harrison, prior to the election of 1890, vetoed a bill that would have provided for a more flexible currency. In order to gain greater support among farmers, the local Republican party would have preferred that the national party not support high tariffs, since many farmers saw these as responsible for the rise in the cost of basic necessities and a decrease in the price of farm products. The margin of victory between Democrats and Republicans was razor thin between 1876 and 1892, and each party was eager to seize on issues that could move voters into its column. The Democrats were quick to appropriate the silver issue, as one way of attracting rural votes, though they also tried to make it attractive to those in the cities by arguing that it would enhance the prosperity of the entire nation.

Fusion, for example, was not an easy pill for Kansans to swallow during Cleveland's second term (1892–96), when he presided over a major economic collapse. This is one reason why the Republicans won the state's gubernatorial election in 1894. The state's Republican party was clearly prosilver, yet it was constrained from offering this as a clear plank in its platform, or doing anything meaningful about it, because the national party favored the gold standard.

I am not suggesting that national platforms or local policies were always carefully crafted by astute politicians in order to get elected. In fact, the evidence suggests that there was a great deal of random experimentation and fumbling about. Concessions were first made to the agrarian and working classes, both in and outside of Kansas, because there was no well-consolidated business class demanding a particular law or policy in its interest. There was agreement at only one level: the ideological. Both Democrats and Republicans, and ultimately the Populist leadership, would argue that they stood for the general principles of growth and prosperity—in fact, for business. So all parties eventually fostered the interests of industrialists and financiers, not because this was a cohesive group making specific demands, but because so many groups—reformers, businessmen, workers—subscribed to the notion that the solution to America's problems was a Hamiltonian one. The garden would be subdivided and factories would be built, while the federal government provided the means. As the decade progressed, the concerns of the farmer receded further and further into the background.

An examination of the major elections within Kansas reveals several important trends, as they relate to the formation of a class for itself. As emphasized in the previous chapter, the Alliance capitalized on three decades of dissent within the state. An agenda had been building, but one which brought together people whose goals were quite diverse. The strength of the movement was rooted in the Alliance, but when the Populist party was created this organization was allowed to wither. Nothing, at least at the grass-roots level, arose to take its place. A gap slowly opened between those who acted and spoke in the name of reform, and those who were supposed to be represented. Mechanisms for debating policy and educating the membership were limited. This meant that, when a strategy such as a fusion was adopted, it was difficult to quell dissent among supporters. Even worse, when a policy failed to produce the desired results, and Populist leaders such as Lease assigned blame to other leaders, the seeds of disorder were sown. The Populist leadership found it difficult to explain its legislative failures, because the leaders did not externalize blame and because they did not have an organizational structure which would allow them to portray the struggle in which they were involved in clear class terms. As the decade progressed, the Populist party came to argue for its legitimacy on the same basis as the other parties, i.e., that it would create prosperity. One of the many ironies of this conflict, then, was that although it was born out of a class struggle, and although a party was formed as a result of class conflict and competition for power, the party system and the organizational structure of the Populist party acted to defuse class conflict and to inhibit the formation of class consciousness.

Elections Prior to 1890

Even before the national economic upheavals of 1873, Kansas served as the birthplace of third-party movements. In 1872, the Liberal Republicans, after endorsing Horace Greeley's doomed bid for the presidency, fused with the Democrats and captured 34 percent of the votes for governor. The state platform of the Liberal Republicans opposed monopolies and appealed to the sentiments of the agricultural sector. They said, "[W]e are opposed to all further grants of land to railroads or other corporations. The public domain should be held sacred to actual settlers." They passed a resolution that "labor is the true wealth of the State, and . . . we demand such legislation as will protect and build up the agricultural and industrial interests of our whole state."[4] Those Democrats who were opposed to fusion, and a few more renegade Republicans, formed the "Straight-Out Democratic Party," and also held a convention. They were "opposed to the policy practiced by the Government for the last ten years in giving away the public domain to rich conspirators, and declare that the public land belongs to the homeless."[5] All third-party platforms addressed themselves to the growing concentration of wealth; Kansans were particularly interested in questions of land and finance.

The first organized effort by farmers to influence politics occurred in 1873, when a Farmer's State Convention was held. (The convention took place in March, two months before the financial panic of 1873 began.) Their demands were very specific. They noted that the basis of all material prosperity was agriculture, proposed a reduction in railroad rates, and argued that the public domain should be for actual settlers and "in no contingency be allowed to fall into the hands of the railroad monopolies and landsharks." The convention also argued that the tariff laws were unjust and asked that the bondholders be required to pay taxes on their gains. Farmers also questioned the wisdom of continuing to pass municipal bonds, saying they "will inevitably bring bankruptcy and ruin on the people." Finally, they demanded a national currency.[6] They did not, however, enter the field as a third party, but expected the Democrats and/or Republicans to heed their cries for reform.

In what was to become a standard maneuver, the 1874 Republican party platform included a number of planks dealing with the concerns of the farmer. "We favor such legislation as will make national banking free to all . . . uniform taxation. . . . and the public lands of the United States [should] be sacredly held for the use and benefit of the actual settlers, and we condemn and disapprove of any further grants to the railroad or other corporations." Like the national party, they argued for specie payments or the gold standard. As a party of moral reform within the state, they reminded the voters of the evils of drink: "drunkenness is one of the greatest curses of modern society, demoralizing everything it touches, imposing fearful burdens of taxation upon the people."[7]

At this stage, both the dominant parties and third parties tended to train their guns on Washington. Calls for legislation concerning tariffs, banking, or land all required the action of Congress. In Kansas voters always tended to expect necessary transformations to occur through established political processes. A third party which did not have a good chance of affecting national legislation could have few long-term claims on people's loyalties. Much third-party voting must be understood as a simple protest vote: against the policies of the dominant parties, and against the actions of politicians within the state.

The Independent Reform party, which became the Greenback party, entered the Kansas scene in 1876. Its convention, which brought together Grangers, Democrats, and reform-minded Republicans, addressed itself to issues important to the farmer and laboring man. It argued for a federal paper currency, decried the "Crime of 1873" (eventually a favorite theme of the Populists), and demanded an income tax "upon all incomes of over fifteen hundred dollars per annum." It also called for an improvement in the state's educational system and excoriated the current administration for having misspent monies on "fraudulent school bonds."[8] The Democrat platform was almost a carbon copy of that of the Reform party.[9] Meanwhile, the Republicans made no reference in their platform to railroads, monopolies, or the needs of farmers, turning their attention almost exclusively to national issues.[10] Yet Kansans seemed content to cast their lot with the state Republican party; in the race for governor, the Reform party secured only 5 percent of the vote, with those votes coming primarily from the Democratic column. Republicans enjoyed the same 57 percent majority they did in 1874.

The Republicans did not ignore the growing interest of Kansans in the Greenback platform. In 1878, the state Republican party came out for an expansion of currency (though holding to the gold standard), if it would not depreciate in value (an interesting compromise between their need to appeal to Kansans while maintaining their loyalty to the national party). They also supported the free coinage of silver and railroad legislation, and they condemned laws that granted monopolies more power.[11] At this point, the Democrats seemed to take most of their cues from the national party, and for the first time came down strongly against tariffs, accusing the Republicans of sponsoring "class legislation."[12]

The Greenback platform of 1878 was clearly the most "radical" of all the party platforms, though the Greenbackers would take care, given the national ideological climate, to declare themselves "unusually hostile to any form of Communism which seeks to appropriate the wealth of others without giving an equivalent." In the following years, the Greenbackers would continue their demands but fail to capture voters. As the economic crisis faded, and farm prices in Kansas continued to climb, the Republicans turned their attention to issues that were not of immediate relevance to farmers or laborers. In contrast, the Democrats, at both the national and local levels, presented themselves as champions of the workingman, in opposition to "gluttonous and selfish corporations."[13] They also continued their argument for the free coinage of silver. Grover Cleveland was elected president in 1884 because of this widely based appeal.

The Republicans were now on the defensive, and in 1888 they adopted a platform designed to attract votes from Greenbackers as well as from Republican profarmer splinter groups. Consequently, they came out for "free schools everywhere," civil service reform, liberal pensions for Union soldiers, a reduction of letter postage to a one-cent rate, protection for the working classes against foreign products (so that they, like the national party, favored high protective tariffs). They opposed cheap immigrant or convict labor, and demanded railroad legislation, lower interest rates, and a break-up of trusts or "combinations that monopolized food supplies or controlled production to the detriment of the people."[14]

That same year, with the fading of the Greenback party, Union

Labor sprang up to demand everything the Republicans had asked for and a bit more. While the Republicans had called for free education, Union Labor asked the state to "publish school text books for the use of public schools, and [to be] furnished by the various school districts at cost."[15] In spite of its name and its call to laborers and farmers to unite, Union Labor was identified in the minds of voters almost solely with farmers and their needs. In 1888, when Union Labor managed to capture approximately 10 percent of the state vote in the gubernatorial election, few of those votes came from villages or urban centers. In Lawrence, Kansas, for instance, only four people out of 2,013 chose the Union Labor candidate. The party did slightly better in Fort Scott, where it earned 13 percent of the votes. Union Labor votes were concentrated, specifically, in the rural townships and in the middle sector of the state; these were the areas where the Alliance would experience its growth and success in the next election.

Certain characteristics seem to be "typical" of the third-party voter, and of the Republican and Democratic voter, in the elections prior to 1890. Louise E. Rickard, focusing on the gubernatorial elections between 1880 and 1888, found that distinctions could be made between these groups on the basis of cultural, economic, and geographic variables.[16] A third-party voter was likely to favor prohibition, was a member of a pietistic religious denomination, and was a native-born white. His farm was likely to have been mortgaged, and the value of his farm crops low, reflecting the fact that he lived in the central counties of the state. Finally, this third-party man lived in the country rather than a village, and was a farmer rather than a worker or merchant.[17]

A typical Republican voter shared some of the same characteristics, such as opposition to liquor, and membership in a pietistic religious group. He was also likely to be a native-born white. Republican voters, however, tended to be more prosperous, as measured by value of farm and farm products, than third-party voters. This meant that Republican votes were concentrated in the eastern third of the state. Finally, like third-party voters, Republicans were more likely to be farmers than laborers, though there were a significant number of laborers and, inevitably, merchants among their ranks.

The Democratic voter emerged most distinctly. Democratic voters were, first of all, most likely to be Catholic, German, non-native-born, and opposed to prohibition.[18] Democratic voters tended to be concentrated in cities and small towns, and were the least likely of all groups to be concentrated in farming. In summary, both cultural and economic variables were important in determining who supported which party.[19] These factors would continue to be important, although it is significant to consider other factors when explaining the outcome of a particular election.

The Election of 1890

Platforms and Issues

The Populist party gave local suballiances considerable freedom in the election of 1890, encouraging them to meet and discuss who to nominate and support in local races. (This was the last election in which they had, or exercised, such autonomy.) Farmers were optimistic about their chances of capturing political power. In the towns, people saw the Alliance as an opportunity to challenge Republican control of the state, and a way to register their concerns about such issues as railroad rates. We saw earlier, for instance, how the merchants of communities such as Fort Scott and Lawrence were as concerned about economic conditions and the railroads as the farmers. Perhaps as many as 10,000 townspeople formed Citizen Alliances to work alongside the regular Alliance when Alliance membership was restricted to farmers.[20] The Populist vote would not, however, be high in the towns.

The Populist platform of 1890 was composed almost exclusively of the St. Louis demands—those principles agreed upon by the National Farmers' Alliance in the winter of 1889. The platform asked for: (1) the abolition of national banks and the substitution of legal-tender treasury notes; (2) the free and unlimited coinage of silver; (3) legislation to prevent speculation in grain futures; (4) laws prohibiting alien ownership of land, with all excess lands held by the railroads to be returned to the public domain; (5) a fair system of taxation; (6) fractional paper currency; and (7) public ownership of the means of transportation and communication. The Kansans also favored pensions for Union soldiers.[21] These seem remarkable demands until they are compared with Republican and Democratic demands. Clearly, the deepening economic crisis in Kansas turned both of the local parties abruptly left.

The Republican platform, in slightly different language, called for many of the same things, and added some of its own: (1) an elected railroad commission; (2) a state board of arbitration for settling labor disputes; (3) an end to free railroad passes; (4) legislation prohibiting the employment of children; (5) laws restricting foreclosure; and (6) free text books.[22] It did not, however, call for the free coinage of silver, or fiat currency.

The Democrats seemed determined to please almost everyone. They advocated the free coinage of silver, and because opposition to Senator Ingalls was a Populist issue, they incorporated a plank specifically condemning his statement that a reformed political system was an "irridescent dream." The most controversial plank was one calling for resubmission of the prohibition amendment. They framed the issue most carefully. Democrats argued that it would be good for business if the amendment were lifted, and claimed that prohibition had resulted only in bribery, corruption, and evil. They suggested a high license fee and proposed that the money be spent on making and improving roads.[23] Many Kansans agreed that the issue should be resubmitted to the voters. The Democratic-Resubmission ticket was headed by Charles Robinson of Lawrence, Kansas, the first free-state governor of Kansas and a long-time Republican who enjoyed considerable prestige in the state. His presence on the ballot definitely affected voting patterns. In terms of the platforms, then, the main differences between the parties were the issue of Senator John Ingalls and prohibition. The Populists had managed to sidestep, for the time being, the questions of suffrage and temperance, which had been raised at their convention.[24]

The Republicans seemed to believe they could not lose the election. They campaigned through vilification rather than through the platform they had adopted. They assumed that Ingalls' seat was safe because senators were selected by a joint ballot of the state legislature, and the Republicans would have at least 39 of the 40 votes in the Senate. They assumed they would have a majority in the House. The work done by the suballiances bore bitter fruit for the Republicans in the election of 1890 and sent a Populist senator to Washington. The Populists captured 91 of 125 seats in the House. Their share of the popular vote was not, however, as impressive.

The Vote

The Republicans had elected the governor by a margin of 7,000 votes (108,179 for the Populists, 115,024 for the Republicans, and 71,357 for the Democrats), but the Populists elected their men at the local and regional levels. As the *Kansas City Times* said, this was accomplished by the intense organizing efforts of local suballiances.

> In our astonishment at the success of the People's party in Kansas, we must not imagine that it was the work of an unorganized and temporary sentiment. The power of organization was never more clearly demonstrated. Neither of the other parties was as strictly organized or as frequently reviewed and drilled. The local Alliances were the backbone of the movement. They met frequently, received instructions from their central officers, pledged themselves to voting the ticket, read their party literature, and acted with the precision of a machine. A sentiment and a reason were the strong springs, but there was everywhere the direction of a pervading intelligence of management.[25]

This report was probably an accurate reflection of the role of the suballiances during this election. Unfortunately, it was not an experience that the Populist party built on in the following elections. The lesson about their party that the Populists learned from this election was that "whenever aided by the Democrats, it swept everything before it."[26] Pressures for fusion would, then, be considerable from the leadership of both the Democrats and the Populists.

The Populists had argued that they stood for the dignity of all laborers, but their popular success in village or urban areas of Kansas was almost nil. In Kansas City, Kansas, for example, the Populists polled only 95 votes out of all those cast.[27] In Lawrence, home of Charles Robinson, the Populists received only 36 votes, or 2 percent of the total. They did slightly better in Fort Scott (receiving 10.5 percent of the votes), where Robinson was less popular. Outside the towns, the picture changed considerably. In the townships of Douglas County, for example, the Populists got 23 percent of the vote, as opposed to 2 percent in Lawrence. In the townships of Bourbon County, the Populist share of the vote was 31 percent. This pattern was repeated throughout the state.

The Democrats' decision to stand for resubmission, and to have Robinson head their party, had two major consequences. It kept the Democratic loss (1888–90) smaller than that of the Republicans, and it shifted counties with a strong German population, or a concentration of foreign-born, over into their column. For instance, Sedgwick County, which had a sizeable German population, gave the Democrats a majority of 50.8 percent, compared to 37.8 percent in 1888. Wyandotte, which again had a number of foreign-born, went from a total of 43.5 percent in 1888 to 52.8 percent in 1890.[28] Populist votes also correlated negatively with the Democratic vote of 1888 and positively with that of the Republican vote, indicating that the election of 1890 was most disruptive to the Republicans in terms of the loss of total number and percentage of voters.[29] But the Democrats were, after all, the minority party, and *any* loss to the Populists was devastating to their electoral chances. There were strong reasons why the Democrats would opt for fusion in the elections of 1892.

The Populist votes in the rural areas of Kansas came from two principal sources: defecting Republicans and an increased voter turnout. (There was, though, a drop in overall voter turnout between 1888 and 1890, as 1890 was not a presidential election year.) As we have seen, the Republicans experienced a significant drop in number of expected voters in 1890, when over 40,000 shifted to the Alliance ticket. In addition, as Argersinger found, there was a higher voter turnout in rural counties than in urban ones, and a higher percentage of these votes went to the Populists.[30]

Argersinger used county-level data to analyze the vote for secretary of state in 1890. He chose the position of secretary, rather than governor, believing that it would more accurately reflect local sentiments. His findings deserve examination. The most important predictor ($r=.52$) of the Populist vote was number of farm mortgages in a county, which meant that it was those farmers in the middle third of the state who were most likely to vote with the third party. The second most important variable ($r=.24$) in determining Populist vote was simply the number of people in a county living on farms. Overall, then, it was the rural nature of an area, combined with economic conditions, that explained half of the vote.[31] The major cultural factor in the election of 1890 was religion. Catholicism was the most important predictor of the Democratic vote.[32] Argersinger's analysis of the 1890 election parallels that of Jeffrey C. Williams, who also found Catholics and other ritualists (e.g., Episcopalians and Lutherans) and/or Germans supporting the Democrats, and pietists (e.g., Baptists, Presbyterians, and Methodists) supporting the Populists. (Pietists did not support the Populists after fusion with the Democrats.)[33]

Having won control of the House in the state legislature, the Populists proceeded in the legislative session of 1891 to unseat Ingalls, and send William "Whiskers" A. Peffer to the United States Senate. More time was spent electing their nominee to the position of state printer, a post of considerable patronage. With those items out of the way, they proceeded to try and make law. They were remarkably unsuccessful, partly because they would not compromise with the Republicans, who controlled the Senate and the governor's office, and partly because the Republicans vetoed any legislation in which they did not have a hand. Some issues were passed: a modified banking act, an eight-hour day for those working on public projects, and a reapportionment of the state into additional legislative districts. This was also an election year for nine district judges, and the Populists showed their vulnerability at the polls by losing seven of the seats. Harrington has argued that the Populists lost because they could not find well-qualified lawyers among their ranks to stand for office.[34] Be that as it may, they also lost heavily in local races, where the Republicans dominated by a margin of 277 to 127.[35] Both Republicans and Populists approached the elections of 1892 determined to win.

The Election of 1892

Platforms and Issues

In 1892, the Populists entered the field as a national party. The People's party reaffirmed its commitment to the St. Louis platform of the Alliance and demanded, among other things, the free and unlimited coinage of silver, as well as a graduated income tax. They voiced their opposition to any and all monopolies, and upheld the principle that "Wealth belongs to him who creates it."[36] At the state level, the Populists added resolutions designed to attract the Kansas voter, e.g., "That we favor a liberal pension law and a law making good to the old soldiers their loss by reason of payment for service in a depreciated currency."[37]

The Republicans were not to be outdone. They nominated a farmer for governor and adopted a platform that favored boards of arbitration, a lowering of transportation costs, government control of the telegraph service, and the free delivery of mail in the country as well as in the towns and cities. These proposals read as though they had come straight out of the Populist platform, and they probably did. As so it went, check and countercheck.

Though Democrats would later in that year fuse with the Populists, they had a platform of their own which continued to call for resubmission, as well as the introduction of legislation which would benefit the workingman. They stood, like their national party, for a reduction in tariffs. The Democrats' desire to fuse with the Populists stemmed from the fact that they wanted to reelect Cleveland as president, and deny Harrison Kansas's electoral votes. After intense debate, the Democratic state convention endorsed the entire Populist slate. With everything in place, the campaign of 1892 began in earnest.

The Vote

The Republicans tried to win Alliancemen back to their party, and received 43,000 more votes than they had in 1890. (The total vote increase for all political parties was 30,000 between 1890 and 1892. The Republicans gained 9.7 percent, while the fusion ticket lost close to 11 percent.) In some districts, the vote was so close that the polls had been closed several days before it was known who had won the elections. When the results were announced, it was found that General Weaver had captured the state's electoral votes for the national ticket, and the Populists had staged a stunning victory over their Republican opponents. They had won the governor's race and elected their candidates to Congress in four districts—the Republicans in three. The new state Senate was controlled by the Populists, with twenty-three members—to fifteen for the Republicans and two for the Democrats. The situation in the House presented a different picture for it appeared that the Republicans would control sixty-three of the seats, the Populists fifty-eight, and the Democrats two. There was one independent candidate, and one district in which there had been a tie between the Populist and Republican candidates. This situation would result in the "Legislative War of 1893."

One of the reasons for the Republican resurgence could be traced back to legislation of 1891, which created nineteen new districts in western Kansas. Alliance strength was confined almost exclusively to middle and eastern Kansas, and by 1892 the population of western Kansas was primarily composed of ranchers and large landowners, not yeomen farmers. In this sparsely settled area, a few votes could easily change the outcome of the election. The Republicans made a concerted effort to reach the few voters in this area, and carried fourteen of the nineteen districts, which alone was clearly enough to swing the balance of power in the House in their favor.[38]

The election of 1892 showed a slight gain in Republican strength in small towns, as well as in some of the urban areas. This was due partly to the fact that a fusion ticket was unattractive to traditional Democratic voters and may have caused some to shift their votes to the Republicans. For instance, in 1890, the Democratic Resubmission candidate for governor, Robinson, carried Kansas City, Kansas. But in the election of 1892, the fusion candidate, Lewelling, received only 47 percent of the city's vote, and 50 percent on a statewide basis. On the whole, the Populists fared less well within cities. This should not be surprising, for the election of 1890 had made it clear that the Populists had little, if any, support within Kansas cities and towns.

One factor that bedeviled the Republicans in 1892 was prohibition. They were understandably dismayed when the Prohibition party decided to run a separate ticket. It escaped no one's attention that if the few votes—around 4,000—going to the Prohibition party had gone into the Republican column instead, the Republicans could well have won the election. Normally, there was little reason for the Republican leadership to push vigorously for enforcement of the prohibition amendment, as it could only alienate ethnic voters. Those who were proreform, and for prohibition, really had no alternative in Kansas, short of forming a third party, than voting Republican. Republican strategy during this period was to argue for the values of temperance and leave enforcement up to the presumed zeal of local officials. Cultural values, as well as economic conditions, continued to be factors in 1892.

In 1892, Republican support came from eastern Kansas, where corn was planted, rather than wheat. They also did well where there were few mortgaged farms and where the value of farm products was high. As the most nativistic party, they drew the bulk of their support from those counties in which there were few non-native-born whites, and in which there was a substantial Protestant population.

The fusion ticket, on the other hand, attracted those farmers with high mortgages, in the middle portion of the state, who grew wheat. It also drew the support of traditional Democratic voters, e.g., those living in towns, Catholics, Germans, and ethnics.[39]

The major change in voting behavior occurring between 1890 and 1892 involved an overall increase in the Republicans' share of the vote. More frequently than in 1890, the vote came from small towns and from wealthier farmers; these trends would continue through the decade.[40] Fusion with the Democrats was sorely tested when the Populists, fresh from their heady victory, arrived in Topeka to assume control of the state government.

The Legislative War of 1893

The Populists had achieved a great victory but they were unsatisfied. Lewelling, the Populist governor, had carried 57 of the state's 106 counties, yet some of these very counties had returned Republican legislators to the House. Election fraud was strongly suspected, and the Populists brought before the state Supreme Court four contests which they thought they had a good chance of winning. The state Supreme Court was, however, controlled by Republicans, who declined to intervene. Both parties were determined to control the lower branch of the legislature, and went into caucuses on the night of the inaugural to lay their plans.

Jerry Simpson addressed the Populist faithful and told them they had beaten the Santa Fe Railroad, "and you must take charge of government. You must organize the Legislature in this Hall tomorrow, and I wouldn't let the technicalities of the law stand in the way. Call this revolution if you will . . . but see to it that you organize the Legislature here tomorrow."[41] They elected a speaker, J. M. Dunsmore, for the session which was to begin the next day, and announced that they would bar eighteen Republicans, whose seats were going to be challenged, from participating in the first session. The Republicans elected their own speaker, George Douglass, and said that precedent should rule: all challenges should be ignored until organization of the House was complete. Then a committee (presumably controlled by Republicans) would look into the matter.

Long before the appointed hour had arrived, partisans began to fill the galleries. Rumor had circulated during the night that both sides would arm themselves and would use force, if necessary, to prevail. The local sheriff swore in fifty deputies, who were stationed about the capitol's grounds. The opposing forces managed to assemble without violence and the first session of the House was called to order by the secretary of state at 1 : 20 P.M. "As soon as the secretary of state left the hall, the house got into action—double action. The floor leaders of the two parties ascended the rostrum, called the house to order (or disorder), motions were put and carried, the members sworn in, officers elected, and two sets of messages sent to inform the senate and the governor that the house (or houses) had organized and was now ready for action."[42]

Reporters from throughout the nation who had come prepared to write about the "first people's government on earth," now turned their attention to the "legislative war." For the next several weeks, local and national newspapers featured exaggerated stories and drawings of the "howling mobs" struggling for control of the state capital. Only a little exaggeration was needed. Eventually, the state militia was rushed from Wichita. They set up camp in the snow on the lawn of the capitol building, with new Gatling guns. Sergeants-at-arms were appointed to keep order in the House of Representatives; they all carried rifles. Some added a pistol or two to their armory. Though Republicans as well as Populists carried arms, it was the Populists who were branded with the labels of anarchist and revolutionary.

In the midst of general demonstrations in Topeka and throughout the state, legislators tried to get on with the business of governing the state. Lewelling, and the Populist-controlled Senate, gave official recognition to the Populist House. From the Populist's perspective, that settled things. The Republicans refused to yield, for they knew that challenges carried forward to the state Supreme Court would probably be resolved in their favor. When the Populists brought mandamus proceedings in the Supreme Court to have four certified Republican members of the House ousted, the court claimed to lack jurisdiction. The Populists offered to submit the controversy to a committee of three, but the Republicans rejected this solution, advocating instead that it be resubmitted to the Supreme Court. The dilemma was that neither house, meeting separately or in joint session with their colleagues from the other house, could muster enough votes to elect several key officials.

The first Populist compromise came with the election of the state printer, the Populist Snow, and the United States senator, the Democrat Martin. *All* members of *all* three groups (the Senate, plus the Republican and Populist Houses) met together for these two elections. Without Democratic support, however, the Populists could do little. In order to elect the next United States senator, eighty-three votes on a joint ballot were required. The Populists had eighty-one official certificates of election, the Republicans seventy-nine, and the Democrats five, giving them the balance of power. The Populists, especially those opposed to fusion, wanted Frank Doster, a former district judge, to serve as U.S. senator, whereas the Democrats favored John Martin, long-time Democrat, and the man who had been responsible in 1892 for getting the Democratic state convention to endorse the entire Populist slate. The Democrats agreed to vote for Snow, if the Populists would vote for Martin. They did so. "It was," said one chronicler of these events, "a bitter dose for the proud Populist party to take. Never before had they endorsed or compromised."[43] The Republicans abstained from voting, and elected their own candidate, knowing full well that the United States Senate, controlled by Democrats, would seat Martin.

With the election of a printer and senator out of the way, legislators turned their attention once more to their war. Eventually Lewelling entered the fray, and began the process of effecting some sort of compromise. It was not one designed to help the Populist cause. After thirty-five days of struggle the House landed in Republican hands. The state constitution limited the session to fifty days; only fifteen remained in which to clear up the backlog of bills passed by the Populist-controlled Senate, and to respond to the governor's original message.

The Republicans seized the initiative, and Douglass came to the floor with a list of ten resolutions that spelled out Republican ideas for the legislative program during the rest of the session.[44] Many were Populist ideas. Few important pieces of legislation made their way to Lewelling's desk, since once a bill was thrown into joint conference, it died for the session. The most significant item that failed to clear the joint conference committee was a bill which called for the public election of the railroad commission and an increase in its powers. The failure of this bill might be laid at the door of the Populists, since, when the struggle for control of the House began, Douglass offered the Populists control of several key committees, as well as full control of the railroad committee, if they would agree to Republican organization of the House.

A number of items did pass both houses: a secret ballot; provision for employees to get two hours to vote on election day without loss of pay; a requirement that candidates file statements of their campaign expenses and list their contributors; provision for property owners to redeem their land up to eighteen months after foreclosure proceedings; and provision to pay employees once a week in cash rather than "store script." The Republicans also added an item of their own: suffrage. Kansans would be allowed to vote in 1894 on whether or not women should be allowed full voting rights.

The Populists came out of the 1893 legislative session greatly weakened. The Republicans were able to take credit for most of the proreform legislation that had passed. One major piece of legislation the farmers had hoped for—that relating to the railroads— was not forthcoming. The pro-Republican press had promoted a view of Populists as irresponsible anarchists, who could not be trusted with the business of running the state. The Populist ranks were torn by the necessity to compromise with the Democrats on Martin's election. Lease, in particular, would claim publicly that Lewelling had betrayed the principles of the Populist party, and that fusion with the Democrats would lead only to further corruption. (Lewelling was also unpopular with some Democrats who claimed he had not delivered on patronage.) These tensions would all contribute to the Populists' loss in 1894.

The Election of 1894

Platforms and Issues

Kansas Republicans were aided greatly by the Cleveland administration. Cleveland had been elected as a protest against worsening economic conditions, repression of labor organizations, and declining farm prices. However, Cleveland managed to alienate both farmers and laborers. Much to the distress of midwestern farmers, he came out strongly for a gold standard. When Coxey's Army of the unemployed marched on Washington in the fall of 1893, to protest the collapse of the economy, Cleveland had the marchers arrested. The depression of 1893 thus benefitted the Kansas Republicans, who could attack the Democrats in Washington and the fusionists in Topeka.[46]

The Republican platform of 1894 shifted away from the detailed proposals of 1892, when they tried to be as radical as the Populists, and back toward a more conservative position. Like the national party, they supported strong tariff laws, adding the sop that "tariff laws should protect the products of the farm as well as of the factory." They denounced the Lewelling administration for its "revolutionary tendencies," and though they did not come out for free coinage, they indicated that they did favor "bimetalism."[47]

The Populist platform did not change, with one exception. The Populists decided to support women's suffrage. This decision was made over the strong objections of the Democratic members of the Lewelling administration and the pro-fusion forces within the party. It has been claimed that one of the reasons suffrage was pushed was precisely because it would drive Democrats from the ranks, and also because the radicals within the party wanted to stand on the principle of reform, whatever the costs. Not everyone demanding that the Populists support suffrage was a part of the Kansas leadership. "Susan B. Anthony . . . forced the Kansas women into the action on threat to withdraw all support of any kind whatsoever from the state if the Kansas women should not consent to force the issue in the populist convention."[48] Divided though they were, the Populists again nominated Lewelling to be their standard-bearer. This time, however, not all Democrats were willing to join in an alliance.

The Stalwart Democrats, as they proudly called themselves, met separately and forged their own platform. They called for a resubmission of the prohibition amendment—always a favorite topic—and said, emphatically, "We oppose woman suffrage as tending to destroy the home and the family, the true basis of political safety, and express the hope that the helpmeet and guardian of the family sanctuary may not be dragged from the modest purity of self-imposed seclusion to be thrown unwillingly into the unfeminine place of political strife." They favored gold, silver, a paper currency, irrigation in western Kansas, restriction of immigration, and endorsed the "wise and patriotic administration of President Cleveland."[49]

The Vote

The Republicans not only carried the state in 1894, they defeated all but one of the Populists against whom they ran. They increased their share of the vote by a full percentage point and held fast the voters they had attracted in 1892. Lewelling received 118,329 votes to 148,697 for his Republican challenger, Morrill. The Stalwart Democrat Overmeyer received 26,709 votes, and the Prohibition party candidate 6,397. Lewelling could not have won, even if he had received all of the votes that went to Overmeyer. The key to the Populist loss was their position on suffrage, which was defeated by a vote of 103,139 to 95,302.

Consider what happened in traditional Democratic strongholds when the Populists opted for suffrage. In 1892, Sedgwick County returned a majority of 53 percent for the fusion ticket in the governor's race. In 1894, however, the fusion ticket received only 37.9 percent of the vote, while the Stalwart Democrats earned 12.4 percent of the vote. In 1896, when Democrats and Populists again came together to support one ticket, they received 57.5 percent of the vote. The same pattern was found in Wyandotte County, which had never shown a preference for the Populists. In 1892, the fusion ticket received 48.2 percent of the vote, but this dropped to 30.8

percent in 1894, and went up to 48.8 again in 1896. Ethnic voters and workers were quick to desert the Populists. This pattern is particularly striking if we look at data from cities.

Atchison, Kansas, was a major railroad center and had in all voting wards a significant number of German voters, as well as immigrants from Britain and the Commonwealth, who favored third parties rather than the Republicans.[50] In 1892, the Republicans received 57 percent of the votes for governor; the fusion ticket got 41 percent, and the Prohibitionists 2 percent. In 1894, the Republicans gained two points, receiving 59 percent of the vote, while the Democrats/Populists lost substantially, receiving only 27 percent in this election. The Stalwart Democrats got 13 percent of the votes, and the Prohibitionists one percent. The same pattern was prevalent in other "industrial" towns in Kansas. In 1892, Leavenworth voters gave the Republicans 52 percent of the vote, and the Democrats/Populists 48 percent. But in 1894, the fusion ticket received only 26.5 percent of the vote, and the Stalwart Democrats received 21 percent.[51] Clearly, then, the decision by Populists to take a stand on suffrage cost them the support of workers, Catholics, and ethnic voters throughout the state.

On the Road to Silver

Once the Republican Morrill took office, he set about trying to undo some of the laws passed during the previous legislative session. In particular, he tried to overturn the eighteen-month redemption law but was prevented from doing so by the fact that the Populists carried over a majority in the Senate. They could thus effectively block any antifarmer legislation, although other than the mortgage bill little was forthcoming.

No longer in power, untroubled by the necessity to distribute patronage or to compromise in the halls of the state capitol, the Populists could set about doing what they did best: attacking the legislative program of the Republicans and pointing out why it did not meet the needs of laboring Kansans. By 1895, however, this work was being done primarily through the reform newspapers in Kansas; the Alliance was for all intents and purposes dead.[52] What distinguished the Populists from the other parties both locally and nationally was an explanation of the nation's economic troubles and a definite program to solve them. Populists advocated reform of the nation's monetary system, and they spoke of the growing division between the money power (eastern banks and capitalists) and the have-nots in the South and West. The solution of the explanation was "silver."

Why just one plank in the Populist party's Omaha platform, which addressed the problems of land, money, and transportation, was picked up while the others were discarded has been endlessly discussed. The reasons are fairly simple. Silver still meant, to many Kansans (this is quite clear from their speeches and platforms), expansion of the monetary supply, fiat currency, and national control over the system of the economy. Money alone seemed to be the problem. The Populists had been successful in their educational campaign; they had convinced a substantial number of Americans that the issue of the tariff was a sham. Silver was seized upon as an easy explanation of what had gone wrong in the country; if Cleveland, it was asserted, had not vetoed legislation allowing for the free coinage of silver at a ratio of 16 to 1, the depression of 1893 would not have occurred. Both Democratic and Republican politicians, prior to the presidential race of 1896, made silver an issue, and the Populists could not sidestep it, or explain to the masses of the country why silver alone would not solve the nation's problems. (The silver issue covered all the complexities of the political economy.)

For a time it seemed the Populists would have the stage all to themselves in 1896. Those favoring a gold standard were firmly in control in the Republican party, and even though Cleveland had suffered a crushing defeat in 1892, he was still a powerful figure in the Democratic party. However, the silver Democrats, comprising those supported by laboring men and farmers and those who owned silver mines in Colorado and Idaho, were in firm control of the Democratic nominating convention, and picked William Jennings Bryan. The Populists, who had delayed holding their convention until the Democrats met, were now trapped. Should they support a man who had long been a friend of the common man and an issue that was important to them, or try to run an independent third-party campaign? They had already seen what had happened in Kansas when they did not have the support of the Democrats. The awkward compromise the Populists arrived at was to accept Bryan as their presidential candidate but to nominate the southern Populist and Allianceman, Tom Watson, for vice-president instead of the regular Democratic candidate, Arthur M. Sewall, a wealthy and conservative banker. Not all Kansas Populists were pleased with the outcome.

> I warned the People's Party that its managers were pursuing a dangerous course in giving undue prominence in their campaigns to free coinage . . .; that should the Democrats nominate free silver candidates on a free silver platform, our resolutions and papers would enable them to condemn us out of our own mouths for even keeping up our party organization instead of joining them.[53]

However, there was much in the regular Democrat platform to attract Populists, for some planks were quite radical. The platform declared the debate over the tariff to be specious, referred to the "Crime of 1873," which "resulted in the appreciation of gold and a corresponding fall in the prices of commodities produced by the people; a heavy increase in the burden of taxation and of all debts, public and private; the enrichment of a money-lending class at home and abroad; the prostration of industry and impoverishment of the people."[54] Almost everything the Populists had stood for, save greenbacks and government control of the railroads, was in the platform. Bryan's condemnation of Cleveland's administration made fusion easier for some Kansans.

The Election of 1896

Platforms and Issues

Populists and Democrats were joined in Kansas by a handful of silver Republicans for the election of 1896. The Democrats and Populists agreed to support one another's candidates on a fusion ticket. The Democrats, determined to elect Bryan, chose all of the presidential electors, and the Populists, in turn, were able to select all of the state-level candidates. Their nominee for governor was John W. Leedy, who would take a probusiness stance in the coming election, explaining how a vote for the state party and Bryan would result in prosperity for all classes. The party advertised its candidates as "sensible, practical, and successful."

The People's party 1896 platform was uncharacteristically bland. It condemned the "Republican house of representatives for failing and refusing to pass the bills sent to them from the Populist senate." Its positive resolutions focused on demands that railroad rates be reduced and the use of convict labor be curbed.[55] The Democrats, who had met in separate session, commended "President Cleveland for the gallant fight he has made for tariff reform," and demanded "the free and unlimited coinage of both silver and gold at the ratio of 16 to 1."[56]

The Kansas Republicans, who up until 1896 had always indicated their support for silver, now had to do a complete about-face, when the national party made its opposition clear. "We are," the Kansans said, "opposed to the free and unlimited coinage of silver at the ratio of 16 to 1." However, they were for irrigation, improved highways, and a more powerful board of railroad commissioners. They made their usual references to "Populist depredations and misrule."[57]

The fusion ticket, too, had its troubles. For many Democratic politicians, a repudiation of Cleveland meant a repudiation of patronage. A few Populists were uncomfortable with a ticket that included the patrician Sewell as the vice-presidential candidate, and were offered in Kansas a Bryan-Watson ticket. There is little evidence, however, that Watson's entry made a difference. His name, along with Bryan's, was on the presidential ballot, as was the Bryan-Sewell ticket. The Watson ticket probably received less than 1,000 out of the 338,000 votes cast in the election of 1896. Perhaps this is as good a measure as any that people wanted to cast their votes rationally—for the person who had a chance of winning and actually making state policy.

Voters, then, had a range of choices in 1896. There were five separate gubernatorial candidates—Republican, a fusion ticket, a separate Democratic ticket, a separate Republican-Populist ticket, and the Prohibitionists—and four possible choices for president. Once again, however, the Populist ticket was to prove successful in Kansas.

The Vote

Bryan carried the state by 173,424 votes to McKinley's 159,719. Nationally, Bryan came very close to being president. He lost to McKinley primarily because of the nationwide increase of two million Republican voters. These voters came primarily from New York, Pennsylvania, and New England, which Bryan had conceded. "The battle ground was in the states of the Middle West, and the election was so close in the states of Indiana, Ohio, Kentucky, and

California, that a change of less than 30,000 votes in those states would have given their electoral votes to Bryan and elected him president."[58] The Populist governor, Leedy, was elected by a smaller margin, 167,941 to 160,507, which indicates that Bryan had more than a Populist appeal. In Kansas City, Kansas, for instance, Bryan trailed McKinley by 400 votes, but Leedy ran behind the Republican candidate for governor by almost 1,000 votes. The Populists in Kansas won all but two of the congressional races, and now controlled both houses of the legislature.

Kansas did not experience the surge in voting that the rest of the country did between 1894 and 1896, mostly because the state was already highly politicized and the vast majority of eligible voters were already participating. The vote for governor, for instance, only increased by 2,000 between 1894 and 1896, though the increase in the vote for president between 1892 and 1896 was about 13,000.[59]

The voting patterns of 1896 were much the same as in the previous year, with the notable exception of the votes cast for Bryan. Baptists had traditionally voted with the Republicans or Prohibitionists, but shifted their allegiance to their Baptist brother, Bryan, in 1896. Williams estimated that Bryan probably decreased the Republican total by 4,500 votes.[60] The ethnic vote was important, once again, for Germans fled the fusion ticket.[61] The Democratic-Populists continued to do best in the central, wheat-growing sections of the state, and worst in the areas of mixed agriculture, i.e., eastern Kansas. The Republicans again dominated in the towns of rural Kansas and in the more prosperous regions.[62]

Even at their most successful, then, Populists just managed to pull even with or slightly ahead of the Republicans, and it repeatedly took a fusion ticket to manage that. It is also clear that the Republicans continued to increase their share of the vote, and that they did so particularly in areas of increased prosperity. Given the importance of economic variables, the future of the Populist party in Kansas depended in large part on the continuation of economic problems. Populist leaders "believed that McKinley, called by his followers the 'advance agent of prosperity,' would fail to restore prosperity under the single gold standard, and that then the nation would turn to silver for relief."[63] Kansans who voted for the state ticket, however, wanted action, and expected the party that had been waiting in the wings for six years would accomplish its goals. They were disappointed.

A Populist Government

The legislative session of 1897 was an active one. Many new laws, some of which had been proposed in previous years, were passed. Some of these laws called for the regulation of the Kansas City stockyards, the weighing and inspecting of grain, uniformity of textbooks, and a reduction in the salaries of public officials. Three major pieces of legislation, however, failed: railroad regulation, a bill to reduce interest rates, and procedures which would facilitate referenda. The fate of railroad legislation revealed divisions within the ranks of the Populist party.

With the aid of both Populist and Republican votes, the Senate offered a bill to expand the powers of the existing railroad commission and give it the power to fix rates. This bill was drafted and supported by Lewelling, the former Populist governor, who was railroad commissioner under Leedy. However, thirteen of the twenty-seven Populist senators signed a protest against the bill, arguing that it "did not go far enough." Debate in the lower house became bitter, but the Senate version of the bill carried. It was then sent to Governor Leedy, who vetoed it. The farmers were left where they began. The radicals, who had demanded a bill that would in all probability have been declared unconstitutional by the federal courts, were unwilling to compromise; when they had achieved agreement with both Republicans and other members of their party, they had increased their demands. The Populist leadership was not able to exercise sufficient control to pass any bill that would allow them to go to the polls in the next election claiming credit for improving the farmers' lot.

The *Farmer's Advocate* summed up the feeling of many of the long-time supporters of the party.

> Many good laws were passed, but unfortunately none of general importance and interest were finally acted on until late in the session when the people had become impatient and had made up their minds that nothing of value was to be accomplished. One of the greatest disadvantages in the way was that too many of the members were inexperienced. They knew nothing of the difficulties and hindrances which must be overcome before anything could be accomplished. Too many members were devoting their attention to matters which would give them notoriety and prestige. Others occupied valuable time looking after patronage for themselves and friends.[64]

The Aftermath

The fortunes of the Populist party continued on a downward spiral through the remainder of the decade, and were affected by both local and national conditions. Within Kansas, Democrats and Populists failed to come together in a number of key races in 1898. The Republicans (more than hypocritically, for they had blocked some of the bills) were quick to point out to Kansas voters that the Populists could not legislate, and failed to execute their campaign promises. Nationally, the Republican administration was overseeing the popular Spanish-American War and taking credit for a dramatic improvement in the country's economic fortunes. Discovery of the Klondike gold fields and the opening of South African mines did much to increase the amount of money in circulation and to raise the price of commodities. Ironically, of course, this inflation validated the position of those who had been arguing for the unlimited coinage of silver.

The Populists lost the governor's seat in 1898 and also control of the lower branch of the House. Populist senators were carried over from 1896. If total votes are a measure of people's interest in politics or a party, one would have to conclude that Kansans were growing weary of the battles that had raged across the state. Though the previous election, of 1896, had coincided with a presidential election, the vote total in 1896 for governor was only 2,000 votes higher than in the previous off-year, 1894. But when we compare the votes for governor in 1896 with those cast in 1898, it is clear that thousands chose to stay home. The overall decline in votes was 44,000: the highest for any of the periods under investigation. Furthermore, the fusion ticket saw a drop of almost 34,000 votes, far more than its expected share.

The Populists made one last attempt to pass railroad legislation. Leedy called the Populist government into special session just before the Republicans were to come into office. A new law was placed on the statute books, replacing the railroad commission with a court of visitation with the power to fix rates. When the Republicans took office, they challenged the law and sent it to the Republican-controlled state Supreme Court, which overturned it. The result was that Kansas was then left with not even a railroad commission, for the previous legislation had abolished it. This does not mean that no further legislation was passed which benefitted farmers or laborers in the state, but it does mean that it was done at the initiative of the Republican party, which received credit for it. (There is a strong evidence that the state Republican party kept an eye on the rural sector, to prevent the kind of jolt they received in 1890.) Much profarmer legislation was introduced by Republican legislators from districts which had previously returned Populist majorities.[65] Reform in Kansas would continue, but it would now be reform shaped and guided by a probusiness tradition. Populism was finished when Republicans simply outlawed fusion tickets in 1900. The Populist party had never been able to broaden its base except, in limited ways, through fusion. An analysis of the voting patterns in three Kansas communities will amplify this point.

Voting in Three Kansas Communities

Lawrence, Kansas, was a bastion of Republican strength throughout the years, and showed little evidence of support for the Populists. Table 8.1 shows that the Republicans received the lion's share of the vote in all wards. Wards I and II, which represented the better socioeconomic areas of town, clearly showed a preference for the Republicans. The Republican vote dips in these two wards in only year, 1890, the year in which Charles Robinson, former Republican governor, ran on the Democratic Resubmission ticket. But even Robinson's personal popularity was not enough to give him a plurality in these two traditional Republican wards. Wards III and IV, on the other hand, present a slightly different picture; they were wards that had the highest concentration of ethnic voters, as well as those wards with the greatest number of workers. When liquor was an issue, as it was in 1890, these two wards move over into the Democratic column but come back to the Republican in the next gubernatorial election. Ward V was also a working-class ward, though it had a high percentage of black voters, but less than Ward VI, which had the greatest concentration of blacks. Clearly, blacks sided with the Republicans, despite direct Populist appeals that their proposals for civil service reform would result in jobs.[66]

Alone, the Populist party was simply not of interest to Lawrence voters, for no ward in 1890 gave it more than a handful of votes. The Populists got their highest number of votes in 1892, the first time they fused with the Democrats, and this was in the most working-class of all wards, IV. However, the next year, when the Populists stood for suffrage, this same ward gave them 11 percent fewer votes. Lawrence's Democratic party vote was clearly a minor-

Table 8.1   Republican and Populist Votes for Governor, 1888–1896:
Lawrence and Douglas County

	1888	1890	1892	1894	1896
			Republican (%)		
Douglas County	62	47	59	51	50
Lawrence Wards					
I	75	52	66	66	70
II	65	64	72	67	73
III	64	49	61	64	66
IV	54	30	53	52	59
V	74	64	75	75	71
VI	85	72	79	82	75
			Populist (%)		
Douglas County	—	15	51	38.5	48
Lawrence Wards					
I	—	2	34	24	30
II	—	4	28	21	27
III	—	1	39	27	34
IV	—	1	47	36	41
V	—	2	25	15	29
VI	—	2	21	12	25

Note: See chap. 8, n. 67, for source of data. The Republican and Populist percentages do not total 100 in some years, e.g., 1894, because there were more than two
tickets in the field.

ity vote, and tended to come primarily from the working-class
wards, though the majority of Lawrence's workers and members of
the lower-middle classes gave their support to the Republican party.

It was only in the townships of Douglas County that the Populists
were able to muster any support in this most Republican of counties. However, in 1890, when the Populists received 37 percent of
the votes for governor on a statewide basis, they captured only 15
percent of the votes in the townships of Douglas County. Those
townships that had the highest percentage of Populist voters were
those farthest from Lawrence, and did not have towns. The fusion
party captured the bulk of the votes in only one election year, 1892,
as table 8.1 shows. Ethnicity was at work in the townships just as it
was in the town of Lawrence. Eudora Township (see table 4.12) had
a sizeable German population, and when the Populists came out for

Table 8.2   Republican and Populist Votes for Governor, 1886–1896:
Fort Scott and Bourbon County

	1888	1890	1892	1894	1896
			Republican (%)		
Bourbon County	62	40	48.5	50	48
Fort Scott Wards					
I	58	40	48	57	50
II	63	50	57	62	59.5
III	61	48	50.5	61	56.5
IV	65	57	57	65	60.5
V	—	52	57	55	50
			Populist (%)		
Bourbon County	—	45	51.5	46	51.5
Fort Scott Wards					
I	—	6	52	27.5	50
II	—	6	43	20	40.5
III	—	8	49.5	27.5	43.5
IV	—	11	43	21.5	39.5
V	—	23	46	34.5	50.0

Note: See chap. 8, n. 68, for source of data. The Republican and Populist percentages do not total 100 in some years because there were more than two tickets in the field. There are no data recorded for Ward V, in 1888, because it was not yet formed.

suffrage in 1894 they received only 28 of Eudora's votes.[67] Fort Scott was not as pro-Republican as Lawrence, because, as I noted in chapter 4, the town had a strong Democratic party composed of people who had fought for the Union. Fort Scott also had more workers than Lawrence, many of whom were employed by the railroads. Even so, in 1888, as table 8.2 shows, the Republicans dominated in all wards of the city and in the townships of Bourbon County.[68] In 1890, the Populists took votes away from the Republicans and the Democrats, especially in the ward (V) that had the greatest number of workers. The wards which had the highest status (III and IV) were the only wards to go Republican that year. Wards I and V had the greatest number of workers. Most of the votes in 1890, however, went to the ex-governor from Lawrence, Robinson. Fusion attracted more voters to the ticket in 1892, though the Populists still carried only one ward. The workers of Fort Scott were as unenthusiastic about suffrage as those in other towns; in

1894, they deserted the ranks of the fusion party by the score, with drops in the range of 20 percent. The Populists' strength lay, as in Douglas County, in the townships, and in those most distant from Fort Scott. Those closer, with higher land values, such as Scott Township, returned a majority to the Republicans in 1890, rather than to the Populists, just as in many of the other townships.

The importance of economic and cultural variables in determining the outcome of an election can be seen clearly in Kansas City, Kansas. We will also see, however, that local political machines affected the outcome. Kansas City had a significant number of ethnic voters as well as native-born workers. The six wards of Kansas City can be briefly characterized as follows.

Ward I. The area surrounding the stockyards, with significant number of Irish, who are later replaced by Slavic and Croatian populations; the lowest-status ward.

Ward II. A portion of the area known as "Strawberry Hill," home of Croatians, mostly packinghouse workers; a working-class ward.

Ward III. The core of the wealthy, with blacks who were domestics, and other laborers for the wealthy; the most prosperous ward.

Ward IV. Catholics (Irish and German), some Croatians; also a prosperous ward.

Ward V. Croatians, Irish, railroad workers; working-class ward.

Ward VI. "Armourdale," a manufacturing area with Irish, Germans, Belgians; a low-status, working-class ward.[69]

In 1888, Republicans carried all wards, save the two I have characterized as the most working-class, e.g., I and VI. The Republican party fared far less well in the election of 1890, though as table 8.3 should make clear, this had little to do with the Populist party.[70] Most of the shift in votes away from the Republicans can be explained simply by the fact that Robinson, and resubmission, were attractive in all but the two most prosperous and least ethnic wards, e.g., III and IV.

In 1892, when there was a fusion ticket, there was a straight across-the-board increase in support for the Republicans. The fusion ticket cost the Democrats votes in every ward. This was even

Table 8.3   Republican and Populist Votes for Governor, 1888–1896:
Kansas City, Kansas

Vote by Wards	1888	1890	1892	1894	1896
			Republican (%)		
I	43	22	45	52	38
II	66	49	60	63	59
III	77	63	67	69	65
IV	56	52	57	61	58
V	58	38	48	57	47
VI	46	30	41	52	47
			Populist (%)		
I	—	3	55	43	62
II	—	2	40	28	41
III	—	3	33	19	35
IV	—	2	43	26	42
V	—	3	52	33	53
VI	—	2	59	37	53

Note: See chap. 8, n. 70, for source of data. The Republican and Populist percentages do not total 100 for some years because there were more than two parties in the field.

more true in 1894, when the voters rejected both fusion and suffrage in favor of the Republicans. Finally, in 1896, with Leedy running on a prolabor and probusiness platform in the area, the Democratic-Populist ticket reestablished itself in three of the city's six wards, losing most heavily in the two "better" wards. Between 1888 and 1900, however, the Democrats only once succeeded in carrying the city in a gubernational election (1890). Workers tended to see the Populist party as a farmer's party, but another factor explained the attraction of the Republican party for many of Kansas City's workers.

The first municipal election in Kansas City came in April of 1886, after considerable labor disorder in the city. The long strike against Jay Gould's railroad had just come to an end, and the political fortunes of the local Knights of Labor had suffered. The business classes, in reaction, tried to nominate a mayoral candidate who would represent their interests, but in a last-ditch effort the Knights captured the Republican nomination, and eventual election, for an Irish-Catholic stonemason, Thomas F. Hannan. Hannan was a reform mayor, who tried to curb the abuses of capital, and in particular of the railroads. In time, however, Alliance reformers in the city would come to refer to the "Hannan ring," and they began to lobby actively against his influence. They were aided and abetted by local Democrats, no longer able to claim the unalloyed support of many of Kansas City's workers. A vote against Hannan became, at one point, a vote against labor influence. In the mayoral election of 1895, Hannan was no longer in power, but Democratic and reform forces mobilized against his ghost. The Republican candidate, a wealthy realtor and "ring candidate," ran on a platform that was designed to attract workers. He openly promised them jobs, saying he would raise taxes and begin street-building. He was elected.[71] Many workers came to see their fortunes as bound up with the Republican party, both in Kansas and nationally. Populism did not appeal to them, and neither did it appeal to most other Kansans.

Summary

Perhaps the high point of the Populist movement came in 1890, when standing alone they captured 37 percent of the vote, rather than in 1896, when, with the aid of the Democrats, they controlled all branches of the state government. In 1890, Republicans, Democrats, and former third-party men came together determined to change the state's system of government. They were primarily from rural Kansas—the villages and farms lying in the middle of the state. This broad base of support would narrow in the ensuing elections.

The election of 1890, and those that followed, revealed how much faith the people of Kansas placed in normal political processes. The strategies they adopted in their attempts to change economic and social realities clearly reflected their belief that well-meaning men could elect others who would be fair. The idea that one would have to compromise principle, and make deals with one's political enemies, was repugnant to the Populists and a major reason they failed to be "effective" legislators. There were subsequent strains within the movement as leaders became interested in the workings of political power and tried to cajole farmer-legislators into compromises they found distasteful.

The Populists were faced with an insoluble dilemma. On their own, they had not been able to swing an election. They could not significantly affect or control the legislative process unless they fused with the opposition party. But fusion with the Democrats

meant a deradicalization of the party, so that, for many, the fusion
ticket came to be seen as "politics as usual." They became, because
of their chosen strategy, part of the very system they hoped to reform. Fusion changed the base of support for the Populists. At the
outset, a majority of farmers supported them; after fusion, they
came to represent the poorest farmers in the middle sector of the
state. The foreign-born also voted with the fusion ticket because of
traditional loyalties to the Democratic party. On the other hand,
the more well-to-do farmers (and there were more of these as the
decade progressed) voted for the Republican party. The Populists
were never able to attract workingmen to their side. When they ran
alone, they received almost no votes in the cities. When they fused
with the Democrats, they did slightly better, except when they
made the strategic political mistake of supporting suffrage in the
1894 election and had to witness mass desertions by workers.

The Populists' fortunes were not determined solely by cultural
and economic factors in the state. The Republican party was also a
major actor. On more than one occasion, Republicans tried to be
more radical than the Populists. In 1892, after suffering the trauma
of the 1890 election, they ran on a number of planks that were designed specifically to attract Alliance voters back to their ranks. In
legislative sessions, one of their defensive maneuvers was to side
with the Populists when it was possible for them to take credit for
the action. There is also evidence that they stalled and delayed legislation when the Populists were ascendant, and then passed the
same legislation when they were in power. There were always many
items in the Populist agenda that a proreform Republican party
could, and did, support. Both Populists and Republicans took
credit for the Australian ballot, arguing that it would bring an end
to "ticket scratching" and corruption. Both supported accounting
reforms for campaign contributions, free texts for school children,
and so on. In short, because of political pressure from farmers, and
because some of the legislation also fit a Republican agenda, many
items became state law in Kansas which on the face of it would appear "contradictory," because they benefitted classes other than industrialists and financiers in the very era of their ascendancy.

The Republicans were masters of the game of politics and were
aided in their efforts by the antireform local press, as well as the
national climate. When the Democrats elected their first governor
and controlled the state Senate in 1892, there ensued the "legislative
war of 1893." Republicans were able to claim that the Populists could

not govern, that they were anarchists and dangerous rebels. The Republicans also delayed the Populists' legislative agenda and then, when the lower house was finally organized, seized the initiative and introduced that very agenda under their aegis. The Populists came out of this particular session weakened by fusion and by the fact that they had not passed the legislation they stood for. The leaders of the party compromised with the Democrats in the election of a United States senator, and sent Martin, rather than the Populist Doster, to Washington. This action, along with other compromises during 1893, divided the Populist radicals, who stood for principle above fusion, against those who were interested in office and patronage. The radical faction, led in part by Mary Lease, would "impose" suffrage on the Populist convention in 1894, thereby driving out many Democrats and assuring the Populists of the loss of many ethnic votes.

The Populists could not place on the statute books those very items that were of greatest interest to Kansas farmers—control of the railroads, and lower interest rates. Lower rates, of course, were something that only the national government could effect—when senators and congressmen who would support a liberalized monetary policy were in Washington. The national party, which had begun with a broad agenda, narrowed it to a focus on the free and unlimited coinage of silver. The Kansas Populists had other interests, and many did not see free coinage as a solution to the farmers' or the nation's problems. For a time the party was unique, pitting itself against the "money power," the gold men, in both parties. The Democrat William Jennings Bryan began to agitate against the policies of Cleveland and the disaster that these policies had brought upon the country. After telling the assembled delegates at the Democratic national convention, "thou shall not crucify mankind upon a cross of gold," he became the man who would lead the fight against McKinley. Though the Populists could have decided not to support Bryan, they did support him because, once again, experience had taught them that, if they hoped to win, they needed the help of the Democrats.

The platform that Bryan ran on was, perhaps, more radical than that of the man who stood for governor on the Populist ticket in Kansas. Leedy did not challenge the money power, nor did he attack industrialists or the business classes in his 1896 campaign. The Kansas Populists, who were no longer infused with the spirit of the Alliance, posed as another party that could bring prosperity to the state. They were distinguished from the Republicans in that election by the fact that the Kansas Republicans had to retreat from their previous support of the free coinage of silver, as their national party came out squarely for a single gold standard.

The reasons for the Populists' ultimate decline in Kansas were economic, organizational, and ideological. Economically, they came to appeal to the poorest farmers. With increased prosperity under McKinley, the party held less appeal. The state Republican party had also achieved ideological hegemony. It was the "Grand Old Party," and Union loyalties remained strong, as indicated by voting patterns in towns such as Lawrence. The Republican party was also seen by many as a party of reform. That is one reason why, when the Republicans began to incorporate significant portions of Alliance and Populist demands into their platform, and to pass favorable legislation, people drifted back to the Republican fold. By these methods, they removed a great deal of the support upon which the Populist party had been based.

Many of the initial recruits to the Alliance were rational, opportunistic voters. The rapid growth of the Alliance meant that many potential voters had not developed strong ties with it, nor had the Alliance had time to develop the necessary organization or discipline for sustained electoral success. When the Alliance offered its first slate of candidates, under the label of the Populist party or endorsed Republicans who pledged to abide by Alliance goals, many farmers cast their lot with them. They had much to gain if the Populists succeeded. When, however, the Populists could not translate discontent into political gain, and the Republican party offered solutions, farmers, once again, voted with the dominant party.

The Populists were not able to maintain the sense of community necessary for the success of a mass democratic movement. As they became increasingly like members of other political parties, as people who held positions of trust and authority came to worry more about their election or reelection than the animating spirit of the group, oligarchy reigned.[72]

The idea that the business of America was business grew out of the agrarian and third-party struggles that took place in states like Kansas at the end of the nineteenth century. Well-meaning farmers lost an important struggle when prosperity came to be defined in terms of industrial growth. The moral overtones of the conflict were important. Early in the postwar years, those who stood for credit, against the concentration of wealth, were labeled as irresponsible agitators. Peace, progress, and prosperity became the Republican party's hymn. When McKinley defeated Bryan in 1896, agrarianism was pushed to the side. The visions of the Alliance reformers, in which each laborer would control his own destiny, in which prosperity would rest on the backs of laboring men and women who would be justly rewarded for their toil, gave way to the ideology of the merchant. Babbitt and his friends would dominate in the twentieth century.

> They went profoundly into the science of business. . . . To them, the Romantic Hero was no longer that knight, the wandering poet, the cowpuncher, the aviator . . ., but the great sales-manager, . . . whose title of nobility was "Go-getter," and who devoted himself and all his young samurai to the cosmic purpose of Selling—not selling anything in particular, but pure Selling.[73]

Could it have been otherwise?

Epilogue
Plowing the Ocean

An early twentiety-century Kansas farmer plowing his field to prevent wind erosion. Courtesy Kansas State Historical Society.

Nineteenth-century farmers did not accept their fate quietly. They did not accept as inevitable their loss of control over how they lived and labored, and over the products of that labor. They saw the dominant political parties acting for the privileged and for monopolies, and came together determined to challenge cynicism and corruption and to demand justice. In so doing, they created themselves as a class, became subjects rather than objects of history. Nevertheless, they failed to make this a democratic country, one in which small holdings and simple equality would be the rule rather than the exception. They failed to get their fellow Americans to rise above racism, sectionalism, and their own narrow self-interests and to stand on principle. They offered America an agenda that called for participation as citizens, debate, and an integration of the public and private spheres. It was rejected in favor of easy answers to difficult problems.

Today, we are so numbed by the distance between public and private, by the absence of any serious debate, and by limitations of the political process, that we forget that once it was otherwise. There is much to be learned from those who came together to form the Farmers' Alliance, and later the Populist party: lessons about how and why people mobilize, as well as what conditions allow people to transform the social order, even temporarily. But above all, their story is the story of a class that failed in its attempt to become a dominant force—morally, politically, and economically—in American history.

A class is not a static entity. It is first and foremost a process. People who see themselves as different, describe themselves as different, and act on this basis, are members of a class. The kind of work persons do, or the way in which they do that work, influences attitudes about the larger social order. When people mobilize, it is often to protect cherished forms of working and living. However, whether people can mobilize and create themselves as an autonomous class has much to do with their ability to organize themselves. The development of class consciousness, the disposition to think and act as a class, is intimately bound up with people's ability to form unique organizations which represent their interests. If a class is to become dominant, or simply survive as a class, there must be an organization, be it a union or political party, which acts in the name of the class. Yet history is full of examples of people mobilizing on the basis of interests that cross-cut class ties and threaten the ability of those people to act in terms of class interests. Class is, therefore, simultaneously structure, ideology, and organization.

For farmers to create themselves as an ascendant class, they needed more than a distinctive position in the occupational hierarchy. They also had to wage an ideological battle, and they needed to form and control an organization—a political party—which would represent their distinct interests. Their ability to do so was determined in part by the structural conditions, as well as by the new structures they created. Our society is not what they hoped for. No matter how rational humans might be, and no matter how active their response to the world, they sometimes make strategic mistakes, and their actions sometimes have consequences they could never have foreseen.

If the Civil War did nothing else, it revealed the contradictions between the dream and the reality of American democracy. Men fought and died for principle, and others grew rich. Many wanted no more than the right to work for themselves, to own a small piece of land, and to prosper or fail as their own efforts dictated. Those who took up the plow were unprepared for the fact that when it came time to ship their grain and hogs to market, the railroads and meat-packing combines lay in wait for them, charging prices for shipping and paying rates for their products that soon made them as desperate as the working poor. They were also unprepared for the fact that their government seemed bent on helping the very men and corporations that had turned their hopes to ashes.

Third-party movements washed in and out with the cycles of prosperity and devastation in the 1870s and 1880s. The collapse of Jay Cooke's empire in 1873 ushered in the first post–Civil War depression, which dragged on for several long years. This depression gave rise to farmer and worker movements throughout the country, but these movements receded as prosperity returned, because little effort had been made to build a strong organizational base among the discontented. But as each movement entered and exited, it left behind a legacy: stories about the "Crime of 1873," when silver was demonetized, about the Crédit Mobilier and government corruption, about the growing concentration of wealth, and political parties that cared far more about reelection than principle. Slowly, a sense of injustice and an agenda were building. A debate was beginning and the very meaning of America was questioned. How should progress be achieved? How could one assure the prosperity of the many? For a growing class of merchants, industrialists, and financiers the answer was that prosperity would result through the efforts of soldier-entrepreneurs, who would mobilize the resources of the country, rather than leaving them in the hands of those who would squander them: workers, agrarians, reformers, blacks, and Indians. There would be no more battles of the Little Big Horn. Capital would not be defeated by "uncivilized" rabble. The rule for the rabble was work or die. On the other hand, farmers and workers argued that it was *their* labor which created wealth. Instead of helping corporations, the government should help them. They were reacting to the country's growing industrialization and, specifically, to changes in the meaning of work.

The men and women who came to Kansas were not isolated from these national debates or trends. They were intimately involved in them. But their circumstances were unique. "Bloody Kansas," which had figured prominently in both pre–Civil War, as well as Civil War, hostilities, had finally been settled as a free state, and the fortunes of the Republican party in Kansas were largely determined by this fact. The state's growth occurred almost exclusively in the post–Civil War period, with former Union veterans coming to claim their land, along with merchants and others who hoped to do well. Those who came found a hostile and unpredictable climate, but their optimism remained surprisingly high. When agricultural prices reached their highest level, in 1881, the rush to the state was on. Some counties, principally those in the middle sector of the state where rainfall was erratic, doubled their population in a two-year period. Many late arrivals had to borrow heavily for their land and for the equipment necessary to turn the prairie sod. Then came the long drought, which began in 1887, and coincided with a drop in farm prices. Homes, animals, and futures were mortgaged. Towns and businesses had been "boomed" right along with the farms, and were heavily dependent on continued agricultural prosperity. However, farmers and town merchants were *not* agreed on what the solutions to the problems should be.

Economic position, everyday experience with the economic system, and values all came together. Farmers were entrepreneurs, independent yeomen, who either owned their own means of production or intended to. Yet, after the Civil War, farmers were inserted into a national and, at times, international economy. Their fortunes were determined by international commodity prices and markets over which they had little or no control. Because farmers were not sufficiently well organized to control market prices, they found their surplus labor "appropriated" by market mechanisms and by those whom they called rapacious capitalists, middlemen, or parasites. They rose up because of their immediate economic immiseration, and they also challenged the new idea of work. Their entire way of life was being threatened.

Though merchants were also entrepreneurs, and suffered as a result of the economic downturn, they experienced economic reality differently. Merchants were not protesting changed definitions of work; in fact, they celebrated the rise of industrial America. It meant larger markets and increased prosperity for them. There was almost no basis for solidarity between hard-pressed merchants and farmers. Merchants and small industrialists saw themselves as the next Jay Goulds, their towns as the next Chicagos. They eagerly adopted the ideology of eastern industrialists who argued that the future of the country lay not in the garden but in the factory. These men and women did everything in their power to boost the growth of their towns. They took on staggering levels of debt to attract the fickle railroads to their hamlets; they issued bonds for commercial enterprises; they tried to entice manufacturers from one town to another with promises of new facilities. Farmers resented the control that merchants exercised over the town's finances and politics, and resented being taxed for bond issues which did them little good. At the same time, the category of worker was a very fluid one on the Great Plains; many workers easily crossed over the line delineating "independent" businessman, carrying their own boxes of tools.

The language that Kansas farmers used to articulate their concerns played a crucial role in bringing farmers together, but it also served to distance workers, to mobilize powerful elites against them, and to inhibit the development of a powerful critique of the developing capitalist system. What unifying force can bring people together and sustain them in solidarity when results are not forthcoming? Language speaks to hope for the future, about how structures can be changed. It plays a central role in determining whether or not people can form autonomous class-dominated organizations. This language comes from two sources: out of the circumstances of people's lives and out of the organizations, or movements, of which they are a part. It, like class itself, is emergent.

The concerns of farmers were primarily land, transportation, and money. Those of Kansas workers centered around a desire to prohibit the use of convict labor and to restrict immigration. Their future hope lay with economic growth. Like the middle-class merchants of the towns, many believed that the rhetoric of the farmer spoke of anarchy and rebellion, and that it would drive desperately needed capital from the state. This was a mistake. The farmer's call was remarkably nonradical—for a control of monopolists and an end to corruption. An important contradiction was, in fact, embedded in the language used to call for change. Farmers wanted a government of the people, one answerable and accessible to them; they did not want bureaucracy. They also wanted a government that would participate actively in regulation and control. They wanted a government which would protect the rights of small property-holders, while curbing the interests of the large property-holder. They wanted, in short, a capitalist system with none of the abuses of that system. They placed great faith in a redeemed political system.

By the turn of the century, with the onset of the Spanish-American War, the fortunes of Kansas farmers had begun to improve. Here an 1897 threshing crew
pauses in their labor for the photographer. Permission of the Joseph J. Pennell Collection, Kansas Collection of the University of Kansas Libraries.

Farmers felt responsible for bringing about this redemption. In
the summer of 1889, hundreds gathered to discuss their problems
and make sense of their plight. The summer encampments in Kansas were responsible for the development of a movement culture.
They were a group of people who saw themselves as occupying a
unique place in the economic order, with a distinctive set of values.
They preached love and charity, and spoke of a commonwealth of
all producers. Solutions to their troubles appeared simple and at
hand. They would act together and elect men who would uphold
the principles for which they stood. They found reason for optimism in their sheer numbers, which created a sense of physical and
psychological unity. No one thought about what to do if things did
not turn out as they wanted them to. The action which was called
for seemed limited and direct—men would vote. The limited nature of the commitment itself attracted many to the Alliance. It was
in a farmer's immediate self-interest to stand with the Alliance. It
was not clear to farmers, however, why it was in their *class* interest
to stay for the duration of the battle. The political strategy of running farmer slates had both positive and negative results. It got
people to act in concert, to think of themselves as members of a dis-

tinct group who could gain if they stood beside one another on the barricades. However, the shift to politics exacerbated existing divisions within the movement.

The Kansas alliances were formed in a one-year period, which meant that people did not have time to learn or develop a coherent ideology or to debate specific strategies. The economic cooperatives which characterized the efforts of the Southern Alliance, and were central in people's political and economic education, were simply not a factor in Kansas. There was also a rapid shift between what was a heterogeneous social movement and the creation of the Populist party. Part of the problem was that organizational mechanisms had not been developed to link the local suballiances with the new party, and part of it was the leadership.

The leadership of the Populist party was composed primarily of former third-party members. This group of people had an agenda that paralleled that of Kansas farmers but did not always reflect farmers' immediate interests. This in itself would not have been crucial had there been some mechanism established for debate, for the education of both followers and leaders. When the Alliance was taken wholesale into the Populist party, the local suballiances withered rapidly away. The leadership developed strategies which made perfectly good sense to them but were not adequately explained to the membership. The high point of the farmers' movement was 1890, when they alone captured 37 percent of the vote. After this, the leadership decided that the only way they could bring about change was by fusing with the Democrats. This decision drove some farmers, particularly Republicans, out of the Populist camp. The Populist leadership also was divided against itself. There were those who vehemently opposed fusion with the Democrats, seeing it as the worst form of treachery and a compromise of principles, and those who wanted the party to take a stand on women's suffrage. More "practical" leaders, however, wanted to avoid suffrage, knowing that it would alienate ethnic voters and possibly the Democratic party. In both state and national politics, winning took priority. The free coinage of silver was seized on as a strategy designed to bring victory at the polls. This strategy deradicalized the movement and allowed it to be swept up by the Democrats when they nominated Bryan in 1896 and took the silver plank as their own creation.

That the Populists accomplished as much as they did is remarkable. Many of the things they stood for were incorporated into law, because the country was in the midst of another major depression, which contributed to the mobilization of farmers and demanded solutions. Nationally, the margin of victory between the dominant parties had been a percentage point or less in four presidential elections. At both the state and national levels, the regular parties were quick to include planks which spoke to the needs of the producing classes. And, in some cases, certainly in Kansas, the state-level parties acted to pass legislation designed to maintain their hold on these voters. Through the technique of selective endorsement, brought on by a system crisis, the regular parties undercut the Populists and eroded their bases of support. In Kansas, as the decade closed, the Populists adopted strategies which reduced politics to the very clichés they had hoped to avoid. They represented an ever narrower base of the farming population. Their deradicalization was complete in 1896, when they ran on a platform almost indistinguishable from that of their Republican opponents.

Could the farmers of America have succeeded in creating a distinct class movement, one which would successfully have altered the face of America, or were all of their activities no more than attempts at plowing the ocean? It is worth recalling just how many imponderables there were that affected the fate of the Populists. McKinley's victory over Bryan was exceptionally narrow in 1896, because the Republican party, under Mark Hanna, was able to bring to the polls thousands of new voters. What would have happened if Bryan had not conceded the northeast? America's workers had not come together as a class, nor had they discovered an effective technique for preventing strikebreakers from keeping plants open. What if they had been successful? What if the Knights of Labor had not lost the strike to Jay Gould? Would farmers and laborers then have been able to come together in a powerful alliance? What if racial and sectional prejudice had not operated so strongly and all of the farming classes could have acted as one? What if the Spanish-American War had not driven prices up and improved economic conditions for both workers and farmers? If none of these things had happened, or if all the right things had happened, would the farmers have been able to create themselves as a distinct class?

My answer is no, but it must be qualified. For a class to become a class for itself, one not confined to the dustbin of history, it must possess structure, organization, and ideology. As Marx claims in the *Eighteenth Brumaire,* if a group of people, occupying a distinctive place in the mode of production, "begets no unity, no national union, and no political organization, they do not form a class" (p. 109). He had grave doubts as to whether members of the petty bourgeoisie—and yeomen farmers were that—could act in their own name. While farmers saw themselves as unique, and acted on that basis, and formed a unique political organization, they could not sustain that organization. They failed because a group of people who did not represent their interests appropriated the movement. As victory became ever more elusive, non-class ties reasserted themselves and the movement died. The lesson seems clear: without a strong organization, acting on behalf of the class, though clearly grounded in the reality of the class, a class movement cannot succeed. Nineteenth-century American history is replete with third-party movements, but they are known only to the archivist and historian. Those whose results are still visible in the form of unions and organizations that act on behalf of distinct class groupings were groups that had a strong, powerful, and centralized organization or party at their core.

Classes, as I have defined them, do not rise spontaneously from contradictions between the social relations of production and the social forces of production. They arise because real people have grievances, because people come to recognize the contradictions as affecting their lives. But other steps are necessary. People must come together and discuss their problems; they must understand both the source of their misery as well as the fact that the solutions lie in collective action. Finally, they must act in concert to change history.

What the Populists originally hoped for was a Jeffersonian state, one in which there was an informed electorate, one in which political debate and action were a normal part of life. They longed for a society in which justice was the rule and inequality the exception. If we still experience such longings, we must create and sustain those organizations that make possible the pursuit of such a society.

Notes

Preface

1. Tocqueville, *Democracy in America,* p. 287.
2. Ibid., p. 514.
3. Quoted in Matthews, *The Radical Politics of Thomas Jefferson,* p. 89.
4. Ibid., p. 112.
5. Ibid., p. 116. Also see Bowles and Gintis, *Democracy and Capitalism,* especially chapter 1, for a discussion of essential differences between Jefferson and Madison.
6. Adams, *Education,* p. 109.
7. Goodwyn, *The Populist Moment,* p. 264.
8. Bowles and Gintis, *Democracy and Capitalism,* p. 8.
9. Quoted in A. Plummer, *Bronterre: A Political Biography of Bronterre O'Brien,* p. 177–78.

Chapter One

1. Cited in Goodwyn, *The Populist Moment,* p. 195.
2. Cited in Morison et al., *The Growth of the American Republic,* 2:173.
3. Cited in Barr, "The Populist Uprising," pp. 1150–51.
4. The figures on Alliance membership must be treated with extreme caution, and will be discussed in detail in chapter 7. The first figure, 100,000, comes from the May 6, 1890, edition of the *Farmer's Advocate,* and the second, of 10,000, comes from a Republican newspaper, the *Lawrence Daily Journal* of March 19, 1890.
5. The figures here refer to Kansas votes in gubernatorial elections and come from Hein and Sullivant's *Kansas Votes,* pp. 27 and 29.
6. Goodwyn, *The Populist Moment,* p. vii.
7. Poulantzas, *State, Power, Socialism.*
8. Thompson, *The Making of the English Working Class,* p. 11.
9. Thompson, *The Poverty of Theory,* p. 295, original emphases.
10. Ibid., p. 8.

11. Ibid., p. 298, emphases in original.

12. See, in particular, Calhoun, *The Question of Class Struggle*, and Hobsbawm, "The Making of the Working Class, 1870–1914."

13. Anderson, *Passages from Antiquity to Feudalism* and *Arguments within English Marxism;* Althusser, *For Marx;* Althusser and Balibar, *Reading Capital.*

14. Porpora, "The Role of Agency in History."

15. Calhoun, *The Question of Class Struggle.*

16. See Burawoy, *The Politics of Production*, pp. 35–40, who defines class in a similar manner; and Meiksins, "Beyond the Boundary Question," for a discussion of why class cannot be defined in occupational terms but must be defined in terms similar to mine.

17. Calhoun, *The Question of Class Struggle*, p. 136.

18. Roy, "Class Conflict and Social Change in Historical Perspective," pp. 497–98.

19. Gutman, "Work, Culture, and Society in Industrializing America."

20. See Sewell, "Ideologies and Social Revolutions," for a discussion of the "independent" structuring role of ideology.

21. Snow et al., "Frame Alignment and Mobilization."

22. Aminzade, *Class, Politics, and Early Industrial Capitalism.*

23. Katznelson, "Working-Class Formation," pp. 17–19.

24. Skocpol, "Political Response to Capitalist Crisis."

25. Levine, "Marxism, Sociology, and Neo-Marxist Theories of the State," and Quadagno, "Welfare Capitalism and the Social Security Act of 1935."

26. Poulantzas, *State, Power, Socialism.*

27. Shefter, "Trade Unions and Political Machines," has provided an excellent description and analysis of the means by which trade unions and political parties channeled and contained class conflicts within the United States.

28. Prezworski, "The Process of Class Formation from Karl Kautsky's *The Class Struggle* to Recent Debates."

29. Marx, *The Eighteenth Brumaire*, p. 124.

30. For a discussion of the problems involved in using the concept of class consciousness see Katznelson, "Working-Class Formation," pp. 17–19.

31. Hahn, *The Roots of Southern Populism*, p. 271.

32. Granovetter, "Economic Action and Social Structure," p. 487.

33. Clawson, "Fraternal Orders and Class Formation in the Nineteenth-Century United States," p. 674.

34. Moore, *Injustice.*

35. Barnes, *Farmers in Rebellion*, makes the explicit argument that the ideology of a protesting group must externalize the blame for failure.

36. Goodwyn, *The Populist Moment.*

37. Barnes, *Farmers in Rebellion*, pp. 160–70.

38. Ibid., and Schwartz, *Radical Protest and Social Structure*.

39. Barnes, *Farmers in Rebellion*, p. 98.

40. McAdam, "Tactical Innovation."

41. Schwartz, *Radical Protest and Social Structure*.

42. McAdam, "Tactical Innovation."

43. Olson, *The Logic of Collective Action*, p. 2.

44. Jenkins, "Resource Mobilization Theory and the Study of Social Movements."

45. Oberschall, "Theories of Social Conflict"; McCarthy and Zald, *The Trend of Social Movements*.

46. Fireman and Gamson, "Utilitarian Logic," p. 10.

47. Jenkins, "Resource Mobilization Theory," pp. 537–38.

48. Klandermans, "Social-Psychological Expansions of Resource Mobilization Theory," p. 592.

49. Hannigan, "Alain Touraine, Manuel Castells and Social Movement Theory," p. 441.

50. Calhoun, *The Question of Class Struggle*, p. 229.

51. Offe, *Disorganized Capitalism*.

52. Schwartz, *Radical Protest and Social Structure*, p. 195.

53. Gamson, *The Strategy of Social Protest*.

54. C. Tilly, L. Tilly, and R. Tilly, *The Rebellious Century;* C. Tilly, *From Mobilization to Revolution;* C. Tilly and L. Tilly, *Collective Action and Class Conflict*.

55. Jenkins, "Resource Mobilization Theory," p. 540.

56. Gamson, *The Strategy of Social Protest*, and "Understanding the Careers of Challenging Groups."

57. Gamson, *The Strategy of Social Protest*, p. 107–8.

58. Tilly, *From Mobilization to Revolution;* Skocpol, *States and Revolution*.

59. Piven and Cloward, *Poor People's Movements*.

60. Ibid., p. 283. My analysis of Piven and Cloward's argument follows that of Hobsbawm, "Should Poor People Organize?" and the page references are from Hobsbawm's citations.

61. Piven and Cloward, *Poor People's Movements*, p. 286.

62. Ibid., p. 290.

63. Hobsbawm, "Should Poor People Organize?" p. 290.

64. Ibid.

65. Ibid., p. 293.

66. Traugott, *Armies of the Poor*.

67. Hicks, *The Populist Revolt*, p. 2.

68. Also see Minogue, "Populism as a Political Movement," whose view parallels that of Hofstadter.

69. The *Democratic Promise* was later published in an abridged form, *The Populist Moment*, which I have used throughout this study.

70. Goodwyn, *The Populist Moment*, p. 9.

71. Ibid., pp. xviii–xxi.

72. Stanley Parsons, "The Role of Cooperatives in the Development of the Movement Culture of Populism."

73. Billings, "Class and Class Politics in the Southern Populist Movement."

74. Argersinger, *Populism and Politics*, p. 303.

75. Ibid., p. 306, emphases added. Lipset, *Agrarian Socialism*, has also argued that one of the major problems of the Canadian populist movement was oligarchy.

Chapter Two

1. Cited in Trachtenberg, *The Incorporation of America*, p. 73.

2. Giddens, *The Constitution of Society*, p. 189.

3. Williamson and Lindert, *American Inequality*, p. 21.

4. Ibid., p. 62.

5. Wilentz, *Chants Democratic*, p. 363.

6. Trachtenberg, *The Incorporation of America*, p. 8.

7. Cited in Barr, "The Populist Uprising," p. 1140.

8. Holmes, "The Concentration of Wealth," p. 593.

9. Original data from Charles Spahr. Cited in Trachtenberg, *The Incorporation of America*, p. 99.

10. Montgomery, *Beyond Equality*, p. 8ff.

11. Ibid., p. 30.

12. Buck, *The Granger Movement*, p. 37.

13. Goodwyn, *The Populist Moment*, p. 7.

14. Sundquist, *Dynamics of the Party System*, p. 104.

15. Ibid., p. 104.

16. Johnson, cited in Montgomery, *Beyond Equality*, p. 337.

17. Montgomery, *Beyond Equality*, p. 347.

18. Blair to Broadhead, cited in McPherson, *Struggle for Equality*, p. 380–81.

19. Motley, *Four Questions for the People*, p. 9–10, 24, 30, 53, 66.

20. Adams, *Education*, p. 265.

21. Sundquist, *Dynamics of the Party System*, p. 107.

22. McNall and McNall, *Plains Families*, p. 9.

23. Taylor, *The Farmers' Movement*, p. 145.

24. Martin, *Behind the Scenes in Washington*. Cited in Taylor, *The Farmers' Movement*, p. 146.

25. Cochrane, *The Development of American Agriculture*.

26. Hicks et al., *The American Nation*, p. 169.

27. Shannon, *The Farmers' Last Frontier*, p. 185.

28. Farmer, "The Economic Background of Frontier Populism," p. 387.

29. Cited in Farmer, ibid.

30. Nash et al., *The American People*, p. 632.

31. William A. Reddy, in his discussion of why French laborers in the

textile industry finally struck, argues that they reacted to a change in the meaning of work. "It was not so much a decline in the standard of living, not the drudgery of machine tending, nor the poor housing of factory towns that afflicted society during the early phase of industrialization, but a loss of independence, the violation of old moral standards by unrestricted competition." Reddy, *The Rise of Market Culture,* p. ix.

32. Bogue, *Money at Interest,* and North, *Growth and Welfare in the American Past.*

33. Hofstadter, *Age of Reform,* and North, *Growth and Welfare in the American Past.*

34. Mayhew, "A Reappraisal of the Causes of Farm Protest," p. 468.

35. Ibid., p. 473.

36. Palmer, "*Man Over Money,*" p. 210.

37. Ibid., p. 217.

38. See ibid., for a discussion and elaboration of these points.

39. Taylor, *The Farmers' Movement,* p. 133.

40. Cited in ibid., p. 164.

41. Sundquist, *Dynamics of the Party System,* p. 111.

42. Ibid., p. 112.

43. Nash et al., *The American People,* p. 554.

44. Ibid., p. 556.

45. Ibid.

46. Ibid., p. 557.

47. Haynes, *Third Party Movements,* p. 106ff.

48. Ibid., p. 107.

49. Sundquist, *Dynamics of the Party System,* p. 113.

50. Haynes, *Third Party Movements,* p. 125.

51. Ibid., p. 113–14.

52. Lloyd, *Henry Demarest Lloyd,* 1:139.

53. Sundquist, *Dynamics of the Party System,* p. 120.

54. Buchanan, *The Story of a Labor Organizer,* p. 426.

55. Haynes, *Third Party Movements,* p. 211.

56. Cited in Goodwyn, *The Populist Moment,* p. 25.

57. Ibid., p. 27.

58. Ibid., p. 40.

59. Haynes, *Third Party Movements,* p. 214.

60. They were, in fact, indebted to mortgage companies and banks. The important difference is that banks and mortgage companies wanted cash, not crops, in payment of debts. There is little evidence that western bankers foreclosed on farmers to gain control of their land; if land was seized, it was only as a last resort. See Bogue, *Money at Interest.*

61. Cited in Nixon, "Cleavage within Farmers' Alliance Movement," p. 29. Also see Nixon for an elaboration of the issues which divided the two alliances.

62. Sundquist, *Dynamics of the Party System,* p. 123.

63. Ibid., pp. 125–27.

64. Hahn, *The Roots of Southern Populism,* p. 284.

65. See Burnham, *Critical Elections,* as well as Skocpol and Orloff, "Why Not Equal Protection," for a discussion of the triumph of regulation in the Gilded Age.

66. *Weekly Iowa State Register* (Des Moines, July 8, 1881), cited in Haynes, *Third Party Movements,* p. 145.

67. Trachtenberg, *The Incorporation of America,* p. 22.

68. Slotkin, *The Fatal Environment,* p. 290, but see all of chapter 13 for a discussion of these issues.

69. Slotkin, *The Fatal Environment.*

70. Foner, *The Great Labor Uprising of 1877,* cited in Trachtenberg, *The Incorporation of America,* p. 71.

71. Cited in Slotkin, *The Fatal Environment,* p. 362.

Chapter Three

1. Bannon, *The Spanish Borderlands,* p. 12.

2. Cited in Sears, *The Sex Radicals,* p. 118.

3. This material is drawn from McNall and McNall, *Plains Families,* pp. 14–15.

4. Cited in Morison, *The Oxford History of the American People,* 2:591.

5. Bailey, "John Brown and the Kansas Conflict," p. 39.

6. Emerson, "On Affairs in Kansas," pp. 42–43.

7. "Conflict Characterized Rise to Statehood," p. 3.

8. Parrish, "Kansas Agriculture Before 1900," p. 403.

9. Clark and Roberts, *People of Kansas,* pp. 10–11.

10. Ise, *Sod and Stubble,* p. 166.

11. Crane, "Nebraska's Bitter Fight for Life," pp. 409–10.

12. Richmond, *Kansas,* p. 133.

13. Cited in Howes, *This Place Called Kansas,* pp. 166–67.

14. Cited in Dykstra, *The Cattle Towns,* p. 192.

15. In Ruede, *Sod-House Days.*

16. Parrish, "Kansas Agriculture Before 1900," p. 440.

17. Ibid.

18. Cited by McNall, In, Foreword, Ruede, *Sod-House Days,* p. xiii.

19. Clark and Roberts, *People of Kansas,* p. 24.

20. Ibid., pp. 49–50, 208.

21. This division into regions is based on ibid., pp. 31–61.

22. Burch, *Kansas As It Is,* p. 141.

23. *Kansas As She Is,* p. 8.

24. Watson, Letters, in P. J. Jennings papers.

25. *Kansas As She Is,* p. 6.

26. Dick, *The Sod-House Frontier,* p. 360.

27. See McNall, "State, Party, and Ideology."

28. Cited in Miller, "The Background of Populism in Kansas," p. 473.

29. Ibid., p. 482.

30. U.S. Bureau of the Census, *Report on Statistics of Agriculture, Eleventh Annual Census*, pp. 84–85.

31. Cather, "Eldorado: A Kansas Recessional," p. 364.

32. Clark and Roberts, *People of Kansas*, pp. 44–48.

33. U.S. Bureau of the Census, *Report on Real Estate Mortgages, Eleventh Annual Census*, p. 161.

34. Miller, "The Background of Populism in Kansas," p. 483.

35. Ibid., p. 487.

36. Ise, *Sod and Stubble*, p. 209.

37. Parrish, "Kansas Agriculture Before 1900," p. 424.

38. Miller, "The Background of Populism in Kansas," pp. 484–85.

39. Malin, "Turnover of Farm Population," pp. 365–72.

40. Miller, "The Background of Populism in Kansas," p. 485.

41. Quoted in Ise, *Sod and Stubble*, p. 183.

42. Bogue, "Farm Debtors in Pioneer Kingsley," and *Money at Interest*; Severson, "The Source of Mortgage Credit for Champaign County."

43. See Zornow, "The Basis of Agrarian Unrest in Kansas, 1870–1890," pp. 455–62, for a discussion of these points.

44. Miller, "Financing the Boom in Kansas," p. 73.

45. Zornow, *Kansas: A History of the Jayhawk State*, p. 190.

46. Ibid., p. 192–94.

47. Some of those who called themselves Liberal or Independent Republicans were Democrats.

48. Reude, *Sod-House Days*.

49. *Osborne County Farmer* (Osborne, Kansas), July 14, 1876, p. 3.

Chapter Four

1. *Fort Scott Daily Monitor*, June 29, 1897.

2. Ware, "A Corn Poem," July 4, 1876, cited in Douglas, *A History of Manufacturers in the Kansas Fuel District*, pp. 1–3.

3. See Lamar, *The Far Southwest*, for a discussion of the concept of internal colonialism.

4. Kansas Board of Agriculture, *Fifteenth Annual Report*, p. 1196.

5. Kansas Board of Agriculture, *Fourth Annual Report*, pp. 502–3.

6. Douglas, *A History of Manufacturers in the Kansas District*, p. 39.

7. Ibid., pp. 43–47.

8. Andreas, *History of the State of Kansas*, 2:1065.

9. For an excellent discussion of how this operated in the development of Leavenworth, Kansas, see Rita Napier, "Squatter City."

10. Hawkins, "Fort Scott: The First Generation," p. 48.

11. *The Fort Scott Democrat*, July 13, 1861.

12. Robley, *History of Bourbon County*, p. 172–73.

13. Hawkins, "Fort Scott," p. 78.

14. Kuhns, "An Army Surgeon's Letters to His Wife," p. 313.

15. Robley, *History of Bourbon County*, p. 205–6.

16. Fort Scott Board of Trade, *Report of the Special Committee of the Board of Trade*, p. 8, original emphases.

17. Ibid., pp. 13, 12.

18. *Fort Scott Daily Monitor*, April 17, 1873.

19. Ibid., June 18, 1873.

20. Fort Scott Board of Trade, *Report of the Special Committee*, pp. 9–11.

21. Pease, "A History of Banking in Bourbon County," pp. 5–22.

22. Kansas Bureau of Labor, *Fourth Annual Report*.

23. Williamson and Lindert, *American Inequality*.

24. Edwards, "Alma: Community and Shire Town of Wabaunsee County, Kansas."

25. Kansas Bureau of Labor, *Ninth Annual Report*, pp. 62, 166.

26. Douglas, *A History of Manufacturers in the Kansas Fuel District*, p. 49.

27. Tripp, "Kansas Communities and the Birth of the Labor Problem," and Walker and Leibengood, "Labor Organizations in Kansas in the Early Eighties."

28. North, *Growth and Welfare in the American Past*.

29. Clawson, "Fraternal Orders and Class Formation." See the discussion of Clawson's work in chapter 1.

30. Lesher, "The History of Bourbon County," pp. 99–176.

31. See ibid., pp. 29–48, for a listing of those whom he considered to be the leaders in Fort Scott. Though there is overlap, my definition of a leader is somebody who held an elected position, e.g., mayor or councilman. My reason for defining these as leadership positions has to do with the fact that people who held these positions had control over scarce resources, e.g., tax monies and jobs that were created by council expenditures.

32. Connelley, *Kansas and Kansans*, 3 : 1227.

33. Andreas, *History of the State of Kansas*, 1 : 1083.

34. Fort Scott Board of Trade, *Report of the Special Committee*, p. 2.

35. Cited in Andreas, *History of the State of Kansas*, 1 : 312–13.

36. Middleton, "Manufacturing in Lawrence," p. 8.

37. Ibid., p. 313.

38. Ibid.

39. Rev. Richard Cordley, cited in ibid., 322.

40. *Herald for Freedom*, January 13, 1855.

41. Rev. Richard Cordley, cited in Middleton, "Manufacturing in Lawrence," p. 10.

42. Middleton, "Manufacturing in Lawrence," p. 25.

43. Ibid., p. 89.

44. G. W. E. Griffith, *Lawrence Daily Journal*, December 18, 1880.

45. Middleton, "Manufacturing in Lawrence," p. 187.

46. *Lawrence Daily Journal,* September 9, 1895.

47. Ibid., September 17, 1895.

48. Kansas Bureau of Labor, *Ninth Annual Report.*

49. Farmer, "The Economic Background of Populism."

50. See the annual reports from the Kansas State Board of Agriculture, 1873–1903.

51. Larsen, "Certain Aspects of Farm Tenure in Kansas."

52. Cited in Parsons, *The Populist Context,* p. 47.

53. Blackmar and Burgess, *Lawrence Social Survey.*

54. Andreas, *History of the State of Kansas,* p. 327.

55. Ibid.

56. Middleton, "Manufacturing in Lawrence," p. 99. All of the information on Bowersock comes from Middleton.

57. Parsons, *The Populist Context.* See, in particular, chapter 3, "The Village."

Chapter Five

1. In this chapter all quotations from working men come from studies conducted by the Kansas commissioner of labor between the years 1885 and 1896. Each year the commissioner sent questionnaires to working men and women throughout the state, and published selections of the unedited responses the following year. According to the commissioner, the response rate was about 30 percent. See, then, the first through the twelfth *Annual Report* of the Kansas Bureau of Labor and Industrial Statistics (1885–96).

2. Ibid. Occasionally, skilled craftsmen, who also were homesteaders, received the questionnaires and completed them.

3. Watson, *The People's Party Campaign Book,* p. 221.

4. Kleppner, *The Cross of Culture,* pp. 369ff.

5. Because the responses of workers were published as received, there are sometimes spelling errors, or spelling which reflects practices at the time. In order to smooth the reading of worker comments, I have changed the spelling to conform to current practices, or simply corrected it. Another reason for making corrections is that some are the result of typesetting errors that were not corrected by the Bureau of Labor and Industrial Statistics.

6. Hofstadter, *The Age of Reform.*

7. Parsons, *The Populist Context.* See, in particular, his chapter 7, "Cultural Conflict During the Populist Era."

8. Ibid., p. 111.

9. Cited in ibid.

10. See Blocker, "The Politics of Reform," for a discussion of the dual issues of prohibition and women's suffrage, as well as the Cincinnati convention, where Populists refused to take a position on suffrage or temperance.

11. The emphases are in the original.
12. Kansas Bureau of Labor, *Eleventh Annual Report,* "Sociology," p. 185. All of the quotations come from pages 185–211 of this report.
13. Ecroyd, "An Analysis and Evaluation of Populist Political Campaign Speech Making," p. 72–73.
14. *Nation* (August 28, 1873): 140–41.
15. *Nation* (July 31, 1873): 68.
16. Ibid.
17. Ibid., p. 69.
18. Miller, "Financing the Boom in Kansas."
19. Harger, "New Era in the Middle West."
20. St. Paul, Nebraska, *Phonograph* (June 10, 1887).
21. Harger, "New Era in the Middle West," p. 276.
22. Malin, "The Kingsley Boom of the Late Eighties."
23. *Kingsley Mercury* (April 30, 1887).
24. Edwards, "Alma," p. 75.
25. *Alma Enterprise,* March 25, 1887.
26. Ibid., February 4, 1887.
27. Ibid., May 20, 1887.
28. *Alma Enterprise* (March 29, 1889).
29. *Alma Signal* (April 11, 1891).
30. See Miner, *West of Wichita,* chapter 17, for a discussion of the reaction of people after the boom collapsed.
31. *Kingsley Mercury* (July 4, 1887).
32. *Kingsley Banner-Graphic* (December 16, 1887).
33. *Kingsley Mercury* (October 17, 1887).
34. *Kingsley Mercury* (October 28, 1887).
35. Rockwood, "The Populist Ideology," p. 35.
36. Diggs, *The Story of Jerry Simpson,* p. 79.
37. Clanton, *Kansas Populism;* also cited in Clanton, "Populism, Progressivism, and Equality," p. 565.
38. Cited in Costigan, Recollections, p. 15.
39. Donnelly, *Caesar's Column,* p. 94.
40. Lease, *Kansas City Star* (April 1, 1891).
41. *Wellington Monitor* (October 5, 1890).
42. Emery, *Seven Financial Conspiracies,* p. 46.
43. Lloyd, *The Social Creator,* p. 107.
44. Donnelly, *The Golden Bottle,* p. 106.
45. Cited in *Osborne County News* (October 30, 1890).
46. The Ingalls quotations come from Sackett, "Reaction and Reform in Kansas."
47. *Walnut Valley Times* (July 20, 1884).
48. Argersinger, "Pentecostal Politics in Kansas," p. 29.
49. *Washington Republican* (February 4, 1887). The information on Wash-

ington's Alliance and the newspaper clippings were graciously provided by Mary Alice Pacey of Washington.

50. White, "What's the Matter with Kansas?" originally printed in the *Emporia Gazette* and reprinted in White's *Autobiography*.

51. Morgan, *The Kansas Day Club*. (This book contains the speeches made at the annual meetings from 1892 to 1901.)

52. Ibid., p. 123.

53. Ibid., p. 195.

54. Ibid., p. 33.

55. Ibid., p. 30.

56. Ibid., p. 118.

57. Ibid., p. 119.

58. Ibid., pp. 127–28.

59. Ibid., p. 115.

60. Ibid., p. 201.

61. Ibid., p. 41.

62. Ibid., p. 26.

63. Ibid., p. 233.

64. Ibid., pp. 98–99.

Chapter Six

1. The Beaver Valley Alliance was formed in July 1889 in Cheyenne County, Kansas. The quotations for the ceremony, with emphases added, are taken directly from the handbook provided to presidents of local alliances. National Farmer's Alliance and Industrial Union, *Ritual* (1890).

2. As Hobsbawm has noted, in "Should Poor People Organize?" one of the means by which a class asserts itself is through a form of class organization.

3. Gramsci, *Selections from the Prison Notebooks*.

4. Goodwyn, *The Populist Moment*.

5. Piven and Cloward, *Poor People's Movements*.

6. Schwartz, *Radical Protest and Social Structure*.

7. Barnes, *Farmers in Rebellion*.

8. Turner, "Understanding the Populists." They were, equally, as Turner has suggested, a means of overcoming the isolation of rural life.

9. *Kansas Farmer* (March 15, 1873).

10. Periam, *The Groundswell: A History of the Origin, Aims, and Progress of the Farmers' Movement*, p. 271.

11. Ibid., pp. 274.

12. Ibid., pp. 104–12.

13. Barr, "The Populist Uprising," p. 1147.

14. Peffer, "The Farmers' Alliance," p. 694.

15. Ibid.

16. Smith, "History of the Grange in Kansas."

17. Barr, "The Populist Uprising," p. 1159.

18. *Kansas Farmer* (January 12, 1888).

19. Ibid. (February 23, 1888).

20. Ibid. (June 17, 1889).

21. Ibid. (July 10, 1889).

22. White, *Autobiography*, p. 432.

23. *Barber County Index* (October 1, 1890).

24. "The Farmer is the Man," circa 1890.

25. *Kansas Farmer* (September 25, 1889).

26. Ibid., (July 10, 1889).

27. Ibid.

28. Ibid. (July 10, 1890).

29. Ibid. (December 25, 1889).

30. Ibid. (March 19, 1890).

31. Ibid. (April 16, 1890).

32. Ibid. (July 16, 1890).

33. Ibid. (November 6, 1889).

34. Ibid. (October 16, 1889).

35. Ibid. (November 13, 1889). The reference to the People's Ticket is not to the Populist party, for that would not come into existence until 1890.

36. Ibid. (January 23, 1890).

37. Ibid. (March 19, 1890).

38. Ibid. (February 19, 1890).

39. *Cheyenne County Herald* (January 18, 1890).

40. *Weekly Review* (January 23, 1890).

41. *Selden Times* (May 30, 1889).

42. *Kansas Farmer* (April 30, 1890).

43. *Weekly Review* (May 1, 1890).

44. *People's Advocate* (May 7, 1890).

45. *Topeka Daily Capital* (March 26, 1890).

46. *Kansas Farmer* (March 26, 1890).

47. Barr, "The Populist Uprising," p. 1163.

48. *Kansas Farmer* (April 2, 1890).

49. Ibid.

50. Ibid. (October 8, 1890).

51. *Osborne County News* (November 27, 1890).

52. *Weekly Review* (August 7, 1890).

53. Ibid. (September 25, 1890).

54. Peffer, "The Farmer's Alliance," p. 698.

55. Scott, *The Champion Organizer of the Northwest.*

56. Goodwyn, *The Populist Moment.*

57. Scott, *The Champion Organizer of the Northwest*, p. 15. Scott, who published his own work, often spelled phonetically, and failed to insert punc-

tuation. I have changed the spelling and inserted punctuation to make his statements easier to read; the meaning has not been changed. I have also been faithful to his use of "dialect" in the telling of his stories.

58. Ibid., p. 63.

59. Ibid.

60. Barr, "The Populist Uprising," p. 1159–60.

61. *Osborne County News* (January 14, 1892).

62. Ibid. (January 21, 1892). Spelling has been changed to conform to modern usage.

63. Ibid. (Feburary 11, 1892). See also February 18.

64. Ibid. (Feburary 25, 1892).

65. Ibid. (March 3, 1892).

66. Ibid. (March 25, 1892).

67. Ibid. (May 5, 1892).

68. Ibid. (August 25, 1892).

69. Ecroyd, "An Analysis and Evaluation of Populist Political Campaign Speech Making," pp. 271–87.

70. *Osborne County News* (October 30, 1890).

71. *Lawrence Daily Journal* (May 7, 1890).

72. *Kansas City Star* (April 1, 1891).

73. Ibid. The quotations from Lease, as well as from other speakers, all come from newspaper accounts, unless otherwise noted. There is good reason to believe that these "reports" accurately reflect what was actually said because Lease, Diggs, and the others usually gave their written speeches to the opposition press, as well as the reform press, ahead of time. This was done primarily to prevent the Republican press from inventing statements about what they did and did not say.

74. "The Great Quadrangle Debate," Salina, Kansas, December 18, 1893. Published as a pamphlet by the Open Church, Salina, 1894.

75. *Concordia Times Press* (original speech given on July 20, 1891 and later published as a separate pamphlet by the *Press*).

76. Stiller, *Mary Lease*.

77. *Topeka State Journal* (November 11, 1892), and *Wichita Daily Beacon* (June 15, 1892).

78. Lewelling, "Inaugural Address," *Kansas State Governors' Messages*, 2:19–21.

79. *Lyons Republican* (June 12, 1890).

80. Peffer, "Government Control of Money," p. 271.

81. Goodwyn, *The Populist Moment*.

82. Nugent, *The Tolerant Populists*, p. 77.

83. Bicha, "Jerry Simpson," p. 292.

84. Simpson, "Speech," *Congressional Record*, 53d Congress, Second Session, appendix, vol. 26, pt. 9, pp. 517–22.

Chapter Seven

1. Scott, *The Champion Organizer of the Northwest*, p. 121.
2. Watson, Thomas E., Introduction, in Barrett, *The Mission, History and Times of the Farmers' Union*, p. 15.
3. Ibid., pp. 15–16.
4. Schwartz, *Radical Protest and Social Structure;* Goodwyn, *The Populist Moment.*
5. Scott, *The Champion Organizer*, pp. 44ff.
6. *Cheyenne County Herald* (December 7, 1889).
7. Ibid. (February 1, 1890).
8. Rightmire, "The Alliance Movement in Kansas," has suggested that organizers were paid a "salary" of between $1.50 and $2.00 a day (p. 4).
9. Garvin, *History of the Grand State Farmers' Alliance of Texas*, p. 62.
10. Scott, *The Champion Organizer*, pp. 152–53.
11. Ibid., p. 91.
12. Ibid., p. 90.
13. Ibid., pp. 46–47.
14. I noted earlier that there were few statewide lecturers—men such as Scott and Taylor—in Kansas, who had as their responsibility the organization of suballiances. It appears to have been the case that the state lecturers also carried the burden for discussing political and economic issues. I suspect that those who have studied the Alliance, and come to the conclusion that there were thousands of Alliance lecturers, may in fact have been counting as lecturers those who were designated as such at the suballiance level. Alliance publications such as the *Kansas Farmer* did, in fact, simply list these people as "lecturers." The point, however, is that this position did not appear to have been an active one.
15. Jarboe, Obert, and Manchester, *The History of the Odessa Church.*
16. Dibbern, "Grass Roots Populism," whose material will be referred to below, found that landless farmers made up the bulk of the alliances' membership in Marshall County, South Dakota.
17. Ibid., p. 117.
18. Ibid., p. 178.
19. Using the records of the Kansas secretary of state, I was able to determine that there were 110 known Alliance cooperatives, which I took to be correlated to membership strength. There were an additional 62 that might have been Alliance cooperatives, and these had the same pattern of distribution as did the Alliance cooperatives.
20. Malin, "Turnover of Farm Population."
21. Turner, "Understanding the Populists."
22. Argersinger, *Populism and Politics.*
23. Malin, *A Concern about Humanity*, p. 195.

24. Schwartz, "An Estimate of the Size of the Southern Farmers' Alliance," p. 768.

25. Hicks, *The Populist Revolt*, p. 167.

26. Parsons et al., "The Role of Cooperatives."

27. McMath, *Populist Vanguard*, pp. 80, 165.

28. McMath's references for the first figure, cited on page 80, differ to the extent that they come from two Alliance newspapers: the *Kansas Farmer* and the Newton *Kansas Commoner.*

29. Argersinger, *Populism and Politics*, p. 35.

30. Scott, *The Champion Organizer*, pp. 96, 110–11.

31. *Kansas Farmer* (March 13, 1890).

32. *Annals of Kansas* (1954): 110.

33. *Cheyenne County Rustler* (June 19, 1890).

34. Scott, *The Champion Organizer*, pp. 116, 39–116.

35. See the Junction City, *Tribune*, April 13, 1890, for information on the location and time of meetings.

36. Dibbern, "Grass Roots Populism," p. 59.

37. In the calculations that follow, the Prohibition party vote, which totalled about 6,000, is included in the total number of votes for the Alliance/Populist ticket. That is because the data source collapses them.

38. In this, and the following chapter, the percentage of eligible voters was calculated by dividing the total number of votes by the total number of males twenty-one years and older. As the census categories collapsed those between twenty and twenty-four, I assumed an even distribution by age over the twenty to twenty-four range, and simply subtracted 20 percent of the total population. Likewise, within a given decade, population growth was assumed to be relatively uniform. The population for any given year, then, was simply extrapolated by taking the base population of males for the preceding decade and adding one-tenth of the total population growth for the decade for each year. The census materials came from U.S. Census, 1930, *Population*, vol. 2:663; and Clark and Roberts, *People of Kansas*. The voting data are adapted from: Cabe and Sullivant, *Kansas Votes: National Elections*, and Hein and Sullivant, *Kansas Votes: Gubernatorial Elections, 1859–1956.*

39. This breakdown of where the Populists' votes came from parallels that of Clanton, who compared the vote for presidential electors in 1888 to the vote for secretary of state in 1890. Clanton, *Kansas Populism*, p. 88.

40. Ibid.

41. Schwartz, *Radical Protest and Social Structure.*

42. Goodwyn, *The Populist Moment.*

43. Parsons et al., "The Role of Cooperatives in the Development of the Movement Culture of Populism."

44. I say, "about," because Parsons et al., uses bar graphs.

45. Smith, "History of the Grange in Kansas."

46. Wilson claims that prior to 1900 there were but fourteen farmers' marketing and purchasing associations. The bulk of them (68.9 percent) were organized between 1911 and 1925. Wilson, *A History of Cooperatives in Kansas*, p. 44.

47. Rightmire, "The Alliance Movement in Kansas," p. 8.

48. Ibid., p. 2.

49. Ibid., p. 3.

50. Ibid., p. 4.

51. Ibid.

52. Ibid.

53. Clanton, *Kansas Populism*, pp. 249–50.

54. Much of the information on the leadership of the Alliance and the Populist party in Kansas comes from ibid., p. 75, and passim.

55. Ibid., p. 82.

56. Rightmire, "The Alliance Movement in Kansas," pp. 7–8; see also Clanton, *Kansas Populism*, p. 95.

57. *Farmers' Advocate* (December 10, 1890). Also cited in Clanton, *Kansas Populism*, p. 101.

58. Goodwyn, *The Populist Moment,* in particular saw the shift to politics as the undoing of the farmers' movement. See also Argersinger, *Populism and Politics,* as well as Clanton, *Kansas Populism.*

59. *Farmer's Advocate* (December 2, 1981). Also cited in Clanton, *Kansas Populism*, p. 112.

60. *Farmer's Advocate* (April 20, 1892).

61. Clanton, *Kansas Populism*, p. 139.

62. *Topeka Capital* (November 10, 1893).

63. *Kansas City Star* (January 2, 1894).

64. Clanton, *Kansas Populism*, pp. 144–47, cites what is probably Lease's autobiography. In that document, she makes clear her hatred of the Democrats, her opposition to fusion, and her desire to see the Republicans triumph. Lease would, eventually, return publicly to the Republican fold.

65. Clanton, *Kansas Populism*, p. 168, analyzed the vote in Crawford and Osage counties, both of which had a substantial working-class vote, and concluded that suffrage cost the Populists the election. I agree that workers failed to vote for the Populist ticket because of their stand on suffrage, although as I will also show in the next chapter, worker support for the Populists was never particularly strong.

66. *Advocate* (January 16, 1895).

67. *Emporia Gazette* (June 18, 1895).

68. Cited in *Advocate* (January 6, 1897), and Clanton, *Kansas Populism*, p. 199.

69. *Marion Record* (December 18, 1896).

70. This parallels Hahn's observations, in *The Roots of Southern Populism,*

about the Southern Alliance, i.e., ties of kith and kin were stronger for Georgia upcountry farmers than were class ties.

Chapter Eight

1. *Kansas City Star* (November 5, 1890). Also cited in Argersinger, "Road to a Republican Waterloo," p. 443.

2. This refers to the gubernatorial race in 1892. All voting data in this chapter, unless otherwise noted, come from Hein and Sullivant, *Kansas Votes: Gubernatorial Elections, 1859–1956;* or Cabe and Sullivant, *Kansas Votes: National Elections, 1859–1956.*

3. See Svenson, "The Effect of Popular Dissent on Political Parties in Kansas," p. 72 and passim.

4. *Topeka Commonwealth* (September 12, 1872). Svenson's "The Effect of Popular Dissent on Political Parties in Kansas," contains an appendix, pp. 143–222, which gives the complete platforms of all of the state's parties between 1872 and 1898.

5. *Topeka Commonwealth* (August 28, 1872).

6. Ibid. (March 30, 1873).

7. Ibid. (August 30, 1874).

8. Ibid. (July 30, 1876).

9. Ibid. (May 20, 1876).

10. Ibid. (August 16, 1876).

11. *Topeka Daily Capital* (August 18, 1878).

12. *Leavenworth Evening Standard* (September 6, 1878).

13. *Topeka Daily Capital* (September 1, 1882).

14. Ibid. (July 28, 1888).

15. *Topeka Daily Capital* (August 30, 1888).

16. Rickard, "The Impact of Populism on Electoral Patterns in Kansas," pp. 35–38. Rickard uses a sample of 79 counties, and excludes the western portion of the state. There are good reasons for doing so in such an analysis, for the western counties were sparsely settled, and a few votes could and did swing the election from one party to another.

17. The correlations (Pearson product-moment) are not strong, and are only suggestive. For example, the correlation between the county-level vote for prohibition and Union Labor was .321 in 1888; that for farm value was $-.29$; and it was $-.38$ for value of farm products. All correlations are based on aggregate, county-level data, and their interpretation is subject to the usual restrictions for ecological correlations.

18. The correlation between a vote for prohibition and a vote for the Democratic party was $-.52$ in 1888; and that for Catholic and Democrat was .50. The correlation between percent German in a county and Democrat yielded a figure of .53; and that between foreign-born and Democrat was .38.

19. Williams, "Economics and Politics: Voting Behavior in Kansas during the Populist Decade," analyzed the vote for governor on a county-by-county basis for the elections from 1888 to 1898. He found that ethnicity and religion were important factors in determining support for the Populists. He found that no foreign-born nationality strongly supported the Republicans, and that the Germans were the only group to support strongly the Democrats. Pietists, e.g., Methodists, Baptists, Presbyterians, were more likely to support the Republicans, except when the Populists ran separately from the Democrats. Ritualists, e.g., Catholics, Episcopalians, German Lutherans, tended to favor the Democrats over the Republicans by a 3-to-1 ratio. Third-party support came from Scandanavians, Irishmen, and Anglo immigrants, e.g., Canadians, Welshmen, Englishmen. Williams, however, argues that much of the vote for Populists can be explained by economic factors. For example, the higher the value of land and farm products, the more likely it was that a county went Republican. His conclusion was that "it was farm workers, the poor, the less competent, and the unlucky who supported the protest parties. And the economic causes of protest were direct ones. It was local drought that caused men to vote Populist, not incomprehensible world markets" (p. 248).

20. The figure of 10,000 comes from Argersinger, "Road to a Republican Waterloo," p. 459. His figure comes from a newspaper report, *Topeka Daily Capital* (August 13, 1890).

21. Svenson, "The Effect of Popular Dissent on Political Parties in Kansas," pp. 201–2. The platform also appears in the "Proceedings of the Twenty-Ninth State Republican Convention," Kansas State Historical Society.

22. Ibid., pp. 197–98.

23. Ibid., pp. 199–200.

24. Harrington, "The Populist Party in Kansas," pp. 412–15.

25. *Kansas City Times* (November 10, 1890). Also cited in Harrington, "The Populist Party in Kansas," p. 415.

26. Harrington, "The Populist Party in Kansas," p. 415.

27. Fink, *Workingmen's Democracy*, p. 135.

28. The material on ethnicity comes from Carmen's exceptional work, *Foreign-Language Units in Kansas*, pp. 268–71, 302–7.

29. Argersinger, *Populism and Politics*, p. 73. Using the county as the unit of analysis, Argersinger found a correlation of .20 between the 1888 Republican and 1890 Populist vote, and a correlation of −.24 for the Democratic/Populist comparison.

30. Ibid., p. 69.

31. Argersinger derived a multiple correlation coefficient of .699 for number of mortgages, number living on farms, per capita assessed valuation, and value of farm products, pp. 62–71.

32. Ibid., p. 72.

33. Williams, "Economics and Politics." Rickard, "The Impact of Popu-

lism on Electoral Patterns in Kansas," found the same patterns as did Argersinger and Williams. Rickard's correlations (pp. 87–88) for a sample of 29 counties are as follows:

Correlations of variables with vote for governor, 1890

Variable	Populist	Republican	Democrat
% of families with mortgaged farms	.252	−.439	−.027
Crop failure, 1890	.456	−.298	−.424
Wheat/corn acres	.272	−.148	−.310
% pop. urban	−.419	−.046	.486
Population density	−.555	.098	.494
% pop. engaged in agriculture	.505	−.007	−.572
% pop. professional	−.512	.105	.517

34. Harrington, "The Populist Party in Kansas," p. 419.

35. Rickard, "The Impact of Populism on Electoral Patterns in Kansas," p. 104.

36. Cited in Harrington, "The Populist Party in Kansas," p. 422.

37. Populist Party Clippings, file of the Kansas State Historical Society, 1:38.

38. Harrington, "The Populist Party in Kansas," p. 425.

39. Rickard, "The Impact of Populism on Electoral Patterns in Kansas, pp. 146–52. My comments are based on the data presented in Rickard's multiple regression summary tables.

40. Ibid., p. 121–23.

41. Cited in Barr, "The Populist Uprising," p. 1183. The account of the legislative war is taken from Barr, as well as Parrish, "The Great Kansas Legislative Imbroglio of 1893," and Harrington, "The Populist Party in Kansas," pp. 425–431.

42. Harrington, "The Populist Party in Kansas," p. 426.

43. Ibid., p. 427.

44. Parrish, "The Great Legislative Imbroglio of 1893," p. 487.

45. Harrington, "The Populist Party in Kansas," pp. 431–32.

46. Zornow, *Kansas: A History of the Jayhawk State*, p. 203.

47. *Topeka Daily Capital* (July 15, 1894).

48. Barr, "The Populist Uprising," p. 1201.

49. *Topeka Daily Capital* (June 20, 1894).

50. The information on ethnicity comes from Carmen, *Foreign-Language Units of Kansas*. The data on voting come from the *Atchison Weekly Champion* (November 10, 1892) and the *Atchison Daily Champion* (November 11, 1894).

51. *Leavenworth Evening Standard* (November 9, 1892, and November 7, 1894).

52. Harrington, "The Populist Party in Kansas," p. 436. Newspaper accounts give Alliance membership as 10,000 in this period, down from the reported high of 100,000 in 1891. See table 7.1.

53. *Topeka Advocate* (June 17, 1896).

54. Cited in Harrington, "The Populist Party in Kansas," p. 438.

55. *Abilene Daily Reflector* (August 6, 1896).

56. *Leavenworth Evening Standard* (July 14, 1896).

57. *Topeka Daily Capital* (August 14, 1896).

58. Harrington, "The Populist Party in Kansas," p. 443. Harrington notes, correctly, that others saw the election as even closer. Bryan, for example, said that a change of 962 votes would have given him California; of 1,059, Oregon; or 142 would have given him all of Kentucky's electoral votes.

59. These figures come from Cabe and Sullivant, *Kansas Votes: National Elections,* and Hein and Sullivant, *Kansas Votes: Gubernatorial Elections.*

60. Williams, "Economics and Politics," p. 251. This decrease in Baptist support occurred in both 1896 and 1900.

61. Rickard, "The Impact of Populism on Electoral Patterns," p. 183. There was a decrease in support for the fusion ticket in areas with a high percentage of German population, but no noticeable increase in votes for Republicans, which means that Germans may have abstained in 1896 and 1900.

62. Rickard also indicates that "Analyses of two samples of precincts selected from the seventy-five counties [that made up the sample for the study] found that previous voting, ethnicity, percent in villages, and wheat growing were important in explaining the distribution of the vote in 1896 and 1898. The Democrat-Populist candidates received more support in rural areas, in precincts with a high proportion of the foreign-born, and in areas with a high percentage of the farmland in wheat. Previous voting patterns were, however, the best predictors of the distribution of votes in 1896 and 1898" (ibid.).

63. Harrington, "The Populist Party in Kansas," p. 442.

64. *Farmer's Advocate* (March 24, 1897), also cited in Harrington, "The Populist Party in Kansas," p. 445.

65. Svenson, "The Effect of Popular Dissent on Political Parties in Kansas."

66. Cox, *Blacks in Topeka, Kansas,* pp. 111–35, argues that the black community in Topeka was favorably inclined toward the Populists. However, an examination of voting patterns in Topeka wards gives no indication that blacks voted for the Populists in significant numbers. The same pattern held there as it did in Lawrence.

67. All of the information on voting by ward and township comes from the *Lawrence Daily Journal* (November 11, 1888; November 19, 1890; November 12, 1892; November 10, 1894; November 8, 1896). The informa-

tion on ethnicity and socioeconomic status was discussed in chapter 4. See the notes for tables 4.10 and 4.12.

68. The voting data for Fort Scott and the surrounding townships come from the *Fort Scott Daily Monitor* (November 13, 1888; November 8, 1890, November 13, 1892; November 6, 1894; and November 7, 1896).

69. The data on ethnicity comes from Carmen, *Foreign-Language Units of Kansas,* pp. 302–7. The socioeconomic characteristics of the wards were determined by self-knowledge, as well as historical maps showing the location of subdivisions, factories, and other places of work. In particular, see *Map of Kansas City, Kansas, 1888,* Ernest Abshagen, C.E., Kansas Collection: University of Kansas, Lawrence.

70. The voting data for Kansas City come from the *Kansas City Gazette* (November 16, 1888; November 13, 1890; November 17, 1892; November 15, 1894; and November 19, 1896).

71. The information on Hannan and the Kansas City elections comes from Fink, *Workingmen's Democracy,* pp. 112–42.

72. Argersinger, *Populism and Politics;* Schwartz, *Radical Protest and Social Structure.*

73. Lewis, *Babbitt,* p. 143.

Bibliography

Adams, Henry. *The Education of Henry Adams*. New York: Modern Library, 1931 (orig. 1918).

"Agricultural Exposition of Corporate Law." *The Nation*, no. 426 (August 28, 1873): 140–41.

Althusser, Louis. *For Marx*. New York: Vintage Books, 1970.

———, and Etienne Balibar. *Reading Capital*. London: New Left Books, 1968.

Aminzade, Ron. *Class, Politics, and Early Industrial Capitalism: A Study of Mid-Nineteenth Century Toulouse, France*. Albany: SUNY Press, 1981.

Anderson, Perry. *Arguments within English Marxism*. London: New Left Books, 1980.

———. *Passages from Antiquity to Feudalism*. London: New Left Books, 1974.

Andreas, A. T. *History of the State of Kansas*, Vol. 1. Chicago: A. T. Andreas, 1883.

"Another Aspect of the Farmers' Movement." *The Nation*, no. 422 (July 31, 1873): 69–69.

Argersinger, Peter H. "Pentecostal Politics in Kansas: Religion, the Farmers' Alliance, and the Gospel of Populism." *Kansas Quarterly* 1 (1969): 24–35.

———. *Populism and Politics: William Alfred Peffer and the People's Party*. Lexington: University Press of Kentucky, 1974.

———. "Road to a Republican Waterloo: The Farmers' Alliance and the Election of 1890 in Kansas." *Kansas Historical Quarterly* 33 (1967): 443–69.

Bailey, L. D. "John Brown and the Kansas Conflict." In Everett Rich, ed., *The Heritage of Kansas*. Manhattan, Kans: Flint Hills Book Company, 1970, pp. 37–42.

Bannon, John Frances. *The Spanish Borderlands Frontier, 1513–1821*. Albuquerque, N.M.: University of New Mexico Press, 1974.

Barnes, Donna. *Farmers in Rebellion: The Rise and Fall of the Southern Farmers Alliance and People's Party in Texas*. Austin: University of Texas Press, 1984.

Barr, Elizabeth N. "The Populist Uprising." In William E. Connelley, ed., *History of Kansas*, vol. 2. Chicago: American Historical Society, 1928, pp. 1137–1204.

Bicha, Denis Karel. "Jerry Simpson: Populist without Principle." *Journal of American History* 54 (1967): 291–306.

/ Billings, Dwight. "Class and Class Politics in the Southern Populist Movement of the 1890s." *Sociological Spectrum* 1 (1981): 259–92.

Blackmar, Frank W., and E. W. Burgess. *Lawrence Social Survey*. Lawrence: Kansas State Printing Plant, 1917.

Blocker, Jack S., Jr. "The Politics of Reform: Populists, Prohibition, and Woman Suffrage." *The Historian* 34 (1972): 614–32.

Bogue, Allan G. "Farmer Debtors in Pioneer Kingsley." *Kansas Historical Quarterly* 20 (1952): 82–107.

———. *Money at Interest: The Farm Mortgage on the Middle Border*. New York: Russell and Russell, 1968.

Bowles, Samuel, and Herbert Gintis. *Democracy and Capitalism: Property, Community, and the Contradictions of Modern Social Thought*. New York: Basic Books, 1986.

Boyle, Ernest James. *The Financial History of Kansas*. Madison: University of Wisconsin. Bulletin no. 247, Economics and Political Science Series, vol. 6, 1908.

Buchanan, Joseph R. *The Story of a Labor Organizer: Joseph R. Buchanan*. New York: The Outlook Company, 1903.

Buck, Solon Justus. *The Granger Movement: A Study of Agricultural Organization and Its Political, Economic, and Social Manifestations, 1870–1880*. Cambridge: Harvard University Press, 1913.

Burawoy, Michael. *The Politics of Production*. London: Verso (New Left Books), 1985.

Burch, L. D. *Kansas As It Is: A Complete Review of the Resources, Advantages and Drawbacks of the Great Central State*. Chicago: C. S. Burch and Company, 1878.

Burnham, Walter Dean. *Critical Elections and the Mainsprings of American Politics*. New York: W. W. Norton, 1970.

Cabe, June G., and Charles A. Sullivant. *Kansas Votes: National Elections, 1859–1956*. Lawrence, Kans.: University of Kansas Governmental Research Center, 1957.

/ Calhoun, Craig, *The Question of Class Struggle: Social Foundations of Popular Radicalism during the Industrial Revolution*. Chicago: University of Chicago Press, 1982.

Carmen, Justice Neale. *Foreign-Language Units of Kansas: Historical Atlas and Statistics*. Lawrence: University of Kansas Press, 1962.

Cather, Willa. "Eldorado: A Kansas Recessional." *The New England Magazine* 24 (1901): 360–65.

Clanton, O. Gene. *Kansas Populism: Ideas and Men.* Lawrence, Kans.: University of Kansas Press, 1969.

———. "Populism, Progressivism, and Equality: The Kansas Paradigm." *Agricultural History* 51 (1977): 559–81.

Clark, Carroll D., and Roy L. Roberts. *People of Kansas: A Demographic and Sociological Study.* Topeka, Kans.: The Kansas State Planning Board, 1936.

Clawson, Mary Ann. "Fraternal Orders and Class Formation in the Nineteenth-Century United States." *Comparative Studies in Society and History* 27 (1985): 672–95.

Cochrane, Willard W. *The Development of American Agriculture: A Historical Analysis.* Minneapolis: University of Minnesota Press, 1979.

"Conflict Characterized Rise to Statehood." In Roberta J. Peterson, ed., *Kansas: The First 125 Years.* Topeka, Kans.: Topeka *Capital Journal*, January 29, 1986, pp. 2–3. (Flyer.)

Connelley, William E. *Kansas and Kansans.* Vol. 3. Chicago: Lewis Publishing, 1918.

Costigan, W. J. "Recollections." Note in the Kansas State Historical Society collections, Farmers' Alliance Clippings, Topeka, Kans.: circa 1890.

Cox, Thomas C. *Blacks in Topeka, Kansas, 1865–1915: A Social History.* Baton Rouge: Louisiana State University Press, 1982.

Crane, Stephen. "Nebraska's Bitter Fight for Life." In Fredson Bowers, (ed.) *The Works of Stephen Crane.* Charlottesville: University Press of Virginia, pp. 408–15.

Darnton, Robert. *The Great Cat Massacre.* New York: Basic Books, 1984.

Dibbern, John D. "Grass Roots Populism: Politics and Social Structure in a Frontier Community." Ph.D. diss., Stanford University, 1980.

Dick, Everett. *The Sod-House Frontier.* Lincoln, Nebr.: University of Nebraska Press, 1979.

Diggs, Annie. *The Story of Jerry Simpson.* Wichita, Kans.: Jane Simpson, 1908.

Donnelly, Ignatius. *Caesar's Column.* Reprint. Cambridge, Massachusetts: Belknap Press, 1960.

———. *The Golden Bottle.* Reprint. New York: Johnson Reprint Co., 1968.

Douglas, Richard L. *A History of Manufacturers in the Kansas Fuel District. Reprint from the Kansas Historical Collections, vol. XI.* Topeka: Kansas State Historical Society, 1910.

Dun and Mercantile Company Records, 1865–1900. Library of Congress.

Dykstra, Robert R. *The Cattle Towns: A Social History of the Kansas Cattle Trading Centers, 1867–1885.* New York: Atheneum, 1976.

Ecroyd, David H. "An Analysis and Evaluation of Populist Political Campaign Speech Making in Kansas, 1890–1894." Ph.D. diss., University of Iowa, 1949.

Edwards, Linnie Baker. "Alma: Community, and Shire Town of Wabaunsee

County, Kansas: Its First Fifty Years, 1855–1905." M.A. thesis, Kansas State College of Agriculture and Applied Sciences, 1956.

Emerson, Ralph Waldo. "On Affairs in Kansas." In Everett Rich, ed., *Heritage of Kansas*. Manhattan, Kans.: Flint Hills Book Company, 1970, pp. 42–46.

Emery, Sarah E. V. *Seven Financial Conspiracies Which Have Enslaved the American People*. Lansing, Mich.: Robert Smith, 1891.

Farmer, Hallie. "The Economic Background of Populism" (Part I), "The Railroads and Frontier Populism" (Part II). Ph.D. diss., University of Wisconsin, 1927.

"The Farmer is the Man." (Song, circa 1890). Cited in William E. Koch, "Campaign and Protest Singing During the Populist Era," *Journal of the West* 22 (1983): 47–57.

Fink, Leon. *Workingmen's Democracy: The Knights of Labor and American Politics*. Urbana: University of Illinois Press, 1983.

Fireman, Bruce, and William A. Gamson. "Utilitarian Logic in the Resource Mobilization Perspective." In Mayer N. Zald and John D. McCarthy, eds., *The Dynamics of Social Movements*. Cambridge: Winthrop Publishers, 1979, pp. 8–44.

Fort Scott Board of Trade, *Report of the Special Committee of the Board of Trade of the City of Fort Scott, Kansas on the Advantages of Fort Scott as a Manufacturing and Business Center*. Fort Scott: Monitor Press, 1884.

Gamson, William A. *The Strategy of Social Protest*. Homewood, Ill.: Dorsey Press, 1975.

———. "Understanding the Careers of Challenging Groups: A Commentary on Goldstone." *American Journal of Sociology* 85 (1980): 1043–60.

Garvin, W. L. *History of the Grand State Farmers' Alliance of Texas*. Jacksboro, Texas: J. N. Rogers & Co., Rural Citizen Office, 1885.

Giddens, Anthony. *The Constitution of Society*. Berkeley: University of California Press, 1984.

Goodwyn, Lawrence. *The Populist Moment*. New York: Oxford University Press, 1978.

Gramsci, Antonio. *Selections from the Prison Notebooks*. Edited and translated by Quintin Hoare and Geoffrey N. Smith. New York: International Publishers, 1971.

Granovetter, Mark. "Economic Action and Social Structure: The Problem of Embeddedness." *American Journal of Sociology* 91 (1985): 481–510.

Gutman, Herbert. "Work, Culture, and Society in Industrializing America, 1815–1919." *American Historical Review* 78 (1973): 531–88.

Hahn, Steven. *The Roots of Southern Populism: Yeoman Farmers and Transformation of the Georgia Upcountry, 1850–1890*. New York: Oxford University Press, 1983.

Hannigan, John A. "Alain Touraine, Manuel Castells and Social Movement Theory: A Critical Appraisal." *The Sociological Quarterly* 26 (1985): 435–54.

Harger, Charles Moureau. "New Era in the Middle West." *Harper's New Monthly Magazine* 95 (1898): 276–82.

Harrington, Wynne Powers. "The Populist Party in Kansas." *Collections of the Kansas State Historical Society* 16 (1923–25): 403–50.

Hawkins, Keith E. "Fort Scott: The First Generation, 1842–1872." M.A. thesis, Kansas State College of Pittsburg, 1957.

Haynes, Fred E. *Third Party Movements Since the Civil War with Special References to Iowa: A Study in Social Politics.* Iowa City, Iowa: The State Historical Society of Iowa, 1916.

Hein, Clarence J., and Charles A. Sullivant. *Kansas Votes: Gubernatorial Elections, 1859–1956.* Lawrence, Kans.: University of Kansas Governmental Research Center, 1958.

Hicks, John D. *The Populist Revolt.* Minneapolis: University of Minnesota Press, 1931.

Hicks, John D., George E. Mowry, and Robert E. Burke. *The American Nation.* Boston: Houghton Mifflin, 1965.

Hobsbawm, Eric. "The Making of the Working Class, 1870–1914." In Eric Hobsbawm, *Workers: Worlds of Labor.* New York: Pantheon, 1984, pp. 194–213.

———. "Should Poor People Organize?" In Eric Hobsbawm, *Workers: Worlds of Labor.* New York: Pantheon, 1984, pp. 282–96.

Hofstadter, Richard. *The Age of Reform: From Bryan to F.D.R.* New York: Vintage, 1955.

Holmes, J. K. "The Concentration of Wealth." *Political Science Quarterly* 8 (1893): 589–600.

Howes, Charles C. *This Place Called Kansas.* Norman, Okla.: University of Oklahoma Press, 1952.

Ise, John. *Sod and Stubble.* New York: Wilson-Erickson, 1936.

Jarboe, Ralph, Jr., Ruth Obert and Evelyn Manchester. *The History of the Odessa Church.* Topeka, Kans.: Kansas State Historical Society. N.d.

Jenkins, J. Craig. "Resource Mobilization Theory and the Study of Social Movements." *Annual Review of Sociology* 9 (1983): 527–53.

Jones, Gareth Stedman. *Languages of Class: Studies in English Working Class History, 1832–1932.* Cambridge: Cambridge University Press, 1983.

Kansas As She Is; The Greatest Fruit, Stock, and Grain Country in the World. Lawrence, Kans.: Kansas Publishing Company, 1870.

Kansas Board of Agriculture. *Annual Report of the State Board of Agriculture.* Vols. 1–13. Topeka, Kans.: State Printer, 1873–1903.

Kansas Bureau of Labor. *Annual Report of the Bureau of Labor and Industrial Statistics.* Vols. 1–16. Topeka, Kans.: State Printer, 1885–1901.

Katznelson, Ira. "Working-Class Formation: Constructing Cases and Com-

338   Bibliography

parisons." In Ira Katznelson and Aristide R. Zolberg, eds., *Working-Class Formation*. Princeton: Princeton University Press, 1986, pp. 3–41.

Klandermans, Bert. "Social-Psychological Expansions of Resource Mobilization Theory." *American Sociological Review* 49 (1984): 583–600.

Kleppner, Paul. *The Cross of Culture: A Social Analysis of Midwestern Politics, 1850–1900*. New York: The Free Press, 1970.

Kuhns, Luther M., ed. "An Army Surgeon's Letters to His Wife, 1862–1863." *Mississippi Valley Historical Review* 7 (1914): 307–13.

Lamar, Howard R. *The Far Southwest, 1846–1912: A Territorial History*. New York: Norton, 1970.

Larsen, Harold C. "Certain Aspects of Farm Tenure in Kansas." M.A. thesis, Kansas State Agricultural College, 1930.

Lease, Mary Elizabeth. *The Great Quadrangle Debate*. Pamphlet. Salina, Kans.: The Open Church, 1894.

Lesher, Leila R. "The History of Bourbon County, Kansas, Since the Civil War." M.A. thesis, Colorado State College of Education, 1942.

Levine, Rhonda. "Marxism, Sociology, and Neo-Marxist Theories of the State." *Current Perspectives in Social Theory* 6 (1985): 149–69.

Lewelling, Lorenzo. "Inaugural Address." *Kansas State Governors' Messages*. Vol. 2. Topeka, Kans.: Kansas State Historical Society, 1968.

Lewis, Sinclair. *Babbitt*. New York: Harcourt, Brace, 1922.

Lipset, Seymour M. *Agrarian Socialism*. Berkeley: University of California Press, 1971.

Lloyd, Henry D. *Henry Demarest Lloyd*. Vol. 1. New York: Harper and Bros., 1894.

———. *Man, the Social Creator*. Reprint. Westport, Connecticut: Hyperion Press, 1975.

Malin, James C. *A Concern about Humanity: Notes on Reform, 1872–1912, at the National and Kansas Levels of Thought*. Lawrence, Kans.: James C. Malin, 1964.

———. "The Kingsley Boom of the Late Eighties." *Kansas Historical Quarterly* 4 (1935): 23–49.

———. "Turnover of Farm Population." *Kansas Historical Quarterly* 4 (1935): 339–72.

Marx, Karl. *The Eighteenth Brumaire of Louis Bonaparte*. New York: International Publishers, 1963 (orig. 1852).

Matthews, Richard K. *The Radical Politics of Thomas Jefferson: A Revisionist View*. Lawrence, Kans.: University Press of Kansas, 1984.

Mayhew, Anne. "A Reappraisal of the Causes of Farm Protest in the United States, 1870–1900." *Journal of Economic History* 32 (1972): 464–75.

McAdam, Doug. "Tactical Innovation and the Pace of Insurgency." *American Sociological Review* 48 (1983): 735–53.

McCarthy, John D., and Mayer N. Zald. "Resource Mobilization and Social

Movements: A Partial Theory." *American Journal of Sociology* 82 (1977): 1212–41.

———. *The Trend of Social Movements.* Morristown: General Learning, 1973.

McMath, Robert C., Jr. *Populist Vanguard: A History of the Southern Farmers' Alliance.* Chapel Hill: University of North Carolina Press, 1976.

McNall, Scott G. Foreword to Reude, *Sod-House Days.*

———. "State, Party, and Ideology: Populism in New Zealand and the United States." *Comparative Social Research* 9 (1986): 3–26.

———, and Sally A. McNall. *Plains Families: Exploring Sociology through Social History.* New York: St. Martin's, 1983.

McPherson, James M. *Struggle for Equality: Abolitionists and the Negro in the Civil War and Reconstruction.* Princeton: Princeton University Press, 1964.

Meiksins, Peter. "Beyond the Boundary Question." *New Left Review* 157 (1986): 101–20.

Middleton, Kenneth A. "Manufacturing in Lawrence, Kansas, 1854–1900." M.A. thesis, University of Kansas, 1940.

Miller, Glenn H., Jr. "Financing the Boom in Kansas, 1879 to 1888, with Special Reference to Municipal Indebtedness and to Real Estate Mortgages." M.A. thesis, University of Kansas, 1954.

Miller, Raymond Curtis. "The Background of Populism in Kansas." *Mississippi Valley Historical Review* 11 (1925): 469–89.

Miner, Craig. *West of Wichita: Settling the High Plains of Kansas, 1865–1890.* Lawrence: University Press of Kansas, 1986.

Minogue, Kenneth. "Populism as a Political Movement." In *Populism,* ed. G. Ionesque and E. Gellner. New York: Macmillan, 1969.

Montgomery, David. *Beyond Equality: Labor and the Radical Republicans, 1862–1872.* New York: Knopf, 1967.

———. "On Goodwyn's Populists." *Marxist Perspectives* 1 (1978): 166–73.

Moore, Barrington, Jr. *Injustice: The Social Basis of Obedience and Revolt.* White Plains, N.Y.: Sharpe, 1978.

Morgan, W. Y., ed. *The Kansas Day Club.* Topeka, Kansas: W. Y. Morgan, 1901.

Morison, Samuel Eliot. *The Oxford History of the American People.* New York: Oxford University Press.

———, et al. *The Growth of the American Republic.* Vol. 2. New York: Oxford University Press, 1980.

Motley, John L. *Four Questions for the People: At the Presidential Election.* Boston: Ticknor and Fields, 1868.

Napier, Rita. "Squatter City: The Construction of a New Community in the American West, 1854–1861." Ph.D. diss., American University, 1976.

Nash, Gary B., Julie R. Jeffrey et al. *The American People: Creating a Nation and a Society.* New York: Harper and Row, 1986.

National Farmers' Alliance and Industrial Union. *Ritual.* Washington, D.C.: The National Economist Publishing Co., 1890.

Nixon, Herman C. "The Cleavage within the Farmers' Alliance Movement." *Mississippi Valley Historical Record* 15 (1928): 22–23.

North, Douglass C. *Growth and Welfare in the American Past.* Englewood Cliffs, N.J.: Prentice-Hall, 1974.

Nugent, Walter T. K. *The Tolerant Populists: Kansas Populism and Nativism.* Chicago: University of Chicago Press, 1963.

Oberschall, Anthony. "Theories of Social Conflict." *Annual Review of Sociology* 4 (1978): 291–315.

Offe, Claus. *Disorganized Capitalism.* Cambridge: MIT Press, 1985.

Olson, Mancur, Jr. *The Logic of Collective Action: Public Goods and the Theory of Groups.* Cambridge: Harvard University Press, 1965.

Palmer, Bruce. *"Man Over Money": The Southern Critique of American Capitalism.* Chapel Hill: University of North Carolina Press, 1980.

Parrish, Fred L. "Kansas Agriculture before 1900." In John D. Bright, ed., *Kansas: The First Century,* Vol. 1. New York: Lewis Historical Publishing Co., 1956, pp. 401–27.

Parrish, William E. "The Great Kansas Legislative Imbroglio of 1893." *Journal of the West* 7 (1968): 471–90.

Parsons, Stanley B. *The Populist Context: Rural versus Urban Power on a Great Plains Frontier.* Westport, Conn.: Greenwood Press, 1973.

———, Karen Tooms Parsons, Walter Killilae, and Beverly Borgers. "The Role of Cooperatives in the Development of the Movement Culture of Populism." *Journal of American History* 69 (1983): 866–85.

Pease, Robert L. "A History of Banking in Bourbon County, Kansas." M.A. thesis, University of Iowa, 1941.

Peffer, W. A. "The Farmers' Alliance." Lawrence, Kans.: University of Kansas, Kansas Collection, n.d., circa 1891.

———. "Government Control of Money." In N. A. Dunning, ed., *The Farmers' Alliance History and Agricultural Digest.* Washington, D.C.: Alliance Publishing Co., 1891.

———. *The Farmer's Side.* New York: Appleton, 1891.

Periam, Jonathan. *The Groundswell: A History of the Origin, Aims and Progress of the Farmers' Movement.* Chicago: Hannaford & Co., 1874.

Piven, Frances Fox, and Richard A. Cloward. *Poor People's Movements: Why They Succeed, How They Fail.* New York: Pantheon, 1977.

Plummer, Alfred. *Bronterre: A Political Biography of Bronterre O'Brien, 1804–1864.* London: Allen and Unwin, 1971.

Porpora, Douglas V. "The Role of Agency in History: The Althusser-Thompson-Anderson Debate." *Current Perspectives in Social Theory* 6 (1985): 219–41.

Poulantzas, Nicos. *State, Power, Socialism.* London: New Left Books, 1978.

Prezworski, Adam. "The Process of Class Formation from Karl Kautsky's *The Class Struggle* to Recent Debates." *Politics and Society* 7 (1977): 64–85.

Quadagno, Jill S. "Welfare Capitalism and the Social Security Act of 1935." *American Sociological Review* 49 (1984): 632–47.

Reddy, William M. *The Rise of Market Culture: The Textile Trade and French Society, 1750–1900.* Cambridge: Cambridge University Press, 1984.

Richmond, Robert W. *Kansas: A Land of Contrasts.* St. Louis: Forum Press, 1974.

Rickard, Louise E. "The Impact of Populism on Electoral Patterns in Kansas, 1880–1900: A Quantitative Analysis." Ph.D. diss., University of Kansas, 1974.

Rightmire, W. F. "The Alliance Movement in Kansas: Origin of the People's Party." *Transactions of the Kansas State Historical Society, 1905–1906.* Vol. 9:1–8. George Martin, ed. Topeka, Kans.: Kansas State Historical Society, 1906.

Robley, Thomas. *History of Bourbon County, Kansas to the Close of 1865.* Fort Scott: Monitor Press, 1894.

Rockwood, Dean Stephen. "The Populist Ideology." Ph.D. diss., Miami University, Oxford, Ohio, 1977.

Roy, William G. "Class Conflict and Social Change in Historical Perspective." *Annual Review of Sociology* 10 (1984): 483–506.

Ruede, Howard. *Sod-House Days: Letters from a Kansas Homesteader, 1877–1888.* Lawrence, Kans.: University Press of Kansas, 1983.

Sackett, S. J. "Reaction and Reform in Kansas Literature of the Nineteenth Century." *Kansas Magazine* (1959): 73–83.

Schwartz, Michael. "An Estimate of the Size of the Southern Farmers' Alliance and Cotton Tenancy, 1880–1890." *Agricultural History* 51 (1977): 759–69.

———. *Radical Protest and Social Structure: The Southern Farmers' Alliance and Cotton Tenancy, 1880–1890.* New York: Academic Press, 1976.

———, Naomi Rosenthal, and Laura Schwartz. "Leader-Member Conflict in Protest Organization: The Case of the Southern Farmers' Alliance." *Social Problems* 29 (1981): 22–36.

Scott, S. M. *The Champion Organizer of the Northwest: Or, My First Sixty Days Work as an Organizer.* McPherson, Kans.: S. M. Scott, 1890.

Sears, Hal D. *The Sex Radicals.* Lawrence, Kans.: The Regents Press of Kansas, 1977.

Severson, Robert F., Jr. "The Source of Mortgage Credit for Champaign County, 1865–1880." *Agricultural History* 36 (1962): 150–55.

Sewell, William H., Jr. "Ideologies and Social Revolutions: Reflections on the French Case." *Journal of Modern History* 57 (1985): 57–85.

Shannon, Fred A. *The Farmer's Last Frontier: Agriculture, 1860–1897.* New York: Farrar and Rinehart, 1945.

Shefter, Martin. "Trade Unions and Political Machines: The Organization and Disorganization of the American Working Class in the Late Nineteenth Century." In Ira Katznelson and Aristide R. Zolberg, eds., *Working-Class Formation*. Princeton: Princeton University Press, 1986, pp. 197–276.

Simpson, Jerry. "Speech." *Congressional Record*. 53d Congress, Second Session, Appendix, vol. 26, pt. 9, pp. 517–22. Washington, D.C.: Government Printing Office, 1894.

Skocpol, Theda. "Political Response to Capitalist Crisis: Neo-Marxist Theories of the State and the Case of the New Deal." *Politics and Society* 10 (1980): 155–202.

———. *States and Revolutions*. New York: Cambridge University Press, 1979.

Slotkin, Richard. *The Fatal Environment: The Myth of the Frontier in the Age of Industrialization, 1800–1890*. New York: Atheneum, 1985.

Smith, J. Harold. "History of the Grange in Kansas, 1883–1897." M.A. thesis, University of Kansas, 1940.

Snow, David A., E. Burke Rochford, Jr., Steven K. Worden, and Robert D. Benford. "Frame Alignment and Mobilization." *American Sociological Review* 51 (1986): 464–81.

———, Louis A. Zurcher, Jr., and Sheldon Ekland-Olson. "Social Networks and Social Movements." *American Sociological Review* 45 (1980): 787–801.

Stiller, Richard. *Mary Lease: Queen of the Populists*. New York: Thomas Y. Crowell, 1970.

Sundquist, James L. *Dynamics of the Party System*. Washington, D.C.: The Brookings Institution, 1983.

Svenson, Karl A. "The Effect of Popular Dissent on Political Parties in Kansas." Ph.D. diss., University of Iowa, 1948.

Taylor, Carl C. *The Farmers' Movement, 1820–1920*. New York: American Book Company, 1953.

Thompson, E. P. *The Making of the English Working Class*. New York: Vintage, 1963.

———. *The Poverty of Theory*. New York: Monthly Review Press, 1978.

Tilly, Charles. *From Mobilization to Revolution*. Reading, Mass.: Addison-Wesley, 1978.

———, and Louise Tilly. *Collective Action and Class Conflict*. Beverly Hills: Sage, 1981.

———, Louise Tilly, and Richard Tilly. *The Rebellious Century*. Cambridge: Harvard University Press, 1975.

Tocqueville, Alexis de. *Democracy in America*. Trans. George Lawrence, ed. J. P. Mayer. New York: Doubleday, 1969.

Trachtenberg, Alan. *The Incorporation of America: Culture and Society in the Gilded Age*. New York: Hill and Wang, 1982.

Traugott, Mark. *Armies of the Poor: Determinants of Working-Class Participation in the Parisian Insurrection of June 1848.* Princeton: Princeton University Press, 1985.

Tripp, Joseph F. "Kansas Communities and the Birth of the Labor Problem, 1877–1883. *Kansas History* 4 (1981): 114–29.

Turner, James. "Understanding the Populists." *Journal of American History* 67 (1980): 354–73.

U.S. Bureau of the Census. *Report on Real Estate Mortgages. Eleventh Annual Census (1890).* Washington, D.C.: U.S. Government Printing Office, 1890.

———. *Report on Statistics of Agriculture. Eleventh Annual Census (1890).* Washington, D.C.: U.S. Government Printing Office, 1890.

Walker, Edith, and Dorothy Leibengood. "Labor Organizations in Kansas in the Early Eighties." *Kansas Historical Quarterly* 4 (1935): 283–90.

Ware, Eugene Fitch. "A Corn Poem." Cited in Richard L. Douglas, *A History of Manufactures in the Kansas Fuel District.* Reprint from the Kansas Historical Collections, vol. 11. Topeka, Kans.: Kansas State Historical Society, 1910.

Watson, Louis. Letters. In the P. J. Jennings Papers of the Kansas State Historical Society. June 8 and October 29, 1875.

Watson, Thomas E. *The People's Party Campaign Book.* Washington D.C.: National Watchman Publishing Co., 1892.

———. Introduction. In Charles Simon Barrett, *The Mission, History and Times of the Farmers' Union.* Nashville: Marshall and Bruce Co., 1909, pp. 15–17.

White, William Allen. *The Autobiography of William Allen White.* New York: Macmillan, 1946.

Wilentz, Sean. *Chants Democratic: New York City and the Rise of the American Working Class, 1788–1850.* New York: Oxford University Press, 1984.

Williams, Jeffrey C. "Economics and Politics: Voting Behavior in Kansas during the Populist Decade." *Explorations in Economic History* 18 (1981): 233–56.

Williamson, Jeffrey G., and Peter H. Lindert. *American Inequality: A Macroeconomic History.* New York: Academic Press, 1980.

Wilson, Lloyd C. *A History of Cooperatives in Kansas.* Topeka, Kans.: Kansas Cooperative Council Publication, 1949.

Wright, Erik O. *Class, Crisis and the State.* London: New Left Books, 1978.

Zald, Mayer N., and John D. McCarthy, eds. *The Dynamics of Social Movements.* Cambridge: Winthrop Publishers, 1979.

Zaret, David. *The Heavenly Contract: Ideology and Organization in Pre-Revolutionary Puritanism.* Chicago: University of Chicago Press, 1985.

Zornow, William Frank. "The Basis of Agrarian Unrest in Kansas, 1870–1890." In John D. Bright, ed., *Kansas: The First Century.* Vol. 1. New York: Lewis Historical Publishing Co., 1956.

———. *Kansas: A History of the Jayhawk State.* Norman, Okla.: University of Oklahoma Press, 1957.

Newspapers

Abilene Daily Reflector (Abilene, Kansas) August 6, 1896.

Banner-Graphic (Kingsley, Kansas) December 16, 1887.

Barber County Index (Medicine Lodge, Kansas) October 1, 1890.

Cheyenne County Herald (St. Francis and later, Bird City, Kansas) December 7, 1889; January 18, February 1, 1890.

Cheyenne County Rustler (St. Francis, Kansas) June 19, 1890.

Concordia Times Press (Concordia, Kansas) July 20, 1891.

Enterprise (Alma, Kansas) February 4, March 25, May 20, 1887; March 29, 1889.

Farmer's Advocate (Topeka, Kansas) May 6, 1890; December 2, 1891; April 20, 1892; January 16, 1895; June 17, 1896; January 6, March 24, 1897.

Fort Scott Daily Monitor (Fort Scott, Kansas) June 29, 1887; November 13, 1888; November 9, 1890; November 13, 1892; November 6, 1894; November 7, 1896.

Fort Scott Democrat (Fort Scott, Kansas) July 13, 1861.

Gazette (Emporia, Kansas) June 18, 1895.

Herald For Freedom (Lawrence, Kansas) January 13, 1855.

Kansas City Star (Kansas City, Missouri) November 5, 1890; April 1, 1891; January 2, 1894.

Kansas City Gazette (Kansas City, Kansas) November 16, 1888; November 13, 1890; November 17, 1892; November 15, 1894; November 19, 1896.

Kansas City Times (Kansas City, Missouri) November 10, 1890.

Kansas Farmer (Topeka, Kansas) March 15, 1873; January 12, February 23, 1888; June 27, July 10, September 25, October 16, November 13, December 15, 1889; January 23, February 19, March 13, 19, April 2, 16, 30, May 1, July 16, October 8, 1890.

Lawrence Daily Journal (Lawrence, Kansas) December 18, 1880; November 11, 1888; March 8, 18, May 7, November 9, 1890; November 13, 1892; November 6, 1894; September 9, 17, 1895; November 7, 1896.

Leavenworth Evening Standard (Leavenworth, Kansas) September 6, 1878; November 9, 1892; November 7, 1894; July 14, 1896.

Lyons Republican (Lyons, Kansas) June 12, 1890.

Marion Record (Marion, Kansas) December 18, 1896.

Mercury (Kingsley, Kansas) May 21, July 4, October 17, 28, 1887.

Osborne County Farmer (Osborne, Kansas) July 24, 1876.

Osborne County News (Osborne, Kansas) October 30, November 27, 1890; January 14, 21, February 11, 25, March 3, 25, May 5, August 25, 1892.

The People's Advocate (Hill City, Kansas) May 7, 1850.

Phonograph (St. Paul, Nebraska) June 10, 1887.

Selden Times (Hoxie, Kansas) May 30, 1889.

Signal (Alma, Kansas) April 11, 1891.

Topeka Commonwealth (Topeka, Kansas) August 28, September 12, 1872; March 30, 1873; August 30, 1874; May 20, July 30, August 16, 1876; August 18, September 6, 1878.

Topeka Daily Capital (Topeka, Kansas) March 26, 1890; November 10, 1893.

Topeka State Journal (Topeka, Kansas) November 11, 1892.

Tribune (Junction City, Kansas) April 13, 1890.

Walnut Valley Times (Eldorado, Kansas) July 20, 1884.

Washington Republican (Washington, Kansas) February 4, 1887.

Weekly Review (St. Francis, Kansas) December 19, 1889; January 23, May 1, August 7, September 25, 1890; January 1, 1891.

Wellington Monitor (Wellington, Kansas) October 5, 1890.

Wichita Daily Beacon (Wichita, Kansas) June 15, 1892.

Index